DISCARD

THE ROAD FROM VERSAILLES

MUNRO PRICE

THE ROAD FROM VERSAILLES

Louis XVI, Marie Antoinette, and the
Fall of the French Monarchy

ST. MARTIN'S PRESS ❧ NEW YORK

www.stmartins.com

ISBN 0-312-26879-3

First published in Great Britain by Macmillan, an imprint of Pan Macmillan LTD

First U.S. Edition: January 2003

10 9 8 7 6 5 4 3 2 1

CONTENTS

LIST OF ILLUSTRATIONS

ACKNOWLEDGEMENTS

This book has taken several years of research across a number of European countries. None of this would have been possible without the help and advice of many people in each, and I am very grateful to all of them.

In France, Henri-François de Breteuil first opened his ancestor's archives to me when I was a PhD student in 1985, and ever since he and his wife Séverine have been a source of help, encouragement and advice. Mme Laure de Breteuil has also been very helpful to my work. The marquis de Gontaut-Biron, a descendant of Breteuil through the latter's granddaughter, kindly allowed me to consult Breteuil's previously unused financial papers in his possession. I am also grateful to Susan Wharton, Director in the Department of Printed Books and Manuscripts at Sotheby's, and Bruno Galland, Conservateur en chef of the Section Ancienne of the Archives Nationales, Paris, for bringing their handwriting expertise to some important and controversial documents, presented in the Appendix.

In Austria, Graf and Gräfin Heinrich von Clam-Martinic generously permitted me access to the Bombelles papers, and gave me much help in examining them. I am also very grateful to Count Jan d'Ansembourg for putting me in touch with the Clam-Martinic family. At the Haus-Hof-und-Staatsarchiv in Vienna, Hofrat Auer and especially Dr Michael Hochedlinger made my research much easier than it would otherwise have been. Magister Günther Jedliczka of the Austrian Academic Exchange Service was of great help in finding me accommodation through the University of Vienna on several of my stays. Christopher Wentworth-Stanley was most hospitable, and also introduced me to Vienna – a major and permanent service.

In Stockholm, Bo Runmark kindly shared the results of his research into Breteuil's period in Sweden, and took me on a tour of the former French embassy, the Palais Bååt on Blasieholmen. More generally, my trip to Sweden would not have been possible without the Vetenskapsstaden International Centre for Researchers and the excellent – and affordable – accommodation it provided.

The research for and writing of the book benefited greatly from the award of a Leverhulme Research Fellowship for the year 1999–2000. I am very grateful to the Leverhulme Trust for this, and also to the British Academy for a Small Personal Grant, which I received in 1995.

I owe a considerable debt of gratitude to my friend and agent Andrew Lownie for all his help and advice with the book over several years. At Macmillan, I also owe much to Becky Lindsey, Catherine Whitaker and Jeremy Trevathan, whose editing has improved it considerably. Stanley Price also read the manuscript and made many helpful suggestions.

The book has also benefited from the advice and comments of several historians, especially John Hardman, Tim Blanning, William Doyle, Philip Mansel, Julian Swann and Jeremy Black. Non-historian friends have also provided important and much-appreciated help. Bénoît and Siân Andrieux loaned me a car at a crucial stage of my researches in France. Adela Gooch helped to find the way to Lövstad and Fersen's tomb. Finally, Simon Cox nobly came out to Burg Clam with a digital camera and photographed the Bombelles papers, thus solving the problem of how best to consult them. As a result, I finally gained access to Breteuil's thoughts and plans in the unlikely setting of a CD-ROM.

Introduction

THE FRENCH REVOLUTION was a protean and immensely complex
phenomenon. At the centre of the storm stood Louis XVI and Marie
Antoinette; their response to events as they unfolded determined
not only their own destiny, but that of the Revolution itself. An
enormous amount has been written about the king and queen, and
especially their terrible fate. Yet their actual policy during the Revolution – whether they were ever prepared to compromise with their
opponents, or simply aimed to restore the old regime – is still
shrouded in mystery. As a result, a significant gap remains in our
understanding of an event that shaped the modern world. The picture
of Louis and Marie Antoinette in these years is still very much what
it was over a century ago, when the available sources were surveyed
by the eminent German historian Max Lenz. Writing in 1894, Lenz
lamented the fact that so many had disappeared, but expressed the
hope that this might one day be remedied:

> Although the memoirs of contemporaries, all of whom have an
> axe to grind, are often untrustworthy, we must be glad that . . .
> a burning desire has now arisen to track down the most
> important sources. It is also my hope that the original material
> concerning our subject has not yet all been exhausted. It is
> possible that a few letters may be missing from the most valuable
> archive, the Fersen collection, and that they are still preserved,
> perhaps in code. And dare we not also hope that the papers
> of other intimates of the Tuileries, of Breteuil, Bouillé, and
> d'Agoult, Bishop of Pamiers, may one day see the light of day?
> No one stood closer to the French royal couple than Breteuil,
> the last prime minister of the old regime. In exile he served
> Louis XVI, not without personal ambition, but at the same time
> with great devotion, and I have no doubt that his memory,
> which has often been blackened, would be greatly enhanced if
> his correspondence, with all its importance both for France and

for Europe, were to come to light . . . I treasure the thought . . .
that my own work might one day be corrected or broadened
through further research, and would be content if other hands
could continue what I have begun.[1]

The aim of this book is to continue the work begun by Max
Lenz. The major obstacle to this has always been the paucity of clues
left by Louis XVI and Marie Antoinette themselves as to their true
policy during the Revolution. This was largely a product of necessity.
From the moment they were forcibly taken by the crowd from
Versailles back to the capital in October 1789, the royal couple were
effectively prisoners of the people of Paris. For their own safety,
while publicly endorsing the acts of the revolutionary National
Assembly, they had to keep their real views and aims as carefully
hidden as possible. Despite the obvious dangers, from the summer of
1790 they embarked on a secret counter-revolutionary diplomacy
aimed at restoring as much of the royal authority as possible. They
burned much of this correspondence, however, on the eve of the
storming of the Tuileries and the final overthrow of the monarchy
on 10 August 1792.

In any case, Louis XVI himself wrote very little during the
Revolution. Possibly this was because he was afflicted with intermittent clinical depression after 1789 -- certainly contemporary descriptions of his state of mind tally with this diagnosis. As a result, most
of the royal family's secret correspondence with their confidants and
fellow European monarchs was undertaken by Marie Antoinette.
Because the greatest part of this was with her two brothers, the
Emperors Joseph II and Leopold II of Austria and their advisers,
many of her letters survive in the State Archives in Vienna and have
been published. Yet in this correspondence the queen was mostly
concerned with the practical details of day-to-day diplomacy; only
very rarely did she reveal a glimpse of the actual political system
she and her husband wished to see emerge from the revolutionary
maelstrom.

As Max Lenz stressed, in the absence of detailed memoranda
from the king and queen, the only hope of properly reconstructing
their secret policy lies in the papers of the tiny band of committed
royalists who helped them, often at great personal risk, to pursue it.

One of them, the Swedish Count Hans Axel von Fersen, has become famous because he was perhaps Marie Antoinette's lover as well as her political confidant. Fersen left substantial papers, which are now in the Swedish State Archives in Stockholm. Many of these were published by one of his descendants, baron von Klinckowström, in the 1870s; along with Louis XVI's few post-1789 writings and Marie Antoinette's letters, these are an essential source for the king and queen's policy during the Revolution. Yet they contain many gaps. All of Fersen's diary for the years up to 1791 has been lost, and Fersen himself burned many of his most secret papers in Brussels in November 1792 to prevent them from falling into the hands of the advancing French armies. A century later, Klinckowström destroyed those parts of his ancestor's correspondence with Marie Antoinette that he felt might harm their reputations, so we shall probably never be able to reconstruct the true nature of the couple's relationship.

The papers that remain, important as they are, also fail to address some crucial questions. Fersen was a doer rather than a thinker, a soldier and not a statesman. All his actions during the Revolution were aimed at one very specific goal – to save the queen. He preserved no memoranda or reflections on the crucial wider issues that the king and queen would have had to face the moment they reached freedom. These problems, over which the royal couple must have agonized during their long months of captivity in Paris, were central: whether all or only some of the reforms made since 1789 should be jettisoned, how to stabilize the country's finances, whether to continue with the existing National Assembly or replace it with another, or simply return to personal rule. Fersen the military man left these questions to the politicians.

The same is true of the second figure Max Lenz mentions, General de Bouillé. It was to Bouillé, commander of the last army that remained loyal to them, in Lorraine, that Louis XVI and Marie Antoinette looked when, in the autumn of 1790, they decided to escape from Paris. From this point until the actual escape in June 1791, Louis and Bouillé kept up a secret, coded correspondence about their plans. Yet Bouillé claimed in his memoirs that he systematically destroyed each letter of the king's after he had received it, since the discovery of even one would have been fatal. Max Lenz could not quite bring himself to believe that the general had burned such vital historical documents, but even if some of them do survive, they have not yet been discovered.

Furthermore it is probable, as in the case of Fersen, that Bouillé's dealings with the king and queen were much more concerned with the practical details of their planned flight from Paris and the necessary military dispositions to take once they had reached safety than with their wider political agenda. Although he did allow himself to speculate on this in his memoirs, written in exile in London, Bouillé specifically stated that he never knew for certain what policy Louis XVI would have adopted if he had regained his freedom.

Yet one man unquestionably knew exactly what the king and queen's true policy was, from the moment they made the decision to flee Paris right up until their deaths. This was the baron de Breteuil, the final figure mentioned by Lenz and by far the most important. A distinguished diplomat and politician, in the context of 1789 Breteuil was a staunch conservative. Indeed, it was his appointment on 11 July 1789 as prime minister to restore order to an increasingly unstable situation that brought about the storming of the Bastille three days later and touched off the revolutionary explosion. Breteuil was forced to flee France for Switzerland, where he lived in semi-retirement for over a year. Yet when Louis and Marie Antoinette, alarmed by the Revolution's increasing radicalism, decided that the time had come to reassert royal authority, it was to Breteuil once again that they turned.

From this moment on, Breteuil became the king and queen's secret prime minister in exile, charged in particular with negotiating the support of their fellow European monarchs for their policy to end the Revolution. Failing the discovery of new material in Louis's or Marie Antoinette's own hand, which must now be highly unlikely, unravelling the mystery of their political aims can only be done through a study of Breteuil. Remarkably, this has never been attempted, and even today Breteuil remains a shadowy and enigmatic figure. This book is an attempt to fill that gap.

The quest for the elusive baron has lasted several years and has led to many fascinating and sometimes remote places. In France, the marquis de Breteuil kindly allowed me access to his ancestor's remaining papers preserved at the Château de Breteuil. Yet a problem was soon apparent. In contrast to the baron's pre-1789 papers, which were voluminous, almost nothing survived from the years after 1789. Either they had been burned during a fire at the château in the mid-nineteenth century or Breteuil himself had destroyed them during the Revolution for fear they would fall into the wrong hands. Breteuil's other collaborators in counter-revolutionary activity within France would almost certainly have done the same thing for the same reasons, so the hunt for the baron's surviving papers had to be pursued further afield. Since Breteuil's main efforts during the revolutionary years were diplomatic, aimed at enrolling foreign support for his beleaguered master and mistress, the best hope of tracing his activities seemed to lie in the archives of those countries whose rulers had been his correspondents.

This trail led first to Sweden, to the State Archives in Stockholm. The brilliant and flamboyant Gustavus III, king of Sweden from 1771 until his assassination in 1792, was an old ally of France, and the only foreign monarch Louis and Marie Antoinette really trusted to help them during the Revolution. Gustavus had also been a friend of Breteuil, a former French ambassador to Sweden, since his childhood. If Breteuil had been likely to confide his plans to any European crowned head, it would have been to Gustavus. Sure enough, a file in the Gallica series in the State Archives yielded several long, and previously unknown, letters written by Breteuil to the Swedish king between 1791 and 1792. They contained much new material about French royal policy during these years. Gustavus's letters to Breteuil had been published in Sweden in 1885; those of Breteuil to Gustavus formed the other half of the correspondence.

In contrast to this, Breteuil's correspondence with Marie Antoinette's brother, the Austrian Emperor Leopold II, and his agents, has long been known to historians. It is preserved in Vienna in the State Archives, the Haus-Hof-und-Staatsarchiv. It has, however, never been fully published. While several research trips to the Haus-Hof-und-Staatsarchiv did not substantially alter my view of Breteuil's negotiations with the Habsburgs in 1791 and 1792, they added considerable detail to the picture of his activities in these years. More important, the archive did contain significant new material about the last phase of the baron's counter-revolutionary diplomacy, in 1793, when his overriding aim was to save Marie Antoinette from the scaffold.

Vienna and Stockholm yielded much that was new and important, but not enough for a full-scale book. Frustrating as this was, it increased my respect for my subject. Contemporaries had often accused Breteuil of being choleric and impulsive. Yet the figure who emerged from my researches was very different: a subtle and discreet politician who never gave away more than he had to, and who was adept at covering his tracks at a time of great tension and danger. He had covered them so well, in fact, cloaking his role in secrecy and keeping his correspondence away from prying eyes, that they remained hidden for over 200 years.

The crucial breakthrough came from a private rather than a public source. Breteuil may have destroyed his own papers, but to carry out the king and queen's secret diplomacy he had had to rely in turn on a handful of trusted agents. The most important of these was Marc-Marie, marquis de Bombelles. Himself a distinguished diplomat before 1789, Bombelles was Breteuil's chief protégé, a substitute for the son he never had. As committed a royalist as his mentor, after 1789 Bombelles was Breteuil's natural choice as confidant and collaborator. Between 1790 and 1792, the baron entrusted him with several crucial secret missions on behalf of Louis XVI and Marie Antoinette; to the Emperor Leopold II, to the Swiss cantons, and finally to Catherine the Great in Russia.

Unlike Breteuil, Bombelles carefully preserved everything he wrote – and he wrote a great deal. From 1780 until his death in 1822, he kept a regular diary. In the early 1900s, Count Maurice Fleury, an amateur historian, had been allowed access to this, and had used it as the basis of two books about the French court and the Revolution. Then, in 1978, a much fuller version of the diary began to be published. This contained significant new material about Bombelles's role in Breteuil's counter-revolutionary diplomacy. Yet, once again, the diary was very much a day-to-day record, and contained little specific detail about the precise aims of Breteuil's, and the French royal family's, policy. On the other hand, it was also clear from the diary that a substantial cache of Bombelles's papers still survived. Gaining access to them now became the first priority.

It soon turned out that Bombelles's papers had had almost as adventurous a life as their author. Grief-stricken after his wife's death in 1800, the marquis had gone into holy orders, and spent most of the Napoleonic years as an obscure Catholic priest in Prussian Silesia. On his return to France after the Bourbon restoration, however, he had risen swiftly through the Church hierarchy, ending as Bishop of Amiens. His sons stayed in Central Europe and entered Austrian service, and the Bombelles soon established themselves as an important Habsburg court family. They acquired estates in Croatia, and it was there that they kept their family archives. As the invading German armies approached in 1941, the papers had been sent for safekeeping to a cousin, Count Georg Clam-Martinic, at his castle in Upper Austria, Burg Clam, where they still are today.

Through the generous help of Bombelles's last direct descendant, Count Jan d'Ansembourg, I was able to secure the Clam-Martinic family's permission to consult their ancestor's papers, and set out again for Austria. Dating from the twelfth century and perched on a rock near the Danube, Burg Clam provided a spectacular backdrop for the last stage of the hunt for Breteuil. The diary Bombelles had so carefully kept for forty-two years was shelved in the castle archives, in ninety-seven manuscript volumes. Yet the real prize lay just next to it. This was a large buff ledger, inscribed simply 'Missions'. It turned out to be a record of every secret mission Bombelles had undertaken on behalf of the French royal family during the Revolution. Just as if he had been a regular ambassador and Breteuil his foreign minister, Bombelles had entered copies of all his despatches to the baron, along with the originals of those Breteuil had written to him. Here, at last, was a detailed account of Louis XVI's and Marie Antoinette's secret diplomacy, written as it unfolded by its two principal agents.

The ledger was stacked on top of a carton which contained a mass of unbound documents. These too were fascinating: copies of Breteuil's correspondence after 1789 with Louis XVI's brothers the comtes de Provence and d'Artois, and with another leading counter-revolutionary, the maréchal de Castries. There were also recollections of key events of the Revolution, such as the flight to Varennes, written by some of those close to or directly involved in them. Clearly Bombelles had seen himself as not only a political actor but also a historian, and these accounts had been written at his request during his twenty-five-year exile.

Obviously, the Bombelles papers did not yield up every secret of

Louis XVI's and Marie Antoinette's true policy, but they certainly revealed a great deal. Taken together with the diaries, they form an immensely rich source for the history of French royalism from 1789 through to the Bourbon restoration. Much work remains to be done – so far, only the diaries up to 1795 have been published, which still leaves twenty-seven years to go. Yet if the Bombelles papers are the single most important new source used in this book, the full story of the king and queen's struggle with the Revolution can only be pieced together if they are combined with the other material scattered across archives in France, Sweden and Austria, as well as with what has already been published. I have tried here to assemble as many pieces as possible of this jigsaw and create a detailed picture of Louis's and Marie Antoinette's actions during their final years.

In taking this approach I am, by definition, concentrating on one particular aspect of the period. The French Revolution has never ceased to be a controversial subject for historians, and the last few decades have been no exception. Since the 1960s there has been a fierce debate over its origins, while the role of cultural and gender history in understanding its complexities is currently the focus of much writing and research. Yet important as these debates are, they do not directly concern my story. The subject here is an essentially political one – how Louis XVI and Marie Antoinette responded to the Revolution, and on what basis they would have ended it if they had been able to. Yet this too has significant implications for the way we view the period. If we stick to the traditional interpretation, that the king and queen simply wished to restore the old regime, by force if necessary, against the wishes of the people, then the Revolution's descent into violence and civil war was tragic, but inevitable. If, on the other hand, we adopt the claims of some more recent historians, that Louis XVI was in fact more willing to accept a compromise than has previously been supposed, then the overthrow of the ideals of 1789 by war and terror, while no less tragic, appears avoidable. In the presence of these questions, understanding the royal couple's motives and actions is of critical importance.

Louis XVI once remarked, cryptically, that he would rather be judged by his silence than by his words. Filling that silence is an extremely difficult task. Many have tried to do so, from the king's contemporaries to more recent historians. Yet ulitmately it can only

be done through the writings left behind by those closest to him —
his wife, certainly, but also his secret servants Breteuil and Bombelles.
I hope that their words will bring us a little closer to the truth about
the fall of the French Monarchy.

EUROPE AND THE FLIGHT TO VARENNES
February–June 1791

London
Stettin
Amsterdam
Hanover
Berlin
Brussels
Cologne
Aix-la-Chapelle
Mons
Dresden
Rouen
Coblenz
Frankfurt
Worms
Paris
Rheims
Montmédy
Varennes
Karlsruhe
Strasbourg
Stuttgart
Nuremberg
Dijon
Munich
Vienna
Solothurn
Bern
Geneva
Lyons
Milan
Turin
Cremona
Mantua
Trieste
Zagreb
Genoa
Bologna
Avignon
Zara
Marseilles
Florence
Rome

1 Leopold II: Vienna to Venice/Mantua/Florence/Cremona/Milan, March–June 1791
2 Bombelles to Breteuil: Florence to Solothurn, early May 1791
3 Artois to Leopold II: Venice to Mantua, 18 May 1791
4 Artois: Mantua to Karlsruhe/Coblenz, late May 1791
5 Bombelles to Leopold II: Solothurn to Cremona (return), 22–23 May 1791
6 Bombelles to Leopold II: Solothurn to Milan (return), 4–7 June 1791
7 Breteuil: Solothurn to Aix-la-Chapelle, late June 1791
8 Royal family: Paris to Varennes, 20–21 June 1791
9 Comte de Provence: Paris to Mons/Brussels, 20–21 June 1791

N

0   50   100   150 miles
0   100   200 kilometres

Chapter One

THE KING AND HIS FAMILY

AT MIDDAY ON 5 MAY 1789, Louis XVI entered the Hall of the
Menus Plaisirs at Versailles to open the first meeting of the Estates
General to be held since 1614. The king took his seat at one end of
the hall, already occupied by 1,200 deputies, on a dais carpeted in
violet interspersed with gold fleurs-de-lys. He was followed by the
queen, Marie Antoinette, the other members of the royal family,
the principal officers of the royal household and the keeper of the
seals, who arranged themselves around the steps of the throne. The
king then removed his plumed hat encrusted with diamonds to greet
the assembly, which had risen to cheer him as he made his entrance.[1]

Even though it had been in abeyance for 175 years, the Estates
General was the chief representative body of the kingdom of France.
In the past, its deputies had normally been drawn in equal proportions
from the clergy, the nobility, and the commoners, the third estate.
Yet on this occasion, in recognition of the great increase in the third
estate's size and importance over the course of the century, the
number of deputies it sent to the Estates General had been doubled.
A daunting task lay before the assembly: to agree with the king a
major programme of reforms to regenerate the kingdom and restore
its ailing finances.

Although nobody present could have conceived it then, scattered amidst the throng of deputies were men who would shortly make a revolution. The marquis de La Fayette, standing in the ranks of the nobility, had already gained fame as George Washington's aide-de-camp in the American War of Independence and as a symbol of French support for the cause of liberty. As commander of the Paris National Guard after July 1789, he would emerge as a dominant figure in the moderate phase of the Revolution. In the third estate, a young lawyer of surpassing eloquence from Grenoble, Antoine Barnave, would soon become one of the outstanding orators of the Revolution, sharing La Fayette's political principles but divided from him by personal rivalry.

An altogether more exalted figure, sitting with the nobility, was the king's cousin, Louis-Philippe-Joseph, duc d'Orléans. Already sensing political opportunity in these uncharted waters, Orléans would swiftly transform himself into a leader of the Left. In 1793, he would vote for his cousin's death, without reprieve. Another nobleman, yet symbolically aligned with the commons as third estate deputy for Aix-en-Provence, was the charismatic, pockmarked and notoriously libertine comte de Mirabeau. Tribune of the people in 1789 and 1790, Mirabeau was to end his Promethean career a year later as secret counter-revolutionary adviser to the king and queen. And somewhere in the body of the hall, anonymous in the sober black of the third estate, was an obscure deputy who would end by eclipsing them all, Maximilien Robespierre.

Everybody present realized the significance of the occasion. The scene around them – the king surrounded by the representatives of the people, the third estate facing him, the deputies of the first estate, the clergy, on his right, and those of the second, the nobility, on his left – vividly symbolized the break with the past. By the very act of convoking the Estates General, Louis XVI had brought to an end over a century of absolute monarchy, by which, in theory at least, the king had ruled without the assistance of a representative body. Reviving the long-dormant Estates General was an exceptional act, as the king reminded the deputies in a short opening speech:

> Gentlemen, the day my heart has long awaited has finally arrived, and I see myself surrounded by the representatives of the nation which it is my glory to command.

A long interval has elapsed since the last meeting of the Estates General, and although the practice of holding assemblies seemed to have fallen into disuse, I have not hesitated to re-establish a custom from which the kingdom may gain new strength and which may open up for the nation a new source of happiness . . .[2]

The future shape of the monarchy ushered in by the convocation of the Estates General was less clear. For traditionalists, probably a majority of the first two estates, their summoning merely signified a return to earlier practice within the context of an already existing constitution. For radicals, on the other hand, who soon came to include a majority of the third estate, the aim was an entirely new political system incorporating equality of rights and many of the ideals of the Enlightenment. Within two months of the king's speech from the throne, the incipient struggle over how best to replace the absolute monarchy, and with what, had led to revolution.

*

THE THIRTY-FIVE-YEAR-OLD monarch welcoming the deputies to the Estates General was and has remained an enigma. He was clearly unlike his predecessors. Apart from the family Roman nose, he bore little resemblance to his Bourbon ancestors with their dark hair and complexions and beady brown eyes. With his blond hair, large blue eyes and heavy build, he owed much more to the German stock of his mother, Maria Josepha of Saxony. Where Louis XIV and Louis XV had been gifted with tremendous physical presence, Louis XVI cut an unimpressive figure in public. Tall by the standards of his time and extremely strong, he none the less had bad posture and an undignified walk. He was also painfully tongue-tied in public, which his ministers could only remedy by supplying him with ready-made phrases in advance of public receptions. Apart from hunting, the traditional sport of kings, his pleasures were simple and manual; he had a forge installed above his study at Versailles, and proved to be a talented amateur blacksmith, specializing in making locks.[3]

This unkingly man had a complex and secretive personality, shaped by a series of early bereavements. Born on 23 August 1754 and christened Louis-Auguste, for the first fourteen years of his life the future Louis XVI had had no inkling that he would eventually rule France. The second surviving child of Louis XV's son and heir Louis-Ferdinand, the 'old dauphin', he only became king in 1774 through a succession of deaths in his family. The cause was tuberculosis, which carried off his three closest relatives in six years. In 1761, it killed his precocious elder brother, the duc de Bourgogne, to whom he was devoted. Four years later, his father too succumbed. Within fifteen months, Louis's mother, Maria Josepha, who caught the disease while nursing her husband, had also died.

The two formative influences on Louis-Auguste were his father, the old dauphin, and his grandfather, Louis XV. Yet by the time the young man was eleven his father was dead, so the dominant figure in his life became the old king himself. Outwardly there was little to unite the ageing monarch, still handsome and imposing in his sixties, and his gauche, retiring grandson. The fact that Louis-Auguste, as he grew up, showed no interest in sex also formed a strong contrast to the obsessive womanizing that so marked his grandfather's life. Despite these differences, Louis XV and his grandson soon grew close, particularly once they had discovered one great passion in common – the hunt. In private conversations on and off the hunting field, the king patiently initiated his heir into the business of government.[4]

The intimacy between the two men was cemented by the fact that in one area their characters were very similar. Both were taciturn, watchful and deeply reserved, and probably derived these qualities from the same source – early experience of bereavement. Louis-Auguste had lost both his parents and elder brother to tuberculosis by the age of thirteen; his grandfather had lost his own mother, father and elder brother to smallpox when he was only two. These traumas were most likely also responsible for a further defect that afflicted both Louis XV and Louis XVI throughout their lives – chronic indecision. Louis XV's vacillation was notorious. As for Louis XVI, his younger brother the comte de Provence once came up with a devastating description of how difficult it was to get him to make up his mind: 'Imagine a set of oiled billiard-balls that you vainly try to hold together.'[5]

Louis XVI's intellectual capacity has traditionally been portrayed as limited. The standard view presents him as dull and phlegmatic, more interested in his hunting and locksmithing than in the business of government. In fact, Louis's surviving work for his tutors depicts a pupil of definitely above-average intelligence, with a particular aptitude for mathematics and geography. This was to persist into later life, in the king's sound grasp of public finance and fascination with cartography. Related to this was his love of the sea and of naval affairs; he was to play a significant role in the direction of the maritime aspects of the American war, and helped draw up the instructions for the explorer La Pérouse's expedition to the South Seas in 1785.[6] He devoured Captain Cook's accounts of his voyages as soon as they appeared. Ironically, Louis XVI only saw the sea once in his life, when he travelled to Cherbourg to open the new harbour there in 1786. This was the only visit he made to any French province before the Revolution.

The future king was also a good linguist, with an excellent grasp of Latin, Italian and, more unusually, English.[7] Throughout his life he was to be alternately attracted and repelled by England, enviably prosperous and powerful and his own kingdom's greatest rival. As king, he always followed closely reports of the proceedings of both the Lords and the Commons. He even kept this habit up during the Revolution. In 1792, during council meetings with the Girondin ministers, whom he despised, he would ostentatiously read the English newspapers, translating them on sight if necessary for the business in hand.[8]

Louis's politcal views were shaped in boyhood by his governor, the duc de la Vauguyon, and his collaborators, the Jesuit Guillaume-François Berthier and the future historiographer royal, Jacob-Nicolas Moreau. Their method was to set before their pupil a series of maxims, on which he would comment in the form of 'reflections'. These 'reflections', the most important of which Louis wrote when he was fourteen, form the best guide to the concept of monarchy he absorbed from his teachers. It was quite uncompromising. In one particularly significant sentence, Louis set out a vision of fair-minded but resolutely authoritarian rule: 'The power of the throne is absolute, nothing can check it, but it must be founded on justice and reason, and must always be open to warning and good counsel.'[9]

These ringing statements of faith prefigured Louis's politics for at least the first thirteen years of his reign. Up until 1787 at the earliest, there is no evidence that he wavered in his commitment to the absolute monarchy he had inherited from his grandfather.

The death of Louis XV on 10 May 1774 transformed the dauphin Louis-Auguste into King Louis XVI, and confronted him with the formidable task of ruling France. It also bequeathed to him the headship of a large royal family, all of whose members had power, status and their own political agendas. Prime among Louis's older relatives were his unmarried aunts, Louis XV's daughters, Mesdames Adélaïde, Victoire, Sophie and Louise. He remained deeply attached to them all his life, particularly since they had helped bring him up when he was orphaned. The strongest character among them was Mme Adélaïde, imperious, masculine and deeply pious, closely followed by the plump Mme Victoire, whose favourite pastime was playing the bagpipes.[10] The four sisters could always be relied upon to support tradition in Church, State and foreign policy. They were, however, too eccentric to carry much political weight. Horace Walpole, who met them at Versailles, described them as 'clumsy plump old wenches, with a bad likeness to their father . . . with black cloaks and knotting-bags, looking good-humoured, not knowing what to say, and wriggling as if they wanted to make water'.[11]

Closest of all the king's blood relations were his two younger brothers, Louis-Stanislas-Xavier, comte de Provence, born in 1755, and Charles-Philippe, comte d'Artois, born in 1757, and his youngest sister, Mme Elisabeth. Intelligent, witty, of a literary bent, Provence was fundamentally cold. He had mistresses, but also possessed a strong voyeuristic streak. This has recently been made clear by the publication of a series of obscene letters addressed by him to his friend the duc de Lévis. Written in English in the style of Smollett, these display a prurient fascination with every detail of Lévis's sexual practices with his mistresses.[12] As his attitude to his elder brother after 1789 was to show, Provence's coldness and cynicism also extended to his politics.

Artois shared neither Provence's corpulence nor his brains. Handsome, athletic and promiscuous, his limited talents were initially devoted to the pursuit of pleasure. The crisis of the old regime was to transform him into the most prominent defender of the essential core of absolute monarchy – royal authority and the social, if not the fiscal, privileges of the first two orders. It was left to Mme Elisabeth to supply the quality Provence and Artois essentially lacked – loyalty to their elder brother. Plump, devout and dedicated to good works, Mme Elisabeth was devoted to Louis, and remained with him to the end.

Around the immediate royal family clustered the princes of the blood – Condé, Conti, Orléans and Penthièvre. The two who were to loom largest in the history of Louis's reign were the king's cousins Louis-Henri-Joseph, prince de Condé, and Louis-Philippe-Joseph, duc d'Orléans. Fifty-three in 1789, eighteen years older than Louis XVI, Condé was the only living Bourbon with a military reputation; as a young general at the end of the Seven Years War, he had won the battle of Johannisberg against the Prussians and Hanoverians. He was both ambitious and strongly conservative. Orléans, seven years older than Louis XVI, was very different. By the outbreak of the Revolution he had still found no suitable outlet for his energies. His attempt to build a naval career had been unsuccessful, and his extravagance and womanizing were notorious. Orléans's relationship with his royal cousin was also difficult. He felt that Louis had not supported him sufficiently when his conduct during a naval battle in 1778 was criticized, and never forgave him for this.[13] The king for his part was well aware of his cousin's hostility. The opening of the Estates General gave Orléans an irresistible opportunity to purge his frustrations.

The final figure on this crowded stage arrived in France on 8 May 1770. This was Louis XVI's future queen, the fifteen-year-old Archduchess Maria Antonia, daughter of the Empress of Austria, Maria Theresa. On 16 May the couple were married at Versailles, the bride's name rendered into French and for posterity as Marie Antoinette.

Outwardly, the new dauphine had all that was needed to please public opinion. She was lively and pretty, with large blue eyes, a high forehead and a short, aquiline nose. The only hint of the jutting Habsburg jaw was a rather full lower lip. Her complexion was good, and her hands and arms elegant and well shaped. Although she was still extremely young, her character appeared promising. She was lively, vivacious and well-meaning, with a straightforward, spontaneous nature. With time, Marie Antoinette was to mould these qualities into a very particular and memorable presence, dignified and imposing yet also simple and unaffected. Her charm was legendary. Something of the impression she made on her contemporaries can be glimpsed in Edmund Burke's famous recollection, in his *Reflections on the Revolution in France*, of her holding court as a young bride, in the days of glory before 1789:

> It is now fifteen or sixteen years since I saw the queen of France, then the dauphiness, at Versailles, and surely never lighted on this orb, which she hardly seemed to touch, a more delightful vision. I saw her just above the horizon, decorating and cheering the elevated sphere she just began to move in, – glittering like the morning star, full of life, and splendour, and joy.[14]

Marie Antoinette's intellectual capacities have received even rougher treatment from historians than those of her husband. She has gone down to posterity as stupid and frivolous, forever associated with an infamous remark about cake that she probably never made. In reality, the queen was far from a fool, although she never shared her husband's love of knowledge for its own sake. She had a sound if ordinary mind, occasionally lit up by flashes of genuine intuition and discernment. Unfortunately, her early education at the Viennese court had been seriously neglected. Until the age of twelve she had had almost no formal lessons.[15] It was only the glittering prospect of her marriage to the heir to the throne of France, as a human token of Austria's fidelity to the alliance of 1756, that jolted Maria Theresa into remedying the situation. Versailles was consulted, and in this unaccustomed role of tutorial agency sent to Vienna an approved teacher, the abbé de Vermond. Of a humble but talented family (his brother was to become Marie Antoinette's obstetrician and delivered all her children), Vermond skilfully made his task palatable to his unintellectual charge, and established an influence over her that lasted until the Revolution. Vermond was an expert at covering his tracks, so that even today his real political power remains impalpable; it is appropriate that the only serious study of him, Eugène Welwert's article of 1921, is entitled 'L'éminence grise de Marie Antoinette'.[16]

The queen's major defect was an extremely short attention span. This can be ascribed partly to her lack of early education and at least initially to her youth. The result was that her interventions in politics were fitful and short-lived, and thus, though often conducted with great sound and fury, usually signified nothing. Unlike her mother, Marie Antoinette did not have the stuff of a statesman, because she simply lacked the patience and application to see a policy through from beginning to end. Further, as defining proof that she was no intellectual, she saw politics as a matter of personalities rather than issues. These failings are minutely attested in the stream of reports on her progress sent back to Vienna over a period of twenty years by the Austrian ambassador to Versailles, the comte de Mercy-Argenteau. They are summed up in Mercy's despatch of 4 February 1782 to Marie Antoinette's brother, the Emperor Joseph II:

> The queen is beginning to show some qualities of foresight . . . but my zeal for Your Majesty's service and for the queen's glory does not permit me to conceal the fact that this august princess devotes neither the time nor the effort necessary to gain the solid and preponderant influence that she could have if she displayed a firm and consistent will . . . The need for constant amusement disturbs the ideas and method that the queen should apply to serious matters; she does not accept this fact, since she occasionally intervenes in politics with vivacity and even force. One points out to her most humbly, not as a real fault but rather as a fear one has for her, that great affairs need great preparation, without which activity displayed only at moments of crisis can only compromise her position.[17]

The ambassador's reports remain the most detailed source we possess on Marie Antoinette's life and political role at Versailles. They also reveal much about their author, who even more than Vermond (with whom he worked hand-in-glove) acted as the queen's confidant, mentor and general minder throughout these years. Florimond-Claude, comte de Mercy-Argenteau, was a native of the Low Countries, born in Liège in 1727, and had been Vienna's representative at Versailles since 1766.[18] As a diplomat, he was shrewd, subtle and experienced; as a man, his austere figure reflected an inner coldness. 'The tall and desiccated form of the emperor's ambassador was espied', was one contemporary description of Mercy's appearance at a Versailles reception.[19] Mercy's private life was as discreet as his public persona: he lived a life of blameless domesticity in Paris with his 'elderly and tedious'[20] mistress, the opera singer Rosalie Levasseur.

Apart from his normal diplomatic duties, Mercy had a further and much more private task, specifically ordered by Maria Theresa. This was to act as her daughter's secret counsellor and constant guide, helping her to navigate the eddies and shoals of politics at Versailles. The secret reports that Mercy sent back with his weekly official despatches to Vienna, first to the empress and after her death to her son and successor Joseph II, are a minutely detailed record of this work of twenty years. His labours give some idea of the importance that Maria Theresa and her collaborators attached to their aim. This was to ensure that Marie Antoinette did everything humanly possible to win the affection and confidence of her husband, and to use this whenever necessary on behalf of her native country. In this scheme, the future queen would be not only an adored and adoring wife but a perfectly positioned mouthpiece for the House of Austria.

It has been claimed that Mercy consistently overstated the extent of Marie Antoinette's power, portraying Louis XVI in comparison as stupid, indolent and increasingly dependent on his wife. This, so the argument goes, was a self-interested strategy by which the ambassador could play up the importance of his own services to his masters (and mistress) in Vienna.[21] Yet although Mercy was certainly guilty of some self-serving distortion, his diplomatic credit also depended on the accuracy of his reporting; if the picture of Versailles he presented to his chiefs had borne no relation to reality, this would soon have been exposed.

One facet of Mercy that remains enigmatic is what he felt personally about Marie Antoinette. Did he ever see her as a human being rather than a political object? She was in many ways his life's work; as her Pygmalion, he had shaped and brought her to life at Versailles as queen of France. Yet beneath the formal protestations of devotion in his correspondence, it is difficult to feel that he had any real affection for her – if indeed he had for anybody. Whatever feelings lay beneath his polished surface, he kept them to himself. On the other hand, his formal respect for the queen remained constant. He never displayed the heartless cynicism of his superior, the Austrian chancellor Prince Kaunitz, who, once Marie Antoinette's limitations became clear, coldly wrote her off as a *mauvais payeur*, a bad investment.[22]

The major obstacle that Mercy faced in helping Marie Antoinette negotiate at Versailles was Austrophobia. The French monarchy and the Habsburgs had been hereditary enemies since 1494, and all the military and diplomatic glories of the reigns of Louis XIII and Louis XIV had been associated with an anti-Austrian foreign policy. This state of affairs had only changed in 1756 with the *renversement des alliances*, by which Louis XV, tiring of the unreliability of Frederick the Great of Prussia as an ally, and deciding that England rather than Austria was now France's principal foe, had substituted for the Prussian connection an alliance with the Habsburgs. Yet the new Franco-Austrian alliance was unpopular from the outset, and almost immediately damned by the disasters of the Seven Years War – the loss of French influence in India and the surrender of all her possessions in Canada – which it precipitated. A large section of the French court and of public opinion continued to view the Habsburgs as France's real enemy, and on her appearance at Versailles Marie Antoinette inevitably became a target. Just seven months after her arrival in France, the new dauphine's position became even more precarious when the duc de Choiseul, the foreign minister who had arranged her marriage, was disgraced, and a rival faction, far more hostile to the Austrian alliance, came to power.

Most alarming of all for Marie Antoinette, these anti-Habsburg doctrines were even echoed by her husband. Louis's father, the old dauphin, whose memory he revered, had been a staunch Austrophobe, and had passionately opposed the *renversement des alliances*. His governor la Vauguyon was a close friend of the old dauphin, and shared these views. La Vauguyon also passed on to Louis a family sentiment shared by all Louis XV's children: a horror of female political influence, epitomized in their eyes by their father's mistress Mme de Pompadour, whose exceptional power they had bitterly resented. Above all they had resented the way in which Pompadour, in partnership with another female politician, the Empress Maria Theresa, had thwarted their opposition to the Austrian alliance in 1756. Thus well before Marie Antoinette's arrival in France, the link between Austrian diplomacy and overbearing women had been forged in Louis's mind. The queen herself admitted this years later, in a letter to her brother the Emperor Joseph II:

> The king's natural distrust was first fortified by his governor, well before my marriage. M. de la Vauguyon made him fear that his wife would try to dominate him, and his black heart took pleasure in frightening his pupil with all the dark legends invented about the House of Austria.[23]

A further, deeply personal factor added to Louis's initial distance from his wife. For the first seven years, the marriage was unconsummated. The reasons for the royal couple's sexual dysfunction remain unclear and have been the subject of much speculation. The problem was long thought to be that Louis suffered from phimosis, in which an excessively tight foreskin makes it difficult – and painful – to achieve a full erection. Marie Antoinette's first serious biographer, Stefan Zweig, concluded that the difficulty was solved by Louis undergoing an operation, probably circumcision, in 1777, after which a first child was quickly conceived.[24] Yet there is no clear evidence that the operation did take place, and other testimonies give different explanations of the royal couple's sexual problem. The most notable of these comes from Marie Antoinette's own brother, the Emperor Joseph II. In April 1777 Joseph visited Versailles, partly to further the Franco-Austrian alliance on the diplomatic level, but also to iron out its more delicate personal aspects. In particular, he was directed by Maria Theresa to discover why Louis and Marie Antoinette had not so far bolstered the future of the alliance by producing children.

A forceful and inquisitive character, Joseph lost no time in subjecting his hapless sister and brother-in-law to the most intimate and embarrassing interrogation. In this capacity, Joseph displayed a ruthless practicality. He described the result of his sexological investigation to his brother Leopold in one of the most explicit letters ever written by a reigning monarch:

> In the conjugal bed, here is the secret. [The king] has excellent erections, inserts his organ, remains there without stirring for perhaps two minutes, then withdraws without ever discharging and, still erect, he bids his wife goodnight. It is incomprehensible, all the more so since he sometimes has nocturnal

emissions. He is quite satisfied and frankly admits that he performs the act from duty alone and takes no pleasure in it. Ah! if I could only have been there once, I should have put things right. He ought to be whipped, to make him ejaculate, as one whips donkeys. As for my sister, she is not amorously inclined, and they are a couple of incompetents together.[25]

Possibly Joseph's real concern here was to exhibit his own carnal knowledge to Leopold and to portray his brother-in-law as a buffoon. Yet this letter remains the most detailed direct account of Louis XVI's and Marie Antoinette's conjugal difficulties. Also, the sheer bizarreness of the situation it describes, of a monarch who had clearly never been taught to connect conception with ejaculation, is testimony to its truth; it is difficult to imagine Joseph making up something so 'incomprehensible'.

Whether the result of their own efforts, an operation, or Joseph's technical advice, in December 1778 Louis and Marie Antoinette finally produced a child. This first offspring was a daughter, christened Marie Thérèse in honour of her Austrian grandmother, and in October 1781 a first son and heir appeared, the dauphin Louis-Joseph, followed four years later by a second, Louis-Charles, duc de Normandie. From the birth of the dauphin, the balance of Louis XVI's and Marie Antoinette's relationship began to shift. The king, in his immense relief at having finally sired a successor, grew both more affectionate and closer to his wife. As a corollary, the queen's power at court began to grow.

This development was encouraged by the fact that in one important personal aspect, Louis XVI broke with family tradition. Except in the rare cases where they were homosexual, the kings of France had usually taken mistresses. Although its main purpose was recreational, this practice also had significant political side-effects. On a symbolic level, in an age in which royal power ultimately depended on the perpetuation of the dynasty, it enhanced the image of the king's sexual competence and potency. On a more practical level, the division of the monarch's sexual favours between a mistress with whom he slept for pleasure but who could lose her position at any time, and a queen who had the secure status of a wife but whose link with her husband was based not on affection but reasons of state, had important implications for the conduct of government. Crucially, it gave the ministers an essential freedom of manoeuvre, and prevented their access to the king for public business from being blocked by a dominant figure from his private life.[26]

In contrast to virtually all his predecessors, Louis XVI never once took a mistress. Remarkably for his time and social station, he was naturally monogamous. As he grew closer to his queen after the birth of the dauphin, his increasing affection for his wife remained unchallenged by the emergence of another female partner. The division between royal spouse and royal lover that had traditionally benefited the king's ministers thus ceased to operate. The queen began to acquire significant influence over appointments in the Church and the army and, eventually, the ministry. At the same time, an ambitious group of courtiers and politicans, known loosely as the 'queen's party', coalesced around her. By the mid-1780s, Marie Antoinette united the emotional ascendancy of a mistress with the permanence of a wife.[27]

By now Marie Antoinette was no longer simply a representative of Austrian interests at the French court. There is evidence that by the eve of the Revolution her Habsburg family feeling had cooled, and that as mother of a dauphin she felt herself increasingly a French rather than an Austrian princess. When her old enemy, the foreign minister Vergennes, finally died of overwork in February 1787, to Mercy-Argenteau's fury she refused to exert herself in favour of the Austrian candidate to succeed him, the comte de Saint-Priest. It was unfair, she told the flabbergasted ambassador, that the court of Vienna should choose the foreign minister of France.[28] Yet public opinion did not recognize the queen's changed attitude. Marie Antoinette would always be seen as a serpent in the bosom of the body politic, bent on abasing France for the benefit of the Habsburgs.

A further aspect of the queen's personality played into the hands of her enemies. This was her penchant for sentimental friendships with women of her own age, whom she loaded with favours and honours. The first of Marie Antoinette's female favourites was the blonde, highly strung princesse de Lamballe, who was liable to swoon at the least commotion. She was particularly allergic to crustaceans, and once memorably fainted at the sight of a lobster in a painting.[29] From the mid-1770s, Lamballe was eclipsed by the comtesse Gabrielle de Polignac. An exclusive coterie, known at Versailles as the *société*, soon formed around the queen and her confidantes. Its key figures were Mme de Polignac's sister-in-law, Diane de Polignac, the talented collector and amateur actor, the comte de Vaudreuil, the king's brother Artois, and the worldly and cynical commander of the Swiss Guard, the baron de Besenval. This was a tightly-knit circle in more ways than one; Mme de Polignac was the mistress of Vaudreuil, while Artois was the lover of her sister, Mlle de Polastron.

The main function of the *société* was innocent – to provide a space in which the queen could relax and act naturally, away from the formality and hierarchy of the court. It was this need that inspired the creation of the famous backdrop to its activities, the Petit Trianon. In 1782, Marie Antoinette began to build a 'hamlet' around an ornamental lake in the park of Versailles, complete with thatched cottages and a model farm. 'There,' she once remarked, 'I can be myself.'[30] Yet there was a price to be paid for this artifical *fête champêtre*. The etiquette and hierarchy of Versailles had a hard and practical function, which the queen in her naïveté ignored. This was to ensure that all courtiers had clearly regulated access to the royal family, and a fair share of the posts, favours and pensions that this implied. By creating a miniature court within a court, and concentrating upon itself the queen's considerable reserves of patronage, the *société* made both itself and its royal patron deeply unpopular. It is no coincidence that many of those nobles who first sided with the Revolution came from great court families like the Noailles whose former credit had suffered particularly from the rise of the *société*.[31]

It was her relations with the *société* that inspired the most savage aspect of the mounting attacks on the queen. Whereas the first pamphlets against her had been political and anti-Austrian, by the time she was twenty-three they had become personal – and pornographic. It is once again very probable that the first of these libels originated at Versailles itself, with courtiers infuriated by Marie Antoinette's exclusive favour for her coterie. By 1780, the trickle had become a flood; to give just one example, the *Essai historique sur la vie de Marie Antoinette*, an obscene autobiographical 'confession' by the queen, was first published clandestinely in 1781, reprinted in 1783 and then annually well into the Revolution.[32]

These works usually took the form of the rather absurd porno-graphic tableaux since made familiar by de Sade. In them, Marie Antoinette was invariably represented as a sexually voracious mon-ster, prepared to copulate in various permutations with whoever and whatever came to hand. Artois, as the best-looking and most virile of the Bourbons, often figured as her partner in these fantasies (this was the theme of one of the more popular pamphlets, *Les amours de Charlot et de Toinette*). Yet the strongest theme of the pamphlets was that of Marie Antoinette as lesbian, with Mesdames de Lamballe and de Polignac as her sexual partners. There is no evidence whatever that the queen or any of her female friends had lesbian or any other unorthodox sexual tastes. Yet none of this affected the spread of the underground literature against Marie Antoinette, nor the remarkable extent to which it was believed by the public. By 1789, the queen's unpopularity had begun to threaten the crown itself.

Ironically, the one personal secret that could have damaged Marie Antoinette never reached the public. This was her relationship with the Swedish nobleman Hans Axel, Count von Fersen.[33] Tall and elegant, with dark hair and well-cut features, Fersen was considered one of the most handsome men of his day. He first met Marie Antoinette during a visit to Versailles in the 1770s before he moved permanently to France in 1783 as colonel of the Royal Swedish regiment. The question of whether Fersen and Marie Antoinette were ever lovers in the physical sense has excited prurient speculation for 200 years. Certainly, as an attractive woman married to a reserved and sexually incompetent husband, Marie Antoinette had every reason to seek solace elswhere. Against this must be balanced the horrific risks that conducting an extramarital affair posed to the wife of a reigning monarch or heir to the throne. If discovered, it would call into doubt the legitimacy of the royal children and fatally compromise the succession.

In the light of these dangers, it is most likely that the queen's relations with Fersen only became physical, if they did at all, after 1789, when she had already produced an heir and the perils of the Revolution left her with little to lose.[34] The truth, whatever it is, can never be known now, since those of Fersen's papers that probably contained his most intimate correspondence with Marie Antoinette were destroyed by a prudish descendant in the 1870s. The surviving letters between the two, however, do point to one unquestionable fact: from the late 1770s the queen and Fersen were deeply in love. This love was only heightened by the Revolution, and Marie Antoinette's ultimate fate lends it an imperishably tragic quality. Its strength is attested at the end of a coded letter, written in the winter of 1791–2 by the queen to Fersen: 'Farewell, most loved and loving of men.'[35]

Although Fersen was never publicly named as the queen's lover at the time, it is possible that some senior courtiers and ministers were aware of the relationship. This is stated as a fact by the comte de Saint-Priest, himself a minister in the 1780s, in his memoirs. Saint-Priest, however, may well have been settling old scores, since his own wife at one point had a torrid affair with Fersen.[36] As for Louis XVI, whether he was unaware of Marie Antoinette's liaison with Fersen, tolerated it because it was genuinely innocent, or even eventually played the part of a complaisant husband, will never be known.

It was an unusual and ill-matched royal couple that faced the crisis of the monarchy. Louis XVI was knowledgeable, fair-minded, and in many areas, particularly foreign policy, a successful ruler. Marie Antoinette, herself no fool, was plentifully endowed with that presence and charisma so crucial to the mystique of majesty. After 1780, the succession no longer gave cause for concern. Yet this picture also contained shadows. The most ominous was the king's tendency to indecision. This was compounded by the fact that, unusually for his time and station, he never took a mistress. Under Louis XV, the scapegoats for the king's many inadequacies had been his string of unpopular mistresses. In their absence under Louis XVI, this unenviable role fell to Marie Antoinette. The fact that she was a Habsburg, scion of France's hereditary enemies, fitted her all the more for the part.

An intelligent but indecisive king; a strong-willed but impulsive queen, whose perceived dominance of her husband made her a magnet for public hostility: in a period of peace and stability, these deficiencies might not have proved serious. In a time of upheaval, however, their effect was fatal.

Chapter Two

THE MONARCHY IN 1789

THE MONARCHY THAT LOUIS XVI embodied at the opening session of the Estates General was still a grand if somewhat dilapidated edifice. Despite significant domestic turbulence and international eclipse during the previous half-century, it remained a coherent intellectual whole. The king ruled by divine right; he was responsible for his actions only to God. The religious basis of his authority was underlined by his honorific titles – the Most Christian King, the eldest son of the Church. Yet this divine sanction also limited the king's powers at the same time as it exalted them. Responsibility to God bound him to behave in a Christian way towards his subjects and not to tamper arbitrarily with their lives or property.

Beneath the façade of absolute authority, the French monarchy was based upon a complex series of tacit compromises between the crown and the social and political elites.[1] Below the king and the royal family, French society, like that of all continental old regimes, was divided into a hierarchy of orders, known as estates. Each one was legally defined, and had its own rights and duties. The clergy ranked as the first estate, their independence underlined by the fact that they owed allegiance not only to the king as head of state, but to the Pope as head of the Catholic Church. As a further concession to their status, they were not taxed directly, but instead voted a *don gratuit*, or 'free gift', to the crown at their five-yearly assemblies.

The nobility too, the second estate, were subjects of the king pure and simple, in contrast to the clergy. Yet in practice the long history of periodic noble rebellion against the crown, and the substantial local power retained by the great families despite Louis XIV's attempt to gather them all under his watchful eye at Versailles, dictated a prudent royal policy towards them that respected their privileges. By the end of the eighteenth century, these were social rather than fiscal. True, the nobility were exempt from the main direct tax, the *taille*, but from 1695 onwards they had been subjected, along with everybody else, to a succession of income-based contributions, in particular the *vingtième* amounting to one-twentieth of the taxpayer's revenue, in 1749. Generally, however, they enjoyed a special status that placed them far above the mass of ordinary Frenchmen. On the land, they derived from the remnants of the feudal system a whole arsenal of dues and obligations from the peasantry. These ranged from a variety of payments, in money or kind, to the right to hunt over their tenants' property. The nobility also enjoyed a monopoly over all the highest offices in Church and State, from bishoprics and archbishoprics to commissions in the army and ministerial and administrative office.

Below the clergy and nobility stretched the third estate, composed of all lay commoners. At its head were the professional and commercial middle class, some of whom were very wealthy indeed. Yet the bulk of its members comprised the urban working class and, above all, the peasantry, who made up fully 80 per cent of the French population.[2] Socially, politically and economically, it was the third estate that paid the price of the unspoken bargain between the monarchy and the privileged orders. Its members bore the brunt of taxation, to which were added tithes to the Church and, in the peasants' case, the burden of feudal dues. In theory, this was justified by the secular protection the king and the nobles gave the common people in times of war and unrest, and the religious comfort the Church gave to their souls. However, by 1789 the menace of foreign invasion and internal strife had receded, and the revenue from taxation, it seemed, was being frittered away in spectacularly unsuccessful foreign wars. The tax burden, on the other hand, never got any lighter.

France's representative body, the Estates General, had first developed at the beginning of the fourteenth century. Unlike the English parliament, however, it had never settled into a regular rhythm of meetings, and only tended to be summoned at times of internal discord or royal minority. It was also unclear whether its status was purely consultative, or whether and how far its decisions were binding on the king. Finally, the way in which the Estates General was composed and functioned, with the clergy, nobility and third estate deputies debating and voting separately in their own chambers, ensured that instead of reaching firm decisions it usually degenerated into bickering between its constituent orders. Although it was never formally abolished, in the early seventeenth century it fell into disuse.

The discarding of the Estates set the scene for the classical period of the absolute monarchy. Yet even at its zenith the royal authority was unable to shake itself free of all constraints. When the Estates went into abeyance in 1614, the country's sovereign law courts, the *parlements*, stepped into the constitutional breach, and remained there until 1789. There were thirteen of them, one to each major province, and by far the most important was that of Paris. It sat in the Palais de Justice on the Île de la Cité, which is still today the home of France's highest law courts. The *parlements* administered the king's justice, and were staffed by a hereditary caste of magistrates, who bought their offices from the state and transmitted them to their sons. This security of tenure also made them formidable potential opponents of the crown, since they could only be dislodged at the price of a tremendous legal and constitutional upheaval.

The *parlements* stepped into the political arena after 1614 through a variety of motives. Nobles themselves, the magistrates were concerned to protect the interests of their own order against the crown's pretensions. Yet they were also genuinely concerned, in the absence of the Estates General, to act as a constitutional counterbalance to the absolute monarchy and prevent it from degenerating into despotism. Claiming that France in fact had an unwritten constitution, based on certain fundamental laws, the *parlements* set themselves up as its guardians. It was never very clear what these fundamental laws were. By the end of the eighteenth century, however, some radical magistrates were claiming that they forbade any taxation that was not approved by the Estates General.

Far more concretely, the *parlements* disputed the legality of royal edicts they had not themselves registered, and used their right to remonstrate against them to delay or defeat government measures of which they disapproved. The result was a bitter debate over the respective powers of the crown and the *parlements* that dominated eighteenth-century French politics and did more than anything else to bring the absolute monarchy to its knees.[3] From the 1740s onwards, this struggle centred on finance. The series of conflicts in which the Bourbon kings sought to enhance their status in Europe and extend their power overseas – the War of the Austrian Succession and the Seven Years War – necessitated major increases in taxation and loans. Alarmed at both these spiralling costs and the lack of French military success, the *parlements* consistently obstructed the crown's financial edicts.

Yet the deficiencies in the old regime's fiscal system went far beyond the recalcitrance of the *parlements*. They were such that by 1787 the French crown was simply unable to raise enough funds to cover the deficit accumulated over the course of the century. The fall of the absolute monarchy had many causes, but the most immediate was this financial collapse. The traditional view is that the prime culprit was the exemption from direct taxation of the nobility and clergy, which ensured that the State's financial burden was borne disproportionately by the much put-upon third estate. Yet this exemption of the privileged orders was by no means general, as the clergy's *don gratuit* and the nobility's *vingtièmes* bore witness. Furthermore, widely varying local conditions, combined with resistance and significant tax evasion, ensured that there was a wide gap between the crown's demand for revenue and its supply. For all the myths about eighteenth-century France groaning under the weight of unjust taxation, she was in fact less heavily taxed than England.[4]

The distribution of the tax burden was only part of the problem. In particular, the administration of direct and indirect taxes was both inefficient and corrupt. Tax collection was farmed out to private individuals, the receivers general for direct taxation and a consortium of farmers general for indirect taxation. This reliance on private individuals inhibited the development of what the government needed most, a proper system of public credit.[5] The remarkable success of England since the Glorious Revolution had shown what could be achieved by a monarchy whose finances were efficiently managed and open to a degree of scrutiny, where loans could be raised by a properly constituted national bank, and where the national debt was guaranteed by the representatives of the people. England, in today's terms, enjoyed investor confidence; France, with its opaque accounting practices, vast opportunities for graft, and hand-to-mouth credit arrangements, did not. Thus at the height of the American War of Independence, the English government was able to secure loans at roughly 5 per cent interest; that of France was forced to pay almost double that rate, between 9 and 10 per cent.[6] For a monarchy determined at all costs to preserve its standing in Europe, the message could not have been more clear – military and diplomatic prestige depended increasingly on sound public credit.

During the first few years of Louis XVI's reign, the crown's finances were relatively healthy. In 1778, however, this situation changed with the king's decision to intervene on the side of the Americans in their War of Independence against England. France's part in the American war was made possible by a new finance minister, the Swiss Protestant Jacques Necker, who funded it through a policy of international loans rather than increased taxation. The total cost to France of the war was 1,066 million livres: 997 million of this sum came from loans, with 530 million raised during Necker's ministry, at exceptionally high rates of interest that have led his detractors to cast him as the chief architect of the monarchy's financial collapse.[7] Yet these vertiginous figures do not prove that the French monarchy's participation in the American war led *ipso facto* to its financial and political collapse. England at the end of the war actually had a higher debt than France, yet her political system survived intact.[8] The difference between English success and French failure lay less in the size of the debt than in the way in which it was serviced. Here again public credit was the key. That of England inspired confidence and thus lower interest rates, that of France, despite Necker's well-advertised best efforts, did not.

It is just possible that had Necker been given a free hand, he could have remedied this situation. His long-term aim was to improve the crown's credit through a policy of economies at court and streamlining of the financial administration. Yet he was never given the chance to realize this. As a Protestant, he could not sit on the king's council with the other ministers, so his main function was limited simply to finding the funds to meet their exorbitant demands. In May 1781, Necker lost patience and demanded from the king a coordinating role over the budgets of all the government departments. His ultimatum was rejected, and he resigned.

The dominant figure among Necker's successors was Charles-Alexandre de Calonne, appointed controller-general in November 1783.[9] Calonne approached the question of credit and confidence differently from Necker, abandoning economies and boosting the economy through public spending. Revenue, however, remained static while expenditure rose. The result, according to the most reliable modern estimate, was an addition of 651 million livres to the debt during Calonne's ministry.[10] By August 1786, Calonne calculated the deficit at 112 million livres, a quarter of annual revenue, while almost half of the government's income was swallowed up in servicing the debt. The fiscal system of the old regime had reached the end of the road.

Calonne's remedy, which he put to Louis XVI on 20 August 1786, was a vast and ambitious plan of revenue-raising and administrative centralization. At its heart was a new land tax, which would replace the old *vingtième* taxes and finally sweep away the fiscal exemptions of the privileged orders. The new tax would be administered by a system of provincial assemblies elected by local property owners at parish, district and provincial level. This central proposal was accompanied by a further package of rationalizing reform, including free trade in grain and the abolition of France's myriad internal customs barriers. This programme, which Louis XVI whole-heartedly endorsed, was the most comprehensive attempt at enlightened reform of his reign. Yet however enlightened, it deliberately left the royal authority intact. Calonne regarded the notables as purely consultative, and had no intention of allowing them the right of giving or withholding consent to taxation. As he put it to Louis XVI as late as 1789, after his own disgrace and exile:

> It is the inherent right of the sovereign power to make the nation contribute to the cost of its own security, and the monarch's duty to protect his subjects presupposes the duty on their part to furnish him with the necessary means.[11]

Unfortunately, the controller-general was the wrong man to sell this visionary scheme to the public. His spendthrift and authoritarian reputation was well known to the *parlements* and had long ago earned him their enmity. This was why he thought it prudent not to submit his programme to the sovereign courts at first. Instead, he decided initially to submit them to a hand-picked assembly of notables composed of the old regime's social and political elite. Yet even this precaution proved inadequate. When they assembled at Versailles in February 1787, the notables were horrified when the extent of the deficit was revealed to them. They naturally assumed that the slippery Calonne was at least partly responsible. On Easter Sunday 1787, two months after the assembly of notables had opened, Calonne was dismissed and hounded into exile. This treatment was unfair on a man who had genuinely tried to make amends for his previous spendthrift policies. As the contemporary writer and wit Chamfort put it: 'He was applauded when he lit the fire, and condemned when he sounded the alarm.'[12]

Yet the fall of Calonne had a deeper significance. As the fiscal and political systems of the absolute monarchy were indissoluble, the financial collapse revealed the unsoundness of the whole edifice. Until Easter 1787, France's finances had been managed on the basis of traditional absolutism: secretly, hierarchically, without public scrutiny of accounts or consent to taxation. For centuries the monarchy had controlled fiscal policy on its own terms. The unmanageable deficit showed plainly that it had failed. One solution was clearly for the government to follow the example of England and open up its finances to greater public control. Politically, this relaxing of the royal grip on finance, the great sinew of power, implied a transition from absolute to constitutional rule. Yet even if Louis XVI baulked at this sacrifice, it was obvious that the status quo was untenable. The assembly of notables thus marked the first stage in the fall of the French monarchy.

*

THE DISMISSAL OF CALONNE sparked two years of growing unrest that historians have given their own, rather cumbersome name: the pre-Revolution.[13] Between 1787 and 1789, the crown's desperate attempts to implement reform ran into increasing resistance from all sections of the public, most ominously from the nobility and clergy, normally the monarchy's firmest supporters. As in all regimes on the verge of collapse, the politics of this period were both fast-moving and highly complicated. While the crown veered from compromise to confrontation with its opponents, ministers and policies changed with bewildering rapidity. The result, however, is clear. By the autumn of 1788, Louis XVI's authority was dangerously undermined, and France stood on the brink of revolution.

Under the impact of this crisis, the king's character began to change. He had enthusiastically supported Calonne's proposals and was shattered when they were rejected. As Calonne grew increasingly embattled from February to April 1787, Louis backed him until his position became manifestly untenable. When the notables' opposition forced him to dismiss Calonne, the king felt this as a personal affront, and never really recovered from the blow. It was his programme as much as Calonne's that the notables had rejected, and this implied vote of no confidence left him deeply disoriented. He had proved a competent ruler within the confines of the traditional monarchy in which he had been raised, yet now the certainties of centuries had collapsed.

From this point on the king began to seem increasingly detached from day-to-day politics, withdrawing into himself and spending longer periods hunting or at table. Observers noted the change, among others the ever-alert Mercy-Argenteau. In August 1787 the ambassador could report to Joseph II:

> The king's personal state robs him of the resources to combat these misfortunes, and his energies are further diminished by his physical routine. He is putting on weight, and his hunting expeditions are followed by such immoderate meals that these lead to lapses of reason and a sort of brusque carelessness that is very upsetting for those who have to put up with it.[14]

One senses here a man beginning to suffer from a depressive illness.[15] From 1787 until his death this had a significant influence on Louis XVI's actions – or lack of them. Throughout the Revolution there are recurring references by those close to the king to behaviour that echoes Mercy's description. At times Louis seemed completely dissociated from his surroundings, in a way suggestive of deep depression, and for periods was prostrated by illnesses which contemporaries hint were psychosomatic.

The king's difficulties were compounded by the new leading minister. Etienne-Charles de Loménie de Brienne, Archbishop of Toulouse, had the confidence of the notables, but was deeply disliked by Louis XVI. Intelligent, equable and witty, his ability was generally recognized. Some contemporaries feared that his talents, while brilliant, were shallow: the writer Marmontel described his mind as 'glittering like a cut diamond from a number of little surfaces'.[16] His most important asset was the favour of Marie Antoinette; with his appointment the queen moved firmly to the centre of the political stage.

To have such an unwelcome figure forced on him, not just by his wife but by the notables he himself had summoned, depressed the king still further and accentuated his detachment from politics. With little other option, Louis accepted Brienne first as finance and then as principal minister, but qualified this surrender by penning cutting criticisms of the archbishop's views on credit and interest rates. He also made symbolic physical gestures of distaste that those around him could not fail to notice. Knowing that Brienne was afflicted with eczema, he ostentatiously insisted on all papers from the archbishop being dusted before he would handle them.

The king's withdrawal massively increased the pressure on Marie Antoinette. Yet this was not, as her enemies alleged, a case of an overbearing queen finally fulfilling her long-held political ambitions. Rather, Louis XVI's depression made his ill-prepared and unwilling consort the only alternative rallying-point for the dynasty in the periodic absence of the monarch. The queen's ill-considered excursions into politics of the previous decade now bore bitter fruit. She found herself isolated and alone at the apex of power, as the winds of unrest began to blow. Marie Antoinette had the self-awareness to know that her education and training were insufficient for the burden she now had to shoulder, and often confided her fears to her intimates. Her maid, Mme Campan, recalls one such occasion, just after Calonne's dismissal, in her memoirs:

> The queen often bemoaned her new position, and viewed it as a misfortune that had been impossible for her to avoid. One

day, as I was helping her to arrange various memoranda and
reports that the ministers had asked her to pass on to the king,
she sighed: 'Ah! I shall never be happy now that they have
made an intriguer of me.' I protested at this word. 'No,' replied
the queen, 'that is the right word. Any woman who meddles in
matters beyond her understanding, and the bounds of her duty,
is no more than an *intriguer*. You will at least remember that
I do not spare myself, and that it is with regret that I describe
myself so. A queen of France is only happy when keeping
herself to herself, and conserving only enough credit to aid the
fortune of her friends and assure the future of a few faithful
servants.[17]

Brienne's initial strategy was to dispense with the notables and
instead concilate the *parlements* by presenting them with a modified
version of Calonne's programme. This decision ushered in almost
two years of constitutional warfare and growing civil anarchy, as the
parlements opposed Brienne's measures and rallied most of public
opinion to the standard of resistance to the royal demands. Many
historians have claimed that the *parlements* objected less to the
imposition of new taxation than to the fact that it would now fall
equally on the privileged orders of which they, as nobles themselves,
formed a part. Yet there is much evidence that the *parlements* and
the elite they represented were genuinely shocked by the crown's
financial mismanagement and unwilling to accept further onerous
instalments of taxation without an element of scrutiny and control by
other sections of society. In this sense, the privileged orders were
only echoing the cry of the American colonists, 'No taxation without
representation!'[18]

As the crisis escalated, a new and significant feature emerged.
This was a growing chorus of calls for the Estates General. After
the failure of a last-minute compromise between the crown and the
parlement of Paris at a 'royal session' on 19 November 1787, the
provincial *parlements* immediately petitioned for the convocation of
the Estates. With considerable insight, and even a degree of modesty,
the magistrates increasingly adopted the view that a more representative body than an unelected judicial elite was now needed to resist
royal despotism. They could not know that once unleashed on the
absolute monarchy, the Estates General would swiftly turn on them.

After six months of political stalemate and growing disorder, Brienne finally lost patience and decided to break the *parlements* once and for all. He and his closest colleague, Chancellor Lamoignon, prepared an audacious plan whereby their opponents were attacked from both above and below. The *parlements* would be stripped of their 'political' rights of registration and remonstrance, which would be vested instead in a central court, known as the plenary court. At a lower level, many of the *parlements*' judicial functions would be devolved to forty-seven lower courts.

On 8 May 1788, the edicts establishing the plenary court and the other reforms were imposed. This *coup d'état*, as it was swiftly dubbed, created uproar throughout the country. For the first time there were signs of serious popular unrest. On 7 June, a crowd in Grenoble rose in defence of their *parlement* and, in the so-called 'day of tiles' bombarded the troops sent to restore order with roofing from their houses. Order was completely lost in Rennes, where a mob drove out the provincial intendant, Bertrand de Molleville (who was to become Louis XVI's minister of marine during the Revolution). Above all, the May coup destroyed the last semblance of cooperation between the crown and the privileged orders. The assembly of the clergy met, voted the minimum possible *don gratuit*, and demanded the Estates General. The nobility of Brittany, a notoriously turbulent body, held illegal assemblies at Saint-Brieuc and Vannes, and despatched a twelve-man delegation to Versailles to protest the edicts. The government's response was authoritarian, but tinged with a note of hysteria. The Breton deputation was arrested and thrown into the Bastille. 'The *parlements*, the nobility and the clergy have dared to defy the king,' thundered Lamoignon, 'within two years there will no longer be *parlements*, or nobility, or clergy.'[19] His prophecy was to come true, though not in the way he intended.

Most ominous of all, a flicker of unease passed over the army. This did not, however, originate in the ranks. In the 'day of tiles' at Grenoble, which left four dead and forty injured, the soldiers showed no hesitation when ordered to open fire on the crowd. Ten months later, during the much bloodier Réveillon riots, their comrades in Paris were just as resolute, killing twenty-five people and wounding at least as many again. It was the officers whose nerve began to give. Whether this was the product of sympathy with the protestors, hostility to the ministry or simple panic, there were many reports of commanders failing to take the offensive or maintain order. This was sometimes an understandable result of age and illness; in Paris the maréchal de Biron was eighty-eight years old, while in Grenoble the eighty-six-year-old maréchal de Vaux was fighting a losing battle with retention of urine.[20] Already these first symptoms of military disintegration gave grounds for alarm, although their most fatal effects would not be felt until July 1789.

Ultimately, it was not political opposition or even army disaffection that destroyed Brienne so much as spectacular proof that the heavens themselves were out of joint. On 13 July 1788, a freak storm producing hailstones the size of grapefruit that killed both men and animals destroyed the harvest of northern France and the area around Paris. Brienne's ministry was already in great financial difficulties, and this natural disaster dealt a crushing blow to its short-term credit. The government was desperately in need of 240 million livres of loans secured against expected tax yields, known as *anticipations*, to balance the books for the year. With the prospect of adequate revenue in 1789 rendered suddenly highly dubious by meteorological disaster, these *anticipations* found no takers. On 16 August, the royal treasury suspended payments and the stock market crashed. Brienne clung on for nine more days amid feverish negotiations to find a successor for him, then finally resigned on 25 August.

Brienne's resignation took place according to the usual forms; the method of choosing his replacement, however, was completely unprecedented. Marie Antoinette was devastated by the crash of 16 August and did everything she could to keep Brienne, who retained her confidence, in place. To this end, she conceived a plan by which he would remain as principal minister, but with Necker, whose popularity and reputation were still intact, taking over the management of the finances. The ubiquitous Mercy-Argenteau, a friend of Necker as well as the confidant of the queen and the Archbishop of Toulouse, acted as go-between. However, these negotiations failed, Brienne finally gave up hope of staying on and Necker returned to office as director-general of finance.

In taking it upon herself to reshape the ministry at a moment of supreme crisis, Marie Antoinette was assuming a terrifying responsibility. She accepted it with fatalism, mixed with genuine fear. This is palpable in her letter to Mercy of 25 August, the day Necker was reappointed:

> I tremble – excuse me this weakness – that it is I who am bringing him back. My destiny is to bring misfortune; and if he fails as a result of infernal machinations, or undermines the royal authority, they will only hate me the more.[21]

The queen did not act this way out of pure ambition and desire to grasp supreme political power. In fact, it is more likely that she only assumed the direction of affairs because the king himself was unable to do so. The crisis of August 1788 offers further evidence that by now Louis XVI was periodically prostrated by a depression that left him incapable of conducting day-to-day policy. Marie Antoinette herself hinted broadly at this in a letter to Mercy detailing her reservations about recalling Necker:

> I fear very much that the archbishop will be forced to leave the field completely, and then who will there be to put in overall charge? Because we must have someone, especially with M. Necker. He needs a brake. The person above me is in no fit state, and as for me, whatever happens and whatever they say, I am only ever in second place, and despite the confidence of the first, he often makes me feel it.[22]

These words are as remarkable for their shrewd assessment of Necker's failings as for the clues they provide as to Louis XVI's state of mind. Unfortunately Marie Antoinette's growing powers of insight could not keep pace with the pitiless march of events. August 1788 saw the ship of state rudderless, with the king out of action and the key decisions in the hands of the queen and the Austrian ambassador. The second stage of the monarchy's fall was complete.

*

SHORT, HEAVY-FEATURED and high-minded, Jacques Necker was fifty-six when he became finance minister for the second time. Both his style and his substance attracted great hatred from his opponents up to and beyond the Revolution. The Genevan's immense egocentricity and self-belief, coupled with his constant appeals to sentiment and virtue, were bound to grate on a court society faithful to the manners and morals of the previous generation. In addition, his most important actions in 1789 carry more than a hint of the self-serving and the demagogic, not improved for being dressed up in moralizing language.

Necker did great damage to the monarchy during the Revolution. This, however, was not through any actions of his own but rather through his very inaction – what Jean Egret has termed his 'systematic abstention' throughout his second ministry.[23] Brought back to power to implement the promise to call the Estates General, Necker did almost nothing to equip the crown with a coherent policy towards the Estates once it had been called. It is still unclear why this was so. Necker certainly believed that a 'great consultation was necessary . . . to regenerate France'.[24] The fact was that in September 1788 the mood of the nation was overwhelmingly in favour of the immediate calling of the Estates. Necker did nothing to stem or direct this current. His passivity at this crucial juncture underlines the most salient feature of his political career. He was above all a populist, brought to power twice by skilful manipulation of public opinion. If public opinion clashed with the interests of the traditional monarchy, as was now the case, he was bound to side with public opinion.

The key issue facing Necker was no longer whether or not the Estates General would be called; his own recall had ensured unquestionably that this would be the case. The central question now was how it would be composed. If precedent was to be consulted, the model was the last time the Estates had met, in October 1614. In accordance with tradition, this meeting had comprised an equal number of deputies, had deliberated and voted separately, and had only authorized conclusions approved by each of the three orders.

In this highly charged area, Necker, most of the other ministers, and Louis XVI himself, betrayed a fatal uncertainty. If tradition – and the interests of the privileged orders so close by birth and status to the crown – were upheld, then it was clear that the forms of 1614 should be respected. On the other hand, the eighteenth-century growth of population, prosperity, literacy and informed public opinion had given greatly increased power to the third estate. This estate did, after all, constitute over 90 per cent of the population of France in 1789. In acknowledgement of this fact, Calonne's provincial assemblies had accorded double representation to the third estate, giving it the same number of deputies as the other two orders combined. In addition, instead of the traditional vote by order, simple majority voting for the whole assembly, known as voting by head, had been decreed.

If these principles were extended to the forthcoming Estates General, the implications were incalculable. If the third estate were to be granted 50 per cent of the seats in the assembly, as well as voting by head, it would gain the whip hand over all legislation, since it was certain that enough liberal noble and clerical deputies would defect from their own orders to give it a simple majority. Thus by the autumn of 1788, the struggle to replace absolute by constitutional monarchy had been superseded by an equally crucial conflict. At its core was the question of whether the constitutional monarchy conceded by the calling of the Estates General should be aristocratic, dominated by the privileged orders, or populist, dominated by the third estate.

In this dangerously charged situation, the king and his council attempted to compromise. On 27 December, they issued a decision, known as the Result of the Council, which they hoped would prove acceptable to both sides. As a concession to the non-privileged, the number of third-estate deputies to the forthcoming Estates was doubled, while to mollify the first two orders, voting by head was not imposed, but only permitted if each order when convened agreed to it. Significantly, as a further indication of her growing power, on this occasion Marie Antoinette attended a meeting of the king's council for the first time. Equally noteworthy, in view of her growing reputation as a reactionary, is the fact that she supported the concession to the third estate. As the keeper of the seals, Barentin, who was present, later wrote in his memoirs: 'The queen throughout maintained the most profound silence. It was, however, easy to discern that she did not disapprove the doubling of the third.'[25]

Yet the Result of the Council did not have the effect its authors had hoped for. In fact, by its provisions the crown got the worst of both worlds. The Result inflamed the ambitions of the third estate by granting it double representation, but drew back from the crucial further concession that alone would give it meaning, by refusing to impose the vote by head in a single assembly where the third estate could take full advantage of its increased numbers. Equally, doubling the third estate alarmed the majority of the privileged orders, and made it much more likely that when the Estates did meet they would reject any moves to obtain voting by head on a voluntary basis. Instead of calming conflicting claims, the government by its actions ensured that the orders would swiftly descend into political warfare.

Necker was not solely responsible for the government's vacillations at this time. His hesitations were shared by the king, the queen, and almost all of the royal council. Yet, as leading minister, he bore much of the responsibility. He compounded this by his failures in organizing the actual elections to the Estates. No attempt was made to secure the election of candidates favourable to the ministry, as was the practice in England, or to prevent the choice of those known to be hostile to it. It is impossible now to tell whether this was the result of a cynical desire to avoid all responsibility in an unprecedented situation, or a more positive but scarcely less disastrous faith in the ability of the people's representatives once assembled to resolve all problems. Either way, it proved a great mistake. France was facing two immense challenges at once: the shift from an absolute to a constitutional monarchy, and the issue of the nature of the representative body called to oversee this change. To make a further comparison with England, 1789 for France was 1688 and 1832 rolled together. The response of Louis XVI's government was to let events take their course.

The elections began in February 1789 and proceeded on a leisurely timetable; the last deputies elected did not take their seats until the following July, two months after the Estates General first met. In all, 1,201 deputies gathered at Versailles on 5 May 1789, the day fixed for the opening session: 300 clergy, 291 nobles, and 610 from the third estate. This impressive total masked a great variety of individual experiences. Mirabeau, desperate to play a role on the national stage, yet barred from standing by the nobility of his native Aix-en-Provence because of his scandalous reputation as a wastrel and libertine, was elected instead by the third estate of the town amid tumultuous scenes. 'Men, women and children poured their tears over my hands and my clothes,' he wrote to a friend, 'and proclaimed me their saviour, their God.'[26] More modestly, the comte de Montlosier, amateur geologist and future counter-revolutionary, set out at the same time from the Auvergne as reserve deputy for the nobility of

Riom. Stopping on the way to examine the unusual rock formations around Fontainebleau, he was so fascinated by what he found that he arrived late for the opening of the Estates.[27] From all over France, the haughty and the humble, dukes, bishops, parish priests and country notaries, those destined to play a famous or an obscure part in the impending Revolution, journeyed to Versailles and their appointment with history.

*

ALL THE COMPLEX and dramatic events of the past twenty years thus led to the Hall of the *Menus Plaisirs* at Versailles, and the imposing gathering of deputies to the Estates General for the first time in 175 years. The king and the royal family made their appearance at midday, and after his brief speech of welcome, Louis XVI sat down to polite applause. The keeper of the seals, Barentin, then rose and spoke, in terms far too conservative to please the third estate, but, fortunately, almost entirely inaudibly. Then it was Necker's turn. He conspicuously failed to rise to the occasion. Instead of uplifting rhetoric, he treated the assembly to a long accountant's audit of the country's finances. It lasted fully three hours; when the minister's voice gave out, he merely passed his papers over to a secretary, who continued to drone lists of figures to the stupefied audience. None the less, when this finally came to an end and the king prepared to depart, there were more loyal cheers of 'Vive le roi!' More remarkably, several cries of 'Vive la reine!' were also heard. According to eye-witnesses, this took Marie Antoinette, who had been visibly nervous throughout the proceedings, completely by surprise. After a moment's hesitation, she dropped a curtsey to the packed gathering, then, as the acclamations redoubled, a second, lower curtsey before leaving the hall.

Yet appearances were deceptive. The king, Barentin and Necker had confined themselves to platitudes. No concrete programme had been proposed to the deputies. Above all, no attempt had been made to grasp the nettle of how the Estates General was to vote. Beneath the superficial show of unity, dangerous tensions waited to explode.

Chapter Three

BRETEUIL IN 1789

NECKER'S INTERMINABLE SPEECH to the Estates General surprised and disappointed the assembled deputies. It raised, for the first time, the possibility that he might prove unequal to his task. One man, however, had anticipated this, and was already waiting in the wings.

That person was not present in the hall. The baron de Breteuil had left politics nine months before and retired to Dangu, his immense château in Normandy. A distinguished and long-serving diplomat and politician minister of the *maison du roi* (now the Ministry of the Interior) since 1783, Breteuil had played a major role in crown policy throughout the last turbulent decade. His relations with Louis had sometimes been difficult; he was above all the queen's man. Resenting the rise of Brienne, he had resigned his ministry in July 1788. As the political ferment grew, to those alarmed by the dizzying speed of change he increasingly seemed the only man capable of restoring order.

Louis-Auguste le Tonnelier, baron de Breteuil, was born at the château of Azay-le-Féron, in what is now the Department of the Indre, on 7 March 1730. His father, Auguste le Tonnelier, baron de Breteuil et de Preuilly, was an army officer; his mother was the daughter of the *intendant* of Rouen. When Louis-Auguste was only eleven, his father died. His mother later remarried; her name and that of her second husband appear on the register at her son's wedding in 1752.[1]

Although the Breteuils were a powerful and distinguished noble house with a long tradition of state service, Louis-Auguste's side was a poor cadet branch of the family. The early death of his father cannot have helped matters. Straitened financial circumstances did not prevent Louis-Auguste from receiving his education at the best school in Paris, the Collège Louis-le-Grand, but did put a question-mark over his future career. At this point, however, the Breteuil family network stepped in, in the person of Louis-Auguste's uncle, Elisabeth-Théodore, abbé de Breteuil, who held the influential position of chancellor to the duc d'Orléans.[2] This formidable oper-ator decided that his young nephew should follow his father into the army. Accordingly, Louis-Auguste joined the Gendarmes de la Garde du Roi, and soon saw action in Germany on the outbreak of the Seven Years War.[3] Then, in 1758 – whether on his own initia-tive or on the advice of his uncle is unclear – he left the army and entered the world of foreign affairs. That same year, he was appointed French minister to the electorate of Cologne. It was the beginning of a remarkable diplomatic career that made Breteuil a leading European as well as French statesman by the last decade of the old regime.

Between 1760 and 1783, Breteuil was successively minister pleni-potentiary to Russia and ambassador to Sweden, Holland, Naples and Austria. In the course of this glittering career he became acquainted with many figures who were to loom large during the Revolution, both as his friends and as his enemies. The first was the future Catherine the Great of Russia, whose lover Breteuil was instructed to become in order to secure her friendship for France. He appears to have disobeyed this order. Worse, his refusal in 1762 to advance Catherine a loan she needed to mount a coup against her insane husband Czar Peter III, which none the less succeeded without French help, left her with a lifelong grudge against Breteuil that had important consequences after 1789.[4]

Breteuil's next posting, to Sweden, provided him with two important friends who would later become crucial collaborators and confidants during the Revolution. The most eminent was the Swedish King Adolphus Frederick's son and heir, the Crown Prince Gustavus.

As King Gustavus III, this mercurial young man developed into one of the most remarkable monarchs of his day, although today he is largely forgotten outside Sweden. Like his lifelong rival Catherine the Great, he was highly intelligent and a disciple of the Enlightenment. In the course of his twenty-one-year reign, he restored the position of the Swedish monarchy and pioneered many rationalizing and humanitarian reforms. Above all, in moments of crisis Gustavus always had the nerve and style to master the situation. The contrast with his fellow monarch Louis XVI is striking.[5]

Gustavus was a complex and flamboyant character. To judge by his behaviour and affections, he was homosexual; according to a persistent rumour, he was only able to consummate his marriage after detailed instructions from his favourite aide-de-camp.[6] He had a passion for the theatre and wrote several plays which he staged at court, with himself naturally taking the leading part. The superb rococo theatre at Drottningholm Palace, which is still in use today, was his creation. His suitably dramatic end – he was assassinated in 1792 at a masked ball – later inspired a famous opera, Verdi's *Un Ballo in Maschera*.

Within a short period, Breteuil won the affection and confidence of Gustavus. This comes across clearly in an unpublished letter of April 1767 from the crown prince to Breteuil, bewailing the latter's imminent departure to a new posting:

I can only imperfectly express, Monsieur, the regret we all share at losing you. Without speaking of public affairs, which will greatly suffer from your departure, you have earned in so many respects the esteem and friendship of all right-thinking people here that your recall cannot fail deeply to affect us all. For myself, I beg you never to doubt the sentiments that gratitude will always dictate to me and that your conduct throughout your embassy has so justly merited on my part. I hope one day to find myself in a position to mark these by my actions; in the meantime, words do not suffice to express them. Their Majesties, who have been much upset by your departure, have instructed Monsieur de Scheffer to express to you their regrets, and I take this opportunity to speak to you of my own. I hope that these sentiments will make you forget my bad spelling.[7]

Over the next twenty years, Breteuil and Gustavus kept in touch through correspondence and the latter's occasional visits to France. Their friendship, however, attained its greatest political importance on the outbreak of the Revolution. As the crisis worsened, Gustavus stood out as the only European monarch who felt genuine concern for the plight of Louis XVI and Marie Antoinette. Admittedly, he was alarmed to lose the subsidy Sweden had traditionally enjoyed as one of France's oldest allies. On the other hand, the spectacle of the French royal family in peril unquestionably awakened his romantic and chivalrous side. During the Revolution, Gustavus was the only foreign ruler Louis and Marie Antoinette really trusted, and the one to whom they revealed their innermost thoughts.

The second great friend Breteuil made from Sweden was to play an even more central role in the French monarchy's struggle with the Revolution. This was Axel von Fersen, the man who may well have been Marie Antoinette's lover. Fersen first came to know Breteuil through his father, Field-Marshal Count Axel Frederick von Fersen, a leading politician during the baron's period in Stockholm. Fersen was still a boy when Breteuil left Sweden, but the connection came into its own when the young man started to visit France. Breteuil helped to launch his protégé in Paris and at Versailles, and treated him almost as one of his family. His daughter was the same age as Fersen, and the two called each other '*frère*' and '*soeur*'; at one time it was even planned that they should marry. These links were strengthened by a further factor. From the early 1780s, Breteuil was both Fersen's friend and patron and the French queen's confidant — Marie Antoinette sometimes even called him 'Papa Breteuil'.[8] If anyone knew the secret of the couple's relations, it was Breteuil. The figures who did most to shape the royal response to the Revolution formed a very close-knit circle indeed.

At the end of 1770, Breteuil got his most spectacular promotion to date and was named ambassador to Vienna. With Austria now France's principal ally, this was the most important posting in the diplomatic service. But no sooner had Breteuil reached this pinnacle than disaster struck, for the second time in his career. On Christmas Eve 1770, the foreign minister Choiseul, his friend and patron, succumbed to the intrigues of his enemies and fell from power. As the disgraced duke's leading protégé, Breteuil was treated with a savagery that shocked contemporaries. He had already furnished his Vienna residence and sent his baggage ahead, but was none the less stripped of his embassy, which was given instead to a candidate of the rival faction, the ambitious prelate prince Louis de Rohan. From that moment on Breteuil hated Rohan, and this feud was to have important political consequences both before and after 1789.

The baron made the best of a bad job and accepted the decidedly second-rate embassy to Naples and the Two Sicilies. Ironically, however, this was to be a first step in the restoration of his fortunes. This was because the Queen of Naples, Maria Carolina, was a Habsburg, the daughter of the Empress Maria Theresa. Breteuil carefully cultivated her goodwill and thus also gained favour with her mother. When, in 1774, Louis XV died and the ministers who had replaced Choiseul were themselves disgraced, Breteuil was again nominated ambassador to Vienna.

Breteuil's seven-year embassy to Vienna was the most successful of his diplomatic career. He helped maintain the Franco-Austrian alliance, while checking the Habsburg tendency to exploit it to their own advantage. Above all, he made a firm friend of Maria Theresa, whose essentially defensive view of the alliance chimed well with French interests. What pleased Maria Theresa, however, was calculated to displease her son Joseph II, Holy Roman Emperor and co-ruler with her of the Habsburg monarchy, whose foreign policy views were significantly more aggressive than those of his mother. It also alienated Breteuil from the third member of the governing troika, Prince Wenzel Anton von Kaunitz, who was well aware that while Maria Theresa, who had only a few years left to live, embodied the past, Joseph represented the future. Chancellor from 1753 until his death aged eighty-three in 1794, Kaunitz had masterminded the Franco-Austrian alliance of 1756. Despite his eccentricity and hypochondria, he was one of the great statesmen of the age, and his formidable status and reputation made him a dangerous enemy.

Breteuil's mission in Vienna was to put obstacles in the path of Joseph's territorial ambitions, while stopping short of provoking an open breach in relations. The watershed came in 1778–9, when Joseph's attempt to acquire Bavaria led to the War of the Bavarian Succession with Prussia. As one of the mediators at the subsequent congress of Teschen, Breteuil played a major part in negotiating an

end to the conflict. This earned him the favour of Maria Theresa.
A more material reward came in the form of the Table of Teschen,
a priceless creation encrusted with precious stones, presented by
another grateful party, the Elector of Saxony. Yet the fact that
Breteuil failed to uphold the Austrian claim to Bavaria infuriated
Joseph and Kaunitz and made them his inveterate though hidden
enemies.

If the friendship of Maria Theresa could not deliver that of
Joseph, it did lead Breteuil to his most important Habsburg patron
of all – Marie Antoinette. Breteuil came to Marie Antoinette doubly
recommended: he was a protégé of Choiseul, the former foreign
minister who had arranged her marriage, and had the approval of her
mother, whom she held in awestruck admiration. The queen deployed
her influence to help Breteuil gain the Vienna embassy and showed
him much favour during the subsequent decade. When in the early
1780s he launched his campaign to enter the ministry, Marie Antoinette became his strongest supporter. 'Let us talk about your business,
Monsieur le baron,' she remarked to him at the time, 'for it is also
my own.'[9] With his appointment as minister of the *maison du roi* on
18 November 1783, the strategy Breteuil had pursued since he first
paid court to Maria Carolina of Naples was vindicated. It was an
object lesson in using the women of the house of Habsburg to
become a leading minister of the king of France.

In 1788, at the age of fifty-eight, Breteuil sat for the great sculptor
Pajou. The bust shows an imposing, now corpulent man, with a
strong, square face, heavy eyebrows and a short, aquiline nose. It
also hints at other qualities: shrewdness, worldliness and considerable
strength of character. Yet Breteuil's personality and abilities were the
subject of fierce controversy among his contemporaries. The divergent comments about him in the correspondence and memoirs of the
time make it hard to believe they refer to the same man. Some of
Breteuil's characteristics certainly gave ammunition to his enemies:
he was blunt, arrogant and appears to have lacked the social polish
that eighteenth-century court society prized so highly. Unable or
unwilling to look beneath the surface, the baron's detractors found it
easy to write him off as a blundering buffoon.

Breteuil's most cogent critics were Joseph II, Kaunitz and
Mercy-Argenteau. Mercy's correspondence with the emperor and the

chancellor was published in the late nineteenth century, and it reveals Breteuil as a favourite object of that withering contempt in which all three were such specialists. Kaunitz sets the tone:

> In truth, I rather fear the hasty temper, ignorance and lack of perception of our friend the baron de Breteuil ... The baron de Breteuil, whose fate seems never to terminate any of his embassies without some disagreeable scene ... I cannot predict just how irrational French policy might become, if in place of M. de Vergennes, the foreign ministry were given to some madman like the baron de Breteuil.[10]

Mercy's despatches echo his master's invective:

> M. de Breteuil, through his ignorance and inbred impetuosity, will always be a difficult partner ... Having little talent or style, he makes his way through self-importance and much activity ... It is probable that M. de Breteuil will not be given a ministry but simply a place on the king's council, where he will have no influence but plenty of opportunity to talk nonsense about foreign affairs.[11]

Occasionally, Joseph himself adds a disdainful note: 'The pompous baron de Breteuil ...'[12]

These judgements must be taken with a pinch of salt. Breteuil was often merely a scapegoat for a French foreign policy that Vienna found increasingly uncongenial as Louis XVI's reign wore on. It is noticeable that Kaunitz's tone towards him only became really venomous after France failed to support Austria over Bavaria; before that point, the chancellor had actually expressed a preference for Breteuil as foreign minister were Vergennes to be dismissed. In attacking France's ambassador, Joseph, Kaunitz and Mercy were simply shooting the messenger, and Breteuil offered them a temptingly large and colourful target.

The baron's most savage detractor, however, was a writer rather than a politician. Sébastien Roch Nicolas Chamfort, the illegitimate son of a married noblewoman and a priest, was one of the most brilliant satirists of his day. Initially an enthusiastic supporter of the Revolution, he ended by taking his life in spectacularly grisly fashion during the Terror. His posthumously published *Maxims* reveal him as a master of aphorism and a pitiless critic of French society at the end of the old regime. Breteuil had the misfortune to meet Chamfort in 1770 when, impressed by the younger man's talents, he offered him a post as his secretary on the ill-fated Vienna embassy that never materialized. Chamfort, who secretly despised Breteuil, paid him back for this patronage by casting him in a starring role in the *Maxims*. Rarely has a public figure been subjected to such a literary demolition.

Of all Chamfort's many dislikes, his most intense was directed at fools. He was careful to define the term:

> What a fool, what a fool; it is easy to accuse me of exaggerating. What is a fool? Someone who mistakes his position for his person, his status for talent, and his standing for a virtue. Isn't everyone like that? Why make such a fuss about it?

Such a proposition called for examples, and it was Breteuil's unhappy lot to provide most of them. The mildest of these merely poked fun at his snobbery: 'One sees from the example of Breteuil that one can jangle in one's pockets diamond-encrusted miniatures of twelve or fifteen crowned heads, and still be a fool.' The most extraordinary was aimed at Breteuil's vanity, which Chamfort compared to the remarkable perversion of the society banker Peixoto:

> A fool, bursting with pride at some decoration, seems to me inferior to that ridiculous man who, to arouse himself, got his mistresses to put peacock feathers in his bottom. At least this gave him sexual pleasure. But the other! The baron de Breteuil is far beneath Peixoto.[13]

Breteuil was unfortunate in his enemies. Joseph II, Kaunitz, Mercy and Chamfort were all major figures who left writings that have greatly influenced posterity. Yet the invective they heap on Breteuil leaves one crucial question unanswered. If the baron was indeed the buffoon they depict, how could he possibly have won the esteem and confidence of such varied and impressive European monarchs as Maria Theresa, Gustavus III and Stanislas Augustus of Poland? The solution to this mystery lies with Breteuil's friends.

The baron's partisans are less famous than his detractors, but they have the merit of close knowledge of the inner man rather than merely his public façade. In many cases they were his lifelong friends, and all worked with him over a period of many years. Prime among them was the marquis de Bombelles, whose portrait of Breteuil in a journal entry of 1781 is very different to that left by his enemies:

> What order, what clarity in the ideas of this great man! The chronicle of the events of the century seems always before his eyes; it is the only one which the genius and liveliness of his mind permit him to read without interruption. Nature has allowed him to dispense with the efforts others must make merely to become ordinary. He has never been able to concentrate on study, but he has forgotten nothing he has seen or heard, his judgements have always been correct, and the lessons of dealing with the leading figures of every country have been to him what the classics are to others. He would have difficulty naming all of Alexander's captains, but he knows perfectly all the mainsprings of European politics over the last thirty years; he has never been able to learn a foreign language, but speaks his own with rare energy and charm. He has a feel for every country and the knack of grasping exactly what people want to say. He should be an object of admiration for anybody who appreciates real merit, while his talent must grieve the pedant who values erudition above good sense.[14]

Where Kaunitz and Mercy-Argenteau deplored Breteuil's lack of social polish, for Bombelles its absence was a positive advantage, since it revealed more solid virtues: a native wit, great shrewdness and a wisdom born of long years of experience. Breteuil was clearly no intellectual and lacked the refinement expected of an eighteenth-century diplomat, but all this shows is that he did not conform to contemporary standards. In many important ways, he was not a man of his time.

Breteuil's sometimes disconcerting frankness was often remarked on. This quality emerges clearly in a remarkable pen-portrait of him by the celebrated writer and wit the prince de Ligne. Among his posthumous papers, Ligne left a literary portrait gallery in which he sketched the leading figures of his time in the then fashionable style of a Persian fairy-tale. Breteuil appears under the pseudonym of Coprogli, and the prince's description of him echoes that of Bombelles in many aspects:

Coprogli is so frank that when he is not (and this is only when, as a diplomat, he cannot be) he fools everybody. He is sincere to the point of brutality, pokes his nose into everything, is a tyrant to his friends, and even to his acquaintances, and always for their own good. He knows how much money they have, calculates what they spend, scolds them or praises them. He is faithful and steady, and remembers his enemies, I think, as much as his friends. In place of talents, and the humanities, and a little science, which have never penetrated his level head, he has only judgement. The brusque manner that goes with his firm character makes him good company: and this original blend of despotism and kindness is very amusing.[15]

The divergent views of Breteuil's friends and enemies are testimony to a striking and contradictory character. But Breteuil was neither a fool nor a buffoon. In private life, he was a domineering but kind man, who could inspire great affection. In public life, he was an able if unconventional diplomat, whose mistakes were the result of rashness rather than incompetence. Perhaps the most objective judgement of Breteuil's political strengths and weaknesses, which the Revolution was to reveal most starkly, comes in a report to Frederick the Great from his exceptionally shrewd minister to Versailles, Count von Goltz:

He has spirit, even vigour, and also courage, coupled with great political ability. But he is impetuous, and this leads to indiscretions which would be unpardonable even in a beginner ... he adds to bumptiousness the most insupportable arrogance whenever he speaks in the name of his king ... But I repeat that he has both finesse and vigour, and if guided by a talented and active minister, could easily become one of his greatest assets.[16]

Although no intellectual, Breteuil had an immense respect for the life of the mind. This was partly the result of inheritance, for he was born into the purple of the High Enlightenment. His aunt was Mme du Châtelet, 'la belle Emilie', Voltaire's mistress and muse and the French translator of Newton's *Principia Mathematica*. It may have been she who was responsible for his lifelong interest in the natural sciences. Breteuil had a particular passion for astronomy: as minister of the *maison du roi*, he collaborated closely with Jean-Sylvain Bailly, the astronomer royal and future revolutionary politician. 'I owe him the favours accorded me from 1785 to 1788,' Bailly wrote of Breteuil,

> I cannot forget him. I was devoted to him because as a man I believed him to be good, sensitive, upright and fair; as a minister always loving whatever was useful, great and brought honour to the nation and to the king. This is the man I knew and to whom I was sincerely devoted.[17]

Breteuil brought the same energy to his emotional and sexual life that he devoted to politics and friendship. For most of his life he was a considerable womanizer. In January 1752 he married Philiberte-Jérôme, the daughter of the wealthy financier Jérôme-Louis Parat de Montgeron, receiver-general of Lorraine. This was an excellent match, and Breteuil had to beat off much competition to achieve it; indeed there was a persistent rumour that he had to sleep with the mother to gain the hand of the daughter.[18] Whatever the truth of this, the marriage was happy. Philiberte-Jérôme was beautiful, but also haughty and arrogant. Despite this, Breteuil seems genuinely to have loved her. In 1757 the couple had their only child, Marie-Elisabeth-Emilie, the future comtesse de Matignon. Then, on 14 March 1765, during Breteuil's embassy to Sweden, Philiberte-Jérôme died in childbirth, aged only twenty-seven. She was buried in Stockholm in the Klarakyrke.

Breteuil never remarried, but consoled himself instead with a succession of mistresses. For the remainder of his time in Stockholm he pursued an affair with Countess Ribbing, and narrowly escaped being thrown out of a window when discovered *in flagrante* with her by the enraged count. Breteuil's next mission, to The Hague, was both sexually and financially fruitful – an agreeable combination. A wealthy Dutch lady, Mme Vriesen, fell passionately in love with him, and when she died in 1781 left him her entire fortune.[19] Above all, Breteuil began an affair here that was to last for the rest of his life. Catherina Frederica van Nyvenheim was a tall, handsome young woman from one of the best families in Holland. She was initially sent to Paris to learn deportment under the care of her elder sister, who had the distinction of having briefly been the mistress of Louis XV. Soon afterwards Catherina returned to The Hague, where she met Breteuil. The rest is described with brio by Bombelles:

Our big Dutch girl came back to The Hague; she had acquired some style and presence; she was young and fresh, and to the liking of the baron de Breteuil, who without ever being dominated by his mistresses, has always attended to them with a consistency and loyalty that do credit to the goodness of his heart. He returned to France, and Mlle de Nyvenheim followed him a short time after. A short time after that, the comtesse de la Marck made a Catholic of her. A short time after that, they made a duchess of her by marrying her off to the old duc de Brancas, who ended by this senile act all the other stupidities of his life.[20]

The marriage of convenience to the senile duc de Brancas fooled no one. The new duchess's son, born in 1775, resembled Breteuil closely, and was generally assumed to be his.[21] This boy, the comte de Brancas, later became one of Napoleon's chamberlains, and was elevated to the peerage in 1830 as duc de Céreste.

The fact that Breteuil never had a legitimate son led him to make up for this elsewhere. He was friend and patron to a number of talented younger men, with whom his relations were paternal; one of these, the future revolutionary leader Barras, describes Breteuil in his memoirs as the 'protector of youth'.[22] The most important of these protégés was Marc-Marie, marquis de Bombelles. Born in 1744 into an impoverished noble military family, Bombelles was launched on a successful diplomatic career by Breteuil, culminating in a series of embassies. Breteuil also brokered a glittering court marriage for Bombelles, to Angélique de Mackau. Breteuil consciously saw himself as a substitute father to Bombelles, describing him as 'a man whose diplomatic career I have guided and whom I love as my own son'. Bombelles for his part reciprocated the sentiment, referring to himself as Breteuil's 'foster-child'.[23]

These close personal and political ties made Bombelles Breteuil's most trusted secret agent during the Revolution. Cultivated, profoundly monarchist, a merciless observer of the society around him, Bombelles was very much a child of his time in all aspects except one – his exclusive fidelity to his wife, whom he loved deeply. Her death in 1800 – again in childbirth – devastated him and drove him to take holy orders.

Posterity owes Bombelles an enormous debt. He had an obsessive need to record everything he saw, and the result was an immense ninety-seven-volume journal, which he began on the birth of his eldest son in 1780 and kept up until his own death forty-two years later. The journal, along with Bombelles's private papers, has survived in the hands of his descendants to this day. An edition of the journal up to 1795 has been published; Bombelles's private papers, the most revealing of all, have not.

Breteuil's need for a surrogate son in the shape of Bombelles in no way diminished his closeness to his daughter. Marie-Elisabeth grew up to be one of the last great beauties of the old regime. Even the abbé Georgel, who hated both her father and herself, could not restrain a note of grudging admiration when describing her in his memoirs:

> The lively and scintillating comtesse de Matignon ... held the sceptre of fashion both in Paris and at court. The most elegant women took her as their model. Haughty, prickly and demanding, she inherited her father's character and peremptory manner.[24]

Yet Marie-Elisabeth had a tragedy of her own. In 1773, her husband, the comte de Goyon-Matignon, was killed in a carriage accident in Naples, leaving her pregnant and widowed at the age of only sixteen. A few months later she gave birth to a daughter, Caroline, but never remarried, living instead with her father and acting as his companion and hostess. The core of the Breteuil household during the Revolution was a widower, his widowed daughter and a young granddaughter born after the death of her own father.

A final figure completed this unorthodox ménage. Charles-Constance-César-Loup-Joseph-Matthieu d'Agoult, Bishop of Pamiers, was Breteuil's second great protégé, the lifelong lover of his daughter, and the real reason she never remarried, since it was by definition impossible for her to wed a Catholic prelate. Tall, handsome, elegant, and ten years older than Mme de Matignon, d'Agoult owed his introduction to the Breteuil circle to the abbé de Breteuil. He was something of an intellectual; through his own efforts he made himself an expert on political economy, and wrote pamphlets on the subject throughout his long life. He was also a libertine and, before the Revolution at least, a freethinker. Bombelles, who rightly saw him as a rival for Breteuil's patronage, noted disapprovingly: 'Pretty women have turned this young head, which seems less infatuated by new-fangled philosophy than carried away by the taste for pleasure.'[25] With this reputation, it took all of Breteuil's influence to persuade the straitlaced Louis XVI to appoint d'Agoult to the bishopric of Pamiers in January 1787.

Before the Revolution shattered his world, Breteuil lived in considerable style and magnificence. In Paris, he lived in a grand town house on the rue du Dauphin. On the abbé de Breteuil's death in 1780 he inherited the grace-and-favour residence his uncle had been given by the duc d'Orléans, the Pavillon du Mail next to the Palace of Saint-Cloud. This charming neoclassical building, with splendid views over Paris to the east, was an ideal country retreat midway between the capital and Versailles. It still survives today, though only a shadow of its former glory, as the International Office of Weights and Measures. Breteuil also owned a sugar plantation on the island of St Domingue, now Haiti. Finally, in 1781, with the money he had been left by Mme Vriesen, Breteuil bought himself a huge château in Normandy, Dangu, which he proceeded to embellish at vast expense.[26]

Breteuil's political views on his entry into the ministry are difficult to fathom. He had served abroad as a diplomat for most of his adult life and so his knowledge of France's domestic situation was necessarily limited. His main ambition was to become foreign minister; this is why Vergennes, who was well aware of this, hated him so much. It is much easier to gauge his views on French foreign affairs rather than domestic policy. In many ways, Breteuil remained a disciple of France's traditional foreign policy which the reversal of alliances had replaced. He had a particular hatred of Russia, which was clearly linked to his unfortunate experiences there. Above all, despite his close personal links to the Habsburgs, Breteuil's attitude to Austria was often extremely hostile, and this is one of the most perplexing aspects of his career. The likeliest explanation is that he drew a distinction between Maria Theresa's moderate interpretation of the Franco-Austrian alliance, which he supported, and the expansionist ends to which Joseph II wished to harness it, which he bitterly opposed. Breteuil's most difficult task, of course, was to reconcile his friendship with Marie Antoinette with his deep dislike of her brother Joseph. Yet in one sense there was no contradiction; for Breteuil, Marie Antoinette was never the sister of the emperor of Austria, but the wife of the king of France.

Breteuil's domestic political views at this time are less clear, but their outline can be discerned. He was a protégé of Choiseul, who had never been a great supporter of the absolute monarchy, and whose followers formed the backbone of the 'queen's party' in the 1780s. The 'queen's party' was a court faction rather than a political party in any modern sense of the term, but its members had a tendency to prefer constitutional to absolute monarchy.[27] It is imposs-ible to know whether Breteuil shared these views. At this stage he was probably still loyal to the traditional conception of an absolute monarchy tempered by the *parlements*. But he was no friend of the abuse of royal power; he had seen all too well in Russia where that could lead.

As minister of the *maison du roi*, Breteuil was remarkably liberal and humane. He instituted many reforms, all of which were inspired by his Enlightenment heritage. The humanitarianism of the Enlight-enment is obvious in his first major action just a month after entering office, his closure of the state prison of Vincennes, where Mirabeau had once been locked up at his family's request. A year later, he introduced restrictions on the use of the infamous *lettres de cachet*, imprisonment orders signed by the king alone without any reference to the courts. (It is through a *lettre de cachet* that the unfortunate Dr Manette is imprisoned in the Bastille in *A Tale of Two Cities*.) Religious toleration was an important part of Breteuil's Enlighten-ment credo. It was he who set in motion the emancipation of France's Protestants, framing an edict that granted them a civil status and was reluctantly registered by the *parlement* of Paris in January 1788. In this historic task, he had two crucial collaborators: his close friend, the historian Rulhière, who wrote articles and books preparing public opinion for the change, and his own cousin, the eminent jurist and botanist Malesherbes, himself a former minister of the *maison du roi*.

Breteuil's long-standing connection with the sciences and the arts also bore fruit under his ministry. Reflecting the Enlightenment concern with the improvement of public health, and assisted by Bailly, he drew up plans to shut down the capital's main hospital, the

insanitary Hôtel-Dieu, and replace it with four new hospitals in the
more salubrious suburbs.[28] He also closed down the pestilential
cemetery of the Innocents, had the corpses buried there transferred
to the Catacombs, and erected in its place the Marché des Innocents,
which became one of the capital's major markets. Breteuil's attitude
to the arts was shaped by a memorandum he had written as long ago
as 1774, entitled 'Reflections on how to make use of men of letters'.
This argued that the monarchy should stop treating writers as
enemies, as Louis XV had done in his last years, and instead make
friends of them through a policy of discerning patronage.

Breteuil made several interventions in favour of freedom of
expression. Most famously, it was to him that Beaumarchais's *The
Marriage of Figaro* owed its first public performance.[29] The play had
been written back in 1773 and passed by the censors, but Louis
XVI had found it subversive and declared that it would never be
performed. Circumventing a decision of the king was a delicate
business. Beaumarchais was invited to give a reading of the play in
front of an informal tribunal composed of Breteuil, several censors,
members of the Académie française, writers and courtiers. He completely won over his audience by a brilliant rendition of the piece
mixed with artful flattery. In the course of the proceedings Breteuil
made a *bon mot*; Beaumarchais immediately added it to the play. The
baron's daughter, Mme de Matignon, who was also present, was
asked to choose the colour of the ribbon worn by Chérubin, the
page. All Breteuil's qualms were dissipated by this *tour de force*. He
decided the play could indeed be performed, but in order to enable
the king to save face, issued the order on his own responsibility.

From 1785, however, shadows began to fall over Breteuil's
ministry. Vergennes had always been an enemy, but now Calonne,
who had been his ally, turned against him. Together, the foreign
minister and the controller-general made too powerful a combination
to dislodge, and Breteuil was condemned to an increasingly impotent
opposition. Yet the queen's support rendered him safe from dismissal.
Ironically, it was to please her that he made the worst mistake of
his ministerial career. On 9 August 1785, the court jeweller Böhmer
sought an interview with Marie Antoinette. He claimed that he had
delivered to the cardinal de Rohan, acting as her emissary, a fabulous
diamond necklace worth 1,600,000 livres, and that the deadline for

payment had now passed. The queen was flabbergasted; she knew nothing of the transaction, and the idea that she would use Rohan, whom she loathed, as a go-between was absurd. Her first instinct was to send for Breteuil. The baron, who had hated the cardinal ever since the latter had replaced him at the Vienna embassy back in 1771, immediately jumped to the conclusion that he had conspired either to obtain the necklace by fraud, or, worse, to compromise the queen. The result was the last great drama of pre-revolutionary Versailles: the arrest of the cardinal de Rohan in the Hall of Mirrors in full ecclesiastical robes as he prepared to celebrate Mass on Assumption Day.

Rohan's arrest, which Breteuil orchestrated, is the best example of the rashness to which he was fatally prone in moments of crisis. For it soon turned out that the matter was not as simple as it seemed. Rohan argued plausibly that he had been duped by the comtesse de la Motte, an adventuress who had claimed to be the queen's go-between.[30] Rohan alleged that she had persuaded him that since Marie Antoinette could not buy the necklace directly for fear of appearing extravagant, he could be reconciled to the queen if he obtained it for her on a promise of reimbursement. The moment the necklace was passed to Mme de la Motte for delivery to the queen, she absconded with it, and the scandal broke. It is still difficult to believe that Rohan could have been so stupid as to believe somebody of the calibre of Mme de la Motte. Yet any evidence that he was her accomplice rather than her victim disappeared when he managed to scribble a note to his secretary instructing him to destroy any compromising papers before he was carted off to the Bastille.

Breteuil had committed a major blunder. To preserve his own reputation, and above all that of the queen, the cardinal's trial had to result in a conviction. It is probable that the baron abused his authority to obtain this end. Rohan's secretary, the abbé Georgel, claims in his memoirs that Breteuil deliberately allowed key witnesses to flee the country so that they could not give evidence exonerating the cardinal. Unfortunately Vergennes, Breteuil's enemy and Rohan's friend, resorted to every method, including kidnapping, to return these witnesses to testify on French soil. In May 1786, Rohan was tried in front of the *parlement* of Paris and acquitted. This verdict was a disaster. Breteuil was pilloried as a vindictive despot, the queen's name was linked to a sordid fraud, and the monarchy itself was discredited. Napoleon was to date the French Revolution from the Diamond Necklace Affair.

Breteuil's actions between 1783 and 1786 reinforce the impression of a complex and contradictory figure. The man who closed the grim prison of Vincennes and reformed *lettres de cachet* could also attempt to manipulate justice to destroy a personal enemy. These ambiguities are only heightened by the last phase of Breteuil's ministry. The baron contributed significantly to Brienne's appointment, arguing fiercely in the king's presence against the recall of Necker to replace Calonne, which several of his colleagues had favoured. Yet he had clearly not bargained for Brienne becoming prime minister, as he did in August 1787, and found himself increasingly out of sympathy with the archbishop. Part of his disaffection was thus the product of a simple struggle for power. As the ministry entered its crisis in the summer of 1788, Breteuil came under heavy pressure from his circle, especially the duchesse de Brancas and Rulhière, to overthrow Brienne and take power himself. Bombelles gives a vivid insight into these intrigues:

> Certain people are doing everything they can to make M. le baron de Breteuil assume a role for which he is not suited. They are trying to persuade him that, as the only man capable of restoring order and confidence in France, he should profit from the present circumstances to remove the prime minister and the keeper of the seals. Rulhière and the duchesse de Brancas are the ringleaders of this clique. When they whisper together, one seems to see Hatred and Discord plotting together the downfall of humanity.[31]

But Breteuil was not about to become prime minister – yet. Instead, on 24 July, he resigned from the ministry. The reasons for his action remain ambiguous. Did he leave the ministry because he thought Brienne was too authoritarian, or on the contrary because he found him too radical? Breteuil certainly let it be known in July 1788 that he was sick of signing increasing numbers of *lettres de cachet* – a liberal pose if ever there was one. Indeed, the immediate cause of his departure was his refusal that month to countersign the orders imprisoning in the Bastille the twelve deputies of the Breton nobility who had come to Paris to protest at the installation of the plenary court.[32] The implication of this is that Breteuil was distancing himself from the worst aspects of the absolute monarchy and signalling tacit sympathy with the opposition. This reading of Breteuil's actions is supported by Bailly's recollections of meetings with the baron at this time:

> I have to say that in several conversations I had with him between the assembly of notables and the Estates General, his tact and good sense had made him feel that the present circumstances required changes in the government and modifications in the royal authority.[33]

Yet probing further, one gets the distinct impression that on this occasion Breteuil's liberalism was less than sincere. Here, the key witness is the baron himself. Four years later, in the midst of the Revolution, he wrote a long despatch to Bombelles, whom he had just sent to St Petersburg to secure Catherine the Great's support for his secret diplomacy on behalf of Louis XVI and Marie Antoinette. Breteuil was particularly concerned to deny rumours put about by his enemies that he favoured a compromise with the Revolution, and flattered himself that time had softened the empress's dim view of him sufficiently to discount them. 'I hope,' he wrote,

> that the empress's old esteem for me will hear you out in such a way as to dismiss from her mind all the lies she has been told about me. You could recount to her how the unfortunate archbishop of Sens [Brienne], whose system was based upon the destruction of the royal authority and the monarchy, and who always found me strongly opposed to the treacherous ideas he induced the king to adopt by abusing his virtues, nicknamed me *the louisquatorzian*, so as to paint me as an extremist in my desire to uphold the rights of the crown.[34]

These unpublished comments are some of the most revealing Breteuil ever wrote about his political views. It is possible that he was tailoring the truth to justify himself to Catherine the Great, but the words of the man himself, written in confidence to his trusted friend Bombelles, must carry very great weight.

Having written his resignation letter, Breteuil's first concern was to preserve his relations with the queen. He wrote asking to take his leave of her in person. At first Marie Antoinette angrily refused, but relented the following day. Breteuil's audience with her at the Petit Trianon only lasted three minutes, but as he left she did tell him to come to her if he needed help in the future.[35]

In his self-imposed retirement at Dangu, Breteuil took up the agreeable life of a country gentleman. He devoted particular attention to his kitchen, which was badly in need of remodelling. But he also kept closely in touch with political developments through a succession of house-parties for his friends from Versailles. Even Mercy-Argenteau paid him a visit. From the grandeur of the château, the company observed the growing ferment of ideas around them with alarm. Breteuil himself viewed the preparations for the Estates General with grave concern and predicted the worst. His increasingly conservative attitude is confirmed by Bombelles:

> I and my two sisters have just dined with M. le baron de Breteuil. He goes back on nothing he has seen or heard: many of our friends have gone mad; anybody who dares to stand up for the old ways is despised, and soon the adjectives fool and royalist will be synonymous. The licence of the press is unbelievable; the lunacy of the opinions it publishes is even more so. The decent man, the honest citizen who regards monarchy as a moderating force against the abuses of liberty, bemoans the fact that we are rushing like madmen to our destruction. We are throwing off a yoke that has always been gentle, and in order to reform some abuses of authority, passing abuses which the nation can all too easily curtail, we are unleashing passions which will lead to far more permanent and incurable ills.[36]

Yet beneath the pose of Cassandra, Breteuil had other ambitions. If Necker failed to manage the Estates General, he himself was the obvious replacement. Even in retirement, he retained the esteem of the king and queen. Though his real views were conservative, he had won round some liberal opinion by his stand over *lettres de cachet*, and by a well-timed resignation had distanced himself from a violently unpopular ministry. At Dangu, Breteuil was perfectly positioned to observe events. There, like de Gaulle at Colombey, he awaited the summons to return.

Chapter Four

THE SUMMER OF 1789

IT TOOK TWO MONTHS for Breteuil to be recalled to Versailles. The crisis that brought him to power began to build the day after Louis XVI opened the Estates General. The issue that sparked it off was small, but it had major implications. For the assembly to begin business, all the election returns had to be verified to ensure that they were valid. Although in his speech on 5 May Necker had carefully offered no opinion on the wider issue of whether the Estates should vote by order or by head, he had stipulated that this preliminary process of verification should be done separately by order. For the third estate this was the thin end of the wedge; if it conceded verification by order, the precedent was set for accepting voting by order. If it accepted this, it could be outvoted on every major proposal put before the assembly. So on 6 May, the third estate declared that it refused to begin verifying the election results for its order. To all intents and purposes, it went on strike.

Ignoring their obstreperous colleagues, the first and second estates proceeded to separate verification. Over the following fortnight conciliation talks between the orders were held to try and find a way forward, but by 26 May these had collapsed. From this point on, the third estate increasingly began to act on its own. On 3 June, it elected

Breteuil's old friend the astronomer Bailly, now one of the deputies
for Paris, as its president. A week later, it issued an ultimatum to the
other two orders to join it immediately for common verification,
failing which it would proceed independently. In the abbé Sieyès's
famous phrase, the third estate was 'cutting the cable' and sailing into
uncharted waters.

The events that followed are among the most famous in European history. On 12 June, in the absence of any official response from
the nobility and clergy, the third estate began its own process
of verification. The following day, amid scenes of jubilation, three
parish priests from Poitou broke ranks with their own estate and
walked into the hall of the third to present their credentials in
common. Over the next few days sixteen other priests joined them.
Emboldened by these cracks in the opposition, the third estate decided
that it alone spoke for the vast majority of the French people, and on
17 June formally declared itself the National Assembly. By this act
alone, it gave birth to representative democracy in Europe. Three
days later, finding themselves locked out of their normal meeting hall
by royal order, the deputies occupied a nearby indoor tennis court
to hold their sessions. Crowded into the limited space, surrounded
by craning spectators packed into the galleries, they swore a solemn
oath not to disperse until France had been given a constitution.
The oath was administered by Bailly as president, standing above the
sea of faces on a pine table borrowed from a tailor next door. It was
a far cry from the decorous discussions about public health across
Breteuil's gilded desk.

The tennis-court oath threw down an unprecedented challenge to
the monarchy. The third estate was claiming that ultimate authority
in the nation belonged not to the king, but to itself. This act of
defiance could not be ignored. Yet a cruel stroke of fate ensured that
it came at just the moment when the royal family was least prepared
to meet it. On 4 June, at the age of seven, the dauphin died. The
cause was the tuberculosis that had carried off his uncle and both his
grandparents. Although the boy had been ill for some time, Louis
XVI and Marie Antoinette were devastated by his loss. As the
political crisis escalated around them, they retired into mourning.
A deputation from the third estate arrived to offer condolences. The
king refused to receive it. The deputies repeated their request, but

only drew from Louis the bitter cry: 'Are there no fathers in the third estate?'[1]

In the first shock of sorrow, the royal family left Versailles and secluded itself in Louis XIV's former retreat at Marly, a few miles to the north. This geographical move had important political consequences. At a time when the future of the monarchy depended on how Louis XVI decided to respond to the third estate, he was isolated from the ministers and deputies, in the midst of a family stricken equally by grief at the dauphin's death and panic at the challenge to the crown. The combination was hardly conducive to wise counsel.

Above all, the royal family was not united in the face of the threat to its authority. Its divisions played a crucial role in the crisis of the summer of 1789, and later became one of the chief factors that sabotaged the crown's response to the Revolution. Each leading member of the family had different views and motivations, and this made the adoption of a coherent policy towards the third estate extremely difficult. The king's attitude was particularly complex. His preference was for enlightened absolutism, as his support for Calonne during the assembly of notables had shown. He had no great sympathy for the nobility and clergy who were now clamouring for him to protect them against the menace of the third estate; after all, it was their resistance to his reform programme that had forced him to call the Estates General in the first place. It was by no means a foregone conclusion that, in the battle looming over voting in the estates, he would automatically support the privileged orders.

The most revealing testimony as to Louis XVI's state of mind at this time comes in the memoirs of the comtesse d'Adhémar, an intimate of the royal family during these crucial months, describing all she witnessed in the summer of 1789. These memoirs make plain the repeated efforts of the queen and her friends to persuade Louis to forbid verification in common. Yet their appeals received a dusty answer from a monarch who, if anything, inclined to the third estate:

> We never ceased repeating to the king that the third estate would wreck everything – and we were right. We begged him to restrain them, to impose his sovereign authority on party intrigue. The king replied: 'But it is not clear that the third estate are wrong. Different forms have been observed each time

the estates have been held. So why reject verification in common? I am for it.'

The king, it has to be admitted, was then numbered among the revolutionaries – a strange fatality which can only be explained by recognizing the hand of Providence.[2]

Further on, the comtesse reveals just how impatient Louis had become with the noble and clerical privileges which voting by order was meant to defend:

The king . . . paid no attention to the queen's fears. This well-informed princess knew all about the plots that were being hatched; she repeated them to the king, who replied: 'Look, when all is said and done, are not the third estate also my children – and a more numerous progeny? And even when the nobility lose a portion of their privileges and the clergy a few scraps of their income, will I be any less their king?'[3]

*

IT SEEMS CLEAR from this that if Louis XVI had followed his instincts in May 1789, he would have conceded verification in common and voting by head. Yet by the time he withdrew to Marly he was, temporarily at least, broken by the death of his eldest son. He had never found it easy to make decisions, and the current tragic circumstances made it more difficult still. In his depressed and vulnerable state, he now found himself surrounded by a family circle determined to stiffen his attitude towards the third estate. Nobody could predict how long he would be able to withstand their pressure.

Of all the royal protagonists in the summer of 1789, Marie Antoinette has received the worst press. She has consistently been portrayed as a pure reactionary, an Austrian harpy poisoning her weak husband's mind against his own people. Hers has been seen as the principal hand behind all the efforts to distance Louis XVI from the third estate and rally him to the defence of the nobility and clergy. Yet while it contains some elements of truth, this picture is far too simplistic. The queen's memories of the nobles' resistance to the royal reform programme of 1787–8 were just as bitter as those of her husband; perhaps even more so, since the principal victim, Brienne, had been her protégé. In July 1788, asked her views on how the forthcoming estates should be composed, she had replied with her well-known quip: 'Oh, I'm the queen of the third estate!'[4] When called to translate these sentiments into action, at the meeting of the council of 27 December 1788, she had done so by lending her support to the doubling of the third.

What made her change her mind six months later? Despite her developing political maturity, Marie Antoinette had only been playing a significant political role for two years. Like her husband, she was prone to indecision, and she continued to view affairs of state in emotional and personal rather than political terms. She was just as shattered as Louis XVI by the death of the dauphin. Added to this, she was herself under massive pressure from her *société*, especially Mme de Polignac and the latter's lover Vaudreuil, to harden her attitude to the third estate and come to the defence of the privileged orders.

The *société* had had a chequered existence over the past few years. Since 1784 a shadow had come between the queen and her bosom friends, in the form of Calonne. The queen hated the controller-general, but before his fall he had artfully managed to win over the Polignacs to his side, largely through paying off their debts and other financial inducements. These intrigues had led to a rift between Marie Antoinette and her circle, to such an extent that in the summer of 1787 Mme de Polignac had taken the unprecedented step of leaving Versailles to take a trip to England. The crisis of the monarchy, however, changed these tactics; the *société* clearly perceived the threat to that old-regime *douceur de vivre* from which it had benefited so disproportionately. Follwing the fall of Brienne, Mme de Polignac, aided by the king's youngest brother Artois, had regained much of her former favour with the queen, which she used as far as she could to influence her in a conservative direction.[5]

Compared to the queen's hesitations and vacillation, Artois's position was much more inflexible – and reactionary. As a supporter of Calonne during the assembly of notables, he accepted the ending of the tax exemptions of the privileged orders, but always within the context of the traditional monarchy rather than a more representative system. When the Estates General became unavoidable, he was the moving force behind the memorandum addressed to Louis XVI by the princes of the blood in December 1788. This begged the king not to agree to either doubling of the third estate or voting by head, and to limit his concessions to the granting of fiscal equality. As soon as the Estates opened at Versailles, he and the Polignacs used all the resources at their disposal to stiffen the privileged deputies' resistance to voting by order. The marquis de Ferrières, noble deputy for Saumur, recalled in his memoirs that Artois wined, dined and met secretly with the most prominent noble and clerical deputies from the provinces, while 'the Polignacs' lodgings were a hotbed of intrigue, the focal point of every cabal'.[6] Above all, Artois detested Necker, whom he regarded as a secret supporter of the third estate. As early as 30 April 1789, he told the finance minister to his face that he was trying to take the crown from the king's head, and in late June even sought to have him arrested.[7]

Louis XVI's brother, Provence, was as usual far more slippery and ambiguous than the younger Artois. The full extent of his ambitions remains unclear, but at the least he saw the crown's troubles from 1787 onwards as a means of enlarging his own political role. He courted popularity by presenting himself as a partisan of moderate reform; in the first assembly of notables he signalled his distaste for Calonne, and in the second he actually came out in favour of doubling the third estate. His signature was ostentatiously absent from the memorandum of the princes of the blood. Yet he never supported voting by head, and by June 1789 he had cast his lot in with Artois's conservative cabal. Provence's about-face underlines a wider truth about the politics of these months. Many noble and clerical deputies arrived at the Estates General undecided as to the personal position they would adopt. Yet the confrontational stance adopted by the third estate on the first day of business alarmed them and led them instinctively to harden their attitudes. To the first two orders, the third estate seemed intent not just on removing fiscal inequality, but on undermining the entire social order. Many motives have been ascribed to the first and second estates and their defenders in the summer of 1789, most of them unflattering, but perhaps the most potent was simple fear.

The other two princes of the blood to play a political role, Louis's cousins Condé and Orléans, tended in very different directions. The prince de Condé was as conservative as Artois, conceivably even more so. Yet he was no fool, a strong character, and respected for his military capacities and experience. He was also ambitious, and may well have seen Provence and Artois simply as tools to make himself the dominant voice in policy-making. 'M. le prince de Condé wants above all else to be party leader,' noted Bombelles, 'and calculates that in joining forces with Monsieur and M. le comte d'Artois, his experience and shrewdness will soon enable him to dictate their opinons, and that soon he will be master of everything.'[8] This combination of talent and deviousness was to make Condé the relative Louis XVI distrusted most during the Revolution, with one exception. The duc d'Orléans's outburst at the royal session of November 1787 had earned him a spell of internal exile on his estate at Villers-Cotterêts. Like Provence, he had refused to sign the memorandum of the princes of the blood, but unlike Provence, this gesture presaged an open alignment with the forces of radicalism. Elected to the Estates as noble deputy for Crépy-en-Valois, Orléans immediately assumed the leadership of the minority of his order who supported the third estate and espoused voting by head. His Paris residence, the Palais-Royal, which he had earlier converted into a public promenade with shopping arcades as a business venture, became the headquarters of the popular movement. Louis XVI and Marie Antoinette were soon convinced that Orléans was deliberately fomenting revolution to seize the crown.

Thus by June 1789 not just the Estates General, but the royal family itself, was getting out of control. Under the pressure of events, the king's relatives were splitting into differing factions, and he himself was powerless to stop them. From this point on, Louis XVI had to contend not only with a gathering revolution but also with a *Fronde*, a princely civil war.

The declaration of the National Assembly, followed by the tennis-court oath, crystallized the challenge to the royal family. The monarchy had either to assert its rights or cede power to the third estate. For Artois, there was only one possible course of action. As the keeper of the seals, Barentin, put it: 'In his view, the illegality of the deliberation of 17 June, and the audacity of the tennis-court oath, had imperatively to be crushed, without hesitations or half-measures which would only be seen as proof of the government's failure of nerve.'[9] While few were as resolutely authoritarian as Artois, all saw the need for the king to reimpose his authority on a dangerous crisis. At four tense meetings of the council, it was decided that the king should make a personal intervention in the Estates General at a 'royal session' on 23 June.

This royal session, and the declaration of 23 June which formed its centrepeice, was a defining moment in Louis XVI's response to the Revolution, the significance of which endured until the fall of the monarchy and even beyond. It was deeply controversial at the time, and has remained so since. This is because not one, but two draft declarations were debated at the council meetings beforehand, a conservative version sponsored by Artois and his ministerial allies, and a more moderate one drawn up by Necker. The conservative draft was adopted and failed, bringing the Revolution a long step closer; Necker always claimed that if his version had been implemented instead, the crisis could have been resolved.

Tantalizingly, Necker's draft declaration has been lost, so it is difficult to put his assertions to the test. He read it out in full to his ministerial allies, Montmorin and the comtes de Saint-Priest and la Luzerne, in the carriage on the way to the first council meeting at Marly. Unfortunately none of them could hear it properly because of the jolting of the carriage wheels on the cobbled road.[10] Yet it does seem clear that on the vital issue of voting Necker proposed a compromise. The king would command the first two estates to accept voting by head on questions of common concern, above all taxation, but would reserve voting by order for issues specific to the nobility and clergy, such as feudal dues and clerical privileges. This is borne out by a letter of Saint-Priest to Louis XVI of 22 June, referring to 'the project presented by M. Necker, and in particular the proposal to command the first two orders of the state to join with the third and vote by head on matters which do not concern the individual interests of each order and certain other stipulated issues'.[11]

The next events were dramatic. At the council meeting, Necker presented his proposal, which met with few objections from the king and the other ministers. The discussion drew to an end, and Louis was about to approve the draft declaration and fix a date for the royal session. What happened next is recounted by Necker himself:

The portfolios were already closing when suddenly we saw an attendant enter; he approached the king's armchair, whispered to him and immediately His Majesty rose, instructing his ministers to remain where they were and to await his return. This message, coming as the council was about to finish, naturally surprised us all. M. de Montmorin, who was sitting next to me, told me straight out: 'Everything is undone; only the queen could have allowed herself to interrupt the council of state; the princes must have got round her and they want, by her intervention, to postpone the king's decision.'[12]

Necker's recollections fix the moment at which Marie Antoinette was finally won over by the arguments of Artois and the Polignacs. For Montmorin's instinct was correct, and she did indeed persuade Louis to adjourn a decision to a further meeting of the council. At the eleventh hour, the conservatives had saved the day.

The next hours saw a coordinated attack on Louis XVI's crumbling defences. Its aim was precise: to sidestep Necker's compromise proposal and uphold voting by order for as long as the privileged orders wished. By the morning of 20 June everything was ready, and Marie Antoinette and Artois went to see the king. The ensuing scene is recounted by the chevalier de Coigny, a key member of the Polignac circle, in a letter transcribed by the comtesse d'Adhémar and written that very day:

... the queen, unable to contain herself, depicted the throne overturned by the men of faction ... adding that none of what was being done was for the good of the people, but to aid a guilty prince [Orléans] in seizing the crown.

Just when this princess was at her most impassioned, a secret deputation from the *parlement* of Paris was announced ... It had come to beg the king to dissolve the Estates General whose existence was compromising the existence of the monarchy; at the same time it gave assurances that the *parlement*, to arrest the tempest, would not hesitate to register such fiscal legislation as might be sent before it, and would furthermore promise to do anything His Majesty wanted ...

Meanwhile, the cardinal de la Rochefoucauld accompanied by the Archbishop of Paris appeared in their turn. With emotion, they threw themselves at His Majesty's feet as soon as they entered and beseeched him in the name of St Louis and the

piety of his august ancestors to defend religion, cruelly attacked
by the modern philosophers who counted among their sectaries
nearly all the members of the third estate . . .

Then our dear duchesse [de Polignac], carrying the dauphin
and leading his sister by the hand, pushed them into the arms
of their father, begging him to hesitate no longer and to
confound the plans of his family's enemies. The king, touched
by her tears and by so many representations, gave way and
signalled his desire to hold a council on the spot . . .[13]

Louis XVI has often been blamed for weakness at this juncture,
but such massive emotional blackmail would have swayed many a
more decisive ruler. The council met immediately; Necker was not
summoned but, in an unprecedented move, Artois and Provence
were. The following day, the court moved back to Versailles, where
two further meetings were held. Necker, who did attend these,
realized something had gone very wrong when he saw Artois and
Provence facing him across the council table.

The results of these deliberations were drawn up in a declaration drafted by the conservative councillor of state, Jean-Jacques
Vidaud de la Tour. Its core was a rejection of Necker's compromise
and the substitution of a much harder line. The nobility and clergy
were exhorted, but not commanded, to discuss and vote by head
on matters of general interest. If they wished, they could stipulate
that any decisions reached in this manner could only be carried by a
two-thirds majority. These arrangements would apply to the present
session of the Estates only. The form of organization of future
Estates, the rights of the three orders, feudal and seigneurial properties and the honorific prerogatives of the first two orders, were
specifically excluded from discussion in common. Yet even though
the declaration did not compel the privileged orders to join the third
estate, Barentin clearly hoped that the king's exhortation to them to
do so would achieve the same result. As he put it in a covering note
to Louis:

Your Majesty will find enclosed the new draft which he charged
M. Vidaud de la Tour to prepare. It has the advantage both of
firmly maintaining the constitution, and of opening up an avenue

of conciliation which, without the king's dictating it, will have the same effects.[14]

An argument has recently been made that the difference between these articles and those in Necker's draft have been exaggerated, and that given the speed at which the crisis was developing, not even the latter would have worked.[15] The loss of Necker's proposal makes it impossible to reach any final conclusion on this view. Admittedly, Saint-Priest, who supported Necker, expressed doubts to the king as to whether the finance minister's concessions were sufficient to satisfy the third estate. 'I shall not conceal from Your Majesty,' he wrote,

> that I fear the third estate, in its present exaltation, may claim those matters which are so justly reserved in the project for deliberation by order. I even fear it will complain about Your Majesty's solemn intervention at this juncture, so heated does [it] . . . appear.[16]

There was, however, a major difference between the king ordering the nobility and clergy to vote in common on general matters and his merely inviting them to do so, with no guarantee of a favourable response. Necker's compromise might just have rallied enough moderates on all sides to salvage both the royal authority and the Estates General. Ultimately it came down to a choice between two words: whether the king should exhort or compel the first two estates to join with the third. Yet the choice Louis XVI made helped to ignite the French Revolution.

The declaration's conservatism on the central issue of voting has obscured its other provisions, many of which were far from reactionary. The king invited the deputies to present proposals for the abolition of *lettres de cachet* and promotion of press freedom in a way that still safeguarded public morality and the interests of the state. All the French provinces were to receive provincial estates with substantial local powers, whereby the third estate would have double representation and all voting would be in common. Above all, any new taxation, loans, and even the royal budget would be subject to the consent of the Estates General. By this article alone, the declaration of 23 June transformed France's absolute monarchy into a constitutional monarchy. The essential attribute of

any constitutional government, consent to taxation by the representatives of the nation, had been conceded.[17]

Yet, as the decision on voting made clear, this was to be a
constitutional monarchy in partnership with the privileged orders, not
the third estate. The declaration ended the era in which the crown,
influenced first by Calonne and then Brienne, had sought the alliance
of the third in its assault on the first two estates' tax exemptions. Now,
in its alarm at the third estate's claims for a greater share of power, the
monarchy had closed ranks with the nobility and clergy in a defence
of privilege. This refusal to meet the aspirations of the third estate was
the declaration's central failure, and its effects were soon felt.

Despite its flaws, the declaration of 23 June was to have a long-
term significance beyond the summer of 1789. The exact details of
Louis XVI's policy towards the Revolution remain a subject of deep
controversy. His detractors claim that from its outbreak his goal was
simply to re-establish the absolute monarchy if at all possible; his
supporters argue that he genuinely sought some form of constitutional
system. Yet in all Louis's and Marie Antoinette's surviving correspondence after 1789, the political programme they refer to most often
is that contained in the declaration of 23 June. Had Louis XVI
recovered his authority at any point after the outbreak of the Revolution, its most likely base would have been this declaration.

The twenty-third of June was a miserable, rainy day. For the
royal session, the full panoply of the traditional monarchy was
displayed for the last time. Louis XVI arrived at the Hall of the
Menus Plaisirs in ceremonial dress, to the sound of trumpets and
escorted by his household troops. Yet he seemed gloomy and ill at
ease. As on 5 May, he was cheered as he entered the assembly, but
with one ominous difference. This time only the nobility and clergy
joined in. The third estate, now re-admitted to the hall for the
occasion, remained silent. As if to underline the third estate's fears,
today there was only an empty chair where Necker has previously
sat. Nobody knew whether the finance minister had voluntarily
absented himself or been dismissed.

After the king's opening remarks, an official read out a fifteen-
point declaration 'concerning the present session of the Estates
General', which nullified the proclamation of the National Assembly
and set out in detail the decision to uphold voting by order for as

long as the first two estates wished. Then followed thirty-five articles creating the constitutional monarchy that would replace the old. It began with the promise that no new tax would be raised nor old one extended without the consent of the representatives of the nation. In conclusion, Louis commended his programme to the deputies in a short peroration. This sounded an unmistakable note of menace:

> Gentlemen, you have just heard a statement of my provisions and my objectives; they conform to my lively desire to act for the good of all. If, by a remote mischance, you were to abandon me in such a fine enterprise, I should effect the good of my peoples alone; alone I should consider myself their true representative . . .[18]

Here, then, was the final threat. The proposals just unveiled represented the final limit of the concessions the crown was prepared to grant. If the Estates General demurred, the king served notice that he would promulgate them on his own authority. This conclusion, like the declaration itself, was to resonate through the remaining years of the monarchy. If all else failed, imposing the declaration of 23 June by force was never discounted, even though Louis XVI shrank from the inevitable consequence – civil war.

The king left the hall, followed by the nobility and the majority of the clergy. The third estate remained, determined to defy him and to continue its sessions as the National Assembly. The scene teetered on the verge of farce as an army of carpenters descended to dismantle the furnishings installed for the royal appearance around seated deputies desperately trying to preserve their dignity. The situation was redeemed by Mirabeau. The court master of ceremonies, the twenty-seven-year-old marquis de Dreux-Brézé, approached the deputies and ordered them to disperse. Mirabeau thrust forward his imposing bulk and flung back his famous reply: 'Go and tell those who have sent you that we are here by the will of the people and that we will not be dispersed except at the point of bayonets.' Cowed, Dreux-Brézé withdrew, still retaining enough composure to walk slowly backwards with his hat on, as etiquette prescribed.

This was Mirabeau's apotheosis, the crowning moment of his career. Yet Dreux-Brézé may well have had the last laugh. In April 1791, having switched sides and become the royal family's secret adviser, Mirabeau died prematurely and was buried in the Panthéon. When his 'betrayal' of the Revolution was discovered on the fall of the monarchy, his remains were dug up and thrown into a pauper's grave. Dreux-Brézé, on the other hand, quietly resumed his office of master of ceremonies at the restoration of the monarchy in 1814. He survived until 1825, and his court post passed smoothly to his son.[19]

Accounts of Louis XVI's reaction to the third estate's defiance vary wildly. The duc d'Orléans claimed that the king went pale with anger and ordered Dreux-Brézé to clear the hall by force, a command that would have been executed if the deputies had not by then already dispersed. The most widely reported version of his response, however, was the opposite: 'Damn! Oh well, let them stay.' Taken together with his obvious unhappiness at the royal session itself, this implies that the king's defence of voting by order was indeed forced on him by family pressure and went against his true instincts. Louis's lack of confidence was infectious and passed right down the chain of authority. The town criers of Versailles refused to proclaim the declaration through the streets, claiming they all had colds.[20]

The most tangible threat to royal authority came from outside the hall. Necker's unexplained absence from the royal session had caused consternation among the spectators and the population of Versailles. Although in fact the finance minister had himself chosen not to appear so as to mark his disapproval of the proceedings, this was not known, fuelling the conviction that he had been dismissed. A crowd over 5,000 strong gathered between the Hall of the *Menus Plaisirs* and the palace. At six in the evening Necker, who had been sitting tight in his official lodgings, received a summons from Marie Antoinette. As he walked over to the palace, the crowd followed him. The household troops were too few to resist; the populace forced the inner gates and poured inside the building, right up to the doors of the royal apartments. Necker had only been inside for a few minutes when a menacing shout went up that he should reappear, to show no harm had befallen him. The minister was forced to come out and show himself, crying: 'Go back, gentlemen, calm yourselves, the king and queen have summoned me!'[21]

This frightening invasion threw the court into a state of terror. No one had expected such a breakdown of public order, no precautions had been taken, and the king and queen seemed suddenly to be at the mercy of the mob. Bombelles, who had been shuttling back and forth between Breteuil at Dangu and Versailles, rushed into the Polignacs' lodgings 'distraught and seemingly out of his wits, shouting: "The king is betrayed! Our master is in the hands of the villain! . . ." He finally blurted out that M. Necker, followed by a horde over ten thousand strong, had gone up to the palace to see the king and was still there.'[22]

The panic penetrated beyond the doors of the royal apartments. Marie Antoinette, shocked out of her previous support for Artois and the Polignacs, begged Necker for twenty minutes not to resign. Or, as Mercy-Argenteau put it more tactfully to Joseph II: 'Although this august princess was briefly swayed by the infernal cabal against the finance minister . . . it is to the queen's moderation and wisdom . . . that we owe the avoidance of even greater disasters.'[23] Marie Antoinette then led Necker in to see the king. There were no witnesses to the interview, which lasted an hour. It seems, however, that Louis XVI lost his temper, a sure sign that he was under extreme stress. One of the royal valets, stationed at the king's door, heard him shouting at Necker: 'It is I, Monsieur, who am making all the sacrifices, making them with all my heart, while you take all the credit; you want to take all the thanks yourself.'[24]

This outburst presaged Louis XVI's conduct throughout the Revolution. At every important juncture after 1789 when he was able to speak freely, he returned to the theme of the sacrifices he had voluntarily made on 23 June. This was to exaggerate his own altruism; after all, the absolute monarchy had ceased to be viable at least two years earlier. None the less, on 23 June the king surrendered on one day powers it took most of his fellow monarchs another half-century to renounce. From his perspective, the crown had made unparalleled concessions, even if it did not look that way to the third estate. To him, these were not niggardly but remarkably generous, and he never ceased to regard them as the foundation stone of a revived monarchy.

In the short term, the failure of the royal session and the humiliating appeal to Necker made the reunion of the orders inevitable. A few days later, Louis XVI called the leaders of the nobility and clergy to him. With tears in his eyes, he protested 'that he would never abandon his nobility, but that he was forced by circumstances to make great sacrifices for unity'.[25] This statement may seem hard to reconcile with Louis's earlier sympathy for the third estate, but at a deeper level it is quite consistent. Not even Necker had proposed that there should be voting in common on all matters; even he had excluded from this the intrinsic rights and privileges of the first and second estates. Yet the pandemonium after the royal session had swept aside any chance of compromise and ensured that now the public would only be satisfied with reunion of the three orders pure and simple. This was one step too far for Louis XVI. He had previously favoured flexibility to accommodate the third estate, but he was outraged to have full reunion of the orders forced on him by the threat of violence and to be compelled to despoil, as he saw it, his nobles and his clergy of their intrinsic rights. The events of 23 June opened an irrevocable breach between the king and his people.

The day also marked a watershed in Louis's and Marie Antoinette's relations with Necker. From that point on they strongly suspected that he cared more about pleasing the populace than serving them. These suspicions had been reinforced by the minister's evening progress to the palace, when it had been unclear whether he was the crowd's prisoner or its leader. They were hardly allayed by his behaviour on leaving his interview with the king. According to the comte d'Angiviller, a close friend of Louis and director of the royal buildings, one of Necker's friends begged him not to excite the crowd further and to exit by a side door. Necker paused for a moment; then, writes d'Angiviller, 'I wish I could have shown you how he suddenly threw up his head, and, by way of answer, walked firmly to the main door and bounded out to meet the multitude.'[26] He was carried in triumph back to his official lodgings, where most of the deputies of the third estate were waiting to receive him.

While fireworks illuminated the night to celebrate Necker's victory, Louis XVI was already planning his riposte. According to several sources, the council met late that night in the palace. The alarms of the previous few hours had demonstrated one hard practical truth: just how vulnerable the royal family was to a sudden crowd movement. It is not certain, but probable, that the decision was taken then to send in stages for substantial troop reinforcements from the provincial garrisons.[27] Whether the prime purpose was merely for the military to defend Versailles or actually to mount an offensive to regain the king's authority, was most likely not discussed, nor at this stage did it need to be. The events of 23 June led inexorably to the next stage in the revolutionary crisis, culminating in the storming of the Bastille. It was a stage in which Breteuil would be the central figure.

*

SINCE APRIL 1789, the pace of events had been quickening at Dangu. Couriers went to and from Versailles, ensuring that Breteuil was swiftly informed of the latest developments. Bombelles in particular spent much of these months on the road between the court and his patron. All this activity had one overriding aim: the return of the baron to the ministry.

Breteuil's recall was heralded by a number of portents. The previous November he had made a brief visit to Versailles and had an audience with Marie Antoinette lasting, as Bombelles noted carefully, 'Twenty-two minutes and I forget just how many seconds'.[28] Hardly less significantly, the Polignacs had also begun to see him as their trump card against Necker. This was a welcome change, since for over three years Breteuil's relations with the duchess and her circle had been strained. Breteuil's path to the ministry in 1783 had been greatly eased by the betrothal of his granddaughter, Caroline de Matignon, to Mme de Polignac's eldest son. Yet soon after his appointment, Breteuil had broken off the engagement and married Caroline instead to the son of the duc de Montmorency. The resulting breach between Breteuil and the Polignacs was just one aspect of the wider split in these years between the queen and her *société*.

Under the imminent menace of the Estates, however, old friendships were revived and more recent enmities forgotten. Artois and the Polignacs were reconciled with the queen and frantically tried to stiffen her resolve against Necker and concessions on the voting issue. Breteuil benefited greatly from this closing of ranks. With harmony restored in the queen's circle, he became the favoured candidate to take over the ministry and restore the royal authority.

Unsurprisingly, the peace overtures from Mme de Polignac at Versailles and Breteuil at Dangu were transmitted through Bombelles. As the marquis noted in his journal on 20 April:

> I found the duchesse de Polignac working hard for the baron de Breteuil's return to the ministry and thinking, given his conversation with the queen, that he should most certainly be recalled to the council to oppose all M. Necker's schemes aimed at destroying the monarchy and the king's authority. I have been charged with assuring the baron de Breteuil that not only will Mme de Polignac and her friends make no attempt to keep him out of politics, but that they would see him return with pleasure, as the only man capable of maintaining the rights of the crown and good order in the government . . .[29]

Yet this intrigue was doomed without the king's assent. Towards the end of June, however, a correspondence between Louis XVI and Breteuil was estabished. On 1 July, Bombelles mentions that Breteuil had written to the king but not yet received a reply, but the following day, Louis's response arrived. The king thanked Breteuil for his zeal, asked him to continue the correspondence, and specifically invited him 'to find the best means of obtaining, through proposals worthy of confidence, the return to circulation, through a public loan, of the immense sums of money currently hidden away in Paris'.[30]

This financial manoeuvre was the main reason why Louis XVI turned to Breteuil in these crucial days of July. To have any freedom of action, the king needed ready money. Yet the deepening political crisis had made the investors of the capital extremely reluctant to advance funds to the government. Once again, the crown was confronted with the factor that had done so much to cause the crisis in the first place – the collapse of confidence and public credit. As to the ultimate purpose of the proposed loan, one can only speculate. The most obvious conclusion is that Louis was preparing to dissolve the Estates General and needed quickly to find an alternative source of funds. On the other hand, he may simply have wished to provide himself with at least some financial means independent of the Estates and thus increase his freedom of manoeuvre.

One fascinating detail that has been ignored by historians lends weight to the second argument. The loan that Breteuil busied himself with preparing was for the sum of 100 million livres. Since Louis XVI had specifically stated in the declaration of 23 June that henceforth no new loans would be raised without the consent of the nation, the raising of such substantial funds in secret appears to point strongly to a plan to dissolve the Estates General. Yet in fact Louis had left himself an escape clause. Although the declaration did indeed state that fresh loans would need the agreement of the Estates, it went on to add that 'in case of war or danger to the nation, the sovereign will have the power to borrow immediately a sum of up to 100 million livres'.[31] It cannot be a coincidence that the loan Breteuil was authorized to negotiate was for precisely the amount that the declaration permitted the king to raise without consulting the Estates.

This revealing touch fits perfectly with an important aspect of Louis's character – his extremely legalistic cast of mind. The king was obsessively scrupulous about keeping his engagements; breaking them required a tortuous process of self-justification. The fact that Louis set Breteuil to raise precisely 100 million livres is powerful evidence that he intended to respect the declaration of 23 June. He would contract a loan for exactly as much as it allowed him to without consulting the deputies, but would stop short of actually dissolving the Estates General itself. From this perspective, Louis XVI had in mind not an outright military coup against the Estates, but simply a return to the declaration of 23 June.

The proposed loan was worked out in some detail. Its moving spirit was Jean, baron de Batz, later a legendary royalist secret agent during the Revolution. A native of Gascony, Batz had made a fortune in the Parisian speculation boom of the 1780s, and retained close financial links with Breteuil from that period. He was essentially an adventurer. Elected to the Estates as deputy for the nobility of Tartas, he had offered to give up his seat to Artois to give the prince further means of influencing the second estate. Under pressure from Necker, Artois had been forced to refuse, but remained grateful to Batz for the gesture. Thus on 5 July, Artois organized a clandestine committee meeting at Versailles, to which Batz's plans for the loan were presented. Batz apparently backed these up with offers of funds from 'the leading bankers in Paris'. It was decided that Batz should see Breteuil immediately, and so at three in the morning he and

Bombelles set off for Dangu. Over the next few days the main details
were thrashed out; an official *arrêt du conseil* was drafted creating
100,000 bonds worth 1,000 livres each, and 33 million livres were
promised in advance.[32]

The action now shifted to Paris, where Bombelles and Batz
headed from Dangu to meet another key figure Breteuil had drawn
into his plans, the duc de la Vauguyon. A notably successful diplomat,
la Vauguyon was currently on leave from his embassy in Madrid,
where he had been posted since 1784. On the afternoon of 7 July, he,
Bombelles and Batz held a secret conference with Hamelin, a former
first secretary of finance, to whom Breteuil had insisted that the loan
proposal be submitted. La Vauguyon then left for Versailles, to work
on a plan of action requested by the king. Bombelles claims that
he and Hamelin managed to dissuade the duke from including in
this the establishment of a sinking fund specially earmarked from
the budget to pay off the deficit, and which should be put under the
authority of the deputies. This is revealing, since it implies that left
to himself, la Vauguyon did foresee a continuing role for the Estates
General in the new dispensation.

The pace of events accelerated the following day. At five in the
evening, Breteuil himself arrived in Paris from Dangu. A conference was held at his house during which the finishing touches were
put to the loan proposal. At midnight, la Vauguyon arrived from
Versailles. He brought the news that Provence and Artois were doing
everything they could to persuade the king to grant Breteuil an
interview. This implies that although Louis was happy to correspond
with the baron, he was not yet ready to readmit him to the ministry.
La Vauguyon then read out his completed plan of action. It did not
inspire Bombelles with confidence. 'It is well set out,' he noted
pessimistically,

> but does not indicate with enough precision what should be
> done in this important crisis . . . I rely more on the faults and
> excess of frenzy of [the king's] enemies than on the sufficiency
> of the means employed for the restoration of peace and the
> royal authority.[33]

At three in the afternoon of Saturday, 11 July, Necker was sitting
down to a family dinner. At that moment, he was handed a letter

from the king. It politely informed the finance minister that he had been dismissed, and ordered him to leave the country immediately. For once Necker resisted his urge for publicity. He said nothing to his daughter Mme de Staël and her husband, who were also at table, but spoke quietly to his wife and called for his carriage. Without changing their clothes, and taking only one travelling-bag, the Neckers climbed in and set off for Brussels.

The following day, a change of ministers was announced. Necker's ally Montmorin was replaced as foreign minister by la Vauguyon. The maréchal de Broglie, a seventy-one-year-old veteran of the Seven Years War, took over the war ministry. First and foremost, Breteuil was appointed *chef du conseil royal des finances*, making him in effect prime minister. The baron had arrived in power.

*

BRETEUIL'S PERIOD IN OFFICE was brief, and has gone down to posterity as the 'Ministry of the Hundred Hours.' Yet these hundred hours spanned the outbreak of the French Revolution. To this day, its aims and motives remain shrouded in mystery. This is because before Breteuil and his colleagues had time to implement their plans, the storming of the Bastille forced them from office. No record of those plans survives, so their exact nature remains a subject of fierce controversy. Did the Ministry of the Hundred Hours mean to dissolve the Estates General by force and impose martial law on Paris? Or was it instead struggling towards a political solution in those fateful days before 14 July?

The traditional view has always been that Breteuil intended to use force. It was best expressed by the eminent French historian Pierre Caron in an article of 1906. Remarkably, between then and now Caron's conclusions have only been challenged once.[34] Caron argues that the new ministry planned to intimidate the Estates General, surrounding it with enough troops to 'use all means' if necessary. The Estates would then have been forced to accept some version of the declaration of 23 June, on pain of dissolution or transfer away from Paris.

The strongest evidence in favour of Caron's view is the military build-up around the capital in late June and early July. There were already 6,000 soldiers from the French and Swiss Guards stationed around Paris and Versailles, but as a result of the decisions taken at the end of June these troops were heavily reinforced. Before the month was out a further 4,000 troops had arrived. On 26 June 4,800 more were ordered up, and on 1 July no fewer than 11,500 received their marching orders. By the time Breteuil came to power there were probably over 25,000 soldiers surrounding Paris. Most worrying for the third estate and its supporters, roughly half of the troops summoned were from Swiss and German regiments of the army. As foreigners, and in many cases non-French speakers, these men would presumably be more immune to radical propaganda, and have fewer scruples about firing on the people, than native Frenchmen.

This imposing concentration of force would seem to have only one possible object: to take the offensive against the third estate and the Parisians, and subjugate them if necessary by military force. Yet there has always been a major stumbling-block to this view. The orders given by the maréchal de Broglie to the military commander of Paris, the baron de Besenval, have survived – and they say nothing whatever about offensive operations. In fact, they state quite the reverse; their provisions are both cautious and defensive. Pierre Caron got round this awkward fact in an ingenious fashion. He attributed the absence of any plan of attack to Broglie's inability to conceive that the undisciplined Parisians posed any military threat. Instead, he presented the marshal's timidity as the result of blind overconfidence, 'the arrogance of a man accustomed to see all bow down before him'.[35]

This argument cannot be sustained. For one thing, it fails to take into account Broglie's age and character. He was elderly and deeply devout; one English observer wrote that the military preparations around Paris were interrupted three times every morning while the marshal went to Mass.[36] The idea of this pious geriatric conducting a *coup d'état* is highly unlikely.

Most important, Broglie's instructions to Besenval make it quite clear that far from underestimating the threat posed by the Parisians, he was only too well aware of it, and that this was the real reason for his defensive strategy. As early as 1 July, he was preparing for some form of insurrection. As he wrote to Besenval at 12.30 p.m. that day:

... if the warnings you have been given of a rumoured attack by the populace today on the discount bank and the royal treasury materialize, the king consents that you assemble all the forces on which you can rely to safeguard the royal treasury and the discount bank ... and that you confine yourself to defending these two positions, the importance of which you fully realize and which fully deserve all your attention at a time when we are unfortunately not in a position to look to everything.[37]

By 11 July the marshal's concern had deepened, and he sent Besenval a further, even more cautious order. One of its phrases has an ecclesiastical flourish -- perhaps he had just returned from Mass.

As I am apprised from many quarters that there is reason to fear a violent insurrection at daybreak tomorrow, I beseech but also enjoin you – as the king writes to bishops – I instruct you, therefore, on the pretext of military exercises, to bring up the battalions of Swiss Guards which are at Rueil and Courbevoie ... before dawn ...

If there is a general insurrection we cannot defend the whole of Paris and you must confine yourself to the plan for the defence of the Bourse, the royal treasury, the Bastille and the Invalides . . .[38]

Broglie's fears were justified, since for several months the situation in Paris had indeed been getting out of control. In April, a riot at the Réveillon wallpaper factory had involved thousands; the French Guards had opened fire on the crowd, killing twenty-five and wounding hundreds more. Ominously, two months later two companies of these same French Guards mutinied, declaring that they would under no circumstances fire on the people. On 30 June, 4,000 Parisians stormed the Abbaye prison where the ringleaders of this mutiny were being held, released them and carried them back to the Palais-Royal. This political unrest was fuelled by economic hardship, as the effects of the previous year's disastrous harvest were felt and bread prices rose steeply.

In this dangerous atmosphere, Broglie was determined to avoid a confrontation with the people, not provoke one. He was acutely aware that bread riots could easily escalate into political disturbances, and he did his utmost to ensure that his troops performed their policing duties with discretion. This is clear from his transmission to Besenval on 5 July of a request by the Paris lieutenant of police 'for assistance in maintaining order in Paris should it be troubled tomorrow by the common people if they cannot obtain bread at the morning market'. Broglie endorsed the lieutenant of police's plea, but added almost two paragraphs of warning:

> As this request is solely intended to afford protection to the citizen and to prevent disorder, I fully authorize you to ... issue the officers commanding the detachments you may be called upon to employ with the most precise and limited orders so that the troops may only act as protectors and scrupulously avoid getting entangled with the people – unless to prevent arson or excesses and pillage which threaten the safety of the citizen.
>
> I trust that you will not have to employ these means and I desire it more than I can express: I am perfectly sure that these are no less your own sentiments.[39]

If the military commanders had no intention of mounting an offensive, was the same true of the politicians? It is difficult to reach a conclusion. Nothing written by Breteuil during this period has survived, while Bombelles, overwhelmed by events, broke off his journal after 8 July and did not resume it until 5 August. The intentions of Breteuil and his colleagues can only be partially reconstructed from fragments of the memoirs of other contemporaries. These do, however, provide evidence that Breteuil spent at least part of his hundred hours of power attempting to resolve the crisis by negotiation. The most susbtantial account of his efforts comes from the duc des Cars, a senior officer and court noble who was particularly close to Artois. 'I was in constant touch with the comte d'Artois and the men whom he wished the king to appoint to his council,' des Cars recalled of this period. 'I sped from Versailles to the baron de Breteuil at Dangu, and from Dangu to Versailles, where I met often with the duc de la Vauguyon and the other members of this party.'[40]

On the morning of 13 July, claims des Cars, one of his associates at Versailles received a letter from the duc d'Orléans. In it, the duke repented of the role he had played as a leader of the opposition, and requested an interview with Breteuil as a first step towards a reconciliation with the king. This is entirely plausible, since by then all the rebellious deputies were alarmed by the menacing build-up of troops around them. Orléans also had particular reasons for channelling his overture through Breteuil. The baron's family had strong connections with the Orléans; his uncle the abbé, who had died in 1780, had been chancellor to the current duke's father and had run his household for twenty-four years. Breteuil himself had close financial ties to the House of Orléans. As his papers reveal, on the very day of which des Cars writes, 13 July, he was sent the half-yearly instalment, worth 7,600 livres, of a life annuity he had placed with the duc d'Orléans. It is one of the small ironies of 1789 that the day before the storming of the Bastille, the man Louis XVI charged with restoring royal authority received a substantial interest payment from one of the principal revolutionary leaders.[41]

According to des Cars, Breteuil did indeed agree to meet Orléans, secretly, in the stables at Versailles. Des Cars even claims to have seen Breteuil, a martyr to gout, being carried to the rendezvous in his blue sedan-chair. He adds that Orléans followed shortly afterwards. Apparently the baron did then arrange for Orléans to see the king. It is unclear, however, whether this meeting actually took place.

A further hint of contacts across the revolutionary divide comes in the memoirs of Saint-Priest, who as minister without portfolio was an ally of Necker's and was dismissed with him. Saint-Priest noted that the comte de Clermont-Tonnerre, one of the leaders of the National Assembly, was Breteuil's cousin, and claimed that the baron aimed to use this link to open a channel of communication with his opponents. 'It seems', he wrote, 'that the baron de Breteuil, counting on the influence of his relative the comte de Clermont-Tonnerre, then president of the National Assembly, hoped to resolve matters by negotiation. This hope did not last long.'[42]

One telling detail of these days implies that Clermont-Tonnerre did in fact try to help Breteuil. On 13 July the National Assembly, shocked by the removal of Necker and his colleagues and fearing the worst from their replacements, debated a motion calling on Louis XVI to recall the sacked ministers. Significantly, Clermont-Tonnerre, as secretary (not president, as Saint-Priest has it) of the Assembly, dissented from this proposal. While firmly supporting all the Assembly's actions since 17 June, he argued, in the name of the principle of the separation of powers, that the king had the absolute right to nominate or dismiss ministers as he saw fit. While he couched his argument in purely abstract terms, it seems more than a coincidence that its most immediate potential beneficiary was his own cousin, who may well already have opened negotiations with him to gain support for his new ministry. Interestingly, Clermont-Tonnerre's viewpoint was supported by his principal allies in the Assembly, those constitutional monarchists later to be dubbed the *monarchiens*, Mounier, Lally-Tollendal and Virieu. This may imply that they too had received overtures from the baron. Yet Clermont-Tonnerre went even further than they did. He disagreed with Virieu's proposal that the deputies renew the tennis-court oath in order to maintain solidarity, no doubt because he felt that in the circumstances this would be too provocative. Beneath its high-flown rhetoric, his speech sounds very like a discreet attempt to secure at least a hearing for Breteuil:

> In times of public calamity, one must stick to first principles. The king has the right to compose and to discompose his council; the nation should not nominate ministers; she can only indicate them by the testimony of his confidence or its disapproval. As to the [tennis-court] oath, Messieurs, there is no point in renewing it: the constitution will survive or we will perish with it . . . .[43]

Predictably, Bailly used his old friendship with Breteuil in a desperate effort to head off the looming showdown. He did not dare to see the baron in person, but on 12 or 13 July he wrote him a letter begging him not to take precipitate action. 'I warned him as a friend not to misjudge the assembly,' Bailly wrote,

> That it was nothing like a *parlement*, but instead the nation; that it would neither go back on its decrees, nor give way to authority; that it was worthy of his character, which I knew, to act for the public good, and to be as much the minister of the nation as of the king.[44]

Bailly later heard that Breteuil had been angered by his letter; in any case he did not reply. Yet he does seem to have tried to protect Bailly individually as the situation worsened. Apparently there was some discussion among the new ministers about arresting the leading rebel deputies. Yet Breteuil defended Bailly as a man of probity and moderation, and argued that he should be spared. As Bailly later put it: 'I did not wish to be singled out like this, but [Breteuil's] action proves that he was prepared to make exceptions.'[45]

In fact, Bailly's activity as mediator did not end there. One of the more surprising claims in his memoirs is that around this time he was approached by a friend of Artois, whom he does not name. This anonymous contact told Bailly that he had actually managed to convince the prince to persuade Louis XVI to compromise with the Estates General. This does not fit at all with Artois's unyielding stance up until then, but perhaps by this point even he was beginning to waver. At all events, Bailly was a sober and trustworthy man, and his recollections are usually reliable. He writes that on the basis of this overture he worked out the draft of a conciliatory speech the king could make to the Estates, although this was soon overtaken by circumstances. While this effort, like those of Breteuil and Orléans, clearly came to nothing, it does shed a revealing light on the events surrounding 14 July. Behind the dramatic confrontation, discreet – and up until now carefully hidden – negotiations were undertaken by both sides to avoid a trial of strength that practically everybody dreaded.

A further matter that remains mysterious is whether Breteuil really wished to return to power at all in such a dangerous situation. He was certainly ambitious, and had been intriguing behind the scenes for at least three months, but even an ambitious man might have thought twice about staking his reputation at such a critical juncture. Indeed, in April 1789 Bombelles described him as 'in no hurry to return to power'.[46] One of the reasons why Bailly was so shocked to learn that Breteuil had replaced Necker was precisely that the baron himself had often assured him he had no intention of doing so. 'I could not conceive how he had decided to come back in such terrifying circumstances,' Bailly recalled.

> He had told me a thousand times that he had no desire to return to public life, and had added that he would certainly not do so

if M. Necker left his post . . . It was clear that grave changes
were being planned, and that M. Necker was being dismissed
for refusing to support them. But had his replacement agreed to
carry them out? This was what tormented me.[47]

Were Bailly's fears justified? Again, very few clues remain. One
is contained in a further entry in Bombelles's journal, which hardly
presents Breteuil as itching to send in the troops. At the end of April,
Artois asked him what should be done to save the situation. The
baron's reply must have infuriated the sabre-rattling prince: 'Nothing,
except to stay calm, remain true to the king and the public good, and
trust to the tutelary genius of France in the absence of the wise
measures that should have been taken.'[48]

One might wonder from this whether Breteuil had any plan at all
in mind when he agreed to become prime minister. One hint that
he did comes in the memoirs of Louis XVI's friend and confidant
d'Angiviller. According to this source, Breteuil and la Vauguyon
thought that the king and the royal family should be moved away
from the danger of mob violence to Compiègne, north-east of Paris,
and the Estates General transferred to nearby Soissons. D'Angiviller
even claims that Louis's chief valet had already been sent to Compiègne with the crown jewels, both for their safety and as security
for a further emergency loan.[49] D'Angiviller was extremely well
informed, and his account has the ring of truth. The plan to move
the king to Compiègne would recur more than once during the
Revolution.

Next to Breteuil, it was la Vauguyon who played the pivotal role
in the Ministry of the Hundred Hours. He comes across strongly as
the most moderate and 'constitutional' of the ministers of 12 July,
and this realism would persist for the rest of a long political career
that spanned both the emigration and the restoration. Unfortunately,
the la Vauguyon family is now extinct and the duke's papers seem to
be irretrievably lost. Yet la Vauguyon did leave some clues to his
position in the summer of 1789, in a pamphlet published in Paris in
1797.

In this work, the duke presented himself as a moderate but
committed reformer at the time the Estates General opened. He
wrote:

I was devoted . . . to the principles that made Louis XVI desire so strongly a salutary reform of the abuses of public administration, and the ways of achieving this had been the object of my most profound meditations. I had for long lamented the successive errors and ill-conceived operations that had so disastrously affected the financial situation. Convoking the notables had not seemed to me the solution; what was required was the Estates General, whose solemn inauguration would no doubt, in more tranquil circumstances, have remedied our ills, and ably assisted the most virtuous intentions.[50]

What had changed his hopes for the Estates General to alarm, the duke claimed, had been the increasing disorder and political radicalism that had surrounded the elections. As a result, he had worked out a plan that he presented to one of the ministers, whom he does not name but who was obviously Necker. Its contents are of great interest, since they clearly indicate la Vauguyon's way of thinking at this juncture. 'My wish,' he states,

was that Louis XVI, informed by the *cahiers* [the lists of grievances which each constituency had drawn up for its deputies] . . . should fashion on this basis a great public charter, and that on the opening day [of the Estates General] he should himself arrive and promulgate it. At that moment people were carried away rather than genuinely revolutionary; those who might have had the sinister design of fomenting disorder did not yet know each other; factions had not yet formed . . . this bold move would unquestionably have snuffed out the first sparks of rebellion.[51]

This plan, of course, was remarkably similar to that adopted by Louis XVI on 23 June, two months too late. But it does show that la Vauguyon was by no means intrinsically hostile to the Estates General; indeed, he saw it as essential, under the right conditions, to the regeneration of France. It is unlikely that by early July, despite the intervening upheavals, he had so completely reversed his position as to argue for its dissolution. It is much more probable that his preference was for Breteuil's ministry to keep the Estates in session, but to ensure that this time it would accept the 'great public charter' he had spoken of — no doubt modelled on the declaration of 23 June — through military pressure, transfer further away from Paris, or both. La Vauguyon's testimony is further evidence that in July 1789 Breteuil and his colleagues were not planning the straightforward destruction of the Estates.

From all this evidence, it seems that a combination of negotiations and military pressure to induce the Estates General to accept the declaration of 23 June is most likely to have been the new ministry's plan. Yet this still leaves vital questions unanswered. Above all, there was an obvious contradiction between the military and political aspects of the plan. For the Estates General to be sufficiently isolated and cowed to cede to the crown, it had to be faced with a carefully calculated military deployment; most important, Paris had at all costs to be contained and prevented from coming to its aid. But there is no hint in any of Broglie's surviving papers of any dispositions regarding the Estates General, while the measures the marshal did take to neutralize the Parisians were wholly inadequate. This disparity between ends and means has always been the abiding mystery of the Ministry of the Hundred Hours.

*

THIS FINAL PIECE of the jigsaw does, however, exist, though it has so far remained hidden. It is contained in the Bombelles papers. The marquis's diary lets slip no clues, since he was too busy to keep it up during those crucial days of July. Bombelles did, however, discuss the events of that summer two years later. In January 1792, he was in St Petersburg on a mission to gain Catherine the Great's support for Breteuil and his policies. He carried with him letters of accreditation from the baron to the empress and to her vice-chancellor, Count I. A. Ostermann. At the end of the month, Ostermann asked Bombelles for a memorandum explaining that aspect of the Revolution that mystified him most, the weakness and division in royal policy since 1789. The marquis duly wrote the memorandum and sent it to Ostermann with a covering note stressing that he had tried to be as objective as possible:

> Your Excellency wished me to write for him a précis of what in my opinion have been the causes both of our misfortunes and

of the lack of coordination in those [royalist] initiatives whose aims have been the same . . . I have set out in the attached memorandum what I think; it has been dictated purely and simply by my own opinion. I have received no order to discredit anyone; I would never be chosen to be the instrument of a cabal . . .[52]

Bombelles begins his analysis with the assembly of notables, but its centrepiece is the meeting of the Estates General. His major revelation, which provides the key to the inactivity of both Breteuil and Broglie that July, is that Breteuil was completely opposed to Necker's dismissal. He was well aware that this would cause an explosion in Paris, and that Broglie did not yet have enough troops at his disposal to counter a full-scale revolt. Breteuil's plan was to keep Necker in place for as long as was needed to bring up sufficient troops to deal with the situation, while surrounding him with enough reliable ministers to prevent further concessions to the third estate. To this end he was prepared to return himself to the king's council. Then, when all was ready, Necker could be dispensed with and a settlement based on the declaration of 23 June imposed.

Bombelles's own diary for the period just before he broke it off confirms this retrospective account. On 24 April, he set down in detail a plan drawn up by Provence and Artois that he had just conveyed to Breteuil at Dangu. Its aim was the creation of a new council to deal solely with the Estates General, and to which the two princes, as well as their cousins Condé and Conti, would be admitted. All the other ministers would be dismissed, except Necker, 'because we must not make him a figurehead for the opposition'.[53] Breteuil would take over as foreign minister, and the king would choose between la Vauguyon, General de Bouillé and the councillor of state Foulon as ministers of war and marine.

This scheme had pitfalls to say the least. The most obvious was Necker's likely reaction when he found his own ministerial allies dismissed and himself surrounded by a council dominated by his enemies. Would he not have simply resigned on the spot? It is possible that retaining him by force if necessary was contemplated, but this was a very risky path to take. After all, Necker's absence from the royal session of 23 June, and the consequent rumours that something precisely of this sort had happened to him, were enough to provoke a mass invasion of the palace that evening; isolating rather than dismissing the finance minister could easily have provoked an upheaval no less dangerous than that which did actually take place on 14 July. At the most, this manoeuvre would have gained a few more days for troops to come up; but perhaps that was all Breteuil wanted.

Up until 11 July, the plan held good. Necker protested against the troop build-up in the council and the Estates passed a resolution calling for their withdrawal, but nothing more happened. Then, just as the final card, the remodelling of the ministry, was about to be played, something went wrong. Instead of being merely ringed by opponents in the council, Necker was actually removed, and the explosion Breteuil had worked to avoid was set off. Bombelles summed it up pithily in his memorandum:

> MM. de Breteuil and de la Vauguyon were summoned, but the king, under heavy pressure to send away M. Necker, completely failed to do what M. de Breteuil had taken the liberty of counselling; this minister wished the king to keep on M. Necker, who was discrediting himself by his mistakes, and who only regained his popularity because he was dismissed too soon.[54]

Again, it is open to doubt whether the Parisians would have been fooled – or fooled for long enough – by Breteuil's plan. Yet Necker's precipitate dismissal undoubtedly ruined whatever chance of success it possessed. Why this happened is still a mystery. On this crucial point Bombelles is reticent, but his inference is clear. Louis XVI was 'under heavy pressure to send away M. Necker', yet Bombelles himself states that Breteuil, his obvious replacement, strongly favoured retaining him. Who else had the necessary influence and charisma to force the king to this fateful decision? The obvious candidate is Artois. In all the accounts of the period it is the prince who appears as the moving force in the resistance to the third estate. As Saint-Priest recounts in his memoirs, by late June Artois had, temporarily, subjugated the queen to his will, so that Marie Antoinette played only a secondary role in the events of July. It is also clear that Artois had a deep personal hatred of Necker. As early as 30 April he had publicly insulted the finance minister, virtually accusing him of treason. Just before the royal session, he even argued for his arrest. We will never know for certain, but it was most likely a sudden impulsive intervention by Artois that brought about Necker's dismissal and completely transformed the situation Breteuil had to face.

The plan may have misfired, but the baron was now too deeply involved to withdraw. Against all advice and his own instincts, he found himself recalled to the council not just as one minister among several, but as chief minister in place of Necker. His position was extremely unenviable. It also condemned him to a waiting game. Although the odds were now heavily stacked against him, he could only play for time until sufficient troops came up. Under the circumstances, it is not surprising that he attempted to open negotiations with Orléans and other opposition leaders. These may not even have been wholly insincere; Breteuil knew that force had its limits, and that some degree of consensus for his planned pacification was well worth the effort. Yet within two days both planks of his policy, the political and the military, had been destroyed by the revolt of Paris.

This interpretation also explains much about Breteuil's later relations with Artois. Assuming that Bombelles's memorandum was accurate (and the marquis had no reason to lie about the past), Breteuil must have been inwardly furious with Artois for so cavalierly wrecking his scheme and, with it, his ministry's chances of success. From that moment on, in contrast to their close collaboration over the previous months, Breteuil and Artois ended all friendly contact. When the baron became head of Louis XVI's secret diplomacy in late 1790, it is not fanciful to discern in his immovable refusal to trust any of his plans to the prince the searing memory of the imprudence that had brought on a revolution.

Breteuil's appointment as chief minister was announced on 12 July. The weakness of his position became apparent within hours. It is just possible that, left to himself, he could have brokered a deal with the deputies at Versailles; what he could not do was contain the capital. At nine that morning, the news of Necker's dismissal and his own elevation reached Paris. The response was immediate. Huge crowds gathered in and around the Palais-Royal; in the early afternoon, inflamed by radical orators, they broke into Curtius's wax museum in one of the arcades, appropriated two busts of Necker and the duc d'Orléans, and set them at the head of a massive demonstration advancing towards the Place Vendôme. Here, for the first time, the people encountered troops, a company of the Royal-Allemand cavalry commanded by the prince de Lambesc. The soldiers were ordered to clear the square, but the press of bodies was too great for them, and they retreated across the Place Louis XV (now Place de la Concorde) into the Tuileries Gardens. In the ensuing violence, one demonstrator was killed. Yet the royal troops were heavily outnumbered by the crowd, which was now strengthened by mutinous companies of French Guards. That night, the commandant of Paris, Besenval, having made virtually no effort to retrieve the situation, acknowledged his reverse by withdrawing his forces right out of the city, west to the Pont de Sèvres.

Necker's premature dismissal thus had precisely the effect Artois should have anticipated and which Breteuil most feared. By the evening of 12 July, the botched attempt to subdue Paris had in fact delivered the city up to anarchy. As Broglie had foreseen, the political aspect of the revolt was reinforced by traditional food riots. That night the customs wall around Paris, hated symbol of taxes on consumption, came under sustained attack. It was demolished in several places. The night was lit up by the flames from forty of its customs houses, which were put to the torch. The following morning, the monastery of Saint-Lazare, which also served as a grain depot, was sacked by the crowd. It was this complete breakdown of law and order, rather than the illusory menace of royal troops, that forced the city council to set up its own authority; paradoxically, this had been made necessary by the absence of soldiers rather than their presence. Just after dawn on 13 July, the capital's electors met at the Hôtel de Ville and agreed to set up a citizens' militia of 48,000 men to preserve order. For the first time since the sixteenth-century wars of religion, Paris had a revolutionary government.

The first task of the insurrection was to search for arms. This had a dual purpose; it satisfied the crowds, who were baying for weapons to defend themselves against the royal troops, and gave the citizens' militia an essential means of control. Throughout 13 July, inconclusive negotiations were carried on with the governor of the Invalides for the 30,000 muskets at his disposal to be delivered up. Not unnaturally, the governor played for time. On the morning of

14 July, the Parisians lost patience, and a crowd 80,000 strong broke into the Invalides and seized the muskets and even some pieces of cannon. Now all that was needed was powder for the guns. This had been stored, on Besenval's orders, at the Bastille.

One of the many remarkable features of July 1789 is that all the royal commanders knew the Bastille was a weak spot. The garrison guarding the powder was insufficient, and the commandant, the marquis de Launay, was recognized as being prone to panic. As early as 5 July, Broglie wrote bluntly to Besenval: 'I will say straightaway that there are two sources of anxiety concerning the Bastille; the person of the commandant and the nature of the garrison there.' He claimed that he was trying to find a replacement (though by the 14th one had still not been found). He also ordered Besenval to reinforce de Launay with thirty Swiss troops. Finally, in what with hindsight must be the most ironic words of the whole summer, Broglie told his lieutenant to send some gunners to the Bastille 'to examine whether the cannon are in good order and to use them if it comes to that – which would be extremely unfortunate but happily is wildly improbable . . .'[55]

As at the Invalides, negotiations to hand over the powder and cannon in the fortress were at first attempted, but were broken off when the crowd spontaneously invaded the outer courtyard and were fired on. From half-past one to five in the afternoon the Bastille underwent a regular siege. This ended when de Launay, with no confidence in his garrison and aware that he had almost no food supplies, decided to capitulate. By then, almost a hundred of the attackers had been killed. This was enough to ensure that the terms of surrender were not respected. Eight of the defenders were lynched. De Launay himself was assaulted and murdered as he was taken to the Hôtel de Ville for trial. His head was cut off and placed on a pike by a cook named Desnot who was chosen, as he later testified, because he 'knew how to work with meat'.[56]

The most perplexing riddle of the revolution of Paris is why, during those crucial two days when the city was given up to the crowd, Broglie and Besenval, with upwards of 20,000 men at their disposal, did nothing. It is clear that Broglie felt he did not have enough troops to contain the 'general insurrection' he feared, but surely even these should have put up more than the pathetic resistance that was offered at the Invalides and the Bastille? As his orders for the early part of July reveal, the marshal's plans were resolutely defensive; extraordinary as this may seem, he refused to alter them one jot even when the situation was transformed by the revolt of the capital. This is made clear by Broglie himself, in a justification of his conduct written for Louis XVI at the end of the month. Amazingly, this remarkable document has never been used or published, despite the fact that it sits in one of the most famous public collections of revolutionary material, the papers found in the *armoire de fer* after the storming of the Tuileries and now housed in the Archives Nationales.

Broglie's letter was written from Luxembourg, where he had fled (contrary to the king's orders) after the fall of the Bastille. It was a vehement protest against the flood of pamphlets and articles accusing him of agreeing to take the offensive against Paris through ambition and self-interest. Indeed, the letter reveals that Broglie had actually refused the offer of a peerage when appointed to command the troops around the capital. The marshal was no less firm in stating that he had never proposed any attack on the capital. 'My conscience reassures me,' he reminded the king,

> that the sole call of duty impelled me to obey you in circum-
> stances that you yourself described to me as so difficult and so
> critical, and I hope that you will not refuse me the justice of
> making it known how far I was from proposing any of those
> violent counsels that are currently being attributed to me.[57]

This must be the truth; Broglie would never have dared to falsify the record in a letter to the king retracing events which both men had helped shape. Confirming that Broglie had no offensive plans, however, gets us little closer to the mystery of *why* he had none. The answer to this can only be found by examining his relations with Breteuil.

The key fact is that Broglie's appointment predated, and was quite separate from, Breteuil's. The marshal arrived at Versailles on the evening of 27 June, in reply to a summons from Louis XVI that was itself a response to the tumultuous scenes of the 23rd. From then on, his hands were full, first with organizing and supplying the large numbers of troops being sent to him at such short notice, and second with stiffening the king's resolve against successive attempts by Necker and the third estate to have them sent away. He had neither the time nor the inclination to draw up offensive plans. Above all, until 12 July he was under the orders of a ministry whose avowed aim was to conciliate, not to break the Estates. Yet for all his opposition to Necker, Broglie does not seem to have had any connection with Breteuil either. He played no part in the baron's plans before the July crisis; in the remodelling of the ministry discussed by Bombelles in April, la Vauguyon, Bouillé and Foulon are mentioned as possible war ministers, but not Broglie. In this light, the marshal's eventual appointment to the war ministry on 12 July appears dictated more by the fact that he was on the spot than that he was a positive choice by the baron and his colleagues.

This lack of military and civilian coordination, and Necker's premature dismissal, are the keys to the failure of the Ministry of the Hundred Hours. The decision to call for Broglie was probably the king's own, taken independently of the cabal headed by Artois, the queen and Breteuil. Once in place, Broglie proceeded with his own plan, which aimed simply at defending the royal family and Versailles from an upheaval. He took these measures separately from, and perhaps even in ignorance of, Breteuil's plans. Both Broglie and Breteuil were taken unawares by the dismissal of Necker; Breteuil because he needed more time to organize a military offensive, Broglie because he had never had any plans for such an offensive in the first place. No doubt Breteuil did aim to incorporate Broglie into his own strategy. Once Necker was satisfactorily isolated and the troop build-up complete, the marshal could have been ordered to take aggressive measures against the capital if necessary. Yet the time needed was not given, and the rising of Paris caught both men unprepared.

The disastrous gulf between Breteuil and Broglie underlines a wider truth about July 1789. Even as the crisis reached its height, there was no systematic plan to remove Necker and crush the Estates. The king, realizing the dangers after 23 June, sent for troops, summoned Broglie and agreed, under pressure from his wife and brothers, to start corresponding with Breteuil. Until 11 July, however, he reached no firm decision about his ultimate policy. In the meantime, the fact that Louis XVI was taking advice from different and unconnected quarters, and that no one faction could wholly gain control of him, utterly compromised the attempt to reassert royal authority. The shrewdest summary of the whole complex situation comes from Necker himself in his memoirs:

> For my own part, I was never made perfectly acquainted with the plans that were in agitation; the whole was a system of secrets within secrets, and I believe the king himself was unacquainted with the final views of his advisers, who probably intended to reveal them only by degrees, and according to the pressure of circumstances . . .[58]

The fall of the Bastille blew all these fragile combinations apart. The news of the Parisian uprising reached Versailles on the evening of 14 July. The reaction was one of consternation. The following morning, Louis XVI went on foot to the hall of the Estates, accompanied only by his brothers Provence and Artois, to announce the withdrawal of all the troops around Paris. This abrupt reversal of policy implies strongly that his heart had never been wholly in Breteuil's plan in the first place. Yet, significantly, the king's capitulation stopped short of a promise that he would dismiss Breteuil and recall Necker. His hardline policy had failed, but he still hoped to hang on to his ministry.

That night a tumultuous session of the king's council took place. Apart from Breteuil and la Vauguyon, the names of only a few of the participants are known, but the atmosphere was panic-stricken. The councillor of state Foulon was in despair, having always argued that half-measures either of repression or conciliation would be disastrous. 'All is lost,' he remarked, 'the king must give way and concede everything.'[59] He could not know that his own death was only a week away. The arch-conservative Barentin, also recorded as present, crumbled even more abjectly. 'I think', he whispered to a friend, 'that we shall have to resign ourselves to a change of dynasty.'[60]

The key decision to be taken was whether, now the attempt to subdue Paris had been given up, the royal family should stay or flee. On this issue, Breteuil's and la Vauguyon's position was firm. They argued passionately that the king and queen should surround themselves with whatever loyal troops remained and retreat to Metz in Lorraine. This would no doubt have ushered in a civil war, but the baron and the duke clearly preferred this to surrender to what was now clearly a revolution. The project had a double significance. In the short term, it reveals Breteuil and la Vauguyon as the only ministers to keep their nerve and resolution after the news of the Bastille's fall broke. In the longer term, the idea of seeking safety with a loyal garrison on the eastern frontier was to form the basis of all major subsequent attempts to retrieve royal authority throughout the Revolution.

The plan almost worked. At 3 a.m. on 16 July, des Cars was woken by Breteuil and la Vauguyon, 'almost dead from fatigue and anxiety',[61] who told him that the king had agreed to go to Metz. Yet five hours later, when the three men met again, the scheme had been wrecked by Broglie, who had said he could not rely on his troops to guarantee the royal family's safety en route. Eighteen months later Louis XVI was to look back on this as the decisive moment when he failed to master the Revolution. 'I know I missed my chance,' he confided to Fersen, 'it was on 14th July, I should have left then, and I wanted to, but what could I do . . . when the maréchal de Broglie, who commanded the troops, said to me: "Yes, we can go to Metz, but what do we do when we get there?" '[62]

It was the marshal's intervention that turned retreat into rout. By refusing either to advance or withdraw, he had ruled out all options other than surrender to the opposition. Yet if this course remained open to Louis XVI personally, it was far too dangerous for the ministers he had appointed four days before, who were not protected from reprisals by royal status. On the evening of 16 July, Versailles witnessed a general *sauve qui peut*. Disguised variously as merchants, valets and chambermaids, the cream of the court took to the roads. La Vauguyon and his son made for Le Havre, Barentin for Brussels, and the Polignacs for the border via Valenciennes.

Even some members of the royal family judged it more prudent to depart than stay. The prince de Condé returned to his château at Chantilly, and from there organized the departure of his family and household for Valenciennes, sending them off separately in four carriages to avoid detection. The most illustrious refugee, however, was Artois. It had always been assumed that the prince fled because he feared assassination in the wake of the Parisian revolution. This view is contested, and much new light besides shed on his departure, by a manuscript account written by the duc de Sérent, who in 1789 was governor of Artois's children. This was composed by the duke in 1800 for Bombelles, who had a historian's desire to gather his contemporaries' impressions of events in which he and they had taken part. Since then Sérent's testimony has lain buried in the Bombelles papers, and has never been used or published.

Sérent's main aim was to refute the whispers that it was concern for his own personal safety that had motivated Artois's flight. The story he tells is rather different. It begins with Artois sending for him at 7 p.m. on 15 July, just after the fateful meeting of the council had ended. Taking him over to a window in the dauphin's apartment, the prince told him that he was leaving that very night for Valenciennes, and that Sérent should escort his children to the frontier separately. When the duke, shaken, asked Artois if his family knew of his decision, he replied: 'The king knows, approves, and has advised me to go; he is being taken to Paris tomorrow, he will be held captive there, and only my liberty can guarantee his own.'[63] This puts a new complexion on both Louis XVI's and Artois's actions after 14 July. At the council meeting the king did indeed take the decision to go to the capital the following day to reassure the Parisians; he thought it quite likely he would be imprisoned there, or even assassinated himself. In this perspective, it is quite credible that he wished to ensure that at least one member of his immediate family was left at liberty and free to speak in the name of the crown. The fact that this version conveniently acquits Artois of cowardice should not in itself lead one to disbelieve it.

Above all, Sérent gives a fresh and compelling picture of what were literally the last hours of the old regime at Versailles. He had insisted to Artois that he needed a personal warrant from the king to guarantee the safety of his charges on their journey. Knowing that the departure was fixed for midnight, Sérent waited until 11 p.m. He guessed that the delay was caused by the prince's agonizing farewell to his family, which he was desperate not to interrupt, but he saw no alternative. Gathering himself, he made his way to the queen's bedroom, where the royal family had assembled, and was admitted. 'I shall never forget the picture that ill-omened room presented,' wrote the duke.

Monsieur, now Louis XVIII, Madame, Mme Elisabeth, Mesdames Adélaïde and Victoire, were lining the walls in stricken

attitudes. The king and Mgr le comte d'Artois were standing close to one another in an angle of the balustrade around the bed, and seemed in a world of their own.

The queen came over to the door, and taking my arm led me across to the king and Monseigneur. Perceiving that they were still in a state of profound distraction, I nerved myself to address the king. I told him that Mgr le comte d'Artois had commanded me to leave that night with his children and conduct them over the frontier, and that I had come to receive His Majesty's orders and to beg him to inform me of his intentions . . .

After giving me all the time I needed to speak, the unfortunate monarch let out a sigh, and turning his eyes to me said in the most searching tone: 'Yes . . . leave now, we know your devotion . . . we trust them entirely to you . . . do the best you can.'

Overwhelmed by emotion, I went down on one knee in an involuntary movement . . . The king had the goodness to raise me up with an expression of the most touching sensibility. I added that it was essential that he communicate to me his precise intentions . . . that I needed to know whether to escort the princes his nephews to Brabant, Switzerland, Italy or Spain.

After a moment's reflection the king said: 'My brother should take the Flanders road . . . but do the best you can . . . I repeat . . . they are like your own children: we trust them entirely to you and we rely on you completely.'[64]

This striking description of Louis XVI virtually sleepwalking through the greatest crisis of his reign reinforces the impression that he was on the brink of mental collapse. The 'state of profound distraction' noted by Sérent fits exactly with eye-witness accounts of the king's reactions at other critical moments during the Revolution: withdrawal and disassociation from the world around him, inability to register words addressed to him, and total inability to make a decision. It would be dangerous to read too much into the evidence, but these accumulated testimonies imply strongly that from 1787 on Louis XVI's ability to govern was seriously impaired by acute intermittent depression.

Indeed, in his succeeding paragraphs Sérent gives a further telling example of this. In answer to his request for a warrant in the king's own hand, Louis had agreed and handed a paper each to himself and to Artois. Passing through the Hall of Mirrors on his way back to his rooms, Sérent glanced at the document the king had given him, and was staggered to find that it was not from Louis at all, but a simple passport signed by Montmorin, who was no longer even a minister. Although aware of the extreme danger in which this would place himself and his charges were they stopped en route, Sérent decided he could lose no more time and set off immediately. He and the princes crossed the border without serious mishap.

*

ONE OPTION THAT Sérent considered and rejected on discovering the king's lapse, was joining the column of troops that was leaving Versailles for Metz that night under Broglie. At the meeting of the council on 15–16 July, the marshal had been categoric that his soldiers could not be relied upon to protect the royal family on a retreat from Paris. He underlined this opinion by abandoning them before they even reached Metz and fleeing over the border to Luxembourg.

The question of the troops' loyalty or lack of it is the final conundrum of July 1789. The standard view is that they could not be counted on. There is much anecdotal evidence for this in contemporary memoirs and letters, but there are also harder facts. By 14 July, five out of six battalions of the French Guards, which were traditionally quartered in Paris, had mutinied. Indeed, some French Guardsmen played a decisive part in the capture of the Bastille, in particular by showing the attackers how to lay their guns. Even the troops called up to the capital from the provinces, especially the French regiments, were not immune from the increasing breakdown of order. In the weeks before 14 July, seventy-nine men from the Provence Infantry deserted, and twenty-nine from the Vintimille Infantry. There were fewer desertions from the German-speaking reigments, but here too there were worrying signs of disaffection.[65]

The unreliability of the troops, of course, offers the best excuse for Broglie's timidity. If it really was apparent that they would refuse to obey orders, then clearly it was folly to order the soldiers to attack Paris, or indeed expose them to any situation in which they were confronted by the people. But the best and most exhaustive study of the army's morale, Samuel Scott's *The Response of the Royal Army to the French Revolution*, casts significant doubt on this assumption. Scott concludes that for all the units that wavered, just as many stayed firm. Again, this was especially true of the foreign mercenary regiments, who were almost all German-speaking. The Royal-Allemand Cavalry, which clashed with the crowd in the Tuileries Gardens on 12 July, had only fifteen deserters for the whole of 1789, as did the Nassau Infantry. Three of the Swiss regiments ordered up to Paris, the Castella, Châteauvieux and Reinach Infantry, between them suffered fewer than ninety desertions between September 1788 and September 1789.[66]

What wrecked the army's morale was not the attitude of the men, but that of the officers, of which Broglie's timorousness is only the most striking example. This was the product of a major and long-standing weakness of the French army, the officers' neglect and lack of concern for their men, and their isolation from them. The purchase system and the ravages of court favouritism had created an inefficient officer caste uniquely ill-equipped to cope with a crisis such as that of July 1789. Disastrously ignorant of the temper of the men, their commanders were thrown into panic by the first sign of disaffection in the ranks. Their conviction that their men would not fight became, as Scott points out, a self-fulfilling prophecy. The breakdown of discipline among the men was primarily a response to their officers' lack of confidence in them, and not vice versa. Tellingly, the vast majority of the desertions suffered by the army in July – all but 185 of a total of 760 – came not before but after the 14th.[67]

Interestingly, this view was shared by Breteuil and la Vauguyon themselves. To the end of their lives both men remained certain that a retreat to Metz on 16 July would have saved the royal authority, and above all prevented the collapse of the army. This telling detail is recounted by Breteuil's confidant des Cars in his memoirs:

I saw a lot of the baron de Breteuil and the duc de la Vauguyon during the emigration, and after our return to Paris we all three often recalled that disastrous morning of 16 July; we were convinced that if the king and the royal family had managed to get to Metz, the National Assembly would have found the king a far more formidable opponent, and that this measure would have prevented the later defection of the troops.[68]

In the light of these facts, Broglie's remarkable failure of nerve appears precipitate. It is quite possible that if he had given his troops the order to fire on the crowds, they would indeed have mutinied. But his own collapse of confidence ensured that this was never put to the test. As Samuel Scott concludes: 'One can barely refrain from speculating what might have been the effects on the royal army and the entire Revolution if self-confident officers had marched their troops to a violent confrontation with hostile Parisians on 14 July.'[69]

Many secrets of these hundred hours remain impenetrable. Yet the new evidence from the Bombelles papers, combined with a re-examination of other sources, does help to resolve some of the abiding mysteries of July 1789. The key to the ministry's failure, unsuspected until now, is that contrary to Breteuil's wishes, Necker was dismissed too soon, probably by a surprise decision forced on Louis XVI by Artois. This left the new government dangerously exposed to a revolt in the capital, with insufficient troops to meet the threat. Its discomfiture was only accentuated by Broglie's glaring inadequacy as a commander. It is conceivable that even at this stage the stiuation could have been saved by a resolute use of troops coupled with willingness to accept substantial civilian casualties. Yet the marshal and his senior officers refused to consider this possibility. The consequences for the history of Europe were profound. On the first day of the French Revolution, the crown had lost the initiative. It was never to regain it.

*

AS HIS MINISTRY collapsed around him, Breteuil stayed obstinately at his post. It is probable that he renewed his overtures to the moderates in the Assembly for support. Before 14 July, these may well have been insincere; after it, they were very much in earnest. An echo of them can be found in the debate on ministerial responsibility to which the Assembly returned on 16 July, having broken it off on the 13th. Clermont-Tonnerre's previous argument that the king had the sole right to appoint and dismiss ministers was taken up again by his ally Mounier, this time against the formidable opposition of Mirabeau and Barnave. Allowing the Assembly to influence the choice of ministers, Mounier claimed, would open it up to continual conflict and caballing 'both to empty and to fill ministerial places'.[70] Yet this last-ditch defence of the royal prerogative became obsolete even while it was being mounted. The debate was interrupted by the news that Barentin and Broglie had already resigned. At 6 p.m. the Assembly learned that Breteuil and la Vauguyon had finally followed suit. To general rejoicing, it was announced that the king was recalling Necker to power.

That evening Bailly went to the palace to report to the king. There was much to discuss: the events of the 14th, and Bailly's own nomination that day by the capital's electors as mayor of Paris. Bizarrely, Louis XVI did not take the opportunity to inform the new mayor that he planned to visit Paris the following day – another possible sign that his mental grip was faltering. Bailly had just left the king's study when something unexpected happened:

> I had hardly gone out, when I was called back. I assumed the king wished to add something. I went back into the study: the king was no longer there. I found instead M. de Breteuil with M. d'Angiviller and one other person. M. de Breteuil took me over to a casement window and said: 'I knew you were here, and I wanted to see you.' I replied that I too was pleased to see him, but was sorry that it should be on such an occasion. He told me he was leaving Versailles the next day. I told him that he could now see that events had borne out what I had written to him the previous Monday. He said: 'So now you are the mayor of Paris; I congratulate you.' He added that the king was going there the next morning, and was astonished that His Majesty should not have told me this. I told him without embarrassment that I was glad to have seen him without failing in my duty, because I was genuinely attached to him; and I left him, deploring for his sake both his ill-considered arrival at Versailles, and his departure, so necessary and so different from the one he had made a year before. I make no secret here of either my actions or my thoughts.[71]

This is a moving description of two men trying to salvage a friendship from the revolutionary chasm that had suddenly opened between them. Bailly never saw Breteuil again.

The baron was now alone. His friends and allies had all slipped away; the time had come to save himself. But first he hurriedly arranged for the safekeeping of his most treasured possessions. The Table of Teschen, symbol of his greatest diplomatic success, was entrusted to his friend, the banker Magon de la Balue, at his house on the Place Vendôme. (La Balue was guillotined during the Terror and Breteuil later had to buy the table back from his heirs.)[72] Then, disguising himself as a Benedictine monk, the baron made his escape. Precisely how he left France remains mysterious, but on the evening of 21 July he arrived in Brussels with Mme de Matignon and Mme de Montmorency.[73] Understandably in need of a rest, he then left to take the waters at Spa.

Chapter Five

THE TURN OF THE SCREW

THE EVENTS OF JULY 1789 marked a decisive victory for the National Assembly. The deputies now took up the task they had set themselves when they swore the tennis-court oath: to give France a constitution. To underline this, from now on they styled themselves not the National, but the Constituent Assembly. Yet the pace of events did not slacken. The fall of the Bastille had touched off a wave of unrest throughout France, especially in the countryside. Throughout the provinces peasants abruptly refused to go on paying tithes to the Church or dues to their lords, and pillaged and burned monasteries and châteaux, concentrating particularly on what remained of the feudal system. To the alarmed deputies at Versailles, it looked as if France was collapsing into anarchy. A motion was put to the Assembly calling for calm, and for the continued payment of tithes, taxes and feudal dues until these could be reformed in due course. On the night of 4 August, however, the debate was taken over by a group of radicals. Led by a young left-wing noble, the duc d'Aiguillon, they demanded not just the reform of feudalism but its outright abolition.

Extraordinary scenes followed. What began as a proposal to redeem feudal dues and abolish serfdom and labour services soon broadened into an assault on all the privileges of the old regime. In a frenzy of patriotic self-sacrifice, noble and non-noble deputies who had benefited from the old order heaped venality of office, plurality of benefices, seigneurial courts, tolls and vestry fees on to the metaphorical bonfire. Complete civil equality and the career open to talent were proclaimed. Yet this orgy of renunciation was also fuelled by bloody-mindedness on the grand scale, as those who had not wanted to part with their special status made sure that the colleagues who dispossessed them were left with nothing themselves. When the Bishop of Chartres denounced aristocratic hunting rights, the duc du Châtelet immediately proposed the abolition of the ecclesiastical tithe.[1]

The night of 4 August dramatically altered the social and administrative landscape of France. The way was now clear for the deputies to construct from first principles their heavenly city of the Enlightenment. Its foundation was laid on 26 August, when the Assembly passed into law the Declaration of the Rights of Man. In place of precedent, authority and tradition, the Declaration declared that 'the fundamental source of all authority resides in the nation', and proclaimed a government founded on inalienable natural rights. Consent to taxation, religious liberty and freedom from arbitrary arrest were guaranteed. Although it was to take until the end of 1791 to elaborate the full constitution, its broad outline was apparent from the first month of the Revolution. At its core was a complete break with the past and the substitution of an entirely new political system.

Louis XVI had supported a measure of reform since 1787, but he had not bargained for this. It was a direct indictment of his own stewardship and that of all his predecessors. A few years previously he had commented on Turgot's *Mémoire sur les municipalités*, which had implicitly criticized his three previous ancestors:

> One does not have to be a genius to see that this document is aimed . . . at discrediting all our old institutions, which the author supposes to be the work of centuries of ignorance and barbarism, as if it were possible for a fair and reasonable mind to class the reigns of my three predecessors along with those of the barbarian centuries.[2]

Now a far more brutal judgement was being made, not just of Louis XIII, Louis XIV and Louis XV, but of all the French kings stretching back to Clovis.

A further straw in the wind was the defeat of those moderate royalists, the *monarchiens*, with whom Breteuil was rumoured to have negotiated in July. In two critical debates that September, their leaders, Mounier, Malouet, Clermont-Tonnerre, Bergasse and Lally-Tollendal, put forward an evolutionary rather than revolutionary view of the constitution. They wished to preserve some privilege, and put a limit on the powers of the Assembly by dividing it into an upper and lower house on the English model. The role of the monarch was to be recognized, along with the separation of powers and the need for a strong executive, by giving the king an absolute veto over legislation. Yet on 10 September, the proposal for two chambers went down to a crushing defeat, followed the next day by the absolute veto, which was replaced by a suspensive veto for two sessions of the legislature only. The king could now only delay, not reject outright, proposed legislation. This was despite the fact that Mirabeau, who was already beginning to see popular anarchy as a greater menace to France than royal power, ranged himself in these debates with the *monarchiens*.

Armed only with a suspensive veto, Louis XVI now had to face the dilemma posed by the abolition of feudalism and the Declaration of the Rights of Man. Inevitably, he felt unable to give his assent to both decrees *en bloc*. Instead, he prevaricated, and, on 18 September, proposed some amendments. In particular, he pointed out the difficulty of abolishing feudalism on the lands within France, in Alsace, owned by German princes whose rights were guaranteed by the treaty of Westphalia. Since this was precisely the issue on which the revolutionary war broke out in April 1792, the king was showing rather more foresight than the deputies.

The Declaration of the Rights of Man also failed to impress the monarch. On 4 October, he declared laconically that it would be more sensible to wait until the constitution was finished before making such grand statements of principle. Yet by now an explosion was brewing, which Louis XVI touched off in September by summoning the Flanders regiment to Versailles to reinforce his guard. On the evening of 1 October, the new arrivals, as was the custom, were given a banquet by the King's Bodyguards. It was held in the opera house of the palace. The event has become legendary, and in the varying reports it is difficult to separate fact from fiction.

Unusually for these occasions, the king and queen made an appearance. Marie Antoinette was holding the four-year-old dauphin and walked around the tables showing him to the soldiers. The band struck up an air from Grétry's popular opera *Richard the Lionheart*, 'O Richard O mon roi, l'univers t'abandonne'. Its relevance to Louis XVI's plight was abundantly clear. This moved the officers and men to a pitch of loyalist enthusiasm. 'We only acknowledge our king!' they cried. 'We do not belong to the Nation! We only belong to our king!'[3] According to some accounts, they then tore off the new tricolour cockade from their hats, and pinned in its place not only the white colours of the Bourbons, but also the Habsburg black of the queen. True or not, in view of what happened to Marie Antoinette five days later this report is significant.

None of this amounted to a counter-revolutionary conspiracy; one regiment in October was hardly going to succeed where a whole army had failed in July. But the exaggerated descriptions of the banquet given in the radical press caused a storm of fury in Paris, exacerbated by the fact that bread prices, which had fallen since July, were now rising again. Nor was the royal family the Parisians' only target; heavily influenced by politicians of the Left, they were increasingly finding their new municipal government too cautious and conservative. On the morning of 5 October, the Hôtel de Ville was besieged by a crowd several thousand strong, largely made up of the capital's picturesque and terrifying market women. It has recently been argued that the attackers' original aim was to mount a municipal revolution against the city authorities personified by Bailly as mayor and La Fayette as commander of the new urban militia, the National Guard. This danger, it is claimed, was shrewdly diverted by the latter into a march to Versailles to demand from the king bread, assent to the August decrees and the Rights of Man, and his transfer to Paris away from the 'counter-revolutionary' atmosphere of the palace.[4] Whatever the precise truth, by 11 a.m. a column of market women and their supporters, numbering at least 6,000, heavily armed and dragging two cannon behind them, had set off for the palace.

At Versailles, a further Parisian upheaval had long been feared. Indeed, on 30 August an earlier attempted march there had had to be broken up by the National Guard. Alarmed, the *monarchien* deputies revived the project Breteuil and la Vauguyon had considered in July, of transferring the royal family to Compiègne and the Assembly to Soissons. The plan was discussed by the council, but this time Louis XVI vetoed it. When the Bishop of Langres, a leading *monarchien*, asked Necker why Louis had done so, the harassed minister replied:

> Monsieur, if you want to know the truth, understand that our role is very arduous. The king is good but difficult to persuade. His Majesty was tired ... he slept through the council. We were for transferring the Assembly, but the king woke up, said 'No', and withdrew.[5]

It may seem extraordinary that Louis could have slept through such a crucial meeting, and the fact that he sometimes did so at councils has often been used to buttress the picture of a ruler uninterested in government. Yet in reality this was a device that the king deliberately employed, as here, to insulate himself from proposals made in council with which he disagreed, making it easier for him to forbid them or postpone a decision.[6]

Louis was out shooting when the news was brought to him that Paris was on the march. He rushed back to the palace and summoned Necker and the other ministers for what was to be the last ever meeting of the council at Versailles. Saint-Priest, now minister of the interior, proposed a variation of the Compiègne project – an immediate flight to Rambouillet, protected by troops. The council split down the middle over the plan. Interestingly, all the ministers with a military background were for it, and all the civilians against. The king was left with the casting vote. Once again, he was unable to make up his mind. What Malouet termed his 'passive courage' was very apparent that afternoon. He was repelled by the idea of flight, and paced up and down, muttering to himself: 'A fugitive king ... a fugitive king...'[7] In the meantime, moves were made to prepare Rambouillet to receive the royal family. Yet in the end Louis opted to stay.

After the council had risen, the king went to find the queen, who had been walking in the gardens of the Petit Trianon, and told her the news. She begged him to reconsider the plan for flight, but in vain. Time was running out, and the urban mob was about to erupt into Marie Antoinette's rural idyll. She was never to see the Trianon again.

Events now moved with brutal speed. At 5.30 p.m. the market women reached Versailles and invaded the Assembly, reducing it to chaos. That evening, under renewed pressure from the deputies, Louis, in tears, sanctioned the August decrees and the Declaration of the Rights of Man. News was then received that La Fayette was about to arrive, having been forced to put himself at the head of 20,000 National Guards determined to bring the royal family back to Paris. Flight was again discussed, and some of the ministers had already got into their carriages to head for Rambouillet when Louis, on Necker's advice, reaffirmed his decision to stay.

It was midnight by the time La Fayette entered the palace and, surrounded by hostile courtiers, went to see the king. He urged the royal family's removal to Paris as the only way of avoiding blood-shed, but Louis, although he promised to consider this, refused to agree immediately. The exhausted La Fayette then went off to bed. This was a fateful decision, since it meant that he was not at his post when the night's next drama struck. Royalists never forgot this, and swiftly dubbed him 'General Morpheus'.

What is truly extraordinary is how, even after flight to Rambouillet had been ruled out, the court neglected to take the most elementary military precautions. The Flanders regiment was not effectively deployed, and, for reasons which still remain mysterious, a large number of the King's Bodyguard were sent over to the Grand Trianon, leaving the palace itself dangerously exposed. Those loyal to the royal family were caught completely unprepared by the appearance of the market women and, later, the National Guard. The confusion in which they rallied to defend their king is vividly captured in an eye-witness account by an anonymous courtier and officer:

> We stood to arms from 4 to 9.30 p.m. in court dress, soaked to the skin by ten successive showers of rain, with hats that should have been carried under the arm on our heads, and ceremonial swords in our hands. These were the clothes my colonel and I were in, since we had both been at Versailles since the Saturday on private business and it had never occurred to us that we might have to serve the king as soldiers.[8]

By two o'clock in the morning, a semblance of calm had descended on Versailles, and the royal family went to bed. Then, at 5.30 a.m., something shocking happened. A group of the market women, led by an immense bearded artists' model from the Academy of Painting and Sculpture named Nicolas Jourdan, slipped into the inner courtyard of the palace through a side-gate that had been left unlocked. Brandishing swords and axes, they rushed up the Queen's Staircase, making straight for Marie Antoinette's bedroom. Their aim was plainly murder; they shouted as they ran that they would tear out the queen's heart and fry her liver. The king's bodyguards who tried to block their way were swiftly despatched. Marie Antoinette herself only escaped through the bravery of the guardsman stationed at her door, who cried out, 'Save the queen!' before he too was cut down. She fled to her husband's apartments, dressed in her nightshirt and clutching her stockings in her hand. Behind her, the mob broke into the room, and finding the bed empty cut it to ribbons with axes and swords.

The National Guards were able to clear the palace, but the wider situation had spiralled out of control. A huge crowd now filled the palace courtyard, brandishing weapons and shouting, 'The king to Paris! The king to Paris!' Above them, impaled on pikes, bobbed the severed heads of two murdered royal bodyguards. La Fayette, now roused from his slumbers, advised that calm could only be restored if the royal family showed themselves to the people. The king did so, but this did not satisfy the throng below, who demanded instead to see the queen. Marie Antoinette, who must have thought her last hour had come, was compelled to walk out alone on to the balcony. Muskets were levelled at her, and she could have been shot on the spot. Her courage, however, made an impression on the vast gathering, and after two electric minutes she was able to go back inside. The final capitulation was now inevitable. The king reappeared on the balcony and, this time to cheers, announced that he and his family would go to the capital.

The full truth about the October Days, as they were soon dubbed, will never be known. The crowd that marched on Versailles certainly aimed to bring the royal family back to Paris, where their freedom of action and political influence would be decisively curtailed. Many contemporaries went further, and alleged that there was actually a plot to murder them. In this version, the chief villain was the duc d'Orléans, abetted by Mirabeau. Orléans's plan, it was argued, was for the march to lead to either the royal family's murder

or flight, leaving the throne vacant for him to seize. In this
perspective the attempt on Marie Antoinette's life was not simply an
unforeseeable tragedy, but part of a much more sinister design. Yet
only anecdotal evidence survives to substantiate this theory, and it is
unlikely ever to be proved.[9]

Unsurprisingly, Marie Antoinette was traumatized by the October Days. She had only escaped death by a door's thickness, and
remained haunted by the memory. On 6 October her hair went white
at the temples. The experience also left her with a hatred of La
Fayette, who she felt had neglected, perhaps culpably, his duty to
protect her. This hatred endured to the end; in 1792 she preferred
the risk of death to rescue at his hands.

The October Days had far-reaching political as well as personal
consequences. In July 1789 Louis XVI had lost the initiative; in
October he lost his freedom. Before October, he was at least at
liberty, and free to bolster his position by leaving Versailles and
withdrawing to a safer retreat; afterwards, he was virtually a prisoner
in the capital. Henceforth, the essential preliminary to any attempt to
reassert the royal authority would have to be escape from Paris.

Although he had been less directly menaced than Marie Antoinette by the events of October, Louis XVI was no less shocked by
them. For him, they represented a final breach of trust, of a piece
with all the upheavals since July. In his view, he had voluntarily
given up a large portion of his power in the interests of his people.
They had repaid him by defying his authority, attempting to murder
his wife, and imposing semi-captivity on himself and his family. As a
result, although he had always accepted the need for reforms, after
the October Days he regarded his consent to the acts of the National
Assembly as extracted under duress and therefore not binding. He
made this very clear on 12 October in a formal protest addressed
to his cousin, Charles IV of Spain, which was smuggled out of
France by his agent Fontbrune. Significantly, the letter confirms the
centrality of the declaration of 23 June in Louis's mind, as the last
free expression of his political will. Through it one hears the king's
authentic voice:

> I owe it to myself, I owe it to my children, I owe it to my
> family and all my house to prevent the regal dignity which a

long succession of centuries has confirmed in my dynasty from being degraded in my hands . . .

I have chosen Your Majesty, as head of the second branch [of the Bourbon family], to place in your hands this solemn protestation against my enforced sanction of all that has been done contrary to the royal authority since 15 July of this year and, at the same time, [my intention] to carry out the promises which I made by my declaration of the previous 23 June.[10]

This crucial letter marks the beginning of Louis XVI's dual policy towards the Revolution. On the surface, the king appeared to accept the reduced role that the Assembly allotted him, up to and including endorsing the constitution. His real aims were expressed through a secret policy which had a very different point of departure. Its twin cornerstones were the declaration of 23 June and escape from Paris, and its prime mover was to be Breteuil.

*

AFTER HIS HASTY FLIGHT from France, the baron had spent three months recuperating at Spa and Aix-la-Chapelle. Soon, however, he had been forced to find a more permanent home. Return to his homeland was out of the question, and continued residence in the unstable Austrian Netherlands did not appeal. The baron decided on Switzerland, then as now a safe haven in times of European turmoil. On 4 October 1789, just one day before the Paris crowd marched on Versailles, he, Mme de Matignon and Mme de Montmorency arrived in Solothurn.[11] This was a good choice for several reasons. Solothurn was the capital of the Swiss confederation, linked to the European diplomatic circuit by the presence of foreign embassies, the air was good for a man past middle age, and it was close, but not too close, to the French border.

Soon after installing himself, Breteuil sat down and wrote a long letter to Louis XVI. Preserved today in the Archives Nationales, it is a remarkable document. Its beginning is surreal, since the baron presents his resignation as prime minister as being caused by the state of his health rather than the fall of the Bastille:

I feel that I owe Your Majesty an account of the use I have made of the permission he granted me to travel outside the kingdom for as long as my health required. I have taken the waters at Spa and Aix-la-Chapelle. I have been [in Solothurn] since the fourth of last month, and plan to spend the winter here.[12]

The real point of the letter lay elsewhere. As Breteuil pointed out to the king, he was now hard up; the revenue from his estates and investments in France was cut off, and he expected that the National Assembly would swiftly take an axe to the royal pensions he enjoyed. His proposed solution, however, was bizarrely unrealistic. He asked the king to reinstate him in his old diplomatic career, by appointing him if possible to a vacant embassy. But, he made clear, not just any embassy:

> The gout that frequently torments me makes a mild climate preferable, and leads me to beg Your Majesty to do me the favour of reserving for me the Rome embassy, if the cardinal de Bernis [the present ambassador] dies before I do. I will be sixty next 7 March; the cardinal must be at least seventy-four or seventy-five.[13]

Breteuil's actuarial expertise conceals a more important truth. Far from rejecting out of hand the post-14 July dispensation in France, at this stage he was actually begging the king to be allowed to serve it in the way he knew best. Far from flinging himself immediately into counter-revolution, as did Artois and Condé, he was trying to pretend that the Revolution had not taken place.

Although the king turned down this request, Breteuil's willingness to cooperate with the new regime became apparent once more a few months later. In the autumn of 1789, the Assembly turned to confront the deficit, which had actually increased as a result of the disorder of the previous months. Its most drastic measure was to nationalize all the lands of the Church, using them to pay off the debt through an issue of bonds known as *assignats*. As finance minister, Necker also proposed a one-off 'Patriotic Contribution' from all citizens of a quarter of their income. Far from ignoring this, Breteuil took the opportunity to give proof of his good citizenship. On 22 February 1790, from exile, he sent in a declaration of his income as a basis for determining his 'Patriotic Contribution'. He estimated his net revenue very precisely as 75,573 livres, 18 sous and 4 deniers, of which his contribution, after some minor deductions, came to 18,225 livres and 19 sous.[14] This was not the act of a man determined to break with the new order.

Yet by September 1790, the baron had changed his mind. That month he wrote the king a memorandum, strongly urging him to escape from Paris. His plan was for the royal family to flee to Lorraine and place themselves under the protection of General de Bouillé in Metz, who had proved his reliability the previous month by crushing an attempted mutiny in the army he commanded. This was simply a variation on Breteuil's original proposal to Louis XVI on 16 July 1789, with modifications made necessary by the October Days. The Bishop of Pamiers, who was making frequent visits to Breteuil's mistress and her father in Switzerland but had not yet actually emigrated, agreed to act as messenger and bring the document to Paris.[15]

At the palace of Saint-Cloud outside Paris, where the royal family had been allowed by the Assembly to spend the summer, the king was still pondering what course of action to take. Breteuil's was not the only proposal for reasserting the royal authority that he had received. As early as the previous October Mirabeau, disillusioned with Orléans and increasingly fearing the prospect of anarchy, had made overtures of his own to the royal family. By the following May, with Mercy-Argenteau as intermediary, he had entered into a clandestine agreement with the king and queen. In exchange for substantial payments, he became their secret adviser, sending them voluminous memoranda on the political situation (the famous 'Notes to the Court'). To seal the pact, on 3 July the queen nerved herself to meet her former enemy in person, in a carefully concealed rendezvous in the park of Saint-Cloud. The interview was a success. Belying his demagogic and lecherous reputation, Mirabeau was humble and respectful. Marie Antoinette responded with her famous charm, though after he left she fainted from horror.[16]

Mirabeau's original plan was for the royal family to leave Paris, but not clandestinely and not for the east: 'To retire on Metz or any other frontier would be to declare war on the nation and abdicate the throne.'[17] Instead, having made sure of enough troops, they should quit the capital openly and take up residence in Rouen, where the surrounding provinces were loyal and there would be no hint of collusion with foreign powers. Then the king would call a national convention to replace the Assembly and revise the constitution. However, as one of the first champions of the Revolution, Mirabeau held no brief for the restoration of the old regime. He was determined to strengthen the executive power as a barrier against anarchy, but also to preserve the achievements of 1789: constitutional government, religious freedom, the career open to talents, and judicial reform. This, coupled with his scandalous reputation, was enough to ensure that Louis XVI and Marie Antoinette never fully trusted him. The Rouen plan was not adopted.

Riding the revolutionary tiger, as Mirabeau suggested, was too alarming a prospect for a monarch who had already experienced the sharpness of its claws. Furthermore, by the autumn of 1790 Louis XVI had fresh evidence that the animal was untameable. The first indication was Necker's resignation on 4 September. A year of revolution had brought no improvement in France's economy or finances, and the minister was made the scapegoat. Throughly disillusioned, he gave up his post and set off back to Switzerland. This time, he did not return.

Far more significant was the religious issue. Between May and August of that year, the constituent assembly embarked on a wholesale reform of the French Church, promulgated as the Civil Constitution of the Clergy. Its provisions were extremely radical: instead of being nominated as before, bishops and priests would now be elected by the laity. This opened up the prospect of Protestants, Jews and atheists participating in the election of Catholic clergy. The Pope was henceforth excluded from any part in episcopal appointments. Finally, in December, the Assembly decided to impose an oath of support for the Civil Constitution on all the Church hierarchy. All who refused to do so were to be immediately replaced.

This action launched the first open battle between supporters and opponents of the Revolution. Almost half of the parish clergy and all but seven of the episcopate declined to take the oath. Instead, the latter rallied round the *Exposition of Principles* drafted by Archbishop Boisgelin of Aix, and signed by thirty of the bishops in the Assembly, giving their reasons for voting against the Civil Constitution. On a wider scale, the 'non-juring' parish priests who would not swear the oath and faced ejection generally had much support among their congregations. The issue of religion thus marked the beginning of popular counter-revolution.

The Civil Constitution presented Louis XVI with the most profound moral dilemma of his life. Under the pressure of circumstances he had given up the majority of his powers as king, but now he was being asked to compromise his personal faith. He had previously been prepared to grant Protestants a civil status and to take from the clergy 'a few scraps of their income'. Yet the new reforms, with their complete reversal of the apostolic principle through the election of bishops and priests, were an entirely different matter. In his heart Louis XVI could never accept them. As the great diplomatic historian of the Revolution, Albert Sorel, puts it:

> He had compromised with 'usurpation'; he could not do so with schism and unbelief ... He had no option but to fight. Where his power and personal safety had been concerned, he had remained patient. Now his salvation and that of those he considered God had entrusted to him were at stake; he felt he had no choice. The king had borne all his humiliations; the Christian could not betray his conscience.[18]

In this agonizing predicament, the king once again temporized. On 24 August, he gave his assent to the Civil Constitution, and on 26 December sanctioned the imposition of the oath. Yet this surrender to necessity tormented him. 'You know', he wrote to the Bishop of Clermont, 'the unfortunate predicament in which I find myself through my acceptance of the decrees on the clergy; I have always regarded my sanction of them as acting under duress.'[19]

On a practical level, the king now started to cast around for the means to end a political situation that had become intolerable to him. The Civil Constitution was as decisive for Louis XVI personally as it was for France as a whole. It marked the moment when he began actively to plan a counter-revolution.

It is no coincidence that Breteuil's scheme for an escape from Paris arrived when it did. It is particularly significant that it directly followed General de Bouillé's brutal reimposition of discipline on his army in Lorraine.[20] Bouillé's action was probably decisive in convincing Breteuil to approach the king. By this time Louis himself was thinking along similar lines. On 4 November, in a letter thanking Bouillé for crushing the mutiny, he had written: 'Look after your popularity; it may be very useful to me and to the kingdom; I regard it as the sheet-anchor which may one day be the means of restoring order.'[21] It is equally revealing that the king wrote his favourable reply to the baron on 20 November, just as the National Assembly was preparing to impose the oath to the constitution on the clergy. One further circumstance, never sufficiently stressed by historians, may also have influenced Louis XVI – the fact that, at the height of his torment over the religious issue, Breteuil's project was brought to him by a non-juring prelate, the Bishop of Pamiers.

Over the previous eighteen months, the bishop had been given ample reason to feel out of sympathy with the Revolution. Alongside undeniable administrative talents, his elevation to the episcopate had revealed the less admirable trait of extreme arrogance. As a result, his clergy had refused to elect him as their deputy to the Estates General, despite his shameless and public checking of which way each of them had voted. Frustrated in his political ambitions, the bishop had turned his hand to pamphleteering. Early in 1789 he published a short treatise, *Reflections on the Principles of the French Constitution*. This argued that the absolute monarchy should transform itself into a constitutional one by conceding that taxation could only be raised with the consent of the nation. Yet he was bitterly opposed to the Civil Constitution of the Clergy, and immediately after his return to Solothurn from Paris published another pamphlet, with the catchy title *Read This and Tremble*. It contained a forthright peroration:

> My brothers, let us remain fervent worshippers of the Lord, faithful children of the Church, and firm upholders of a holy and consoling religion, which today Judaism, Calvinism and libertinism in alliance with the impiety of modern philosophy are attacking with a fury that can only be inspired by Hell.[22]

The bishop was a forceful character, who later even upbraided Marie Antoinette. Louis XVI had always been suspicious of him, disapproving in particular of his private life. But under such radically changed circumstances, the appearance of this eloquent prelate, representative of a menaced faith which commanded the king's deepest allegiance and armed with a bold plan of counter-revolution, was bound to influence the monarch.

The bishop's visit bore fruit in November 1791, a month after his return to Solothurn. It came in the form of a plenipotential power, or *plein pouvoir*, from the king, giving Breteuil full authority to act on his behalf. In practical terms, this meant organizing an escape from Paris. The letter is still preserved today at the Château de Breteuil.

> Monsieur le baron de Breteuil, conscious of all your zeal and fidelity, and wishing to give you a new proof of my confidence, I have chosen to confide to you the interests of my crown. Since circumstances do not permit me to give you my instructions on every specific subject and to hold a regular correspondence with you, I am writing you this letter to serve as a plenipotential power and authorization with regard to the different Powers with whom you may have to treat on my behalf; you know my intentions, and I leave it to your prudence to make whatever use of them that you judge necessary for the good of my service. I approve everything you may do to achieve the aim which I have set myself, which is the restoration of my legitimate authority and the happiness of my peoples. Where-upon I pray God, Monsieur le baron, to take you into His holy protection. Louis.[23]

This is a truly remarkable document. The powers it gave to Breteuil were exceptionally broad, made necessary by the king's semi-captivity and the baron's exile across the border. As Breteuil himself later put it to Bombelles: 'I do not think anybody has ever received any which are so wide-ranging.'[24] It made him a virtual viceroy, speaking for his monarch *ex cathedra* and relaying to the European powers privately what Louis XVI could not express in public. As such, it was to form the basis of Breteuil's authority and actions right up until the king's execution.

Breteuil's *plein pouvoir* has recently become the starting-point of a radical reinterpretation of Louis XVI's conduct during the Revolution by the French historians Paul and Pierrette Girault de Coursac. These scholars claim that from 1790 onwards, unknown to her husband, Marie Antoinette carried on a separate policy of her own, aided by Fersen and Breteuil. They even contend that the queen planned to flee Paris without the king. For the Girault de Coursacs, the essential difference between Louis and his wife was their attitude to foreign intervention to restore their position: the queen, as an Austrian, had no qualms about this, while the king, as a patriotic Frenchman, refused to contemplate it. This is an ingenious, if complex, way of purging Louis XVI of the damning taint of treason, and redirecting all the blame on to Marie Antoinette.[25]

The Girault de Coursacs' most sensational claim is that, to further this policy, Marie Antoinette and Fersen forged Breteuil's *plein pouvoir*.[26] The baron, they argue, was thus the agent not of Louis XVI's clandestine diplomacy, but of a substitute one concocted by Marie Antoinette and presented to the world as that of her husband. Whenever the baron wrote, as he often did, of having received the king's orders, he really meant those of the queen, and all the authority he claimed emanated in reality from her.

There is some evidence to back up this theory. There were indeed long-standing foreign policy differences between Louis XVI and Marie Antoinette. Marie Antoinette was a Habsburg, so it is not inconceivable that she had far fewer qualms than Louis in looking to Austria for military support. Her letters to Mercy-Argenteau and her brother the Emperor Leopold dealing with the preparations for the royal escape also show some curious features. In several, the queen sometimes writes 'I' before crossing it out and substituting 'the king', thus showing inadvertently that she is speaking for herself rather than her husband.[27] She also expressed to Mercy ideas on foreign policy so far-fetched that it is difficult to believe that Louis could have approved them.

The detailed arguments for and against the authenticity of the *plein pouvoir* are too complicated to be set out here. The essential question, however, is one of handwriting. It therefore seemed advisable to submit it to two recognized handwriting experts. Their conclusion, published here in an appendix,[28] endorses the Girault de Coursacs' contention, that the *plein pouvoir* is indeed a forgery.

No handwriting expertise can be absolutely infallible, but the opinion of these two recognized authorities is very compelling. Their finding means that the received picture of Louis XVI's and Marie Antoinette's policy towards the Revolution can never be quite the same again. It now seems that on one vital occasion, the queen colluded in the forging of her husband's handwriting to further a course of action he had not formally approved. Not only did she have political views of her own, she was determined at this critical juncture that they should appear to be the king's as well, and she was not scrupulous about the means she employed to ensure that this was so.

Yet one must be cautious about the wider implications of this revelation. In October 1790, Louis XVI may well have been unwilling, or have hesitated, to give Breteuil's daring plan his approval. But the following June he did indeed accompany the queen in escaping from Paris, and it stretches credulity to believe that all the detailed planning of the intervening months was carried on without his knowledge or approval. To make the picture even more ambiguous, a later letter of the king's about a subsequent diplomatic initiative, which again specifically accredited Breteuil as his only authorized spokesman, was also examined by the experts who had analysed the *plein pouvoir*. This time, they concluded that the document was unlikely to be a forgery.[29]

This dramatic yet contradictory new evidence has one probable explanation. It is highly unlikely that the king's and the queen's political views diverged greatly during the Revolution – on the contrary, there are many indications that they collaborated in pursuit of the same goals. However, as we have seen, at crucial moments Louis XVI became incapable of making a decision. It is entirely plausible that the autumn of 1790, when he was faced with a choice between continuing the policy of cooperating with the Revolution that he had followed for over a year, and the tempting but extremely risky dash for freedom proposed by Breteuil, was one such moment. In this situation, while he no doubt listened sympathetically to Breteuil's plan as outlined by the Bishop of Pamiers, the king may well have avoided a formal commitment. Yet Breteuil needed some sort of authorization from Louis to pursue the project, since otherwise he would have no credibility. It was this that Marie Antoinette, with Fersen's help, took it upon herself to provide. Since October 1789 she had been a desperate women, and in these circumstances desperate measures were needed.

What this does not mean is that from late 1790 on Marie

Antoinette systematically deceived her husband and pursued a secret diplomacy of her own that she passed off as his. There is too much evidence pointing in the other direction, and even if she had done so, her conduct would have aroused much more suspicion than it did at the time. In fact, no contemporary ever accused her of counterfeiting her husband's policy. Both king and queen shared the same aims. The only difference between them was that he baulked at the decisions needed to achieve them, whereas she did not. In the autumn of 1790, the most crucial choice of all – whether or not to escape from Paris – had to be made, and the queen, if necessary by dubious means, resolved to make it for him.

We shall never know whether Breteuil himself was aware that his prized *plein pouvoir* was a forgery. If he did, and continued with his plan regardless, he was taking a considerable risk. Paradoxically, the moment of greatest danger would come if the escape from Paris succeeded; at that point, Louis XVI would inevitably learn of the deception. If Breteuil did know that his authorization was not genuine, he must have been very confident that the glow of success would deflect the king's anger, and above all that the queen would shield him by taking responsibility on herself.

However this was achieved, the despatch of the *plein pouvoir* to Breteuil marked a turning-point both for himself and for Louis and Marie Antoinette. To all intents and purposes, the baron was now the chief minister and spokesman of the captive king of France, with formal accreditation to prove it. Yet the royal authority he invoked for his actions was currently being challenged by a rival force in France, the National Assembly. Most dangerous of all, the policy he was being authorized to pursue ran directly contrary to the one Louis XVI had ostensibly agreed with the Assembly. If a whisper of Breteuil's secret negotiations leaked out, the royal family would be in grave peril. The plan to flee Paris, and the fate of the king and queen, depended on the deepest secrecy.

Chapter Six

MIRABEAU VERSUS BRETEUIL

THE VISIT OF THE Bishop of Pamiers, bearing Breteuil's proposals, set in motion the royal family's plan to escape from the capital. Yet Breteuil's was not the only plan for flight that Louis XVI considered. By this time too Mirabeau, still the court's secret adviser, had revised his opinion that the only feasible refuge for the king if he left Paris was loyalist Normandy. With the rapid spread of economic crisis, political radicalism and military disaffection, a retreat further into France no longer seemed safe. Like Breteuil, Mirabeau now cast his eyes in the direction of Lorraine, to the only disciplined army still at the king's disposal, that of General de Bouillé.

Mirabeau did not discuss these thoughts in his Notes to the Court; the evidence that he pursued them comes from Bouillé's own memoirs.[1] François-Claude Amour, marquis de Bouillé, had come to occupy a unique position in French politics in 1790 and 1791. A hero of France's intervention in the American War of Independence, in which he had captured Grenada from the English, he was widely regarded as the best general in the army. He was no blind reactionary, but a partisan of moderate reform. Yet his thorough repression of the mutiny among his troops at Nancy in August 1790 had revealed him as above all a man of order. He thus swiftly came to the notice of all those who, whatever their political backgrounds, wished to put a curb on the Revolution. He became a powerful warlord in a country on the brink of civil war, courted by a variety of political suitors, from Louis XVI himself to Breteuil, Mirabeau and even La Fayette (who presumed rather too much on the fact that he was Bouillé's cousin). The most concrete proposals Bouillé received, however, came from Breteuil and Mirabeau.

The general's first visitor was the Bishop of Pamiers, returning to Solothurn after his mission to Paris. The bishop arrived in Metz with a short, laconic letter of introduction in Louis XVI's own hand, dated 23 October 1790. While this gave nothing away, the bishop did, telling Bouillé that the king intended to escape from Paris and make for Lorraine at some point the following spring. Before leaving, the bishop outlined to him Breteuil's plan. From this point on a secret, coded correspondence began between Bouillé and Louis XVI.[2]

Then, on 5 February 1791, Bouillé received a mysterious letter from the king. It warned him that he would shortly receive a visit from the comte de la Marck, a great noble from the Austrian Netherlands but also a French landowner and noble deputy to the National Assembly. La Marck was a close associate of Mirabeau and would, Louis hinted, be carrying proposals on his friend's behalf. The king wrote:

> Although [Mirabeau and his circle] are not estimable men, and the former has cost me a lot of money, I none the less think that they have their uses. You may find some interesting things in Mirabeau's project; listen to it but keep your own counsel, and let me know what you think.[3]

The very next day, 6 February, la Marck did indeed arrive at Metz, and outlined Mirabeau's plan. Mirabeau's aim was to dissolve the Constituent Assembly, on the twin grounds that the deputies did not have sufficient authority to alter France's antique constitution, and that since October 1789 the king was no longer a free agent. This would be achieved by means of a public petition backed by as many as possible of the departments of the kingdom (Mirabeau claimed he already had the support of thirty-six) and calling for a new assembly and liberty for the king. In the meantime, Bouillé would bring his troops up to the capital, ready to take safe delivery of the royal family and instal them at either Fontainebleau or Compiègne.[4]

By February 1791, Bouillé was thus being canvassed on behalf of two deeply contrasting plans, both of which the king was exploring. Mirabeau's involved a compromise with at least some of the revolutionaries, and ensured that certain of their achievements would be preserved in the context of a new assembly and constitution. Breteuil's, on the other hand, relied simply on Bouillé's troops. Interestingly, Bouillé preferred the first plan. According to his memoirs, he cynically advised Louis XVI to adopt it,

> to shower Mirabeau with gold, and to . . . promise him whatever he wanted, pointing out that things had gone beyond the stage where virtuous and honest men could save the monarchy . . . whereas only the scoundrels whose talent and audacity had caused the trouble in the first place, had the insight and the means necessary to cure it.[5]

A further difference between Mirabeau's and Breteuil's plans lies in the element of risk each involved. Mirabeau's project, based as it was on constitutional devices like a grand petition, enabled Louis and Marie Antoinette to act through proxies in the Assembly and the departments and thus to some extent protected them. Breteuil's scheme, on the other hand, with its cloak-and-dagger escape from the Tuileries, carried a very real danger of confrontation or pursuit if the royal family were intercepted.

One person who had no illusions about the perils of Breteuil's enterprise was Mercy-Argenteau, who was informed of it by Marie Antoinette in February 1791. While remaining ambassador to France, Mercy had in October 1790 been sent as the emperor's personal representative to resolve the crisis in the Austrian Netherlands, which were also in a state of revolutionary upheaval. There is a strong hint of personal cowardice in Mercy's behaviour during the Revolution. He fled precipitately from the Paris uprising in July 1789 and did not return for four months, and was to show a similar reluctance to resume his duties in the capital after his mission to the Austrian Netherlands ended. One senses that this failing equipped him better than most to appreciate the dangers the escape posed. 'The most important thing to ensure is the flight's safety,' he advised the queen in April 1791. 'There must be an escort at intervals along the route; one shudders to think what horrors might result from being betrayed and stopped.'[6]

Mirabeau and Breteuil were now engaged in a long-distance duel. At stake was the king's confidence, and with it the future shape of the French monarchy. There is no record of what the two men thought of each other. Given the deep secrecy in which the royal family's plans were cloaked, it is not even certain whether Mirabeau and Breteuil knew that they were rivals for the king's confidence. Mirabeau may have suspected something, since in his Notes to the Court he dropped the occasional hint that he was aware of Breteuil's continuing influence. When in June 1790 he was consulted about the despatch of a special envoy to Madrid to renegotiate France's alliance with Spain, he suggested the baron's old friend and publicist Rulhière, who had briefly defected to Necker but had now returned to his old allegiance. 'If only experienced diplomats are to be considered,' Mirabeau wrote,

> ... I would propose ... M. de Rulhière, who undoubtedly has his drawbacks, but who is a man of much spirit and of whose loyalty I am almost certain, and who no longer works for Necker but once more serves a man who will always be devoted to the queen.[7]

This shrewd reference to Breteuil would not have been lost on Louis and Marie Antoinette. The baron, however, always maintained an oracular silence on important matters, and his views on Mirabeau were no exception. By March 1791 he certainly knew of the rival project, since Bombelles told him about it, but he passed no comment.[8] Whether he would ever have considered an accommodation with its author is dubious. This would have required substantial concessions, and there is little evidence that Breteuil was prepared to make them.

Whichever plan Louis XVI adopted, however, the essence of both was secrecy. Here, the views and activities of his brother the comte d'Artois posed a grave danger. After fleeing France in July 1789, Artois, the prince de Condé and their families had installed themselves in Turin, in the court of the former's father-in-law, the king of Sardinia. From there, Artois had set himself up as the rallying-point of all those Frenchmen who remained faithful to the regime and rejected all compromise with the Revolution. At the same time, he launched a series of intrigues to raise counter-revolution in the French Midi. This culminated in the so-called 'conspiracy of Lyon' which was unearthed and suppressed by the authorities in December 1790. The effect of Artois's actions was disastrous. Public opinion could never believe that they did not have the secret approval of his brother Louis XVI. The prince's posturing, from the safety of northern Italy, exposed his family still inside France to the very real danger of a fresh burst of popular fury. This danger became even more acute in early 1791 when Condé moved from Turin to Worms, in western Germany, to establish a base there for armed counter-revolution.

The activities of Artois and Condé underline a wider truth about royalist politics after 1789. The princely emigration after 14 July had ensured from the start that the conflict between revolution and counter-revolution would be international. This meant that the planning for the royal family's flight could not just be limited to France. In fact, in the spring of 1791 the king and queen had to coordinate events in three different countries from the Tuileries: France itself, where Bouillé's dispositions were crucial, Germany where Condé was now established at Worms, and northern Italy, which was not only Artois's centre of operations but also, between March and July 1791, that of the Emperor Leopold II. It is thus impossible to divide the royal escape from Paris neatly into 'French' and 'foreign' compartments. It was a European event, played out on a European chessboard.

As the Tuileries' secret representative, Breteuil's activities extended into all these areas. Since it was increasingly clear that Artois had to be contained, his gaze was inevitably drawn to northern Italy. Between December 1790 and June 1791, all the baron's diplomatic skills were needed in a highly delicate correspondence with Artois, attempting to prevent him from acting as a loose cannon, while at the same time hiding from him the king and queen's inmost secrets. Only a few of these letters have been published. The originals are lost. Copies of them, however, remain in the Bombelles papers, and these are of great significance. They reveal that Breteuil's contacts with Artois before the flight to Varennes were much more extensive than previously thought. They also shed new light on the attitude of both Artois and Breteuil towards Louis XVI himself.

Breteuil's first letter to Artois, written on 6 December 1790, was a polite but firm warning to him to cease his provocative intrigues in the Midi. Interestingly, in an indication of his reticence towards Artois, the baron made no mention at this point of the *plein pouvoir* he had just received, but wrote in a purely personal capacity, as 'an old servant of the king, faithfully devoted to the interests of his majesty and his crown', whose eyes had been 'constantly fixed for the last eighteen months on the misfortunes of the monarchy and those of the king and queen themselves'. He did, however, make a veiled threat that if Artois persisted in his escapades, Louis XVI might formally disavow him.[9]

Artois swiftly replied, justifying his actions. Beneath the refined politeness of their phrases, one senses the start of a ruthless duel between the prince and the baron. Breteuil had insisted in his letter on the necessity of the king's presence to any successful counter-revolution. Artois riposted with a telling argument: no one would welcome this more than he, but up until that point Louis XVI had shown no inclination to break his chains. 'Convinced more than anyone of the need for the king to escape,' he wrote,

> I have used every means I know: prayers, supplications, plans, reasoning, even threats, but up to now all have been useless, and even at the moment I write to you, my hopes are virtually destroyed and my fears livelier than ever.[10]

This is a remarkable passage. It reveals the full extent of Artois's suspicions of his elder brother, and his obsessive fear that left to himself, Louis XVI would arrive at some form of compromise with the Revolution. In 1790 at least, these fears were not unjustified. The king had not tried to escape while he had the chance, and had tamely allowed himself to be dragged back to Paris by the crowd in October 1789. Once in the capital, he had made no further effort to flee, even when his move to Saint-Cloud during the summer of 1790 had made it relatively easy for him to do so. Instead, he had opened secret negotiations with Mirabeau, one of the founding fathers of the Revolution. However unwillingly, he had sanctioned the August decrees, the Declaration of the Rights of Man, even the Civil

Constitution of the Clergy. Just how far this had strained his relationship with his younger brother is made clear by Artois's extraordinary admission that he had actually issued threats to the king.

Although the evidence for this is now lost, there must have been some coordination between Breteuil's actions and those of the Tuileries, for at the end of December a secret messenger arrived at Turin from Paris. He brought a categorical order from Louis XVI to Artois to call off the planned insurrection in the Midi. If this were not done, the king went on – and it can hardly be coincidence that here he used almost exactly the same phrase as Breteuil – he would be forced publicly to disavow his brother.[11] After a heated and bitter meeting of the council that Artois, for all the world like a reigning monarch, had formed to advise him, it was decided to honour Louis XVI's wishes.

The previous month, the princes in Turin had been joined by a particularly fateful figure. At the end of November, Calonne arrived from England and quickly established himself as the leading figure on their council and their *de facto* prime minister. Since his disgrace at the hands of the assembly of notables, the former controller-general had been leading an adventurous life. He had first fled to England, then returned to France to present himself as a candidate for the Estates General. He was immediately mobbed by a hostile crowd and had to flee again. As early as July 1789 he met Artois and Condé, in flight from France, at Namur, and became their confidential agent. When he eventually rejoined them in Turin, Artois greeted him as his saviour: 'Thank Heaven, I have him at last!' he exclaimed.[12]

The prince had, of course, been a friend and supporter of Calonne both before and during the assembly of notables. Yet to give such a welcome – and position – to a man the king himself had dismissed and who had always been the queen's bitter enemy was tactless, to say the least. The worst suspicions of Louis XVI and Marie Antoinette were confirmed: John Hardman has claimed that the king's despatch of the *plein pouvoir* to Breteuil may well have been a direct riposte to the news of Calonne's arrival in Turin. This underestimates the role played by the Civil Constitution of the Clergy in Louis XVI's action, but certainly it may have contributed to his decision. It is understandable that Marie Antoinette could write to Leopold II: 'We would have no secrets from the comte d'Artois, if he were not surrounded by M. de Calonne and the prince de Condé, in whom we can never have confidence.'[13]

Against this darkening background, Breteuil returned to the attack. On 8 February 1791, he wrote a long reply to Artois, remarkable both for its frankness and its firmness of tone. He defended Louis XVI forcefully against Artois's accusation of inertia, pointing out that Louis XVI had only remained passive so far because the moment was not yet ripe for him to seize the initiative. 'This, I feel,' he wrote,

> is the only way to view the king's dreadful situation and the criticisms, as ceaseless as they are unfounded, that have been made of his excessive patience. Doubtless I am too far away and too much on the sidelines to judge whether it would have been possible for the king to escape, as Monseigneur seems to think he could have done in the letter with which he honoured me on 15 December. But, here in my remote retreat, I am free to turn my thoughts and the reflection of my love for my king to the great question of whether His Majesty should indeed have surrendered to this natural wish, at a time when the mutiny of the troops as well as their officers seemed irresistible, when popular frenzy was at a peak everywhere, and when the foreign powers by whom the king could hope to be supported were themselves in the midst of embarrassments which only permitted them to aid him with words.[14]

This was the best defence that a counter-revolutionary could make of Louis XVI's conduct during 1790. Having allowed himself to be taken captive in October 1789, it made sense for the king to see just how much of his power he might be able to retain in the context of the emerging constitution, while not excluding flight should this settlement prove unacceptable. Breteuil's argument, that a royal escape in 1790 was folly given the mutinies in the army, is also very revealing. It offers further evidence that he only decided a flight was feasible once Bouillé had made sure of his own soldiers' loyalty.

In future, Breteuil proposed, Artois should make no further overtures to any of the Powers without Louis XVI's prior approval.

The prince should also (and Breteuil felt this point sufficiently important to underline it) dismiss the many extremist and indiscreet *émigrés* who now crowded round him in Turin. It is not difficult to discern in this recommendation a first sally on the baron's part against his old enemy Calonne. Breteuil ended his letter with a peroration whose obvious sincerity is rather moving. Beneath its florid phrases, one catches a glimpse of the man beneath the politician, pierced to the quick by the overturning of his world:

> I wish I could strengthen my arguments with insight and means in equal measure, but I can only offer the pure devotion and the calmest possible reflection on the part of a man who must preserve himself from rash impulses born of his love for the king, through that habit of respect for the rights of the crown and its power which he has seen displayed by the whole of Europe as well as the king's own servants; and who joins to his opposition to everything that offends the royal prerogative the necessity of guarding against the anger in his soul, tortured by every kind of pain, sacrifice and personal misfortune.[15]

Artois's reply, written from Venice on 21 February, was better written than his previous efforts. One discerns in it the hand of the subtle Calonne rather than that of the impulsive prince. Presumably Artois was now relying heavily on his new adviser to help frame his diplomatic correspondence. If this was the case, it lends an added piquancy to his exchanges with the baron; in effect, he was merely providing a façade behind which Breteuil and Calonne, who had hated each other since 1784, could resume their long political vendetta.

Artois's letter underlines just how tense relations between the Tuileries and Turin had become over the previous few months. The prince once again defended the stridency of his recent messages to Louis and Marie Antoinette. 'I have spoken to [the king] as well as the queen', he proclaimed,

> in the language of honour. My expressions have been strong, severe, even harsh if you wish; but the purity of my motives excuses all of this, and everything I saw and heard compelled me to speak out; but at the same time as I was trying to help and enlighten my all too unfortunate relatives, I was doing

everything possible to conform to their intentions. . . . You
yourself should know this better than most, if you recall the
conversation you had with M. de Calonne at Solothurn.[16]

In this self-justificatory passage, Artois lets slip a remarkable fact. It
has never been realized that Calonne stopped off in Solothurn to see
Breteuil on his way to Turin, and that the two old rivals had a
political discussion. It is generally assumed that Breteuil and Calonne
were at daggers drawn throughout the Revolution, and that during
this time they had no personal contact. Yet the fact of their meeting
in late 1790 implies that at this point their differences were not yet
unbridgeable. It was the planned royal escape from Paris, and the
intrigues which surrounded it, which caused the decisive breach
between the two men.

Despite the doubts Artois expressed to Breteuil, at the Tuileries
plans for escape were gathering pace. After la Marck's visit to Metz
with Mirabeau's project in February, Bouillé had made it clear to
Louis XVI that he greatly preferred it to Breteuil's. He did not
succeed in changing the king's mind, and the baron's original
proposal was retained. None the less, it seems that Mirabeau's plan
continued to be discussed. Throughout March a steady drip of
information trickled through to Artois and Condé that Louis was
about to agree to a compromise scheme, almost certainly that of
Mirabeau, which would resolve the revolutionary crisis. Amazingly,
the most concrete evidence came from Bouillé himself.

Besieged as he was by emissaries from all quarters, it is not
surprising that the general inadvertently let slip something of the
plans afoot. The evidence, once again, comes from Bombelles, whose
diary for the spring of 1791 is particularly detailed. Soon after the
storming of the Bastille, the marquis had left Versailles for Venice,
where he had been ambassador since just before the Revolution.
When Artois came to Venice in January 1791, he stayed with
Bombelles, and soon incorporated him into his circle of advisers. The
marquis, who felt he could be of most use in combating Calonne's
wilder ideas, did not disdain this new role.

Bombelles was thus present in Venice on 19 March when Calonne
read out to Artois's council a letter he had just received from his
niece, the marquise de Fouquet, whose husband was serving with

Bouillé's army at Métz. Growing suspicious of the clandestine comings-and-goings around Bouillé's headquarters, Calonne had asked his niece to investigate. In this she was successful. Bouillé was remarkably forthcoming, and confided in her the details of a plan which was clearly the one Mirabeau had broached with him via la Marck the previous month. The marquise promptly wrote them all down and sent them to Calonne.[17]

Mme de Fouquet's letter described in detail the project Bouillé outlined to her. The general, she wrote,

> claims that there is a party in the Assembly that supports the king, that the comte de Mirabeau is at its head . . . and that the plan is to enable the king to go to Compiègne, where he can be protected by troops from Flanders, and that there he should freely sanction those decrees he feels able to approve.[18]

Yet the marquise also revealed a further, highly significant element to the plan, which was never mentioned anywhere else – that, as part of the deal, Calonne himself would return to office, as 'a form of Chancellor of the Exchequer'. As she herself put it to her uncle:

> Once the king is free, they want to place beside him someone of recognized capacity, and it is of you that they are thinking. I was astonished that Mirabeau does not see himself in this post. The reply was that he is well aware that he cannot appear too prominently, given his reputation. Everyone concerned has been pleased with your work [Calonne's pamphlet of late 1790, *On the Present and Future State of France*], but unhappy about the attempted rising at Lyon and your journey to Turin.[19]

Listening to this, Bombelles must have felt he was stepping into a political Wonderland. Calonne was bitterly unpopular inside France, both as a failed controller-general with a reputation for corruption, and subsequently as an adviser to the most extreme wing of the counter-revolution. Yet there is no reason to doubt the joint testimony of Mme de Fouquet and Bombelles, which so exactly echoes what we do know of the compromise plan. Further, looked at more closely, the scheme has a number of features, artfully combining shrewd logic and sheer fantasy, that plausibly reveal the hand of Mirabeau. The tribune had known Calonne for years, and had acted as his publicist for several years during his ministry. Given this background, it is by no means impossible that he saw Calonne as a potential instrument in his secret policy. If the general compromise he planned were to succeed, sooner or later the princes would have to be included in it, and to have Calonne, their most trusted adviser, on his side would pay dividends. Mirabeau knew the full scope of Calonne's ambition, and his overture is best seen as an audacious attempt to exploit this as a means of reconciling the emigration to the Revolution.

To judge by Calonne's reaction, the scheme worked. Bombelles's diary depicts the former minister buoyed up by hope and excitement at Artois's council, the marquise's piece of paper in his hand: 'Before beginning to read it, he once again protested at the horror of a possible arrangement with Messieurs de Mirabeau, de Lameth and other rogues of that type.'[20] Yet Calonne quickly went on to qualify that disapproval:

> It is dreadful to have to negotiate with traitors. It is probable that their work will prove impossible to reconcile with the aim of restoring a true monarchy. But there comes a time when one must accept what one is unable to prevent. If certain decrees [of the National Assembly] can only be repealed by agreeing to some painful amnesties, this price is worth paying . . .[21]

In aiming at Calonne's most salient feature, his opportunism, Mirabeau had scored a bull's-eye. Even more remarkably, his scheme seems at least temporarily to have won over most of Artois's council. As Bombelles put it: 'The conclusion was that, however frightful a conciliation of this sort, it is preferable to civil war.'[22] Here, the marquis's diary reveals a hitherto hidden facet of the French Revolution. It offers strong evidence that, belying their later reputation for intransigence, in early 1791 Artois and his supporters contemplated a compromise with the Revolution.

Any plan that restored Calonne to favour by definition meant leaving Breteuil out in the cold, and since the latter was known to have influence with the king and queen, here too a reconciliation had to be sought. In fact, Bombelles claims that it was Breteuil who had first been mooted as an adviser to Artois, and that he had only been rejected at the insistence of Condé, who had been at odds with the baron since the 1780s.[23] Now, however, Calonne was only too pleased to be magnanimous; presumably his visit to Breteuil on his way to Turin had been intended as an olive branch. In the context of the vast scheme under discussion, he intimated that he would be happy to divide his ministry with Breteuil. He confided all this to Bombelles, hoping no doubt that he would pass it on to the baron. By this time, Bombelles had got the measure of Calonne, and his description of this overture has a satirical edge:

> M. de Calonne talked to me of forming a ministry as if he was already in his armchair at the council table and in possession of unlimited power. He wants control of justice and finance. He thinks that M. le baron de Breteuil can be left all matters concerning foreign policy and that the two of them, as the preponderant ministers, would need only subaltern ministers, responsible to them, to run the war and marine departments and the provinces. I said yes to everything. One must leave these big children to play at being grown-ups when it amuses them, just as if they were naughty boys.[24]

The very next day, more news arrived of a projected bargain between the king and the Assembly. This time, the information came from Paris, from a well-connected, semi-secret royalist club, the *salon français*. This added a further piece to the jigsaw – the dissolution of the National Assembly in the context of the pact, and the establishment in its place of a new, two-chamber legislature on the English model. The third estate would be transformed into a House of Commons, and the nobility and clergy into a Chamber of Peers.[25]

Like the plan to restore Calonne to office, reviving the idea of a bicameral legislature so soon after its crushing defeat in September 1789 seems one more castle in the air. If the only source for this was the *salon français*, it should not be taken too seriously, given the strong streak of fanciful paranoia common to most royalist intelligence-gathering networks during the Revolution. Yet there is strong evidence that the bicameral option was once again coming to the fore, as an integral part of Mirabeau's planned compromise. Significantly, the *salon français* report mentioned the transfer of the royal family to Compiègne as forming part of the 'two-chambers' scheme.[26] It would make a great deal of sense if Mirabeau had toyed with the idea of a bicameral legislature as a means of rallying royalists and moderate revolutionaries under the same banner. The reason the 'two-chambers' idea refused to die after September 1789 was that it continued to hold out a compromise solution to the fundamental issue that had caused the Revolution in the first place – the composition of the nation's representative body. As a middle way between the radicals' egalitarian insistence on a single sovereign assembly and the diehard royalists' unbending allegiance to the 'antique constitution', it had great attractions. To conservatives, a Chamber of Peers presented a bulwark against democracy and anarchy, while to moderate constitutionalists it guaranteed that there would be no return to the Estates General and its three orders.

It is entirely plausible that by February 1791 Mirabeau thought the time had come to dust down the 'two-chambers' idea to gain the support of those deputies who now wanted to 'end the Revolution', and particularly the remaining *monarchiens* in the assembly. Yet he may well have been looking further afield, beyond the borders of France. Bombelles's diary offers strong evidence that Mirabeau saw Calonne as an essential instrument in his scheme to reconcile the princes to his compromise plan. Indeed, a few months previously, Calonne had published his pamphlet *On the Present and Future State of France*. This proposed a constitutional monarchy based on a two-chamber legislature, with the king retaining much of the initiative in legislation – exactly what the *monarchiens* had proposed in September 1789. What better way for Mirabeau to build bridges to Calonne than by taking up his most recent suggestion?

More concrete evidence that Mirabeau had definitely adopted the 'two-chambers' project comes in the memoirs of the old *monarchien* Malouet, who after his party's defeat in the Assembly in September 1789 was now involved in the efforts to reconcile Mirabeau and the court. Malouet claimed to have been shown at this time a long memorandum of Mirabeau's detailing his plan to restore the royal authority. According to Malouet, the fourth item of the plan was the division of the National Assembly into two chambers.[27]

Like most of Mirabeau's schemes, his plan to free the king and end the Revolution was tortuous and labyrinthine. It was essentially secret, and can only be pieced together from widely scattered sources: Bouillé's memoirs, Bombelles's diary, Calonne's papers and Malouet's memoirs. Yet from all this a clear picture does emerge. In the spring of 1791, Mirabeau was working on a project to set the royal family at liberty and dissolve the National Assembly by constitutional means. As part of the plan, Bouillé's army would approach Paris and guarantee the king's security once he was installed at Compiègne or Fontainebleau. A new ministry would then be formed, conceivably including Calonne as the price of the princes' support, which would oversee the replacement of the Assembly by a two-chamber legislature on the English model. The prince de Condé, who loathed and feared the whole idea, termed it a detestable mixture of 'egoism, *amour-propre* and Anglomania'.[28] It would be fairer to see it as a significant effort to end the Revolution by installing a strong constitutional monarchy.

Could the scheme ever have worked? Probably not; it was altogether too grandiose, and relied for its success on combining too many disparate elements and individuals. Its historical importance, however, lies less in its ultimate feasibility than in the fact that it was so seriously considered. Unravelling its development sheds a new light on the policy of both Mirabeau and the royal family in the first months of 1791. It shows the range of options that Louis XVI was considering to have been much wider and more complex than previously thought.

Then, on 2 April 1791, Mirabeau died suddenly at his house in Paris. His conduct over the past months had thrown his former friends on the Left into a frenzy of suspicion, and there was a wave of rumours that they had had him poisoned. In fact, no trace of foul play was found. Tubercular illness, complicated by the effects of drinking and womanizing, is a much more plausible diagnosis. The disappearance of its moving spirit probably dealt a decisive blow to the plan Mirabeau had conceived. Yet by March 1791, as Bombelles noted in his diary, it was clear that the secret was already out. If Mirabeau's claim as recorded by Bouillé, that he was certain of the support of thirty-six departments for his grand petition, was correct, then many people inside France must have known of the scheme, not to mention the *émigrés* at Worms and Turin. It is difficult to see how the scheme could have survived both the death of its author and its own increasing publicity.

By the time of Mirabeau's death, Louis XVI had also lost faith in the plan. Almost a month previously, in early March, the king had written Bouillé another coded letter that made it clear he had finally opted for Breteuil's project. He informed the general that he would make his escape by the beginning of May at the latest, and went into detail about the route he proposed to take. For the final stage of his journey, he wrote, he intended to take the Varennes road.[29]

The writing of this letter marked a personal watershed for Louis XVI. It also puts into perspective the controversy surrounding Breteuil's *plein pouvoir*. Between October 1790 and March 1791, it was unclear which plan for escape the king would adopt, Mirabeau's or Breteuil's. This tense and evenly balanced contest gave Marie Antoinette yet further reason to have the *plein pouvoir* forged, to enable her candidate to steal a march on his rival. The baron could thus begin to prepare the scheme, even while Louis XVI was still being persuaded to give it his endorsement. By March 1791, Mirabeau's eclipse and the queen's urgings had finally secured the necessary consent.

The attitude of the royal couple's most trusted servants to both plans is symbolized by Bombelles's conduct at this juncture. On 20 March he was prepared to accept, with grave misgivings, Mirabeau's scheme as reported by Calonne. Nine days later, however, he received a letter from Breteuil in Solothurn informing him secretly of his *plein pouvoir* and his own project for a royal escape, and his attitude changed completely. His distrust of the planned compromise and its advocates redoubled. Implicit in the marquis's about-face was a recognition that the essence of Breteuil's scheme was a bid to regain much more of the royal authority than Mirabeau was prepared to contemplate. On 31 March, two days after receiving Breteuil's message, Bombelles confided to his diary his final, negative conclusion on the rival plan. 'It would be frightful to be reduced to bargaining with the leading traitors, and everything points to the danger of being deceived by their cunning propositions.'[30] Though couched in oblique language, the aims the baron had let slip to his protégé were very different: 'It is enough that you be certain of the king's determined resolution to hazard his crown, if necessary, to win back his just prerogative.'[31]

The marquis now reverted to what he had always been: Breteuil's most faithful subordinate. He remained in Venice, but more as the baron's secret agent than Artois's adviser, and began a clandestine correspondence with Breteuil. Now that he knew the king's real intentions, it became essential to dispose of what remained of the compromise plan. This meant discrediting Calonne, a task which Breteuil must have been only too happy to direct. The method was for Bombelles to use information supplied by Breteuil to sow suspicions in Artois's mind that Calonne was only supporting the conciliation project through personal ambition. As the marquis reported on 10 April:

> It is possible that I will be able to make good use of your last letters because, although he has said nothing, M. le comte d'Artois has sensed how much M. de Calonne has come round to the conciliation plan since the moment he saw, or thought he saw, that he would be summoned either to Compiègne or elsewhere.[32]

By April 1791, the baron's strategy was coming together. The escape proposal he had put to Louis XVI had finally been accepted, and he had the precious *plein pouvoir* to prove it. His rival for the king's ear, Mirabeau, was dead, and his alternative compromise scheme had been shelved. Breteuil could now proceed with his own plan to save the monarchy.

Chapter Seven

PREPARATIONS

ON HIS ARRIVAL IN SOLOTHURN in October 1789, Breteuil had installed himself in a comfortable house on the outskirts of the town. During the 'calm year' of 1790, he whiled away his enforced leisure by constructing a leafy promenade nearby so that he could take the air. It remains today much as he left it, and is still known as the 'Allées de Breteuil'.[1] It was in this agreeable setting that he planned the royal family's escape from Paris.

The main reason the baron had been sent the *plein pouvoir* was so that, as an experienced diplomat, he could coordinate international support for the projected flight. In these months, the affairs of Europe preoccupied Breteuil just as much, perhaps even more than, those of his native land. Unlike Mirabeau, who had been determined that the French should solve their own problems, the baron was convinced from an early stage that the Revolution could only be ended with the help, in one form or another, of the other Powers. Indeed, as he never ceased to point out in his letters, it was in their interest to aid Louis XVI to regain his authority, since the Revolution's attack on monarchical power could easily prove contagious.

Yet the European scene in 1791 was not at all propitious to an international effort to help rescue the king of France. The Habsburg monarchy, linked by its blood tie to Marie Antoinette, and essential to any plan for escape through the proximity to France of its Belgian possessions, was itself in the throes of a major crisis. Taking advantage of Joseph II's ill-advised war, in alliance with Russia, on the Turks, Austria's Belgian and Hungarian possessions had begun to plot insurrection. In November 1789, influenced by the French example, the Belgians rose in revolt and drove out the Austrian forces; the following January they declared independence as the 'United States of Belgium'. Although a string of much-needed victories over the Turks in late 1789 pulled the monarchy back from the brink, Joseph's health had given way and his spirit was broken. He died on 20 February 1790. His epitaph, he muttered bitterly, should read: 'Here lies Joseph II, who failed in everything he undertook.'[2]

Having no posterity of his own, Joseph was succeeded by his intelligent, cynical and sexually voracious younger brother Leopold. Grand Duke of Tuscany since 1765, Leopold was known as 'the Florentine' on account of the taste for duplicity and intrigue he had developed through his long residence in Machiavelli's home city. The change of emperor did not bode well for the embattled French royal family. Unlike Joseph, Leopold had little family feeling for his sister; moreover, having always displayed liberal and Enlightened leanings, he was inclined to think that his sister and brother-in-law should reach an accommodation with the Revolution.[3] Above all, he was barely able to contain the upheaval he had inherited in his own lands, let alone help resolve that in France.

As it turned out, Leopold's domestic policy was extremely successful. The Belgian revolution was skilfully mastered by playing off the different rebel factions against each other; by the end of 1790 Habsburg control had been re-established. Here the *éminence grise* was Mercy-Argenteau, from October 1790 Leopold's minister plenipotentiary to the province. For him, even the uncertainties of Belgian politics were preferable to the horrors of Paris.

The principal foreign problem Leopold now faced was posed by his Prussian neighbour. In 1786 Frederick the Great, who for the past twenty years had pursued a generally pacific foreign policy, had died, to be succeeded by his belligerent and opportunistic nephew Frederick William II. Seeing a chance for gain in Austria's difficulties, Frederick William mobilized his army, and a further war that would have proved disastrous for Leopold was only averted at the last minute by the convention of Reichenbach in July 1790. By this time, the crises in Belgium and Hungary and the Turkish war were mostly on the way to resolution. The European states system, however, had been given a considerable jolt, and until the beginning of 1791 none of the major Powers could afford to show much concern for French affairs.

It was against this unstable diplomatic background that Breteuil set to work. His first move, unsurprisingly, was in the direction of Mercy-Argenteau, whom he had known for thirty years. Mercy was still nominally ambassador to Paris, even though he was now resident in Brussels. By this time he had substantial influence in the Austrian Netherlands, which would be crucial if Louis XVI's plans required foreign support. On 12 January 1791, the baron wrote Mercy a long letter, enclosing a copy of the *plein pouvoir*. He had prepared the ground carefully the previous October by sending the ambassador a polite note congratulating him on his Belgian appointment. Mercy's *pro forma* reply gave him the opening he needed.[4]

Breteuil began with some general reflections on the nature of the French Revolution. These are interesting for their clear recognition that the Revolution was unlike any previous political event, and completely incompatible with the established order in Europe. In early 1791 this was a conclusion that few politicians and commentators, with the exception of Edmund Burke, had yet drawn. 'I agree with you, my dear ambassador,' the baron wrote,

> that our revolution is different from any other of which history tells us; and above all that none has ever been so feebly opposed. But if this remark is only too true, the reflection you add is no less so. It is impossible that such a state of affairs can endure physically, morally, or geographically.[5]

Breteuil went on to outline the escape plan, making clear how heavily it relied on the loyalty of Bouillé's troops. On this score, he was optimistic. 'I have ... no doubt', he wrote, 'that as soon as the king is able to show himself, the numbers that will rally to him will be incalculable. We can count on the loyalty of several regiments and the repentance of more.' But he also dropped a broad hint that he hoped the threat of force, rather than force itself, would accom-

1. *Above. Opening of the Estates General at Versailles on 5th May 1789*, by Louis-Charles-Auguste Couder.

2. *Right.* Louis XVI, an unflattering portrait by Joseph Boze. When Sir Winston Churchill was shown this picture, he remarked: 'Now I understand why there was a French Revolution.'

3. *Marie Antoinette with Children*, by Elisabeth Louise Vigée Le Brun, painted in 1787, when the queen's extravagance had already made her deeply unpopular. When the portrait was exhibited at the Salon of that year, an anonymous note reading, 'Here is the deficit!' was pinned to it.

4. Count Hans Axel von Fersen, friend of Breteuil and probable lover of Marie Antoinette.

5. The comte de Provence, later Louis XVIII, by Joseph-Siffred Duplessis.

6. *Left.* The comte
d'Artois, later Charles X,
by Henri-Pierre Danloux.

7. *Below.* Calonne, a portrait
by Elisabeth Louise Vigée
Le Brun, who was also said
to be his mistress.

8. *Right*. The baron de Breteuil by the sculptor Augustin Pajou, commissioned in 1788 by the Academy of Science.

9. *Below*. The baron de Breteuil, by François-Guillaume Menageot.

10. *Above. The Models*, by Jean-Baptiste Le Prince, a friend of Breteuil's. Breteuil, shown leaning over the painter's shoulder, is taking an obvious interest in the proceedings.

11. *Left.* Breteuil's daughter, the comtesse de Matignon, painted c. 1772. 'Lively and scintillating, she held the sceptre of fashion in Paris and at Versailles.'

12. Breteuil's ministerial portfolio.

13. The marquis
de Bombelles as a
young diplomat.

14. The comte de Mirabeau, by Joseph Boze.

plish his aims. He wrapped this in an artful compliment on the way Mercy himself had pacified Belgium: 'You have proved what power sensible reasoning has over the wildest of men, when, in displaying the armed force that compels respect, it combines with this the benevolence that instils love.'[6] This revealing sentence proves the essential continuity of Breteuil's policy towards the Revolution. He had no desire immediately to put it down with fire and sword, as did some of the more hot-headed *émigrés*. Instead, exactly as in July 1789, while prepared to use troops in the last resort, he preferred to keep them in reserve, as a device to inspire fear in his opponents and thus incline them to compromise. Yet the stick of military force was accompanied by a carrot; the promise of the king's 'benevolence' would hold out to the revolutionaries some hope of a generous settlement.

Knowing the Habsburgs' difficulties in Belgium, the baron tactfully refrained from any direct mention of the possible need for Austrian military support. He must have known he would get a dusty answer. Instead, he tried another tack. For his challenge to the Revolution to be viable, Louis XVI needed money, yet his credit had collapsed and floating a loan on the European markets risked arousing suspicions in France. Breteuil's first concern, again as it had been in July 1789, was to provide his master with funds. The most effective way for the emperor to help the king, he told Mercy, would be to lend him 15 million livres 'to help in the first moments' of his freedom.

To judge by Mercy's report to his superior, Chancellor Kaunitz, ten days later, this letter was not well received. Once again, the dislike of the baron that had united both men before the Revolution reasserted itself. 'I swiftly sent back [Breteuil's messenger]', wrote Mercy,

> with a reply that was generally meaningless, but extremely precise on my view that it will be impossile for the emperor to concern himself with anything but the interests of his own monarchy for a long time to come, and that above all he is to preoccupied with restoring to his Belgian provinces an order and tranquillity that they still lack, to wish to expose them to upheavals from abroad.

Even the fact that Breteuil had been unable to find a trustworthy secretary was turned against him. 'On reflection,' Mercy added in a PS, 'I have decided that Your Highness would have too much trouble deciphering the horrible scrawl of M. de Breteuil, who wrote to me in his own hand. I have therefore kept the original and sent you a legible copy.'[7]

Six weeks later, still with no response from Mercy on the vital question of the 15 million livres, Breteuil's pleas became more urgent:

> I hope every day for a positive reply to the requests that you kindly agreed to pass on to your court, and every day I become more distressed by the uncertainty in which you leave me regarding the 15 million for which the king hopes in token of the emperor's friendship.

The baron's increasingly desperate tone reflected the perils to which the Austrian delay was exposing the whole project:

> I cannot beg you strongly enough to obtain a response from the emperor to this capital question, which will determine both our measures and the date of the enterprise. Each instant's delay increases our difficulties, and the experience that has taught me that the greatest secrets can only be kept for a certain time, makes me tremble every day that some accident may lead to discovery.[8]

Breteuil also mentioned here for the first time the possibility of Austrian military support for the plan. In the light of Mercy's repeated assertions that all the troops currently in Belgium were needed to maintain order in the province, he approached the subject gingerly:

> I can imagine what you must think about the danger of scattering your imposing forces, and it is to accommodate your essential interests in exactly the same way as I am sure you would our own, that the king has decided to ask you to make only a show of force, which would in no way lessen your watch on the Belgians, but would greatly aid our plans; that is to say, he asks that, without moving a single soldier beyond your frontiers, you should simply position a large corps of troops

near our own which, if skilfully placed, would signal the most fraternal intentions . . .[9]

The baron's whole point, however, was that he was certain these troops would never be needed. To this end, he repeated to Mercy his confidence in the loyalty and quality of the army in Lorraine:

> His Majesty acquires every day more certitude that the moment he has regained his liberty, the majority of his troops, and the best of them, will rush with as much enthusiasm as energy to help him recover his legitimate authority; I no longer have any doubt as to the success of his courageous enterprise, as soon as he has broken free of his chains.

Yet Breteuil's confidence was belied by his final sentence: 'I leave you to imagine the agitation in my soul.'[10]

In fact, this letter crossed with Mercy's reply to the previous one. Once again, the count maintained a deafening silence on the key question of money. Breteuil did not write his next letter until 20 April. This, as he explained, was because he had been unwell:

> I was chained to my bed, my dear ambassador, by a severe attack of gout in both my feet when your letter of 28 March arrived; I think it is coming to an end, but I fear I will not have the full use of my legs for some time, since they are still as weak today as they were two days ago. My feeble bodily state has prevented me from replying as swiftly as I would have wished to your letter.[11]

At this point a curious feature of the correspondence becomes apparent. Breteuil's letters of 12 January and 3 April had been frank and open, because he had been able to entrust them to reliable friends who were travelling to Brussels. His letter of 20 April, however, had to be sent by post, and the baron was worried that it might be intercepted and read. He therefore resorted to a rudimentary code. The escape plan was disguised as a lawsuit he was undertaking, with Louis XVI figuring as his 'business agent'. As a means of accommodating the Austrian response, Breteuil maintained the fiction that this lawsuit was being judged by the imperial high court, the Aulic Council, and that he was currently waiting for a decision. Under this cover, he and Mercy could both send and receive information.

The object of Breteuil's coded letter was, once again, money. His lawsuit had every prospect of success, he wrote, but at the moment he could not pursue it for lack of funds. Mercy had clearly promised to help raise a loan in the Netherlands, 'but your letters give me no news on this capital point'. The most revealing lines, however, come in a PS. Just as Breteuil had finished writing, a letter arrived from his 'business agent'. It announced that 'everything impels him to act now, and that he holds firmly to his resolution to do all he can to hasten the great judgement. All his plans are laid, and will be put before the court between the 15th and 20th of next month, if an absolute lack of money does not render this impossible.'[12] The letter to which Breteuil refers is clearly the one Fersen wrote to him on behalf of Louis and Marie Antoinette on 2 April, informing him that the escape would take place during the last fortnight of May.

By 17 May, as Breteuil's next letter made clear, there was still no concrete news from Mercy. By now he had even written to Kaunitz but, unsurprisingly, with little success. 'I think I told you,' he informed Mercy bitterly,

> that I had written in great detail to Prince Kaunitz about my lawsuit. I must tell you that I received a prompt reply that was most gracious to me personally, but so perfectly unhelpful about my business, that I would have been happy to have waited longer before being reminded of all the troubles that afflict a supplicant.[13]

It was now clear that nothing could be expected from Austria's chancellor or her minister plenipotentiary in Belgium. Breteuil resolved to play the only card left to him – the emperor himself. He was aided by a major stroke of luck: on 15 March Leopold left Vienna to take a long journey through his beloved Italy. His ministers, including Kaunitz, were left behind in the capital. This was the chance the baron had been waiting for. If he sent an emissary to the emperor now, to plead the cause of his sister and brother-in-law in the absence of the hostile chancellor, the escape plan could still be saved. Breteuil's gout and his duties at Solothurn precluded his going himself, but fortunately an ideal candidate was at hand. Bombelles had resigned his embassy the previous January, unable to take the oath to the constitution that was now required of diplomats as well as clergy. He was still in Venice, however, trying to calm the effervescence of his unwelcome guests the comte d'Artois and Calonne. From there, he was perfectly positioned to intercept Leopold on his arrival in northern Italy.

On 12 March Breteuil sent Bombelles a copy of his *plein pouvoir* and a long set of instructions recalling him, as it were, to the colours. The marquis was to gain an interview with the emperor and sound out his dispositions regarding the French royal family. 'You know', Breteuil stated bluntly,

> how little Prince Kaunitz wishes to encourage these in our favour, and how my friend Mercy, who at bottom is more warmly disposed to us, does not possess the necessary character to decide our great question, so that we must find the force we need in the person of the emperor rather than his ministers.[14]

Bombelles was to seek Leopold's support on the two crucial issues of troops and money. To counter the standard Austrian reasoning that all available troops were needed to maintain order in Belgium, he was to argue that his province could never be truly secure until the similar, but much greater, disorders across the border were ended, and that 'a double stroke is thus needed, to secure the country which concerns [Leopold] most'. The marquis was also to stress, as the baron had done previously to Mercy, that very few Austrian troops would in fact be required: 'As soon as the king has unfurled his banner, the majority of his army will swiftly rally to him, especially if the vanguard sees itself supported by Austrian regiments.' Whatever Louis XVI's personal intentions may have been, Breteuil himself made little distinction between the French and foreign elements in the plan.

Loyal as ever to his patron, Bombelles immediately accepted this mission. In doing so, however, he was faced with a problem. Breteuil was not the only French exile who was closely watching the emperor's movements. Artois and Calonne, still enjoying Bombelles's hospitality in Venice and regarded by Kaunitz with even more horror than Breteuil, saw in Leopold's presence in Italy an opportunity to further their own plans. They knew perfectly well that the emperor fully shared his chancellor's suspicion of them and would refuse to see them if they asked him directly for an interview. It would be better, they decided, if the way was first smoothed by an acceptable emissary – their host Bombelles. The marquis, who had been dragged into their counsels well before he received Breteuil's summons, did not feel able to refuse. As a result, he found himself entrusted with an extremely awkward 'double mission'. Bombelles now became, literally, the servant of two masters. Throughout the following two months, his and Breteuil's deadly serious negotiations with Leopold constantly threatened to descend into *opera buffa*, on the numerous occasions when these cut across Artois's increasingly lunatic plans.

Breteuil's own letter began the comedy of errors. He gave it to a trusted servant, a footman of his daughter named Davier, to take to Bombelles in Venice. Unfortunately, Davier was arrested at Altdorf near Schwyz by a suspicious prefect, and held there for thirteen days.[15] In the meantime, Leopold II arrived in Venice and Bombelles, unaware that a courier from Breteuil was on his way, wrote to him asking for an interview on behalf of Artois and Calonne. On 28 March, this was granted. It is a measure of the marquis's diplomatic skill that he was actually able to secure the promise of an interview for Calonne at Bologna. To do so, he had to calm Leopold's fury at Calonne, who had recently disobeyed his orders and tried to gain access to him in Vienna. Forbidden once in the capital to set foot outside his lodgings, Calonne had promptly headed off to a masked ball, where he had spent the evening persuading his friend the prince de Ligne to intercede for him with the emperor. With his usual frivolity, he wrote afterwards to Ligne: 'If there is gossip about your long conversation with another masculine mask, bring it up short by saying, with your usual straight face, that I am an extremely pretty boy with whom you are varying your pleasures.'[16]

The morning after Bombelles's meeting with Leopold, Breteuil's courier finally arrived. The marquis immediately realized that he had been pitchforked by the length of a day into a deeply compromising situation. Had Davier managed to reach him before the interview, he could probably have managed to keep Artois and Calonne at arm's length from the emperor. Now, however, direct contact had been established, with the marquis himself as its impresario. All Bombelles could do was make the best of a bad job; he transferred his main energies to Breteuil's mission, which after all emanated from the king himself. At the same time he attempted to reconcile this with the task

Artois had set him, by using all his influence to persuade the prince to do nothing rash.

Bombelles launched this strategy in the course of a second meeting with Leopold, appropriately on 1 April. He revealed to him his new instructions from Breteuil, and the decision the royal family had taken to escape from Paris. Deciding that the emperor's agreement to meet with Calonne, and perhaps Artois as well, could even be turned to advantage, he enlisted him in his plan to contain them. If Leopold himself told the prince and his adviser to hold back and do nothing to compromise the safety of Louis XVI and Marie Antoinette, this would be much more effective than any warning from Bombelles or Breteuil. Fully aware of the danger Artois posed to his policy of non-intervention in France, Leopold agreed to this with alacrity.[17]

Interestingly, in his long despatch of 3 April describing to Breteuil this second, two-hour interview with the emperor, Bombelles nowhere mentioned his solution to his double mission. Presumably it was too delicate to be committed to paper. Tacitly, however, he agreed to go on advising Artois, but to report everything back to Breteuil as his unofficial agent. The baron, convinced that this equivocal conduct was necessary, enthusiastically supported it. He was terrified by the indiscretion of Artois's entourage, and was convinced that revealing his own position would compromise the royal family's escape from Paris. He preferred to keep his role secret, even at the risk of a rupture with the king's brother. Breteuil's attitude towards Artois throws into relief a crucial aspect of these months. In themselves, the prince's antics were irrelevant, because they were backed by neither Louis XVI himself nor any major power. Their importance lay in the alarm they inspired elsewhere, in the king, the queen and Breteuil. The fear that any delay might result in Artois sabotaging the planned escape caused an atmosphere of suppressed panic both at the Tuileries and at Solothurn that was not conducive to wise decisions.

The core of Bombelles's discussions with Leopold was the request for immediate financial aid for the escape preparations. The emperor's response was ambiguous. Bombelles, who observed him closely throughout the conversation, came away convinced that he sincerely wished to help his sister and brother-in-law. But Leopold was equally determined to make no commitments, particularly financial ones, until he was absolutely sure that they really did intend to escape. Leopold added that he was expecting at any moment a messenger from Paris who would bring him precise details of the plans for flight.

The emperor's scepticism underlined the very real damage that Louis XVI's passivity since July 1789 had done to his own cause. The allies who would probably have helped him earlier had he shown more initiative, were now reluctant to expose themselves in support of a new policy that, to judge by past form, might be jettisoned at any time. Bombelles received proof of this a few days later, in conversation with Mme Giustiniani, 'a beautiful and very stupid Venetian lady' with whom Leopold had become infatuated. Mme Giustiniani reported that the emperor had told her 'that he very much wanted to help his sister, but that his brother-in-law would have to show more resolution. I shall not repeat here', noted Bombelles, 'the injurious terms His Imperial Majesty used on this occasion. They are as misplaced as they are unjust, since before accusing the king of cowardice he should first ascertain whether up until now this unfortunate prince has had any opportunity to escape from his captivity.'[18]

These comments are just as damning about Leopold II's promiscuity and indiscretion as they are about Louis XVI's alleged lack of courage. Yet Breteuil was certainly aware of the doubts about the king's moral fibre, and these increased the pressure on him. Certain telling phrases constantly crop up in his letters to Leopold, Mercy and Bombelles, as part of a clear attempt to combat these assumptions; his stress, for example, on Louis's 'unvarying resolution' and 'courageous enterprise'. By 27 May, he felt compelled to write the emperor a whole paragraph in this vein:

> In my last letters of the 23rd, the king writes that it is still his firm intention to leave Paris in a few days and put himself at the head of his army; His Majesty's own measures leave me in no doubt as to the success of his enterprise, and the calm with which he contemplates this action only fortifies my hopes.[19]

Bombelles also informed Leopold II of Mirabeau's alternative plan, unaware that its author had died the previous day. Leopold immediately warned against adopting Mirabeau's project, because it would involve a compromise with the revolutionaries. 'The emperor', Bombelles reported back to Breteuil,

> declared immediately that the adoption of this conciliation plan
> would consummate the ruin of the monarchy, but he added that
> he could not believe this was really the intention of the king
> and queen, even if they had decided that the only way they
> could escape from their enemies was by deceiving them about
> their true aims.[20]

Bombelles's words shed interesting light not only on the persistent rumours of compromise, but also on Leopold II's whole attitude to the plight of Louis XVI and Marie Antoinette. The standard view is that a combination of lack of family feeling, the delicacy of his own international position, and a certain personal liberalism made the emperor determined not to intervene in France. Yet Leopold's comment here that the conciliation plan would 'consummate the ruin of the monarchy' shows him as less liberal and constitutionalist, in French matters at least, than was previously supposed. Bombelles's reports tend to bear out Breteuil's original instinct; that left to himself, away from the coldness and caution of Kaunitz and Mercy, the emperor was genuinely concerned to help his French family. As a realist, however, he would only commit himself once he knew that the king and queen had a workable plan for escape and would definitely carry it out.

Leopold may have dismissed the likelihood of the conciliation plan, but it was still destined to make a final appearance. On 6 April, from Parma, Artois wrote Marie Antoinette a frankly menacing letter, warning her that he knew of the project, and hinting that he would do all he could to frustrate it.

> Everything leads me to believe that you have a plan. I think I
> even know every detail of what has been put to you, and who
> is involved. Ah, sister, how can the king distrust me so? I will
> add only one word: it may be permissible to make use of your
> enemies to escape from captivity; but you must refuse any
> bargain, any convention with villains, and above all you should
> calculate carefully whether your real servants, your real friends,
> could consent to the conditions you may have accepted. In the

name of all that is dear to you, remember these few words, and
rest assured that I am well informed.[21]

Artois was not yet informed, however, that by the time he put pen
to paper Mirabeau's project had died with its author. Its legacy, none
the less, continued to poison the relations between the Tuileries and
the princes.

*

THE CENTRE OF EVENTS now moved back to Paris, where a small
escape committee was in place in the Tuileries. It consisted of three
people – Louis XVI, Marie Antoinette and Fersen. In January 1790
Fersen, then with his regiment at Valenciennes, had received instructions from Gustavus III to move to Paris and act as an unofficial
liaison between the Swedish king and the royal family. He had
promptly done so, and over the succeeding months had become
deeply involved in the plans for flight.

We shall never know the precise relationship between the
king, the queen and Fersen. Whatever his initial hesitations, Louis
XVI was now convinced that the royal family had to escape from
Paris. Yet how far he and Marie Antoinette worked together or
separately, how much the king confided in Fersen, and whether at
this point Fersen and Marie Antoinette were lovers, remains impenetrable. The difficulty of achieving the necessary privacy to discuss
their secret plans, together perhaps with the king's periodic depres-
sions, meant that Louis XVI and Marie Antoinette did not thrash
out every detail of their plans together. Rather, it is probable that
the queen took down general instructions from her husband when
she was able to meet in secret with him. She then transmitted them
to her brother Leopold in her own letters, and also passed them on
to Breteuil in despatches written by Fersen to which she herself
added comments. This was probably not just a matter of practical
convenience, but a political necessity reflecting considerable courage
on the queen's and Fersen's part. They realized that if the worst
came to the worst and the plot was discovered, at all costs Louis
XVI must not be implicated. In the final analysis, they knew they
were expendable, and were thus prepared to take full responsibility
if the escape plan were betrayed. If by sacrificing themselves they

could still preserve the monarchy in the person of the king, they were willing to do so.

Much of the trio's method can be discerned in Fersen's first surviving despatch to Breteuil, of 2 April 1791. It is written in Fersen's own hand, but the queen added notes of her own in the margin. It is these that give the key to how the royal couple organized the operation. In the body of the text, the king's name is often invoked, to give Breteuil the necessary authority to proceed with his efforts. It is clear, however, that Marie Antoinette and Fersen decided certain details without reference to Louis XVI. This is revealed by an extremely significant marginal comment by the queen, advising Fersen to tell Breteuil how they had come to employ their previous agent to Spain, Fontbrune. 'It would perhaps be wise', she writes, 'to confide in the baron what M. de Fontbrune was first used for, and why we are humouring him; this idea is entirely my own, I only thought of it after I had seen the king.'[22]

The fact that Marie Antoinette here makes a clear distinction between herself and her husband is highly important. If she and Fersen had been counterfeiting the king's policy wholesale, she would hardly have bothered to point out this minor example of the practice in a private communication between them. Her exact manner of proceeding is revealed by her reference to seeing the king. It is surely not too speculative to presume that after the private talk with Louis she mentions, she dictated the results to Fersen for transmission to Breteuil. On the matter of Fontbrune, however, Fersen did permit himself a slight economy with the *vérité*; instead of preserving the queen's careful distinction between Louis and herself, he simply wrote to Breteuil: 'The king wished you to be informed of this fact, and of our reasons for humouring M. de Fontbrune.'[23]

The despatch also reveals much about Breteuil's side of the correspondence and how it was processed at the Tuileries. This is in fact the first topic it addresses:

I have received . . . your despatch of 11 and 16 March, but your efforts to be mysterious have rendered you virtually unintelligible, and I was almost unable to understand you. The ink you used was so faint that it could only be deciphered by holding it up against the window, and to enable the king to read it I had to copy it out in full; as I dare not trust anybody to do it for me, this took a very long time.[24]

One suspects that these are the queen's own words as dictated to Fersen. The tone of authority is hers, and the lament about not being able to trust anybody recurs frequently in her correspondence. The content is also very important: the reference to the despatches of 11 and 16 March shows that Breteuil kept up a secret correspondence with the king and queen which is now lost. Once they had been smuggled into the Tuileries, the baron's letters were probably handed to Marie Antoinette who, with or without Fersen's help, decoded or transcribed them before passing them to the king.

The testy complaint about the mystery in which Breteuil enveloped his reports, a mystery made necessary by the constant fear of interception, underlines just how dangerous a business transmitting this correspondence was. We know little about how Breteuil's despatches reached the Tuileries, except that some were passed via the diplomatic bag by the ambassador to Switzerland, the marquis de Vérac. There exists, however, a remarkable account of how Louis XVI's and Marie Antoinette's letters were smuggled out in the other direction, to Breteuil, Mercy-Argenteau and Leopold II. This comes in the memoirs of the comte d'Allonville, and has never been cited before. Twenty-nine years old in 1791, d'Allonville was a courtier and officer closely connected with the royal family during the Revolution. His own clandestine activities on behalf of the king and queen are suggested by his biography during these years: emigrated 1791, returned to France soon afterwards, emigrated once more, returned again to France under the Terror, fled to Switzerland 1794. One of d'Allonville's functions was precisely to spirit out letters from Louis XVI and Marie Antoinette, and he describes in detail how this was done. As the only first-hand account of the operation, this is worth quoting in full:

The correspondence of the king and queen with their friends abroad involved some danger, which could only be averted through secrecy, and on Marie Antoinette's part, this was organized through the chevalier d'Esclans, a ... deputy of the constitutional party, his friend Terrier-Monciel, and the [marquis] de Bombelles, who had refused to swear the oath to the constitution and resigned his embassy to Venice.

On Louis XVI's side [the correspondence passed] through the Bishop of Pamiers, who often travelled to and from Switzerland to bring the king's despatches to the baron de Breteuil. None the less, on many occasions the post had to be used; but, to avoid interception, His Majesty had the idea of hiding his letters in the hollowed-out bindings of very pro-revolutionary books. Then, since he feared being surprised in this work, surrounded as he was by spies, these books were given either to the abbé d'Agoult [the Bishop of Pamiers's brother] or the abbé de Tressan, who took them to the marquise de Maupeou's house twenty leagues from Paris; from there they were handed into the post-office at Rebais addressed either to M. de Burckhardt, a former aide-de-camp of M. d'Affry [the commander of the Swiss Guards], or to another man of the same name, a merchant at Basel who was sincerely attached to the royalist cause.

This is how the correspondence never came to be interrupted or intercepted; and if I have knowledge of this, it is because, as a friend and neighbour of Mme de Maupeou, I often helped her in this way to conceal and pass on the king's letters.[25]

All those involved in smuggling out their letters, from d'Allonville to the Bishop of Pamiers, were under no illusion as to what their fate would be if they were discovered. The previous year, the marquis de Favras, a royalist noble who had been involved in a mysterious plot to help the king escape from Paris to Péronne, had been hanged for treason in front of the Hôtel de Ville.

In the spring of 1791, two dramatic events served notice on the king and queen's secret network that the escape could no longer be delayed. The first came from an unlikely quarter: Louis XVI's elderly aunts, Mesdames Adélaïde and Victoire. Horrified by the Civil Constitution of the Clergy, these two pious old ladies decided to signify their disapproval by going to Rome for their Easter devotions. In the increasingly tense political climate, with emigration mounting and the air thick with rumours of the royal family's flight, the effect was explosive. On 19 February, with a small escort of twenty, Mesdames set off; almost immediately, an attempt was made to arrest them near Fontainebleau and had to be beaten off.

Meanwhile, in Paris, a large crowd, convinced that this was just a preliminary to the escape of the rest of the Bourbons, gathered at the Luxembourg Palace, the comte de Provence's residence, forcing him to appear in public to show that he had not absconded. But the perils of Mesdames were not yet over. On their arrival at Arnay-le-Duc in Burgundy, they were arrested again and this time held for eleven days. The two spinsters showed both spirit and some cunning. Unperturbed by the uproar around them, they washed their scanty linen daily, and went to bed early to ensure that it was dry by the following morning. To their embarrassed captors they pointed out that by going to Rome they were only exercising the religious freedom the new constitution guaranteed.[26]

Back in Paris, the news of Mesdames' arrest caused consternation. Radical politicans defended the action; the Centre and Right saw it as a gross violation of individual liberty. Eventually Mirabeau, in one of his last interventions in the Assembly, persuaded the deputies that since the king's aunts had broken no law by departing, they should not be prevented from continuing their journey. Mesdames were allowed to proceed, and made their way to Rome, stopping off on the way in Parma to tell their great-nephew Artois about their adventures. They never returned to France.

The arrest of Adélaïde and Victoire was just a dress-rehearsal for a much more serious incident. This took place on 18 April, and crucially demonstrated the constraints on both Louis XVI's religion and his personal liberty. Once again, it concerned the issue closest to the king's heart: the struggle between his conscience and the Civil Constitution of the Clergy. With Easter looming, the king could not bring himself to take communion from a constitutional priest so, to avoid giving offence to the new order, he decided that the royal family should make a brief return visit to the palace of Saint-Cloud, where they could discreetly attend the service of a non-juror. At midday on the 18th, the royal family descended to the courtyard of the Tuileries, to find a huge crowd massed outside on the Place de Carrousel, determined to prevent their departure. The National Guards on duty even refused to open the palace gates to let the royal party through; on being reproached for this they replied that the king was 'a fucking aristocrat . . . a fat pig . . . that he was paid far too much and should do as he was told'. Finally, after two and a quarter hours sitting trapped in their carriage, surrounded on all sides, Louis and his family turned back. As they re-entered the Tuileries, Marie Antoinette remarked to the soldiers around her: 'At least now you can see we are not free.'[27]

The confrontation of 18 April shocked Europe and starkly revealed the very real dangers the royal family now faced. Inside the Tuileries, the king and queen concluded that their situation was now intolerable, and nerved themselves for an imminent escape. Their state of mind comes across clearly in Marie Antoinette's letter two days later to Mercy-Argenteau. This also reveals that Louis XVI was quite as determined upon flight as his wife.

> The event which has just occurred makes us even more resolute in our plans. The chief menace comes from the [national] guard that surrounds us. Even our lives are not safe. We have to give the impression of agreeing to everything until the moment we can act, and for the rest our state of captivity proves that nothing we are doing is of our own free will. . . . Our position is dreadful; we have to get out of it by next month. The king desires this even more than I.[28]

One last calculation entered into the royal family's plans. The final draft of the constitution was expected to be ready by July 1791. By late 1790 the constitutional committee charged with drawing it up had seemed to be coming round to the idea of strengthening the royal power – probably a further reason why Louis XVI did not immediately agree to Breteuil's proposal for escape. Yet by the following spring the radicals were gaining the ascendant: the king was not to be allowed to reside more than twenty leagues from the Assembly, he was to lose his prerogative of mercy, and sitting deputies were to be ineligible for the next legislature. If Louis were ever to flee Paris, he would have to do so very soon, before his hands were tied by a constitution that reduced him to a cipher.

This sudden radicalization of politics was in large part the work of the Jacobin club, to which most of the left-wing deputies in the assembly belonged. From its headquarters in the former convent of the Jacobin order in Paris, the club set out to form public opinion through a network of affiliated clubs in most of the French cities and provinces. Exercising its power by means of mass petitions and putting up lists of candidates for elections, it was an embryonic political party, and far more effective and better organized than its rivals. Much of the credit for this must go to Robespierre, who was soon to use the machinery he had created in his own bid for power. By the early summer of 1791, one crucial result of these efforts was already apparent. The primary elections for the legislative assembly that was to succeed the constituent assembly were beginning, and the Jacobins were clearly gaining ground. The primaries were scheduled to end on 5 July, providing an additional incentive for a royal flight to halt the process.

In the critical situation the king and queen now faced, an answer from Leopold II on the question of money and troops became ever more essential. The only person in a position to extract this was Bombelles, who was still in Italy, vainly trying to reconcile his two missions from Breteuil and Artois. The marquis was finding his position increasingly untenable. On the evening of 19 April, the indefatigable Davier arrived once more in Venice, bringing Breteuil's two despatches of the 13th and also a letter that Bombelles was to give to Artois. This immediately aroused the prince's suspicions as to where Bombelles's loyalty really lay. The result was an ominous scene. As the marquis noted in his diary:

> Monseigneur was angrier with me than he had ever been before, but this only made my very respectful resistance firmer. When I heard him draw a distinction between reasonable and craven obedience to the king's wishes, I dared to point out to M. le comte d'Artois that such reasoned, conditional submission differed little from disobedience, and that faced with the choice between this course or obeying the king too promptly, I would always prefer to be accused of carrying obedience to excess.[29]

One could hardly find a better description of the fine line Artois was treading.

Matters were further complicated a few days later by Calonne's arrival in Venice, back from Florence where he had had the interview with Leopold II that Bombelles had arranged for him. The marquis soon regretted having, as Breteuil put it, 'procured for our ex-controller-general [this] satisfaction to his vanity'.[30] By now Calonne's policy had changed; realizing that the death of Mirabeau had put paid to his hopes of resuming his ministry with the consent of the National Assembly, he had lost interest in the conciliation project. He now put forward a precisely opposite scheme for a march on Paris by *émigrés* supported by Austrian troops independent of any escape of the royal family. It is clear from this that Calonne's only consistent aim was to return to power by whatever means necessary; his hopes of doing so by accommodation with the Revolution having faded, he was now prepared to try armed force, regardless of the acute danger in which this would place the king and queen. Indeed, he attempted to prove to Leopold that Louis XVI and Marie Antoinette had no intention of leaving the capital, and that his plan was thus the only way of restoring the royal authority. Completely distorting the truth, Calonne now claimed that in Florence Leopold had actually agreed to this wild project. This was not the last time he would make fiction out of fact.

To make Bombelles's position even more uncomfortable, Leopold himself had very indiscreetly dropped a hint to Calonne about Breteuil's role in Louis XVI's secret diplomacy. Calonne lost no time in retailing this to Artois in Bombelles's presence. As the marquis reported to the baron: 'The emperor told M de Calonne that you were one of the king's principal agents, and M de Calonne, with a sly smile, insinuated to M le comte d'Artois that [he could only have known of this] through me.'[31]

Bombelles found a diversion from his worries with the arrival in Venice of a strikingly beautiful Englishwoman. Emma Hart, better known to posterity as Lady Hamilton, was passing through the city with Sir William Hamilton, to whom she was secretly married. On the evening of 21 April, she attended a dinner party given by Bombelles, and afterwards gave a special performance of her famous *tableaux vivants* taken from classical legend. As the marquis noted in his diary:

Mme Hart, who has received from nature a beautiful face, splendid physique and an immense amount of hair (whose colour, quantity and quality set off her features remarkably), has studied in Rome and Naples the best of what antiquity has left us, and has taken from it its noble attitudes, its characterization, and what up until now has been termed, in sculpture and painting, the *beau idéal*. Terrifying in the attitude of Medea, she communicates to her audience the maternal terrors of Niobe; she passes from the wanton, yet decent, gaiety of a Bacchante to the noble bearing of a Vestal, to the frenzy of feeling of a saint praying with a passion that touches the skies. It is with [Indian shawls] that Mme Hart composes the rich and varied draperies which support and accompany her different postures . . .[32]

To the embattled Bombelles, the postures of Emma Hart must have been a welcome relief from the posturing of Calonne.

This agreeable interlude, however, was brief. Already armed with new instructions from Breteuil, the marquis now received a new set from Artois. He was to see the emperor again, and ask for Austrian troops to support the invasion project, as well as a loan of two million livres. The refrain that Louis XVI and Marie Antoinette were fatally inclined to compromise with the Revolution was to be replayed: Bombelles was to furnish proof that 'if there is no word from the Tuileries, it is because they have nothing to say now that Mirabeau is dead'.[33] On 26 April, the marquis set off for Florence.

Arriving in the Tuscan capital on 28 April, Bombelles made the grave error of committing his thoughts to paper in a note to Leopold. He enclosed both a letter of accreditation from Breteuil, which made mention of the *plein pouvoir*, as well as one from Artois. He added, by way of explanation:

> When I have the liberty of speaking with Your Majesty, he will not be surprised to see that I have a double commission, but I must assure him in advance that, however much I may wish to justify the confidence of M. le comte d'Artois, my duty as a faithful subject will always come first.[34]

Bombelles was granted his interview the following day, in the Crocetta Palace. On the issue of money, it was inconclusive, but less so on that of troops. Leopold reiterated that he would only act once he was absolutely convinced that his sister and brother-in-law were really going to flee, but he did agree to move reinforcements from the Tyrol up to Swabia, and to order 2,000 soldiers from his garrisons in Belgium to prepare themselves for a march on the Rhine.

No sooner had Bombelles returned to his inn than he received the news of 18 April. 'A horde of cannibals', he wrote, 'has prevented [Their Majesties] from leaving the Tuileries for Saint-Cloud, where they wished to spend Holy Week.'[35] He immediately wrote to the emperor passing on the news, hoping that this would lead to a further interview that day. As evening drew on, the tragedy shaded into farce. Bombelles knew that Leopold was spending the night in the same hotel as himself with his new mistress, Milady Monck, a compatriot of Emma Hart's, but was far too discreet to disturb him.[36] He knew only too well that in Italy in 1791, alluring Englishwomen provided the only distraction from the cares of counter-revolution.

The following morning a courier arrived from Breteuil, bringing a memorandum for Bombelles to present to the emperor. The events of 18 April had thrown Breteuil too into consternation. He was only calmed by a letter from Fersen in Paris, assuring him that the king and queen were safe, and still more determined to make their escape. 'I have received your letter of 22nd of this month,' he replied. 'I was in need of the swift action it announced, to ease my distress about the cruelties of the 18th.'[37] Under the pressure of these alarming developments, Breteuil had once more let his professional mask slip, to reveal the emotional man beneath, tormented by the anxieties of his situation.

Back in Florence, Bombelles went straight over to the Crocetta Palace, only to be told that Leopold was feverish and receiving nobody. 'His activity will kill him,' the marquis noted cryptically in his diary.[38] By the following day, however, the emperor had recovered. Bombelles found him 'acutely and justly affected by the position of Their Most Christian Majesties, and more than ever aware of the necessity of resolving it'.[39] He handed over Breteuil's memorandum, which extracted every ounce of emotional blackmail from Marie Antoinette's plight: 'The emperor, having more reason than anybody to avenge the insults suffered by the daughter of the Caesars, is the sole sovereign who could and should give a lead to all the others.' In the rest of the memorandum, the military option was very much to the fore: Leopold should order his troops in Flanders and on the borders of Alsace to make demonstrations to support the royal flight, use his forces in the Breisgau to rally the western German princes, and call on Spain, Sardinia and the Swiss for reinforcements. Otherwise, 'crimes without remedy' might be committed – a clear hint that the king and queen might well be murdered. The document ended with a flourish: 'If democracy is not stopped in its precipitate and terrifying path, no throne will ever again rest on secure foundations.'[40]

The increasing emphasis on Austrian military support was a significant development. As the situation in France deteriorated, the fiction that Louis XVI would be able to hold out at Montmédy backed only by native troops wore increasingly thin. As early as 13 April, in his letter to Kaunitz, Breteuil had broached the possibility of Austrian cavalry crossing the French border to stiffen Bouillé's army. The pressure for Austrian help came from Bouillé himself, who as the weeks dragged on was becoming increasingly jumpy about the loyalty of his soldiers. 'The troops are on the point of mutiny,' he wrote to Fersen on 18 April,

> which will lose us those who still remain faithful. . . . [I] therefore strongly wish that from the beginning of May there should be a corps of ten or twelve thousand Austrians around Luxembourg . . . with orders to join up with the king's army as auxiliaries when required. . . . Everything will become impossible if we let May slip by . . .[41]

Historians sympathetic to Louis XVI have always maintained that he drew a clear distinction between relying on domestic and foreign aid. The evidence they most often cite is his insistence that at no point in his flight should he cross the border into Austrian territory. In reality, this distinction was extremely faint. By the summer of 1791, everything pointed to the king's arrival in Montmédy touching off a civil or even a European war.

Leopold II was sufficiently moved by Bombelles's pleas to entrust him with a letter to Marie Antoinette for Breteuil to smuggle across the border. In this note, he repeated that he only remained inactive because he was still waiting for a messenger from the Tuileries to bring him the royal family's latest plans. He added that, 'with Bombelles's help',[42] he had so far managed to contain Artois. Leopold had spoken too soon. Bombelles set off for Solothurn to report back to Breteuil; stopping off at Vicenza on 3 May, he found an incandescent Artois waiting for him. The messenger who had brought him the news of 18 April in Florence (and who had probably also been instructed to spy on him) had found in his hotel room a draft of the letter to the emperor confessing his 'double commission'. The marquis's dual loyalties were now out in the open. Artois accused him violently of bad faith for concealing his mission from Breteuil. When Bombelles countered that he was only obeying the king's orders, the prince burst out: 'And what is the king? Monsieur, at this moment I alone am king, and you owe me an account of your conduct.'[43] This was an extraordinary piece of self-incrimination. In taxing Bombelles with lack of honesty, Artois had blatantly revealed his own disloyalty to Louis XVI.

The climax of Bombelles's 'double mission', with its multiple misunderstandings and intricate sub-plots, could have come from the pen of Marivaux or Beaumarchais. Yet its results were serious, destroying the last remnants of trust between the princes and the Tuileries. From now on, Artois could excuse his disobedience by claiming his brother and sister-in-law had deliberately deceived him about their plans; for their part, the queen and Breteuil would argue that the risk of confiding anything important to him had been simply too great. In the coldly calculating world of eighteenth-century diplomacy, this family split had disastrous consequences. No major power was about to intervene on behalf of Louis XVI and Marie Antoinette for purely altruistic reasons, and in 1791 none of their vital interests was threatened by the French Revolution. The division among the Bourbons, and the consequent confusion about who was really Louis XVI's legitimate representative, gave the other monarchs of Europe a perfect excuse to play one off against the other, and commit themselves to nothing.

Bombelles arrived in Solothurn on 11 May. 'After embracing M. le baron de Breteuil with great joy', he handed him Leopold II's letter to the queen. 'Feeling himself authorized to open it', Breteuil had it encoded straight away so that it could be sent off that day.[44] The two men then went into conference. The most immediate necessity, and the one on which the emperor had given least satisfaction, was money. Bombelles agreed to return to Italy and press the point with Leopold. The instructions Breteuil gave him were highly specific. Assuming that the fifteen million livres requested could not be found immediately, an advance of four million should be raised as soon as possible from the electors of Trier and Cologne or the wealthy monasteries in their domains, and sent to Luxembourg in readiness for Louis XVI's arrival at Montmédy. The emperor could then repay this through loans issued in Holland and Genoa. Knowing that Leopold was now on his way to Milan, Bombelles set off to intercept him.

By the time the marquis reached Leopold, however, Artois had mounted a further provocation, in a way that dramatically increased the dangers facing the royal family. On 18 May, accompanied by the comte de Durfort, who had recently arrived in Italy with news from the Tuileries, Artois had an interview with the emperor himself at Mantua. His aim was to persuade Leopold to support his planned invasion of France with Austrian troops. After the meeting had ended, Artois sent Durfort back to Paris with his own version of what had been agreed. The paper Durfort presented to Louis XVI and Marie Antoinette has become known as the 'Mantua forgery'. It claimed that Leopold had promised Artois four million livres and 35,000 soldiers for an expedition that would be ready by 15 July, and had agreed that in the meantime the king and queen should sit tight and wait to be rescued. Yet Leopold later insisted that he had said no such thing, and on the contrary had told Artois he would take no action until Louis XVI and Marie Antoinette had reached safety.

The importance of the 'Mantua forgery' lies in the effect it had on Louis XVI and Marie Antoinette. The instructions that Durfort brought them, that they should not try to escape but simply wait for an *émigré*–Austrian invasion scheduled to begin on 15 July, caused consternation. Marie Antoinette wrote two frantic letters to Mercy-Argenteau, and one to Leopold, expressing disbelief that her brother could have agreed to such a plan.[45] On 12 June, the emperor replied, reassuring her that he had done nothing of the sort,[46] but the damage had been done. Just when the king and queen had most need of *sang-froid*, as they were making the final arrangements for flight, they were thrown into a panic that was hardly conducive to careful planning. Above all, the 'Mantua forgery' irrevocably ruled out any further postponement of the escape. It was clear that even if Durfort's news were unreliable, Artois or Condé might at any moment mount some spectacular provocation. At the least, this would redouble the Parisians' watchfulness and make flight impossible; at the worst, it might even threaten the lives of the royal family. As Marie Antoinette herself put it: 'The princes, the comte d'Artois and everyone around them are determined to act; they have no real resources and will destroy us even though we do not approve what they are doing.'[47] The royal family's escape from Paris was undertaken as much to pre-empt Artois as to put an end to the Revolution.

Who was telling the truth about the 'Mantua forgery', Artois or Leopold? The solution to the mystery lies with a remarkable document still preserved in the State Archives in Vienna, and entitled 'Eighteen articles read to the emperor by the comte d'Artois on 18 May 1791'.[48] This is an original transcript of the Mantua conference, sent by Leopold to Kaunitz. It lists all Artois's requests to Leopold. The emperor dictated his replies, and Artois himself took them down in the margin. One can still read Leopold's words today, copied in Artois's own hand.

The traditional view is that after Artois had taken down Leopold's replies, the princes' confidants concocted a distorted version that exaggerated what the emperor had promised, which Durfort then brought to Paris. Yet this conclusion ignores a crucial feature of the original document. This is that in writing down Leopold's replies Artois himself omitted certain key qualifications. The emperor had to correct this himself on the copy he retained. The marginalia on the paper are thus in two hands, those of Artois and the emperor, a fact that has never fully been appreciated. It is possible that Artois's mistakes were accidental. Given his views and character, however, it is more likely that he made them deliberately, to exaggerate publicly Leopold's commitment to the French royal cause and force the emperor to back his own plan.

Artois's clumsy distortions are most obvious in the answers to his three crucial demands: for an army of 30,000 to 35,000 Austrian troops to be deployed in Belgium by the end of June, for the publication of a manifesto demanding the liberty of the French royal family, and for the simultaneous entry of two Austrian columns into France, one led by Artois himself. On each point, there is a clear difference between Leopold's replies as taken down by Artois, and as rectified by the emperor himself. Leopold states bluntly that the manifesto cannot appear; Artois only that it will have no point if Louis XVI has escaped from Paris by that time. Artois writes that the Austrian army will be made ready by the end of June, but Leopold adds that this will only be 'when circumstances in Belgium permit, and without giving cause for alarm in France' – a condition that was unlikely ever to be fulfilled. As to the invasion itself, Artois notes that Leopold approves it, but again the emperor inserts a crucial caveat, that his agreement is conditional on the other European powers lending their support.[49]

Having sown alarm and confusion from Mantua to Paris, Artois now set off for the Rhine. His destination was Aix-la-Chapelle in the Austrian Netherlands. Inevitably, this would mean that he would pass through Worms and see the prince de Condé. A meeting so close to the French border between Artois and Condé, whose head was still fermenting with plans for a military attack on the Revolution, was bound to be reported and could not fail to ring alarm-bells in Paris; collusion between the Tuileries and the princes would automatically be suspected, and the guard on the king and queen redoubled. Louis XVI and Marie Antoinette were thrown into panic, and a flurry of letters was despatched to prevent the potentially disastrous journey.

These letters present some curious features. Some went to Breteuil via Fersen in the Tuileries, but Louis XVI sent one directly to Artois himself. While their basic aim was the same – to stop the prince completing his journey – their instructions as to where he should go next did differ slightly. This could be seen as evidence that the king on the one hand, and the queen and Fersen on the other, were still pursuing separate politics. A less conspiratorial explanation, however, is more plausible. In one exchange, Breteuil refers to an order from Louis XVI which is now lost. This was almost certainly from the king himself, and not transmitted like the others via Fersen, since otherwise the latter would have preserved it with them in his papers. In addition to the instructions he received from Marie Antoinette through Fersen, it thus seems probable that the baron had a correspondence of his own with Louis XVI himself.[50]

Assuming that Louis XVI and Marie Antoinette on occasion wrote separately to Breteuil resolves the most perplexing aspect of his and Fersen's letters – the interchangeability with which both refer to the king and queen. As we have seen, in writing to Breteuil Fersen invested the orders he had most likely received from the queen with the authority of the king: 'The king wishes', 'the king approves', 'the king thinks as you do'. Breteuil extended the formula in his own letters to Leopold II: informing the emperor that the king had written to him on the 23rd, he was in fact referring to Fersen's communication of the same date. Unlike Fersen, on other occasions he drew a clear distinction between his instructions from the king and those from the queen. Sometimes, however, he seems to have mixed the two up completely. The height of this confusion was reached in his letter to Leopold of 30 May, which enclosed a decoded one from Marie Antoinette. 'I . . . have the honour', he wrote,

> to send this letter of the queen's . . . to Your Majesty. The king hopes, sire, that the confidential details the queen gives you regarding the imminent execution of the king's project, will make you realize that the effective marks of friendship you wish to extend to Their Majesties cannot be put off for an instant . . .'[51]

None of this has the air of a subtle plot to substitute Marie Antoinette's policy for Louis XVI's. If there were such a plot, then Breteuil would surely have been far more careful to cover his tracks and ensure that all differentiation between the king and queen was eliminated. Instead, it is far more likely that his letters simply mirrored informal working practices, and on occasion confusion, at the Tuileries. Policy came from the king, but was usually transmitted by the queen via Fersen. Sometimes, however, Louis XVI wrote directly to Breteuil or Artois, and sometimes Marie Antoinette added details of her own. In these cases, the messages became garbled, as with the instructions to Artois to change his route. Yet essentially the king and queen were working together on the same strategy, a fact that was tacitly recognized by all their closest confidants, and whose most eloquent testimony is the lack of distinction Breteuil drew between them.

In his alarm, the baron sent not one but two letters to the errant Artois. In the first, he made clear his assumption that the prince now knew in outline the royal family's escape plan. 'I have reason to believe,' Breteuil wrote, 'that Monseigneur has now been informed of the king's resolutions in a way which must satisfy him, and fulfil all his good wishes for His Majesty, the glory of his crown, and the public good.'[52] This olive branch was met with an icy silence. Eight days later, on 22 May, Breteuil himself broke this, acting on instructions sent by Fersen to halt Artois's journey to Worms and Aix-la-Chapelle at all costs. It was in this letter that Breteuil finally informed Artois about his *plein pouvoir*.[53] The baron eventually received his reply in a note from Karlsruhe dated 10 June. It was insultingly brief. 'I have received your letter, Monsieur,' Artois wrote, 'and hasten to respond to it. I am perfectly aware of the king's intentions, and no one respects them more than I do. In the light of this I am greatly astonished by your letter.'[54] The breach between Artois and Breteuil was now formal.

Meanwhile, Louis XVI's own letter had reached Artois. The prince's reply to his brother was more cordial than that to Breteuil, but still fell short of obeying his orders.[55] He did agree not to meet Condé at Worms. On the other hand, using the specious excuse that if he retreated back into Germany he would be suspected of intriguing either with the Austrians or the Prussians, he informed Louis XVI that he would stay in the Rhineland, at Coblenz. This was hardly satisfactory; it was still close to the French border, and no great distance from Worms. For the following year, it was to be Artois's base, from which he would continue his provocations and still further compromise the safety of the king and queen in Paris.

While Breteuil was frantically trying to restrain Artois in Germany, Bombelles was toiling over the mountains to the emperor in Milan. Bombelles's efforts in these months were as much a feat of physical endurance as of diplomacy. Between April and June 1791, he crossed the Alps five times between northern Italy and Solothurn. On this occasion, he went over the Mont-Cenis, which was 'quite terrifying'; his carriage had to be dismantled and carried piece by piece over the pass by mules, guided by bad-tempered muleteers who overcharged him outrageously.[56] He found the emperor in Cremona, where he had two interviews with him, at 10 p.m. on 22 May, and at 3 p.m. the following day. The result was disappointing; Leopold still avoided saying either when the first 4 million livres would be ready, or how long it would take to raise the remaining 11 million. Bombelles left empty-handed, arriving back at Solothurn on 29 May after three sleepless nights on the road.

Hardly had he returned than Breteuil sent him off again. Marie Antoinette's letter of 22 May had just been delivered and had to be taken to the emperor. To it Breteuil added one of his own for

Leopold. This time Bombelles went over the Saint Gotthard pass, his curiosity at his surroundings undiminished by his exhaustion. 'The women around here are well set-up,' he noted, 'but they are disfigured by goitres, and I think I encountered several cretins.'[57] Despite these distractions, he made a swift journey. In the early afternoon of 4 June, he arrived in Milan and went straight to the ducal palace. The emperor was standing on a side balcony, recognized him, and had him sent up. Bombelles immediately handed him Marie Antoinette's letter. This was an answer to Leopold's of 2 May, complaining that he had not yet been informed of the royal family's plans. Slightly late in the day, it detailed the escape plan in full, and the roles of Breteuil, Bouillé and Bombelles.

In the course of the following two days, Bombelles had three further meetings with the emperor. Their main topic, this time, was troops. The letter Bombelles brought from Breteuil was his most urgent and specific yet about the need for Austrian military support. The baron transmitted Louis XVI's request for 9,000 to 10,000 reinforcements to be concentrated near Luxembourg, with orders

> to join up with the French troops as soon as the king asks for them, and to place themselves entirely at His Majesty's dispo-sition within the kingdom. The degree of loyalty and reliability of the king's own troops will determine whether His Majesty will actually need the help that Your Imperial Majesty's goodwill may put at his disposal; in my view, the discipline and spirit of Your Imperial Majesty's soldiers will serve as a great example to our own . . .[58]

Breteuil's words again reflected Bouillé's increasing anxieties and demands. On 9 May the general had expressed to Fersen a fear that the promised Austrian troops might not arrive. 'However,' he added,

> it is absolutely essential to make sure that if they do not act as auxiliaries, the king is able to take seven or eight thousand of them into his own service; this reinforcement is necessary to maintain the order of the troops we shall gather together who, even though they are almost all German, could be corrupted, whereas if my suggestion is adopted, we will be able to do what we like, and the loyalty of our own men will be assured.[59]

Thus as the weeks wore on, the chances of a successful escape were growing slimmer and slimmer; disaffection in the army was beginning to spread even to Bouillé's German-speaking troops.

Despite Breteuil's renewed pleas, Leopold did not change his position; the soldiers were promised, but only after the royal family were free. On the subject of Artois, however, the emperor was reassuring. He repeated that he was doing everything he could to contain him, and confirmed that Durfort had brought no formal accreditation for the prince from Louis XVI.

One important aspect of Bombelles's conversations with the emperor both at Cremona and Milan concerned the international system. The implications for French diplomacy of the royal family's escape have rarely, if ever, been considered. In fact, in addition to a domestic policy, Breteuil also had a foreign policy that he was preparing to implement in the event of a successful royal escape. This is hardly surprising, given his thirty years' experience as an ambassador in the courts of Europe. The baron's overall aim was to strengthen France's main alliances, with Austria and Spain, and to direct them against the perceived menace of England and Prussia, now grouped with Holland in the triple alliance. England was assumed to be casting covetous eyes on France's remaining overseas possessions, while Prussia too saw opportunities in France's weakening international situation.[60]

Breteuil specifically instructed Bombelles to raise these matters with the emperor. In the short term, he wished to ensure that England and Prussia did nothing to compromise the restoration of the royal authority. In the long term, he wanted cooperation with Austria to redress the balance of power that had tilted in favour of the triple alliance. He was encouraged by the fact that Frederick William II's manoeuvres in eastern Europe were just as alarming to Leopold II as his opportunism further west was to Louis XVI. On 13 April he wrote to Bombelles:

> In your interview with the emperor you will make clear your opinion as to the necessity of strengthening our links with him and forming an alliance capable of surmounting that of the king of Prussia with the maritime powers. You will not hesitate to transmit my various views about the king of Prussia, and the

possibility offered by the mediocrity of his talents to diminish his power.[61]

In the Tuileries, Marie Antoinette was also turning her attention to these foreign-policy questions. In her long letter to Mercy-Argentau of 3 February, she sketched out a rather wild scheme for a grand European confederation of Spain, Austria, Russia, Sweden and Denmark against the triple alliance.[62] Breteuil, however, proposed a more modest strategy. To regain the royal authority, he preferred instead to rely on the king and queen's own relations, and those secondary powers directly bordering on France. In practice, this meant gaining the support of Austria, Spain and Sardinia, and negotiating with the Swiss for a force of mercenaries to back up Bouillé's army.[63]

However, even as these combinations were being put in place, the European scene was changing rapidly. With the Turkish war in its final throes, Austria and Prussia were moving towards a rapprochement. At Cremona, Leopold II spoke to Bombelles 'much more positively than he had at Florence' about His Prussian Majesty's favourable dispositions. 'They are such', added the emperor, 'that I feel certain they will soon be consolidated by a treaty of alliance.'[64] Bombelles, alarmed that this might dilute the emperor's commitment to Louis XVI, replied that this would greatly distress him. He was sufficiently worried to send Leopold a letter as soon as he had returned to his hotel, warning him against Frederick William's siren song. 'The emperor, Spain, the king of Sardinia and the Swiss,' he wrote, 'these, our neighbours, have the prime interest in the return of order to France. Any other power that acts [i.e. Prussia] will have dangerous motives.'[65] This was a clear reflection of Breteuil's own views.

There was a further matter to be considered. As the cynical Mercy pointed out to Marie Antoinette, 'One cannot ignore the generally acknowledged principle that great Powers never do anything for nothing.' To encourage their efforts, Mercy himself proposed that Louis XVI make a series of territorial concessions: part of Navarre to Spain, and the sacrifice of independent Geneva as well as frontier areas in the Alps and the Var to Sardinia. England posed the knottiest problem of all. Mercy, along with all the royal family's closest advisers, was convinced that she represented the main foreign obstacle to a successful counter-revolution. To ensure English neutrality, he argued that France should buy her off too, though he did not specify how.[66] Bouillé, in Metz, was more forthright. In April, he wrote to the king proposing to ensure English neutrality by ceding some, or even all, of France's remaining possessions in India, reserving only trading rights. On 18 April, Fersen reported that the king was awaiting Breteuil's advice on the matter, but it is unclear whether this was ever received.[67]

On 11 June, the exhausted Bombelles arrived back at Solothurn. Over the past eight months, he and Breteuil had achieved a great deal. Since October 1790, the baron's scheme had survived the rivalry of Mirabeau, the equivocation of Austria, and, most dangerous, the terrifying indiscretion of Artois. The diplomatic preparations for the royal flight were in place. Events within France rather than abroad would now determine the fate of the French monarchy.

Chapter Eight

THE FLIGHT TO VARENNES

IN THE TUILERIES, in Metz, in Solothurn, the principal actors were making their final dispositions. By the beginning of June, Breteuil and Bombelles had done all they could to ensure foreign support for the escape. All now depended on General de Bouillé, and on Louis XVI himself.

The exact details of the flight were minutely worked out in a secret correspondence between Bouillé in Metz, and Fersen, acting for the king and queen, in the Tuileries. Louis XVI, Marie Antoinette, their twelve-year-old daughter Marie-Thérèse, the dauphin Louis-Charles, and the children's governess the marquise de Tourzel, would slip out of the Tuileries in separate groups under cover of night. Just outside the palace they would rendezvous with Fersen who, posing as a cab-driver, would take them in his hackney coach to the Barrière Saint-Martin, one of the eastern gates of Paris. There they would transfer to another coach, of the type known as a *berline*. They would then set off as swiftly as possible on the road to Châlons via Meaux and Montmirail. At Pont-de-Sommevesle, the first stop after Châlons and the beginning of Bouillé's military jurisdiction, a detachment of forty hussars commanded by one of his colonels, the duc de Choiseul, would meet the carriage and act as an escort. The route would then pass through the small towns of Sainte-Ménehould,

Clermont-en-Argonne, Varennes, Dun and Stenay, to Montmédy. At each place there would be a fresh relay of horses and a further cavalry detachment, which would fall in at a certain distance behind the *berline* as it passed. Between Dun and Stenay, Bouillé himself would be waiting with fifty troopers from the Royal-Allemand regiment (the same that had charged the Paris crowd on 12 July 1789), to accompany the king into Montmédy.

At Montmédy itself, Bouillé had concentrated a small army of 10,000 men. Significantly, it was almost entirely German-speaking. Of the six infantry regiments, four were German (Royal Hesse-Darmstadt, Nassau, Bouillon and Royal Deux-Ponts) and two (Castella and Reinach) were Swiss. Added to them were detachments from ten cavalry units. It was fervently hoped that by the time the royal family arrived, Leopold II over the border would have finally moved up Austrian troops in support. This, coupled with the king's own presence, would ensure the army's loyalty. With the military situation secured, Breteuil would then arrive to unfold his political strategy.[1]

The escape was originally scheduled to take place on 6 or 7 June. Then came a last-minute hitch – one of the dauphin's servants, Mme Rochereuil, who had pro-revolutionary sympathies and probably suspected something was afoot, had just come on duty and would not finish until the 11th. The flight was fixed for the 12th, but Mme Rochereuil again spoilt it by staying at her post for an extra week. The 19th was then decided upon. Fersen alerted Bouillé to this change of plan, but the general was now alarmed. All troop movements had to have the authorization of the minister of war; if Bouillé sent off his detachments for the 19th and there was a sudden further delay, he would have acted without orders and his position would become untenable. The general sent Choiseul to Paris to inform the king 'with respect, but all possible firmness',[2] that the 20th was the absolute deadline. To his horror, on arriving at the Tuileries Choiseul found that Mme Rochereuil had managed to hang on to her duties for one extra day. His ultimatum, however, decided Louis XVI to escape on the 20th at all costs. The flight to Varennes took place at the last possible moment.

Mme Rochereuil was packed off on the morning of the 20th. At 9 p.m., according to custom, the comte and comtesse de Provence dined at the Tuileries. The king had informed his brother earlier about the planned escape and ordered him to make his own preparations for flight, but had told him nothing about its timing or destination. He now told Provence that he was leaving that night for Montmédy, and instructed him to follow suit and head for Belgium. At 11 p.m. Provence and his wife left to make their own escape. Meanwhile Marie Antoinette had left the table, woken the dauphin and Marie-Thérèse, disguised her son as a girl, and accompanied the children and Mme de Tourzel across the courtyard of the Tuileries to Fersen's waiting hackney coach. The courtyard was 'lit up as if in broad daylight'[3] and patrolled by National Guards, one of whom even bumped into Marie-Thérèse. For the queen to cross this open space, hand her children into the coach, then return alone to the palace, was extremely risky and took considerable courage. She was back with her guests by 10.45 p.m.

After Provence and his wife had left, Louis and Marie Antoinette withdrew to their separate apartments. The king then went through his normal ceremony of retiring to bed. Rather unexpectedly, La Fayette turned up to attend it and Louis, who detested him, pointedly chatted to him for longer than usual to make clear that nothing out of the ordinary was afoot. By 11.30 p.m., the king was alone. He immediately jumped out of bed and slipped into an adjoining room where he dressed in a set of simple clothes that had been left out for him: a brown suit, green overcoat, grey wig and round hat. Walking-stick in hand, he then left the palace and sauntered through the courtyard, making for the rue Saint-Honoré, where Fersen's coach had now moved. Halfway across, one of his shoe-buckles came undone; in an act of modest bravado, he stopped very deliberately and did it up. When he got to the coach, his sister Mme Elisabeth was already there. Now only the queen was absent. The little group was beginning to get anxious when she finally arrived, having had some alarming adventures. First, she had lost her way; then, leaving the courtyard, she had almost collided with La Fayette going home in his carriage.

The hackney coach set off, moving east. Fersen, however, decided to make a detour, so that it did not reach the Barrière Saint-Martin until approximately 2.30 a.m. There the changeover to the *berline* was made, and the occupants settled into the roles they were to adopt as cover. Mme de Tourzel played the leading part, as a Russian noblewoman, Baroness Korff. Louis XVI was her steward M. Durand, Mme Elisabeth her companion Rosalie, the royal children became two girls named Amélie and Aglaë, and the queen their governess, Mme Rochet. Three former royal bodyguards disguised as couriers, and Fersen's coachman, Balthazar Sapel, completed the party.[4]

At Bondy, the first posthouse on the route, Fersen left the royal family to make for Belgium on his own. At first sight, it is surprising he did not continue with them; certainly his presence of mind was to be sorely missed later on. One suspects, however, that he foresaw that if he stayed with them and they were arrested, the revolutionaries would seize on his relationship with the queen to destroy her. Earlier that evening, he had received a note from Marie Antoinette, signed by the king and herself, asking Mercy-Argenteau to make over to Fersen 1,500,000 livres they held in Belgium 'as one more agreeable expression of our gratitude and as compensation for all his losses'. For his part, a few hours before the flight began Louis had simply said: 'Monsieur de Fersen, whatever may happen, I will not forget everything you have done for me.'[5]

As a means of transport to Montmédy, the *berline* has been much ridiculed. Its size, slowness and prominence are generally held to have been fatal to the flight's prospects. The Jacobin Fréron referred to it as 'the hearse of the monarchy'; the journalist Mercier added that it was 'a miniature Versailles, lacking only a chapel and orchestra'.[6] None of this is accurate. As Mme de Tourzel, who ought to have known, later wrote: 'There is nothing remarkable about the king's carriage: it was a large *berline*, rather like my own.'[7] After the horrors of the October Days, the royal family had sworn never to separate. Aware of this, Fersen had had the *berline* made specially to accommodate all of them. On the outside, it was not particularly striking; the bodywork was painted dark green, the wheels and undercarriage yellow, with green taffeta blinds at the windows. The inside was comfortable rather than opulent, equipped with provisions, a silver dressing-case, and an ample supply of chamber-pots.

The most difficult part of the plan was the escape from Paris; once the *berline* was out of the capital and rolling towards the east the atmosphere inside palpably relaxed. All the party now thought success was certain. Louis began to make homely quips: 'Once I've got my bum in the saddle again, I'll be a new man'; 'La Fayette should be feeling pretty stupid right now.' Amateur geographer that he was, he ticked off each of the towns they passed through on his map.[8]

Unfortunately, this new-found and exhilarating sense of security caused the royal party to abandon precautions they had previously thought essential. Louis in particular made no effort to hide himself. At the posthouse at Fromentières, he got out of the carriage and spent some time chatting to the local peasants about the harvest. One can sympathize with him; this was only the second journey he had ever made outside Paris and Versailles, and he must have found it fascinating. One of the bodyguards, Moustier, remonstrated with him about the need for secrecy, but Louis replied: 'I don't think that's necessary any more; my progress now seems quite safe from accident.'[9]

The first person to realize the king's identity was the postmaster at Chaintrix. Luckily, he was loyal. He even refused payment for his services. Marie Antoinette, touched, gave him a pair of mono-grammed silver porringers (which are still in the possession of his descendants). It was the same at Châlons, the one major town on the royal family's route. 'We were unquestionably recognized there,' Marie-Thérèse wrote later, 'many people praised God for the sight of the king, and offered up prayers for his safe passage.'[10]

This was all very well, but the fact that after Châlons rumours of the king's presence went before him gave those ahead who might be more hostile time to organize. In addition, the delays since leaving Paris were beginning to build up; it had taken longer than expected to get clear of the capital, and just outside Chaintrix the carriage traces broke and half an hour was lost repairing them. Bouillé's detachments were on a very tight schedule, and a long wait was bound to make them restive. Yet as they left Châlons on the road to Pont-de-Sommevesle and its forty waiting hussars, the royal family felt very close to safety.

*

AT SOLOTHURN, Breteuil was making his preparations to join the king at Montmédy. At 5 a.m. on 16 June, he woke up Bombelles to read him a letter that had just arrived from Paris, announcing that the escape would take place on the 19th. The baron made a swift decision. The Bishop of Pamiers was sent off immediately in the direction of Trier and Luxembourg, so that he could cross the border and join the king the moment he reached Bouillé. This was a change of plan. The bishop had originally been destined for Brussels, 'to light a fire under the cold comte de Mercy'.[11] He was to have stopped off on the way, at Aix-la-Chapelle, to concert his measures with an even more august figure, Gustavus III of Sweden. Officially, Gustavus was taking the waters, but in reality he had known of the planned flight from Fersen, and had been unable to resist the lure of action. As the royal family toiled towards Montmédy, across the border the spectators were drawing up their seats.

On 14 June, Breteuil had written a letter for the bishop to take to Mercy. He introduced him as 'my friend the Bishop of Pamiers, with whom I have divided my work since the king confided to me his affairs outside the kingdom'.[12] Presumably, when the bishop's route was changed, the letter was sent to Mercy by other means. However, the baron's words underline the increasingly central role the bishop was now playing. With Bombelles criss-crossing northern Italy, it was he who sat by Breteuil's side in Solothurn making policy. Breteuil soon came to rely heavily on the bishop, particularly in the area where he claimed his greatest expertise, public finance. The bishop was especially insistent on the need to proscribe the *assignats* as soon as possible.

Breteuil also informed Mercy of his own plans, which had been laid with meticulous detail. 'His Majesty having expressed his wish that . . . I should join him as swiftly as possible,' he wrote,

> I shall leave [Switzerland] on the 20th of this month and travel towards Aix-la-Chapelle. I hope that on the way I shall hear good news to make me turn off for Luxembourg, but if I end up waiting for it at Aix-la-Chapelle, I will only have a short journey to join the king compared with the road from here straight to Luxembourg.

The baron had planned for every eventuality, and with typical care for his domestic arrangements. In the event that the king's flight was delayed or aborted, he had even found a house for himself in Aix-la-Chapelle. 'You know', he told Mercy,

> that in any case I have rented M. Crumpipen's house, but it is completely unfurnished, and it would be very helpful if M. Crumpipen would furnish it himself and raise the rent in proportion. The Bishop of Pamiers is happy to talk to M. Crumpipen about this, and I would be very grateful if you would support my case with him.[13]

Breteuil's final dispositions before leaving for Montmédy concerned Bombelles. The marquis was to stay behind, and as soon as he heard of the king's safe arrival was to negotiate an immediate levy of the Swiss militia to support Bouillé's army. Bombelles spent 19 June copying down Breteuil's instructions for him and discussing his plans with the marquis de Vérac, the French ambassador to the Swiss cantons. A staunch royalist, Vérac had been let into the secret of the flight three days before. His response had been enthusiastic cooperation, especially as he was told that in a few days Bombelles might be foreign minister. The conversation continued into the evening. Unaware of the extra day's delay, both men assumed that at that moment the royal family would be starting their journey. 'As we were talking,' Bombelles wrote,

> the hour approached when we supposed that the king and queen would set their plan in motion, and we felt our hearts beating the whole evening. If, at this moment, Their Majesties are slipping out of the Tuileries, what must they and their servants be going through? . . . this morning I began a novena, and call with all my heart on the Holy of Holies.[14]

The following day passed slowly; the little group were painfully aware that matters were now completely out of their hands. Just after midnight, the Bishop of Pamiers's brother, the vicomte d'Agoult, arrived breathless and confused. He had come straight from Paris, bringing what he thought was a vital message. In fact, this was just a ruse to get him out of the capital, in response to an urgent plea from his brother. The bishop had begged that if the vicomte was not chosen to accompany the royal family, 'he should not be left exposed to the first upheavals that will follow the discovery of this great enterprise'.[15] By now, having heard nothing to the contrary, the household assumed that the king and queen had made their escape. At 6 a.m. on 21 June, Breteuil climbed into his own carriage and set off for Montmédy.

Bombelles's first task, once he had heard that Louis XVI had reached Bouillé, was to present his credentials as the king's special envoy to the Diet of the Swiss cantons at Zürich. These were signed, with a flourish, 'Given at Montmédy', and dated 23 June.[16] Breteuil must surely have noticed the coincidence of the date with that of the king's declaration two years before; it may even have been deliberate. In the meantime, Bombelles was to strengthen his hand by going to Bern and taking the city's chief magistrate, the *avoyer* Steiger, into his confidence. Steiger was well disposed to the French royalists, had great influence throughout the cantons, and would make a powerful ally. Accordingly, Breteuil left a note for Bombelles to present to him. Just as he had assured Mercy when asking for Austrian military support, the baron stressed that the Swiss militia were unlikely to be used in battle and would not be needed for long:

> The king is sure of the loyalty of the overwhelming majority of his troops, but since his main wish is to avoid spilling any of his subjects' blood, His Majesty desires to have such imposing forces at his disposition, that even the most audacious rebels will have no other option than to submit. . . .
>
> The plan calls for the French and auxiliary soldiers less to give battle than to overawe and contain the excesses of a multitude of so-called National Guards, with no unity, no discipline, and who for the most part either lack arms and ammunition or do not know how to use them.
>
> Everything thus announces that numerous faithful subjects of all classes will soon be gathered to restore the rights of the throne, yet prudence and the long-term maintenance of order demands that the king increase the number of foreign regiments in his service. This will very shortly be done, and will bring forward the time when the militia will be able to return home.[17]

This letter sheds important light on Breteuil's thinking in the last days before the flight to Varennes. His consistent wish ever since July 1789, that the threat of force rather than its actual use should prove sufficient to restore the royal power, is more clearly expressed than ever. While prepared for civil war, he hoped to avoid it if it was humanly possible. Yet his prediction that the king would have to enrol more foreign regiments betrayed his basic lack of faith in the loyalty of French troops. Shrewdly, he turned this to advantage in his overture to Steiger: the promise to recruit more of their soldiers would be a powerful incentive to the Swiss, for whom hiring out mercenaries was a traditional and lucrative source of income. Whether they were used or not, the restoration of Louis XVI's authority would rest at least in part on foreign bayonets.

*

THE FIRST PERSON in Paris to realize that the king had fled was his valet Lemoine, who at 7 a.m. on 21 June drew back the curtains of the royal bed to find it empty. By 8 a.m., the capital was in uproar; La Fayette, wrongly suspected of complicity in the escape, had almost been lynched, and a vast crowd was massing outside the Tuileries. An hour later, at the beginning of the Assembly's morning session, its president, Alexandre de Beauharnais, announced the news of the flight. The Assembly declared itself in permanent session, and the deputies passed an extremely anxious day. The tension was broken that afternoon by La Porte, intendant of the civil list, bringing, as the king had instructed, a *Declaration to the French People* he had left behind justifying his flight. Some of the deputies opposed its reading, fearing that this would legitimize Louis XVI's action, but the majority, led by Charles de Lameth, defeated them. The secretary of the Assembly then read out the document amidst a shocked silence.

While the Assembly debated, La Fayette acted. On his own initiative, he dictated an order claiming that the king had been abducted by enemies of the Revolution, and commanding all good citizens to rescue him and ensure his return to Paris. Mounted National Guardsmen bearing copies of this order were then despatched along all the routes out of Paris on the royal family's trail. One of them, Captain Bayon, headed east towards Châlons.

*

IT WAS NOW 6.30 p.m on 21 June, and the royal family were approaching Pont-de-Sommevesle. At any moment, they expected to see the sky-blue jackets of the forty hussars waiting there. They also expected to find the duc de Choiseul, who had left Paris twelve hours before them to take command of the escort. Pont-de-Sommevesle was not even a village; simply a large farm beside a pond that doubled as a posthouse. As they drew level with it, the travellers were horrified to see no sign of either the hussars or Choiseul. As the horses were changed, the king stared out of the carriage window, looking 'as if the ground had opened up beneath him'.[18]

The disappearance of Choiseul's detachment was the first great misfortune of the journey. The duke had arrived at Pont-de-Sommevesle at eleven that morning and gone to a room in the posthouse to change into his uniform. As he was doing so, the forty hussars arrived. They had spent a difficult twenty-four hours. They had met up with the forty dragoons stationed at Sainte-Ménehould, the next town on the route, the previous evening, but the sudden appearance of two detachments of cavalry had aroused local suspicions. The municipality issued 400 muskets to the townsfolk and called out fifty of the National Guard; the following morning, it even seemed they might oppose Choiseul's departure for Pont-de-Sommevesle by force. In the event, the detachment managed to depart without a confrontation, but left behind a thoroughly aroused population.

The pattern repeated itself at Pont-de-Sommevesle. As bad luck would have it, the local peasantry were in dispute with their landlord; the authorities had upheld the latter and were threatening to send troops to enforce their verdict. It was immediately assumed that the hussars had arrived with this purpose, the tocsin was sounded, and Choiseul's command soon found itself menaced by a hostile crowd. Choiseul claimed repeatedly that he was simply there to escort a pay-wagon for Bouillé's army, but nobody believed him. In this increasingly tense situation, all he could do was buy time until the royal party was sighted. It was here that the earlier delays in Paris and Chaintrix had their worst effect. The *berline* was meant to reach Pont-de-Sommevesle at 3 p.m., yet two hours later it had still not apepared. At 5.30 p.m., Choiseul decided he could hold on no longer, and announced loudly for the benefit of the peasants that the pay-wagon must have passed through before he arrived. At 5.45 p.m.

he left Pont-de-Sommesvesle, three-quarters of an hour before the king's carriage arrived.

It is difficult to see what else Choiseul could have done up until then. His next actions, however, were less excusable. Retreating from Pont-de-Sommevesle, he did not think to leave anybody behind who could at least let the royal family know what was happening if and when they did appear. He compounded this error by informing the detachment commanders at Sainte-Ménehould and Clermont that the *berline* would not be coming through that day – an unwarranted assumption, which spread confusion further down the chain of escorts. Finally, given the hostile reception his troops had received, he decided to fall right back to Varennes, and skirt round Sainte-Ménehould and Clermont. Night fell and he got lost, heading northeast 'through every wood in the Clermontois'.[19]

With no other option before them, the royal family continued towards Sainte-Ménehould, which they reached at 8.30 p.m. Here, finally, they saw some signs of an escort: several troopers of the Royal Dragoons regiment lounging outside the Auberge du Soleil in the main square, talking and drinking with the townspeople. As the horses were being changed, the commanding officer, Captain d'Andoins, came up and outlined the situation to the king and queen. 'Leave as soon as you can,' he advised, 'if you don't make haste you are lost.'[20]

The carriage was soon ready, and the royal family prepared to depart. It was then that they encountered their nemesis, the postmaster Drouet. This functionary had been in a bad mood since the previous evening, when the Royal Dragoons had arrived and, instead of renting his stable for their horses, had used the one at the Auberge du Soleil. The appearance of the *berline* added suspicion to his anger. He did not, however, take immediate action. The spur to this came from the townspeople themselves. Alerted by a day's worth of unusual activity, as soon as the carriage had left Sainte-Ménehould several citizens jumped to the conclusion that it contained the king and queen. This was confirmed by d'Andoins swiftly ordering his men to saddle up. An angry crowd formed to prevent them leaving. It was at this point that Drouet walked over to the Hôtel de Ville and voiced his own conviction that the king had just passed through.

He and a companion, an innkeeper named Guillaume, were chosen to ride after the carriage and stop it. An hour and a half after the alarm was sounded, they set off in pursuit.

Meanwhile, the *berline* was rolling through the forest of the Argonne. The longest day of the year, 21 June, was coming to a close. As night fell, the royal family entered Clermont. Here again it was the same story: 140 dragoons, commanded by their colonel, the comte de Damas, were meant to be waiting, but the unexpected appearance of troops had alarmed the inhabitants so much that the count had thought it prudent to lodge part of his detachment in a neighbouring village before dispersing the rest for the night. The onlookers' suspicions were aroused by the profound respect Damas, himself a great noble, showed to the occupants of the carriage; several times he instinctively began to remove his helmet, but stopped himself. Once the *berline* had changed horses and departed, the townspeople gathered, the tocsin was sounded, and Damas and his soldiers were surrounded.

Just outside Clermont, according to plan, the carriage changed direction. Instead of continuing along the main road to Metz, it took a secondary route leading through Varennes, Dun and Stenay to Montmédy. Here fate intervened once more against the royal family. Drouet, riding hell-for-leather in pursuit, assumed they would head straight for Metz. Approaching Clermont, however, he met his own postilions bringing the last relay of horses back to Sainte-Ménehould, and learned that the *berline* had turned off for Varennes. If not for this chance, Drouet would have continued on towards Metz and missed his quarry completely. Skirting Clermont, he and Guillaume set off through the forest on a short cut to Varennes. Unknowingly, they only narrowly missed Choiseul's hussars, who were picking their way along the same path and, to add to the chapter of accidents, were at that point only half a league away from the *berline*. Had the hussars intercepted either Drouet and Guillaume, or the carriage, before Varennes, things would have turned out very differently.

At 11 p.m. the carriage reached Varennes. It still had a half-hour lead over Drouet. With a quick change of horses, it could have carried on to Dun, within reach of Bouillé and the Royal-Allemand. It was here that the final blow fell. In contrast to the previous towns on the route, Varennes did not have a posthouse. Bouillé had therefore left a relay of his own horses there for the *berline*. The royal party thought they would find this at the first house in the town; they did not know that it was in fact at the Auberge du Grand Monarque, just across the river that ran through the town. Whether this was a misunderstanding, or an omission on Bouillé's part, has never been made clear. Mystified and increasingly alarmed, the king himself got out of the carriage. Approaching the nearest house, he banged on the door and demanded where his relay was. A voice from inside replied that it was certainly not there. Baffled, Louis searched up and down the street. The scene, with its desperate, wandering king, was Shakespearean. There was, however, one difference: Richard III had offered his kingdom for a horse, but Louis XVI needed six to save his kingdom.

Finally the travellers decided to continue to the Auberge du Grand Monarque and see if the relay had been placed there. The half-hour lost was crucial. It gave time for Drouet and Guillaume, coming up behind, to spot the carriage, circle round it, enter the town and gather a search-party. Near the river, an arch spanned the main street; the group took up station beneath it, while behind it the bridge was quickly barricaded. As the *berline* approached the arch, a challenge came out of the dark: 'Halt or we fire!' Peering out of the carriage window, Mme de Tourzel saw seven men armed with muskets. Behind them, in his nightshirt and holding up a lantern, stood M. Sauce, the local grocer and *procureur* of the commune.

Even then, all was not lost. The party's passports were handed over and M. Sauce pronounced them perfectly in order. He would have let the carriage pass if Drouet had not lost his temper, shouting that the king and queen were inside and that if the townspeople let them proceed they would all be guilty of high treason. This scared everybody, and it was decided that a decision was best left until morning. The travellers were politely escorted to Sauce's grocery and shown to an upstairs room. An hour later Choiseul finally appeared and drew up his hussars outside. At the same moment Destez, a local judge who had been fetched because he had once seen the royal family at Versailles, was mounting Sauce's stairs. As he entered the upstairs room, he caught sight of Louis XVI, exclaimed 'Ah, sire!' and went down on one knee. 'Yes,' replied Louis, 'I am indeed your king.'[21]

All pretence was now at an end. With tears in his eyes, Louis embraced each of the municipal officers who had crowded into the room, saying that his family had been in deadly danger in Paris and that he had come to seek refuge among his faithful subjects. Soon afterwards Choiseul came in, followed by his second-in-command, Goguelat, and Damas, who had only managed to extricate six of his dragoons from Clermont. They immediately took the king and queen aside. 'What do we do?' asked Louis. 'Save you, sire,' replied Damas. Choiseul proposed to mount the royal family on horses and, if necessary, cut a way through with his hussars. The longer his men were left outside in contact with the townsfolk, however, the greater the risk that their discipline would break down. 'There is not a moment to lose,' he warned the king, 'in an hour the troops will have defected.'[22]

Louis XVI now made a major mistake. He knew that messengers were already on their way to inform Bouillé at Stenay, only eight leagues away, of what had happened. By four or five in the morning, he calculated, the Royal-Allemand would be at Varennes. All he had to do was sit tight and await rescue. A breakout, on the other hand, involved risks, particularly for his wife and children. 'Can you guarantee', he asked Choiseul, 'that in this unequal combat a musket shot might not kill the queen, or my daughter, or my son, or my sister?'[23] Obviously Choiseul could not, so his plan was dropped. Yet Louis's reasoning contained fatal errors. It failed to take account of the increasing numbers of local people, alerted by the tocsin and the extraordinary news, flooding into Varennes from all around. It also ignored the danger they posed to the discipline of any troops brought into prolonged contact with them. If Bouillé, for whatever reason, was delayed, the game would be lost. On this occasion, as on so many others during the Revolution, Louis showed only passive courage where action was necessary. This passivity was his downfall, and was to cost him his throne and his life.

The next few hours vividly illustrated the point. Outside Sauce's grocery, the townsfolk crowded round the exhausted hussars, repeating the same question: would they charge the people if they were ordered? At first, the troopers did not understand, but by four in the morning a woman who spoke German had been found. Fraternization began, lubricated by large quantities of local wine. At that moment

Goguelat stepped outside, took in the situation, and ordered the hussars to form up. They refused; some even cried 'Vive la nation!' in German. Goguelat raised his sabre, and was shot and wounded by a major of the National Guard. As the atmosphere in the town deteriorated, a further detachment of hussars, commanded by Captain Deslon, arrived from Dun. Deslon had ridden for Varennes with a hundred men the moment he heard the king was there, but found the defences that had now been thrown up too strong to charge. He therefore left his troops where they were and rode in to confer with the king.

A précis in the Vienna State Archives of the events of Varennes, based on Deslon's own account, shows clearly the paralysis that descended on the king as his last chance of safety slipped by. It depicts Deslon explaining to Louis that he could not charge the barricades himself, but that Bouillé would soon arrive:

> The king was in such a state of prostration and weakness, that M. Deslon feared that His Majesty had not heard him, though he repeated himself three times. Finally he asked him what he should tell M. de Bouillé. 'You can tell him that I am a prisoner, that I fear he can do nothing for me, but that I ask him to do what he can.'

Deslon then moved over to the queen, but since some National Guardsmen were next to her, addressed her in German. After a moment Louis interrupted them. 'M. Deslon having been told by the king to speak no further with the queen, he took his leave and boldly asked for his orders. The king replied: "I am a prisoner and have no orders to give." '[24] Deslon's recollections, with their vivid depiction of Louis's almost disassociated state, are revealing. They echo Fersen's verdict on Varennes in his diary: 'The king lacked firmness and presence of mind.'[25]

By now the crowd outside was growing restive. One cry was heard with increasing frequency: 'To Paris!' At 5 a.m. Radet, the local artillery commander, came out of the grocery and told the people that the king still wished to go to Montmédy. 'No, no, to Paris!' they shouted back, 'To Paris, or we'll shoot him in his carriage!' The stalemate dragged on until six-thirty, when two officers of the Paris National Guard arrived. They brought a decree from the

Assembly ordering that the royal family be stopped wherever they were and held pending further instructions. Louis XVI took it and read it through quickly. Then he simply said: 'There is no longer a king in France.'[26]

Although the decree specified merely that the fugitives be detained rather than sent back, it was clear that only an immediate return to Paris would satisfy the crowd. The royal party made desperate efforts to obtain one last delay. Clutching at the hope that Bouillé might still arrive, Louis begged the Assembly's emissaries to wait until eleven. But the clamour outside was growing menacing, and his plea was rejected. Breakfast was served; the king ate a little, then pretended to nod off to gain time. The moment he opened his eyes, one of the queen's maids, Mme Neuville, staged a fainting-fit, but the doctor who was quickly brought declared her well enough to travel. There was only one thing left to do. Louis XVI asked for a moment alone with his family, which was granted, with M. Sauce standing guard. Immediately he and Marie Antoinette rushed over to the *procureur*. They told him tearfully that they had only left Paris because the duc d'Orléans would have had them murdered if they had stayed. The only favour they asked of Sauce was to go to their carriage and bring them a box of papers hidden there that must not fall into their enemies' hands. Sauce did so, and the royal family spent their last moments in Varennes burning a heap of compromising documents. No doubt letters from Breteuil and Bouillé fed the flames.

At 7.30 a.m., the king and queen finally descended Sauce's staircase and climbed into the *berline*. They were obviously in torment; Marie Antoinette appeared overwhelmed, while Louis seemed 'in profound pain'.[27] The carriage moved off, surrounded by a vast throng. At 9 a.m., Bouillé's cavalry came within sight of Varennes.

*

FOR 200 YEARS, there has been fierce controversy over why the flight failed. This was first kindled by the surviving participants. Bouillé and Choiseul, in particular, engaged in a bitter public dispute, each blaming the other for the disaster. Bouillé, who emigrated immediately after the king's arrest, published memoirs in 1800 claiming that the fatal error had been Choiseul's retreat from Pont-de-Sommevesle. Choiseul, who only narrowly escaped being lynched after the royal family left Varennes, brought out his own justification in 1822. This emphasized instead the confusion at Varennes over the change of horses, and Bouillé's own slowness in riding to the royal family's rescue. Since then, every stage of the *berline*'s journey has been argued over by historians, raising disputes as impenetrable as the forest of the Argonne. From this tangle a few key factors that ruined the enterprise stand out. Some were human errors: Choiseul's failure to leave a messenger behind at Pont-de-Sommevesle, the mistake in placing the relay at Varennes, and the strangely long time it took Bouillé to cover the eight leagues between Stenay and Varennes. Others were pure bad luck: the accident at Chaintrix, and above all Drouet hearing that the carriage had turned off for Varennes.

If these mishaps were incidental, there was one structural flaw. Far from protecting the royal family, the detachments along their route in fact proved their undoing. They were not sufficient for a major confrontation, as events at Varennes dramatically proved. All their presence achieved was to stir up the local inhabitants and alert them that something unusual was going on. The two upsets that did most damage, Choiseul's premature departure from Pont-de-Sommevesle and the alarm at Sainte-Ménehould, resulted directly from this. The king and queen would have had a better chance of safety if they had abandoned the idea of an escort altogether, and trusted entirely to swiftness and secrecy. Significantly, this is exactly what the comte de Provence did. Travelling in a fast carriage, disguised as an English merchant and with only one companion, he arrived safely in Belgium on 23 June.

It is unclear whether the idea of posting detachments originated with Bouillé or with Louis XVI himself. Bouillé states in his memoirs that Louis ordered him to provide them. Since he himself destroyed the king's letters to him, we shall never know for certain. Yet Fersen was well aware of the plan's dangers, and issued a warning. 'Everything should depend on speed and secrecy,' he wrote to Bouillé on 26 May, 'and if you are not sure of your detachments, it would be better to have none at all, or only to place them after Varennes, so as not to excite attention in the countryside.'[28] Fersen's prescience is chilling, even down to his instinct that the soldiers' discipline would not survive close contact with the people.

The fact that order broke down in three of the escorts poses the larger question of how reliable Bouillé's army would have proved even if the king had reached Montmédy. At first sight, the loyalty of the detachments, and by implication that of the army of which they formed part, seems to have been very precarious. Yet the picture is more complex than that. Two units, the royal dragoons at Sainte-Ménehould and Choiseul's hussars at Varennes, eventually mutinied. However, the latter's discipline held throughout the confrontation at Pont-de-Sommevesle and the long night ride past Clermont, and only broke down after hours of crowd pressure outside Sauce's grocery. Their defection was helped along by the large quantities of wine with which the civilians plied them. Alcohol also jeopardized the situation at Sainte-Ménehould; by the time the *berline* arrived, the dragoons had been drinking all day.

The blame for these military failures lay not with the soldiers but with the dispositions that caused them to spend the day dispersed among alarmed and volatile townsfolk. At Clermont, Sainte-Ménehould and Varennes the troops were heavily outnumbered at the critical moment, while their cohesion had already been undermined by several hours' fraternization with their hosts. From Pont-de-Sommevesle on, the escorts found themselves in an exceptional situation which any troops would have found difficult to control. There was no parallel between their position, isolated in the midst of armed urban crowds, and that of Bouillé's main army, concentrated in its own camp away from the people, and commanded by a tough and capable general. The fact that the escorts along the way eventually mutinied offers no proof that Bouillé's main force would have done the same.

A further consideration is the effect the king's presence would have had on the troops. On the road to Montmédy, Louis XVI was preparing to act a military part for the first time in his life. In readiness for this, he had packed a magnificent red uniform. This was the same one he had worn to inspect the new harbour at Cherbourg five years before, the only other time he had visited the French provinces. On arrival at Montmédy, his first act would be to promote

Bouillé from the rank of general by presenting him with the bâton of a marshal of France. There was, however, a last-minute hitch: there was no spare bâton available, and it was clearly imprudent to ask the war ministry for a new one. Fortunately, Choiseul had one to hand, which had belonged to his late father-in-law the maréchal de Stainville, and he lent it to the king.[29]

Bouillé's promotion ceremony was intended to bolster the troops' morale and raise it to a pitch of royalist enthusiasm. It was scheduled for 23 June, which must have been deliberate. 'The king, the queen and the royal family', Choiseul wrote,

> were to enter the camp, attend a military mass, with the troops under arms, review the army after the service, and then, having ordered it drawn up in a hollow square, the king was to give M. le marquis de Bouillé the marshal's bâton, to the cheers of the troops and amid general rejoicing.[30]

Whether this grand spectacle would have worked is impossible to tell. However, the symbolism of king, queen and dauphin entrusting themselves to their last faithful army might well have had the desired effect.

*

BACK IN THE CAPITAL, the news of the royal party's arrest was greeted with immense relief by the Assembly. The deputies immediately chose three of its members as special commissioners, not to parley with Louis XVI but to escort him and his family safely back to Paris. Two of these, Barnave and Latour-Maubourg, were moderates; the third, Pétion, was of the Left. They were accompanied by Mathieu Dumas, adjutant-general of the army. The commissioners left Paris at four in the morning of 22 June. Just outside Épernay, they saw the *berline* coming towards them, moving at a snail's pace and surrounded by a huge crowd.

The royal family had spent a ghastly day. They had left Varennes escorted by 7,000 townspeople and peasants. It was hot, and the travellers were soon covered with dust and sweat. There was little privacy from the throng on all sides, whose mood was often alarmingly hostile. At Sainte-Ménehould a local landowner, the comte de Dampierre, with remarkable courage rode up to the *berline* to pay his respects. He was pulled from his horse and hacked to death virtually under the eyes of the royal party. Further on, at the village of Chouilly, the tension reached breaking-point; those nearest to the carriage shook their fists at the occupants and spat in the king's face. All of this convinced the inhabitants of Chouilly that the king and queen would not reach Paris alive.

The fullest description of the royal family's return comes in a remarkable yet little-known document, the *Relation of the Journey to Varennes*, by the Archbishop of Toulouse, François-Gilbert de Fontanges. The archbishop was a deputy in the Assembly, a polished courtier, and a close confidant of Marie Antoinette. This worldly prelate, however, ended his life in saintly fashion; transferred to the see of Autun, he died of typhus there in 1806, tending Austrian and Russian prisoners. His manuscript has a curious history. In the early 1800s Bombelles, knowing how close he had been to the queen, wrote to him from emigration asking for his recollections of her. The archbishop replied with the *Relation*, which Bombelles later passed to *émigrés* in London for publication. Its chief value lies in its principal source. As the archbishop put it to Bombelles: 'My aim is not to give you a completely accurate history, but simply to set down faithfully and impartially everything engraved on my memory from my conversations on the subject with the queen herself.'[31] The *Relation* is the closest Marie Antoinette came to writing her own account of the flight to Varennes.

The narrative contains little new material on the flight and the arrest. However, its description of the last stage of the return, from the meeting with the commissioners, is remarkably vivid and detailed. Through the archbishop's words, one can hear Marie Antoinette herself speaking. It was decided that two of the commissioners should get into the *berline* with the royal family. A moment of farce followed as the new arrivals fumbled around in the cramped space. As the *Relation* puts it: 'Barnave, who was fairly thin, placed himself on one seat between the king and queen, Pétion on the other between Mme Elisabeth and the young princess; the dauphin on the knees first of his mother, then his aunt, then his sister.'[32] This seating arrangement had important political consequences, since it enabled the queen to start a discreet conversation with Barnave, and form an alliance with him that helped shape royal policy for the following year. Had Barnave been any fatter, this might never have come about.

The encounter got off to a bad start. This was Barnave's fault. Getting into the carriage, the archbishop wrote,

> he began with ... an impertinence. He glanced first at one of the bodyguards on the outside seat, and then at the queen, with a brief, sly and knowing smile. Since it was rumoured that the comte de Fersen had been one of the three men arrested with the king, and the queen knew of the calumnies circulating about her relations with this Swedish nobleman, she guessed what was in Barnave's mind. She swiftly disabused him ... by making clear the identity of the three men on the seat.[33]

This anecdote is remarkable. It is one of the rare testimonies that gossip about Marie Antoinette's friendship with Fersen was current at the time, and that the queen was actually aware of the fact.

After this, matters could only improve. Louis XVI broke the ice by engaging Barnave in conversation about aspects of the Revolution and the constitution. A friendly argument ensued, in which Barnave sustained his point of view with deference and politeness. After the contretemps over Fersen, the queen had pulled her veil down over her face and resolved not to utter a word for the rest of the journey. Now, however, she decided it might be worth talking to Barnave after all. The archbishop's description of how she won him over captures the quality of her famous charm: 'Little by little she joined in the conversation, adding that grace, charm, presence of mind and easy manner that she better than anybody could blend with the majestic pride fitting to her birth and rank.'[34]

The result was that Barnave conceived a chivalrous admiration for Marie Antoinette, which was strengthened by pity for her situation. Whether his feelings went further than this remains mysterious. Like Fersen, his desire to become the queen's knight-errant probably contained some sexual element, although it is inconceivable that this was ever fulfilled. Marie Antoinette for her part was not immune to Barnave's charms; he was young, handsome and surpassingly eloquent. The peculiar friendship between these two completely different figures is summed up by the Archbishop of Toulouse:

It is from [the return from Varennes] that one can date the sort of confidence that the queen always had in Barnave, which not only effaced the bad impression that his hot-headed extremism at the beginning of the Revolution had made on Her Majesty, but which later led her to seek his advice in difficult circumstances. The form of attraction she felt for Barnave never extended to his friends like Lameth and Duport, even when events forced her to ... have dealings with them.[35]

As the *berline* approached Paris, all this lay in the future. The carriage entered the capital at the Barrière de Montceau. It then rolled slowly down the Champs-Elysées, through a vast, silent crowd held back by National Guards with reversed arms. When the royal family arrived at the Tuileries, violence erupted; a mob tried to lynch the three bodyguards, and one was severely beaten before they were dragged to safety in the palace. With remarkable *sang-froid*, Louis XVI behaved as if nothing had happened in the last two days, and he and the queen mounted the grand staircase to their apartments. They were accompanied by La Fayette, now more than ever their gaoler. Louis then went into his study and wrote some letters, which he made a show of presenting to the general for his approval. La Fayette protested that he was not there to act as a spy. He then made as if to leave, and asked the king for his orders. Louis smiled. 'It seems,' he replied, 'that I am much more at your orders than you are at mine.'[36]

*

AT DAWN ON 25 JUNE, the marquis de Bouillé's son, who had just fled across the border, was galloping along the road to Brussels. Just outside Arlon he encountered a light carriage, travelling at speed the other way. It contained the Bishop of Pamiers, on his way to join the royal family at Montmédy. Bouillé hurriedly told him of the catastrophe.[37] Shattered, the bishop turned his carriage round and the two men headed north. At the little town of Marche-en-Famenne they found the comte de Provence, also making for Montmédy. Provence was regaling the company with amusing stories about his escape from France. In their character of English merchants, he and his companion had loudly repeated stock-phrases, like 'Come along with me', in that language for the benefit of passers-by, and had taken pains to talk French to their coachman with an English accent. The new arrivals swiftly ended this jollity. Provence later wrote that he had wept when Bouillé broke the news of his brother's capture. According to Bouillé, however, 'there was no trace of tears in his eyes, which were entirely dry . . . and bore only their usual duplicitous expression'.[38]

At Aix-la-Chapelle Gustavus III, whom Fersen had told of the planned escape, could barely contain his impatience. Throughout 21 June he paced up and down, his pocket-watch in his hand. On the 24th, a letter came from Fersen describing the royal family's arrest. Fersen himself had crossed the border at Mons and sped down the other side of the frontier, intending to rejoin the king and queen at Montmédy. At midnight on the 23rd, at Arlon, he learned what had happened at Varennes. He immediately sat down and wrote two letters. The first, official, one was to Gustavus. The second, more personal, was to his father in Sweden: 'All is lost, my dear father, and I am in despair. The king was arrested at Varennes, sixteen leagues from the frontier. Imagine my pain and pity me.'[39]

On 25 June, having heard nothing of the royal family's fate, Bombelles set off for Bern to negotiate for Swiss troops with the *avoyer* Steiger. The *avoyer* was delighted by the news of the king's escape and promised his support. On the 27th, Bombelles returned to Solothurn. By this time he was receiving a flow of information about the events at Varennes. It was completely contradictory: some reports claimed that the king and queen had been arrested, others that they had been rescued by Bouillé. A letter arrived from the cardinal de Rohan stating that the king was safe at Metz, followed by another from Bouillé's wife placing the royal family at Mons. It was only on the 28th that Bombelles finally abandoned his illusions.[40]

There is no record of how Breteuil received the news of Varennes. Although he knew all the risks of the enterprise, the blow must still have been devastating. He had been a day away from entering Montmédy in triumph to rejoin the liberated king. Now his own future, like that of the royal family, was cruelly uncertain. The most pressing question was where to go next. There was nothing left for the baron in Switzerland. Whatever lay in store, it was better faced in Belgium, where at least he could lobby Mercy-Argenteau and the Austrians. With a heavy heart, he took the road to Brussels.

Chapter Nine

THE KING'S SECRET

THE GREATEST MYSTERY OF the flight to Varennes is not why it failed, but what were its ultimate aims. What did Louis XVI and Marie Antoinette intend to do once they had reached Montmédy? What political plan, if any, did they have to end the Revolution? Did they intend to turn the clock back completely and restore the old regime, or did they wish instead to broker a constitutional compromise? The decision to escape from Paris forced the king and queen to think more deeply than ever before about what sort of settlement to the revolutionary crisis they really wanted. The conclusions they drew shaped not only their flight from the capital, but their policy towards the Revolution to the very end.

The king, the queen and their closest confidants guarded the secret of their real aims jealously, both at the time of the flight and afterwards. They had good reason. If the truth had leaked out at any point after the royal family's recapture, the consequences would have been disastrous. In the face of these dangers, discretion was very much the better part of valour. Looking back later on the policies the king had been preparing to adopt, Bombelles remarked: 'The cruel catastrophe of Varennes wrecked all these plans, which were then fortunately buried in a profound silence.'[1]

On the night of his escape, Louis XVI did leave behind one clue to the plan he was contemplating. This was his lengthy *Declaration to the French People*, which he composed himself for communication to the National Assembly. The *Declaration* was essentially a public attempt by the king to justify his action in fleeing Paris. As such, it was a critique of the existing political situation, and of the excesses that had driven him to flight, rather than an outline of what he intended to do once he was free. None the less, it does offer one glimpse of his aims. In the course of a long retrospective account of the sacrifices he had made to his people since 1789, Louis XVI laid particular emphasis on the declaration of 23 June. 'Well before the meeting of the Estates General,' he wrote,

> the king had made clear that he recognized that taxation could only be raised with the agreement of the nation's representatives, and that he no longer wished to tax his people without their consent. All the mandates of the deputies to the Estates gave the highest priority to restoring the finances; some wished other matters to be resolved beforehand [a reference to the clash over voting by order or by head]. The king resolved these difficulties by taking the initiative and according, in the royal session of 23 June, all that had been asked.[2]

Significantly, Louis XVI here reaffirmed what he had already made clear on 23 June, that by the act of calling the Estates he had willingly accepted the essential attribute of a constitutional monarchy, that taxation depended on the consent of a representative assembly. Elsewhere, however, he used some disingenuous prose to gloss over the major failing of the declaration of 23 June, its refusal to compel the privileged orders to accept voting by head. He presented the union of the orders, which in fact had been forced on him by the crowd pressure at Versailles, as having been conceded voluntarily: 'the uniting of the orders by the king's will'.[3] This was scarcely accurate; while Louis had personally desired voting by head on some issues, he had drawn back from imposing this on the nobility and clergy.

The *Declaration to the French People* thus implies, but no more, that if Louis XVI had regained his freedom in June 1791, he would have returned to his previous declaration of 23 June 1789 as a basis on which to end the French Revolution. Marie Antoinette, on the

other hand, went much further than this, in her letter to Mercy-
Argentau of 3 February 1791. Here, she gave the most detailed
description left by either of the royal couple of their intentions once
they had fled the capital. 'The king', she confided,

> is busy assembling the material for the manifesto that must be
> issued once we have left Paris. He must first explain the reasons
> for his flight; pardon those who have merely been led astray,
> flatter them with expressions of love; exempt from the pardon
> the chiefs of the rebels and Paris itself, if it does not return to
> its old order, as well as anybody who has not handed in their
> weapons by a fixed date; restore the *parlements* simply as law
> courts, with no power to meddle in administration or finance.
> Finally, we have decided to take as the basis of the constitution
> the declaration of 23 June 1789, with the modifications that
> circumstances and events make necessary. Religion will be one
> of the key points to exploit.[4]

Some recent historians have argued that Louis's declaration and
Marie Antoinette's programme sketched out here have nothing in
common. The first, they point out, lays out no conditions or timetable
for a return to obedience, makes no mention of the *parlements* and
little of religion, and only refers to the declaration of 23 June without expressly making it the basis of any future dispensation. This
resurrects the theory that the king and queen were pursuing separate
programmes. Yet in fact it is perfectly possible to reconcile Louis
XVI's and Marie Antoinette's statements. Each document was meant
for a different audience: the king's to reassure the public, and the
queen's for purely private consumption. Given that the king's
document was meant as a critique of the Revolution rather than a
royalist manifesto, its references to the declaration of 23 June, with
its subtle revision of the commitment to voting by order, are quite
compatible with the queen's invocation of 'the declaration of 23rd
June ... with the modifications that circumstances ... make
necessary'.

At first sight, there seems a more obvious difference between
the king and queen over religion. Marie Antoinette clearly wanted
to exploit the division over the Civil Constitution of the Clergy,
while Louis XVI merely expressed a wish that 'our holy religion' be

respected. But this difference should not be exaggerated. Louis XVI's hostility to the Civil Constitution was fundamental, and the events of 18 April, which had redoubled his determination to escape, were directly linked to the religious schism.

The man who held all the threads of these policies together was Breteuil. If anyone was privy to what the king and queen really intended to do once they were free, it was he. Had he ever revealed the secrets he held, much of the remaining mystery about the flight to Varennes would now be plain. Yet the baron kept his information, and his own aims, carefully to himself. The only small confidences he let slip were to Fersen. On 30 April 1791, he informed him that he would not be able to reach Montmédy until several days after the royal couple, and set out the immediate steps to be taken in his absence:

> As it is impossible, however much haste I make, that the king will not arrive some days before me at his destination, I ask that except for the military operations, where [Bouillé's] views must be neither hindered not postponed, His Majesty should take no decisions in matters of either personnel or policy until I have been able to put myself at his orders. Nothing is more essential for the king's service than to avoid precipitate actions which might then have to be taken back. I dare to add that it is no less important that His Majesty makes clear down to the last details the extent of the confidence with which he deigns to honour me in the conduct of affairs. The king may discern ambition beneath this request dictated by the purest zeal; if so I should become incapable from that moment on of being the slightest use in the difficult situation in which the kingdom finds itself; you will judge the truth of this as well as I.[5]

This gives nothing away about what Breteuil thought Louis XVI should ultimately do, but it does make clear his determination to retain unchallenged authority, next to the king, over all aspects of policymaking at Montmédy. The baron's point about personnel is also significant. He had seen at first hand in the 1780s the havoc wrought by divisions in the ministry (indeed, he had contributed much to them himself). He was determined that this should not be repeated in 1791, and proposed to ensure this by insisting on approving all ministerial appointments himself. He had already marked Bombelles down for the foreign ministry.

Fersen's reply to Breteuil contains further clues to the flight's ultimate aim. It informed the baron that Louis XVI had agreed to all his conditions, but added a tantalizing request. 'As no precipitate actions should be taken that might later have to be reversed,' Fersen wrote,

> but nonetheless circumstances may arise in which decisions might have to be taken before your arrival, the king wishes you to put down in writing some general ideas and insights to serve as a basis for conduct, and as a guideline for a constant and uniform policy. This document should be taken by a trustworthy person to Luxembourg, in sufficient time to be delivered to the king on his arrival at Montmédy.[6]

Thereafter, much of Fersen's correspondence with Breteuil was devoted to the arrangements for the safe arrival of this vital paper. On 22 May, the baron replied to Fersen, informing him that he was entrusting it to his valet, Fresnoy. A week later, he reported that Fresnoy had left for Luxembourg on the 27th, adding:

> As we don't know where he will be staying, you will have to send round the inns to ask for him. The packet he is carrying is addressed to M. de Dampierre. Don't forget that the memorandum, although it appears to be in code, is in fact written in invisible ink, and that the code is meaningless.[7]

The cloak-and-dagger secrecy of these instructions underlines the document's importance.

Fersen's published correspondence, however, contains few clues as to the actual contents of Breteuil's memorandum. On 23 May, as it was being written, Fersen passed on Louis XVI's thoughts on the immediate financial measures that would need to be taken. These concerned above all the National Assembly's new paper currency, the *assignats*, and the necessity or otherwise of declaring a bankruptcy. 'As to the *assignats*,' he wrote,

> the king thinks that the clergy should be given back its property, while reimbursing those who have bought some, on condition that it buys back, in silver, those *assignats* currently in circula-

tion according to their value at the moment of his departure. This will probably result in a loss of 20 per cent, which will reduce the total value of the *assignats* to nine hundred million; one could ask the clergy for a thousand million. As for the bankruptcy, the king thinks that it should only be a partial one, and should guarantee all annuities, so as to create less discontent; this is also the view of several people I have spoken to.[8]

On 29 May, Breteuil wrote his reply to Fersen. In it, he gave the first concrete hint of the policy he was proposing to adopt. The only action the king should take straightaway, he advised,

> should be limited to military matters, which M de Bouillé alone should direct; any decision relating to bankruptcy or even to the declaration of 23 June would be premature. I have given the reasons for this, as well as the only measures I regard as urgent, in the memorandum that I have instructed Fresnoy to bring to Luxembourg.[9]

This statement confirms the centrality of the declaration of 23 June to the flight to Varennes, but is open to two interpretations. It could be seen as proof of caution and flexibility on the part of a pragmatic politician who wished to close off no options, even if that meant going beyond the provisions of the declaration. On the other hand, it could conceal a reluctance for Louis XVI to make any concessions whatever, and certainly none until the baron himself had reached Montmédy. Either way, only the memorandum itself could provide the answer.

Unfortunately, after 29 May the document drops completely out of sight in the published sources. Fresnoy was sent off to Luxembourg on the 27th, but what happened after that is unknown. Ever since, Breteuil's memorandum has been assumed to be lost.

Yet one copy does exist. It rests in a carton in the Bombelles papers at Burg Clam, and is published here for the first time. It has no title; across the top is simply written: 'Sent to Luxembourg. Left Solothurn Friday, 27 May 1791.'[10] It is thus undoubtedly the document referred to by Fersen and Breteuil. A further letter in the Bombelles archives, this time from the Bishop of Pamiers, makes clear its provenance. The bishop wrote this letter on 9 March 1792 to Bombelles, who was then in St Petersburg negotiating for Russian support for the royalist cause. He instructed Bombelles to use it, in the strictest confidence, to help convince Catherine the Great that the king had had no intention of compromising with the Revolution when he left for Montmédy.[11] It is easy to see why the bishop sent the paper, and why he did so in such secrecy. In the absence of any conclusive proof of the king's real feelings on the matter in his own hand, this is the closest to them we are ever likely to get.

Breteuil's memorandum first broached the central issue the king had to face: what attitude to adopt to the National Assembly once he had arrived at Montmédy. 'In a situation where everything requires adapting one's conduct to the extent of one's power,' wrote the baron,

> it appears impossible to fix any plan in advance, either regarding the principles of government, or the finances. Perhaps it will be easier than one thinks, to avoid a new convocation of the estates general. On the other hand, perhaps prudence dictates that one should make a point of not dispensing with them, even if this could be done without great inconvenience.[12]

At first sight, therefore, Breteuil appears undecided about whether representative government should be continued or abandoned. On one matter, however, he was absolutely clear: there could be no negotiations with the current National Assembly. This alone is a decisive blow to claims then and now that Louis XVI was contemplating any form of compromise with the moderate revolutionaries when he set off for Montmédy. Indeed, Breteuil even went so far as to attach to his memorandum a draft declaration for the king, dissolving the National Assembly in the most forthright manner. Its flavour is obvious from the first two articles:

We order the following:

Article 1
That the deputies elected by virtue of our letters of convocation to the Estates General of our kingdom, and currently sitting in the so-called National Assembly, withdraw immediately into their respective constituencies.

Article 2
That the said so-called National Assembly immediately cease all
its functions and sittings, on pain of the contravening deputies
being pursued as guilty of high treason, traitors to the fatherland
and unfaithful to their constituents, and punished according to
the rigour of the laws.[13]

While breathing fire and sword against the sitting National Assembly,
Breteuil appeared not to rule out summoning a fresh Estates General.
The subtext of his memorandum, however, makes plain his strong
preference for dispensing with the Estates. This, then, was the real
reason why he told Fersen that any swift decision regarding the
declaration of 23 June would be premature. The declaration had
promised periodic meetings of the Estates, and Breteuil was determined to avoid an immediate reaffirmation of this that would tie
Louis XVI's hands. Thus in the course of his memorandum he
referred to the declaration only twice, and each time in a back-
handed way designed to postpone its implementation:

I confess that I can conceive of no possible case that could
compel the king [immediately to declare his intentions], unless
one supposes that the troops to which His Majesty will entrust
his person demand this as a condition of their loyalty, which is
utterly unlikely; for, even supposing that the king's presence did
not have the expected effect on French soldiers, and further that
they were not kept in check by fear of the emperor's forces and
those of the allied powers, and that they wished so to abuse
their position as to put a price on their services, they will not
demand the declaration of 23 June, or a guarantee of the
national debt, but rather confirmation of those decrees of the
Assembly which have improved the condition of the soldiers . . .

I do not see how the National Assembly could have the
audacity to call on the king to declare his intentions, but
this Assembly, which could perhaps embarrass His Majesty if
it confined itself to pressing the king to announce whether
he intends to implement the declaration of [23] June, cannot
possibly ask this question, which would annul not only all its
decrees, but even its existence.[14]

Significantly, Breteuil devoted a whole paragraph to warning the king about the need for the deepest secrecy with regard to his plans. He did so in a manner that clearly assumed that Louis XVI, once free, would adopt a hardline attitude to the Revolution. To this end, he fully accepted the necessity of deception:

> If the king is convinced by my reasoning and wishes to adopt the policy I have the honour to propose to him, I dare to beg His Majesty carefully to conceal his plan even from his most trusted servants; it is equally necessary that while seizing every opportunity of expressing his wish to make sacrifices for the well-being of his peoples, to claim only a moderate share in government, to honour not only his own engagements and those of his predecessors, but also those contracted by an illegal assembly, His Majesty lets nothing slip of his preferred plan regarding either the Estates General or the national debt. The least words of sovereigns have such importance: so many people have an interest in guessing their intentions, that it is very difficult to avoid them gaining some publicity, and in the current circumstances the most impenetrable secrecy is, of all measures, the most essential to the government; without it the most imposing display of force dissipates and loses all effect.[15]

The same caution and secrecy applied to Breteuil's views on the matters of financial policy. Since any action the king took in this area was bound to create some losers, it was best to keep his opponents guessing for as long as possible. 'Here,' the baron wrote,

> order can only be restored in three ways: by a more or less hard-hitting bankruptcy; by appropriating some of the property of the clergy, or by substantially raising taxes: but, whether His Majesty prefers to trust exclusively to one of these plans, or whether he decides, as prudence seems to dictate, a middle way which would wisely combine the advantages of all three, this course is bound to create a certain number of malcontents, who could swell the numbers of the partisans of the Revolution, or at least favour them. Our aim is to restore the royal prerogative, and to achieve this it would help, for a little while, to cover with a vague silence a decision that must necessarily collide with an infinity of personal interests.[16]

The only matter on which Breteuil advocated immediate action was the *assignats*. This was no doubt because here, via Fersen, the king had gone into detail. Breteuil agreed that Louis XVI should guarantee to reimburse their holders, but argued forcefully that at the same time he should forbid their circulation forthwith. This was because the existence of a paper currency over which it had absolute control, and could print in vast quantities if necessary to pay its troops, gave the National Assembly an advantage that the king, who would be obliged to pay his own soldiers *in specie*, lacked. On the other hand, an announcement prohibiting circulation of *assignats* would swiftly rob them of much authority and value, since it would be clear that in the event of a royal victory their days would be numbered. 'The mere disquiet that such a declaration would cause', the baron wrote, 'would be sufficient to make those concerned obey it, so that there would not be one demagogue who would not wish to avoid receiving payment of considerable sums in paper money.'[17] Implicit in this vision, of both the king and the National Assembly needing to find ways of paying troops, was an assumption of civil war.

Breteuil's memorandum is compelling evidence that Louis XVI had no intention of compromising with the Revolution when he set out for Montmédy. It does, however, run counter to the recollections of two other participants in the royal escape, Bouillé and Choiseul. Bouillé's belief, set out in memoirs composed at the end of his life, was that the king intended throughout to seek an agreement with the moderate revolutionaries, and would only have used force as a last resort.[18] Choiseul, in an account of the flight to Varennes that he claims Louis actually read and approved, goes further. At Montmédy, he states, the king would have 'accepted reasonable proposals from Paris' for a revision of the constitution that strengthened royal authority. Then, when the new constitution had been freely discussed and received his sanction, he would have installed himself at Compiègne to oversee its implementation.[19]

Yet there are gaps and confusions in both Bouillé's and Choiseul's accounts. Bouillé admitted in his memoirs that he never actually knew what Louis XVI's precise intentions were, and, once at Montmédy, what his conduct towards the National Assembly would have been.[20] If so crucial a figure as Bouillé was uncertain about the king's ultimate plans, it is unlikely that Choiseul, further down the chain of command, had any clearer idea. It is probable that the compromise plan he recalls, with Louis XVI going to Compiègne, was Mirabeau's discarded project, which he confused with the hard-line one actually adopted.

Stronger evidence that a negotiated settlement to the Revolution was in the air comes from the other side, in the reaction of some of the leaders of the Assembly when they learned that the king had fled. Choiseul claims that once this was known, the deputies of the Centre and the moderate Right secretly chose a deputation from the consti-tutional committee to follow him and open negotiations. The go-between was to be the comte de Gouvernet, a well-connected nobleman who had also been Bouillé's aide-de-camp. 'He was to leave at 10 p.m. to announce to the king, at Montmédy, the arrival of the commissioners,' wrote Choiseul. 'The horses had been ordered, and he was about to get into his carriage, when, at 9 p.m., news came of the arrest.'[21]

This account is confirmed by Gouvernet himself, in two letters written to Bouillé after the king's arrest and published by the latter in his memoirs. The first, dated 15 July, reached the general in Luxembourg, where he had taken refuge. 'At the risk of adding to your sorrows,' Gouvernet began,

> the result of my observations and my meetings with the deputies during the king's absence, all led me to believe that, if the king had got through, this great political crisis would have ended inside a month, with a good constitution and without a drop of blood being spilt.[22]

These words provide evidence that some politicians in the Assembly did welcome the royal family's flight as hastening a compromise settlement to the Revolution. Yet the intentions of the deputies did not necessarily reflect those of the king. Many moderates may have acted in the belief, or rather the hope, that Louis XVI, from the safety of Bouillé's army, would be prepared to negotiate. Gouvernet himself based his conviction that a compromise was possible not on his knowledge of Louis XVI, but simply on his faith in the good sense of his old commander Bouillé. 'I knew nothing of the king's projects,' he wrote to Bouillé, 'but I recognized your own moderation, and it was this that made me certain of an accommodation.'[23] Yet as we have seen, Bouillé himself had no clear idea of what the king really planned to do once he had reached safety.

Barring the discovery of new material in Louis XVI's own handwriting, Breteuil's memorandum offers the most important insight so far into what the king's policy would have been in the event of a successful escape. Yet it is not absolutely certain that, had he found the document waiting for him at Montmédy, Louis would have adopted all its provisions. Conceivably, he could have found it too reactionary. Breteuil was not the only adviser available to him; he even considered taking another former minister, Saint-Priest, with him on his flight, and this possibility is mentioned in Fersen's correspondence.[24]

This embryonic division between Louis XVI and Breteuil could be traced back several months, to the forging of the *plein pouvoir*. Breteuil certainly had the queen's confidence, but even now did he fully have that of the king? Yet as usual, Louis's actions belied his initial hesitations. Ultimately the more moderate Saint-Priest was not chosen to advise the king once he had reached freedom, and Breteuil was. Above all, once the royal family were safely at Montmédy, the queen would have gained an even greater ascendancy over her indecisive husband, while the organizer of the successful escape would have enjoyed immense prestige as the saviour of the monarchy. If Louis XVI had still had doubts about accepting Breteuil's proposals, Marie Antoinette and the baron would together have made short work of them. Bombelles, who was well placed to know, was certain that it was the baron's ideas, and not a more moderate plan, that Louis XVI would have adopted. He said as much in a letter to his close friend the chevalier de Las Casas, the Spanish ambassador to Venice, on 8 August 1791: 'the advice [the baron de Breteuil] would have taken the liberty of giving the king would, I think, have gained the approval of His Majesty and of all sensible men'.[25]

One further key witness was convinced that Breteuil's memorandum would have formed the basis of Louis XVI's policy had the flight to Varennes succeeded. This was the Bishop of Pamiers, who would never have sent Bombelles a copy of the document had he thought it implied otherwise. In fact, the reason he did so was precisely to dispel rumours that Artois's followers were putting around the Russian court in early 1792, that Breteuil had espoused the *monarchiens'* plans for an English-style constitutional monarchy. As he wrote to Bombelles in his covering letter:

> I am also sending you a copy of the memorandum that was sent from Solothurn to Luxembourg on the king's wishes a short time before his departure [for Montmédy]. I think that you could not have a more decisive proof with which to combat those epithets, which are quite unjustified, of *monarchiste* or *monarchien*. This is between the two of us, and if you do find a use for it, I am sure that prudence imperiously dictates that you allow no one to make a copy of it, since the smallest indiscretion of this sort, alerting the demagogues to His Majesty's real intentions at the moment of his departure, would confirm all their worst fears and put his life in danger.[26]

The last word should go to Bombelles himself. Almost a decade after the flight to Varennes, in August 1800, he found himself serving in the *émigré* army of his erstwhile opponent, the prince de Condé. On the evening of 23 August, Condé came round to his lodgings, and the two men got into a discussion about what Louis XVI would have done had he reached Montmédy in 1791. Bombelles recounted the incident in an unpublished entry in his diary. Once again, this dispels any notion that Louis XVI would have compromised with the French Revolution had the flight succeeded. Eight years after the king's execution, it is also a last ringing statement of faith in the absolute monarchy:

> Mgr le prince de Condé this evening . . . spoke to me about the baron de Breteuil, in the belief that this minister was working to preserve part of the constitutional regime in the event of the king's successful escape. I think I managed to convince His Highness that nothing could be more false than this supposed intention, and that if His Majesty had not been arrested at Varennes and had arrived at Montmédy, he would have found the baron de Breteuil determined to support him in the clear intention and necessity of a general return to order, that is to say the restoration of the monarchy not as it was after the formation of the provincial assemblies [in 1787], but as it was before the tampering began with the admirable edifice founded,

raised, completed by the master hand of that most excellent monarch Louis XIV, Louis the Great, the truly great, who knew to perfection what was necessary for our nation to tower above all the other countries of the globe.[27]

Chapter Ten

THE KING AND THE CONSTITUTION

THE ROYAL FAMILY immediately felt the consequences of their failed escape. On 25 June, the day they returned to Paris, the king was suspended from his functions. At the Tuileries, extraordinary precautions were taken to ensure that escape would henceforth be impossible, and the palace became a prison. Its courtyards were filled with troops, a virtual army camp was established in its gardens, and sentries were posted on the roof. Inside, the surveillance was even more oppressive. The queen bore the brunt of this; two guards were posted in her bedroom with orders not to let her out of their sight day or night. For several days, she was forced to to go to bed, get up in the morning, dress and undress in front of them. One might Marie Antoinette was unable to sleep, lit her bedside lamp and began to read. The guard on duty, noticing this, poked his head through the bed-curtains and said familiarly: 'You can't sleep? Let's have a chat. That'll do you more good than reading.' The queen tactfully persuaded him that she preferred to get on with her book.[1]

The flight to Varennes changed the political situation dramatically. Even before the royal family had returned to Paris, on 24 June, the most radical political club, the Cordeliers, had delivered a petition to the Assembly calling for the king's deposition. The next few weeks saw, for the first time, the emergence of republicanism as a serious political force. The gap between moderates and the Left was now clear, and the revolutionary front was split as never before.

The catalyst of this radical surge was the assembly's proclamation, contrary to all appearances, that the royal family had not in fact fled, but had been kidnapped by counter-revolutionaries. This absurd fiction was dictated by the determination of the moderate deputies, still in the majority, to retain the constitutional monarchy despite the embarrassment of Varennes. Ironically, they were aided in this by Bouillé who, in a chivalrous attempt to protect his royal master, wrote to the Assembly from Luxembourg on 26 June taking upon himself the whole responsibility for the flight. This exculpation of the king, however, infuriated the Left. On 15 July, the day the Assembly published its decree attributing sole blame for the escape to Bouillé, there was a tumultuous meeting at the Jacobin Club. The hall was invaded by a crowd of 4,000, who forced the publication of a petition that Louis XVI should be deemed to have abdicated, and should not be replaced unless a majority of the people wished it. In essence, this was a call for a republic.

The immediate result of this upheaval was, temporarily, to destroy the Jacobin Club. Almost all the deputies who had previously belonged to it, headed by Barnave, seceded the very next day and founded a rival club based at another former convent, that of the Feuillants. They were headed by Barnave and his allies Duport and the Lameth brothers, and were swiftly joined by La Fayette. Only six deputies, including Robespierre, remained with the Jacobins. This rump, however, went ahead with the preparations for presenting the anti-monarchical petition. It was decided to hold a mass signing ceremony on the altar to the fatherland that had just been erected on the Champ-de-Mars. The following day, a crowd of 50,000 gathered there. As the throng was queuing up to sign, a hairdresser and a cripple with a wooden leg were discovered hiding under the altar. They had probably stationed themselves there to peep up the women's skirts as they came forward, but were immediately assumed to be counter-revolutionary spies and lynched.

At the Hôtel de Ville, this news finally forced the moderates to act. As mayor of the city, Bailly declared martial law and sent La

Fayette at the head of the National Guard to break up the crowd.
The troops arrived on the Champ-de-Mars flying the red flag of
warning, and the general called on the gathering to disperse. It did
not do so, but instead replied with shouted defiance and a hail of
stones. La Fayette gave the order to fire; fifty people were killed, and
the rest fled. The 'massacre of the Champ-de-Mars' was followed by
a wave of arrests of prominent radicals, and those who escaped
prudently went into hiding. It was a grim irony – the only military
offensive against the Parisian people during the entire Revolution
had been the work not of the king's soldiers, but of the revolutionaries themselves.

The spectre of republicanism, and the vigorous steps taken to
exorcize it, created a favourable atmosphere for compromise between
the moderates and the court. It was Marie Antoinette, encouraged by
the rapport established during the return from Varennes, who took
the initiative of opening negotiations with Barnave in the first days
of July. Barnave and the two other Feuillant leaders, Adrien Duport
and Alexandre de Lameth, responded with enthusiasm. A regular
correspondence was swiftly set up, which was to continue until the
following January. It was conducted with extreme secrecy. To avoid
detection, an intermediary was used – the comte de Jarjayes, a
devoted royalist and the husband of one of the queen's maids.
Jarjayes acted as a human letter-box; Marie Antoinette would write a
note to Barnave, seal it, and place it in the comte's pocket. Jarjayes
would then arrange a rendezvous with Barnave, who would take the
letter, read and reseal it, then replace it in Jarjayes's pocket. To
ensure his own handwriting was not recognized, Barnave dictated his
replies to Jarjayes, who passed them on to the queen.[2]

Barnave actually saw Marie Antoinette only rarely after the return
from Varennes. His colleagues Duport and Lameth probably had
several meetings with both the king and the queen during the summer
of 1791, but he himself was too closely watched by his enemies on
the Left to risk being seen entering the Tuileries. According to Mme
Campan, who stayed on as the queen's chief maid until the fall of the
monarchy, visits from Barnave only became possible after September,
when the guard placed on the palace was relaxed following Louis
XVI's acceptance of the constitution. Yet these remained perilous
affairs. The first had to be delayed after Barnave bumped into a

republican spy on his way into the Tuileries; since he had no way of letting those inside know what had happened, first Mme Campan, and then the king himself, waited for hours at the agreed rendezvous, an unlocked door at the side of the palace.[3]

The negotiations between Marie Antoinette and Barnave aimed at forging a common policy between the crown and the moderate revolutionaries. In this sense, Barnave was simply picking up the baton dropped by Mirabeau at the moment of his death. This was deeply ironic, since Barnave had hated Mirabeau, while Lameth had often been accused of poisoning him. Yet in less than six months the situation had changed dramatically. Having previously denounced Mirabeau for selling out to the court, these erstwhile left-wingers were now forced to adopt his policy. The Revolution had to be ended before it spun completely out of control.

The policy the Feuillants submitted to the queen aimed to curb the radicals, and restore stability to France, in three ways. The king should undertake to accept the constitution, suitably revised so as to give more power to the executive, when it was presented to him in a few months' time. On the diplomatic front, the queen should use all her influence with the emperor to persuade him to recognize the constitution, thus placing the Franco-Austrian alliance on a new, more durable basis. The princes and the *émigrés* should also be encouraged to return. By these last two measures in particular, Europe and the Revolution would be reconciled.

When Marie Antoinette's correspondence with Barnave was first discovered and published in 1912, many leading historians of the French Revolution refused to accept it as genuine. Barnave's partisans, in particular, were indignant at the slur these supposed secret dealings with the court cast on his revolutionary purity. The exhaustive handwriting expertise carried out in 1934, however, removes any doubt as to the letters' authenticity.[4] It is clear that in the months after Varennes, the rapid deterioration of the political situation forced Louis XVI and Marie Antoinette into an improbable alliance with the Feuillants in a last-ditch attempt to save the monarchy.

What remains mysterious is just how sincere the partnership was on both sides. Since the main negotiations took place between Marie Antoinette and Barnave, it is their relationship which has come under the closest scrutiny. At first sight, there is plentiful evidence that the queen acted in bad faith throughout. On 19 October, she wrote to Fersen:

> Have no fear, I am not joining the wild men; if I see or have dealings with some of them, it is only in order to make use of them, and they fill me with too much horror to think of ever going over to them.[5]

The previous August, in a letter to Mercy-Argenteau, she had expressed her contempt for the constitution's supporters. 'Our only plan is lull them and inspire them with confidence, the better to confound them afterwards.'[6] Yet her feelings towards the Feuillant leaders themselves, and especially towards Barnave, were both more complicated and more sympathetic. Another letter to Mercy, of 31 July, is proof of this:

> I have reason to be satisfied ... with Duport, Lameth and Barnave. I currently have a sort of correspondence with the last two which nobody, not even their friends, knows about. To do them justice, although they stick obstinately to their views, I have so far seen nothing in them other than great sincerity, forcefulness, and a real desire to restore good order and in consequence the royal authority.[7]

The only way of reconciling these varying opinions of Marie Antoinette's is to place them in chronological context. In July, fearful for her position and even her life after the disaster of Varennes, she had eagerly grasped Barnave's helping hand. Yet once the situation had stabilized and even improved after the Jacobins' split and the 'massacre of the Champ-de-Mars', she grew both more confident and more aware of the gulf that separated the Feuillants' political views from her own. While remaining personally impressed by the Feuillant leaders, and sentimentally attached to Barnave, she resolved to use their friendship to play for time and no more. As Georges Michon, whose 1924 study of Duport is still the best work on the Feuillants, puts it: 'If [the queen] felt personal sympathy for the triumvirs, she never ceased to display an invincible distrust of the constitution.'[8] Or, in Marie Antoinette's own words to Mercy on 1 August: '[The triumvirs] have been useful to me, and still are; but however good their intentions, their ideas are far too extreme ever to suit us.'[9]

A further and probably decisive factor in the queen's disillusion with the Feuillants was the revelation, as summer wore into autumn, of their increasing powerlessness in the Assembly. The basis of the bargain was that the triumvirs would use their eloquence and resources to forge a solid parliamentary majority for the crown and ensure a revision of the constitution in a monarchical direction. Yet the Feuillants themselves were divided by personal and political rivalries. Despite their temporary display of unity in the face of the republican threat, the triumvirs and La Fayette always loathed one another. There were also differences of principle: La Fayette supported the constitution in its entirety, while the triumvirs wanted it modified. Worse, the solid bloc of 250 royalist deputies whose votes were essential to a constitutional revision were even more suspicious of the moderates than the radicals. Ultimately, they preferred the prospect of anarchy to a monarchy that fell short of their ideals. That September, in an act which coined the eloquent phrase *la politique du pire*, they joined with the Jacobins in voting down revision.

For the time being, and not yet aware of the Feuillants' weaknesses, Marie Antoinette lent their policies her support. The first task, which only she was in a position to achieve, was to broker an understanding between her brother Leopold and the triumvirs. Her indispensable counsellor in this, as always, was Mercy-Argenteau, who was far more accessible in Brussels than Leopold was in Vienna. Mercy, for his part, initiated two of his own informants in Paris into the secret. These were the comte de la Marck and Jean-Joachim Pellenc, respectively Mirabeau's closest friend and his former secretary. Their influence underlined the continuity between Mirabeau's earlier rapprochment with the court, in which Mercy himself had been instrumental, and the policy to which the Feuillants now turned.

The queen understandably felt that Mercy, who had never formally given up his embassy, would be more useful to her in Paris than in Brussels, and she put considerable pressure on him to return, writing to him on 29 July:

> The position in which I find myself makes me urgently desire your presence at Paris ... I fear I may make mistakes along the path to be taken; I am in need of your advice, of your attachment to me, and of your presence here.[10]

Yet Mercy obstinately refused to leave Brussels. His motives remain mysterious, but his cold replies to the pleas from all sides for his return give an impression that all that really mattered to him in this terrible crisis was his own safety and that of his possessions. On 6 July, he wrote to his embassy secretary, Blumendorff:

> It is possible, even probable, that all foreign missions [in Paris] will be withdrawn . . . in that case I shall have to smuggle out my furniture and even my wine-cellar; you will have to get permission for a lot of crates to leave the country.[11]

Replying to his close friend the banker Laborde, who had begged him at Marie Antoinette's behest to return 'for the good of France, the sake of [the queen] and that of the empire you represent', he let slip just how frightened he had been by the violence he had witnessed in 1789 and 1790:

> The blackening and distortion of my conduct [as ambassador] has exposed me to much unpleasantness; I have felt it necessary to avoid situations where this might recur. I have protected myself by breaking off after 10 October [1790, the date he left Paris for Belgium] all those contacts which had become unprofitable to the cause and dangerous for myself. I am thus without influence in the very place where it will be most necessary to profit from the information that may be revealed to me. I am happy to spread abroad anything that could smooth the path of conciliation. It is the wisdom of the leaders of the French Revolution that must furnish the means for this by searching for a common interest founded neither on menaces . . . nor on the principle that the fate [of other nations] should depend on the unreserved adoption of new principles of liberty and equality whose advantages can only be proved by time and experience . . .[12]

The sound of Mercy washing his hands of Marie Antoinette is almost audible. From this point on, his attitude to French affairs began noticeably to harden. On 13 July he wrote to Blumendorff that 'any compromise with the Assembly would be harmful'.[13] One suspects that the reasons behind this stance were personal as well as political; the more hopeless the situation in Paris could be made to appear, the less chance there was that he would be sent back there to bail out the royal family.

With or without Mercy-Argenteau in Paris, the effort to reconcile the triumvirs with the emperor still had to be made. On 30 July, Marie Antoinette, at the triumvirs' dictation, wrote a long letter to Leopold offering a renewal of the Franco-Austrian alliance in exchange for his recognition of the completed constitution. At the same time she informed Mercy that a secret emissary from the Feuillant leaders, the abbé Louis, would soon be arriving in Brussels on his way to secure the agreement to the scheme of the emperor in Vienna and perhaps even Louis XVI's brothers in Coblenz. She begged the ambassador, whatever he really thought of the proposal, at least to make an appearance of taking it seriously. The abbé Louis did indeed turn up in Brussels in the first days of August, but returned to Paris discouraged, without having visited Vienna or Coblenz.[14]

Leopold's response to his sister came in the form of two letters written within days of each other, on 17 and 20 August. Although formally addressed to Marie Antoinette, they were really intended for the triumvirs, and set out clearly his terms for cooperation. Belying his Machiavellian reputation, these were eminently frank and sensible. The emperor welcomed the rapprochement between the Feuillants and the court, but warned the former that he would judge them on their actions rather than their words. The litmus test had to be the nature of the finished constitution. Leopold announced that he would only recognize it, and regard his brother-in-law's acceptance of it as genuine, in so far as it met the criticisms that Louis XVI had raised in the last unquestionably free expression of his will, the declaration he had left behind on the night of his escape. A viable settlement, the emperor pointed out,

> can only tend to the maintenance of the most essential aspects of monarchical government, the inviolability, personal safety and dignity of the king and his family, his due influence on the government and the execution of those laws which assure this to him; and finally a system compatible with a proper chain of authority and the upholding of public order.[15]

Without these guarantees, Leopold warned, the constitution would not be worth the paper it was written on.

The critical issue thus became the precise terms of the constitution; on these depended not only the king and queen's support for the Feuillants' domestic policy, but that of Austria for their foreign policy. It was here that the Feuillants' failure became most apparent. The final version of the constitution was to be drawn up by the Assembly's constitutional committee synthesizing all the diverse laws voted over the previous two years into a draft for the deputies to vote on. This committee had substantial discretionary powers to modify or even omit altogether individual decrees that were not to its taste, and since the Feuillants controlled the committee, this gave them a significant chance to remodel the constitution in a conservative sense. Yet all the major proposals of the constitutional committee foundered in the Assembly on the rock formed by the unholy alliance of the extreme Right and the extreme Left. In the final constitutional debates of August 1791, the moderates gained only a few successes. The most important was the reclassification of the Civil Constitution of the Clergy, as well as the abolition of the king's prerogative of mercy, as ordinary laws, which could be repealed in the normal course of events, and not constitutional laws, which could only be altered after ten years. A new royal bodyguard of 1,200 infantry and 600 cavalry was established, and a declaration inserted that Louis XVI was the 'hereditary representative of the nation' rather than merely its 'first functionary'. Yet none of this came near fulfilling the hopes for constitutional revision the Tuileries had originally held out. By mid-August it was clear that the Feuillants could not fulfil the promises they had made to Marie Antoinette.

The swift and ignominious failure of the Feuillants has made it difficult to gauge their wider aims. They had very little time to formulate their policy -- from late June to early August 1791 -- and did so in deep secrecy. Neither Barnave nor Duport ever set down in detail what their ultimate goals that summer had been. These can only be pieced together from the fragmentary glimpses afforded by their correspondence with Marie Antoinette, from what the queen relayed to Mercy-Argenteau, and the insights provided by Mercy's own informants and other eye-witnesses. It is probable, however, that the triumvirs' constitutional project was far more ambitious than the meagre results they actually achieved, and included the resurrection of the absolute veto, an equal share for the king in the framing of legislation, the nomination of judges by the crown, and the establishment of a bicameral legislature.

The fact that the Feuillants rallied to this type of programme is highly significant. It was precisely the same as that which the *monarchiens* had openly championed, and Mirabeau had supported from late 1789 until his death, as the irreducible minimum necessary to achieve a stable settlement of the Revolution. It is highly debatable whether this project for an 'English-style' monarchy in France had any more chance of success in August 1791 than it had had the previous February or in September 1789. Its tragedy was that throughout the Revolution, its supporters never rallied at the right moment and in sufficient numbers. The various groups of moderates whose early adhesion to it *en bloc* would have ensured its success, only came over to it slowly and at different junctures, so that it was never able to gain a secure majority in the Assembly.

The most characteristic feature of this 'Anglo-Saxon' constitutional model was the bicameral legislature, the famous *deux-chambres*. There is evidence that the Feuillants tried hard to establish this in the summer of 1791. The plan raised its head above the parapet twice between August and September, once openly and once in disguise. In one of the Assembly's most important constitutional debates, on 8 August, the old *monarchien* Malouet forcefully pointed out the disadvantages of a one-chamber legislature, and begged his colleagues to reconsider their support for it. According to Malouet's own memoirs, this was in fact a ploy concocted by himself, Barnave and the Feuillant leaders. Malouet offered to get up and attack the whole of the draft constitution, permitting the Feuillants to pose as its defenders, while drawing the fire of the Jacobins towards himself. Barnave's colleague le Chapelier would then rise, and under the guise of answering some of Malouet's objections, propose key modifications that would weaken the legislature and strengthen the royal authority. This seems a rather transparent manoeuvre, and it is difficult to imagine the Assembly being duped by it. As it was, it was never even put to the test; halfway through Malouet's speech, alarmed by the hostility it was provoking from the Left, le Chapelier cut short the stratagem by jumping up and denouncing Malouet himself. As the session descended into chaos, Malouet's last plea for the two chambers was barely heard.[16]

The Feuillants' second attempt to establish the principle of a second chamber was stealthier. It came during the debate over how, if at all, the constitution was to be revised in the future. When a proposal was voted that this should be effected by a special assembly, Duport, Barnave and their allies saw in this a means of promoting a bicameral legislature. The Assembly's constitutional committee, which they dominated, decreed that the mooted special assembly should be elected at the same time as the deputies to the ordinary legislature, but on a separate list, thus creating the nucleus of a second chamber. Frochot, the deputy who had first proposed a special assembly, later claimed that he protested to Duport about this distortion, observing that it seemed to be an attempt to impose two chambers by stealth. 'So?' Duport allegedly replied. 'And what if that is our intention?' Yet in the end a majority of the deputies rebelled against the plan, and so limited the powers of the proposed special assembly that it could never develop into a second chamber.[17]

By the summer of 1791, the attempt to end the Revolution by reviving the idea of an 'English-style' monarchy was probably doomed before it began. Yet one ingredient for its success was always needed over and above the support of the Assembly: the acquiescence of the king and queen themselves. What Louis XVI and Marie Antoinette actually thought about the plan for a constitutional monarchy based on a bicameral legislature remains mysterious. Of all the blueprints for a constitutional monarchy, the 'two-chambers' project had the best chance of rallying support from across the political spectrum. It was ultimately the preferred option of all the most serious and influential moderate politicians: Malouet, Mounier, Clermont-Tonnerre, Duport, Barnave, Lameth and probably Mirabeau. The attitude of the king and queen towards this particular scheme is thus a crucial test of their willingness to accept constitutional monarchy in general.

There was considerable public speculation at the time as to whether the royal couple favoured the 'two chambers'. Certainly some of their friends, like the conservative *monarchien* Montlosier, were genuinely convinced they did.[18] The *émigrés* at Coblenz spared no effort, in their newspapers and pamphlets, to give the same impression, but for a different reason. In intransigent royalist circles, the epithet *deux-chambres* had by 1791 become a convenient shorthand for describing anybody with even mildly constitutionalist tendencies, and thus damning them as prepared to bargain away the most sacred rights of the nobility and clergy. Applying the term to Louis XVI and Marie Antoinette was thus one more attempt by the *émigrés* to discredit them and advance the claims of Provence and Artois.

It is easier to trace the queen's views on the subject than the king's. This is because much of Marie Antoinette's most intimate political correspondence, with Leopold, Mercy and Fersen, has survived, whereas almost none of Louis's has. As these letters make plain, throughout July 1791 the queen was favourably impressed by the triumvirs and was genuinely prepared to give their policy a chance. However, her attitude quickly hardened. The strongest evidence that the triumvirs did indeed favour the 'two chambers', and that Marie Antoinette unambiguously rejected it, comes in her letter to Mercy of 1 August. In it, she describes a memorandum written by the Feuillant leaders, which has not survived. 'After some sensible reflections on the present situation,' she wrote, 'it sets out the whole system of the two chambers . . . As the king must never, for the good of the country, adopt the two-chambers scheme, the rest of the document seems irrelevant to me.'[19]

The almost complete silence of Louis XVI during this period once again raises the question of how much he approved, or even knew, of Marie Antoinette's negotiations with the Feuillants and with Austria. Yet the memoirs of the queen's maid Mme Campan and of the *monarchien* politician Montlosier present the king as involved in the discussions with the triumvirs.[20] After Varennes, it had become even more vital that no direct link should exist between the king and a secret policy that, if discovered, could destroy him. In any case, in negotiations with the Habsburgs it obviously made sense for Marie Antoinette to play a pivotal part. The Feuillants themselves showed their recognition of this by their repeated stress on the queen's vital intermediary role between themselves and the emperor.

The pressures of playing a leading role placed immense strain on Marie Antoinette, and this is palpable in her most personal correspondence of all, that with Fersen. She found the sheer physical effort of writing for hours at her desk, which she had never had to do before, exhausting. She wrote on 7 December 1791:

I am in better shape than I would have expected, given the
prodigious exhaustion of spirit which comes from going out so
little; I don't have a moment to myself, between all the people I
have to see, writing, and the time I spend with my children.
This last, which is not the least, is my only solace.[21]

Even more wearing was the constant duplicity made necessary by her
dealings with politicians whose views and policies she secretly
despised. Only to Fersen did she reveal how much this cost her, and
how much she longed one day to throw off her mask and exact
revenge for her humiliation:

> You must understand . . . my position, and the part I am forced
> to act every day; sometimes I lose the thread myself and find it
> difficult to believe that it is really me speaking; but what can
> one do? All this is necessary, and believe me, we would be
> much worse off than we are now, if I hadn't immediately
> adopted this policy; at least this way we gain time, and that is
> all we need. What joy if one day I could triumph enough to
> show all these rogues that I was never their dupe![22]

None of these intrigues could postpone the moment of truth that
the king had to face in September – whether or not, now that
revision had failed, to accept the constitution when it was presented
to him. The powers that the final draft accorded the crown fell well
short of the minimum Louis XVI thought necessary for effective
government. The king was to appoint ministers, although they were
forbidden to sit in the legislature, he was assigned a civil list of 25
million livres per annum, and his right to command the armed forces
and to conduct foreign policy was recognized. On the other hand,
his veto over decrees by the Assembly remained suspensive rather
than absolute, to last for two legislatures only, and while he had the
power to declare war and draw up peace treaties, these actions were
only valid if ratified by the legislature. Above all, the king was given
no rights of initiating legislation, which became the exclusive prerogative of the Assembly. At a stroke, Louis XVI was deprived of the
attribute that in his eyes defined monarchy – the active making of
laws. His powers were thus far more limited than those of the most
prominent constitutional monarch of the time, George III of England.
Small wonder that in a letter to Breteuil that December Louis referred

to 'the absurd and detestable constitution which gives me less power than the king of Poland used to have'.[23]

Under these circumstances, the king was faced with an acute dilemma. If he were true to himself, he would refuse to swear allegiance to the constitution. This would have the merit of honesty, but would unquestionably provoke civil war, if not the immediate imprisonment or murder of the royal family by the Parisians. If he felt forced to accept it, he could do so in one of two ways. Without approving it in his heart, he could attempt to carry out faithfully his oath to observe it, hoping that in time enough of his fellow citizens would come to share his views to enable it to be revised as he wished. The other, more dangerous path, was to swear publicly to uphold the constitution, but privately to do everything possible to overthrow it by means of internal counter-revolution or foreign invasion.

On 14 September, Louis XVI finally took the oath to the constitution. He endured the humiliation of swearing to uphold it on his feet and bareheaded, in front of an assembly of seated deputies with their hats firmly on their heads. It was a bitter reversal of the roles at the Estates General just two years before. The sole deputy with the courage to remove his hat and stand while the king took the oath was Malouet. The queen watched the ceremony from a box. As soon as the couple returned to the Tuileries, the king threw himself into an armchair and pressed a handkerchief to his eyes. 'All is lost!' he cried. 'Ah, Madame, that you should have witnessed this humiliation! That you should have come to France to see . . .'[24] The rest of his words were choked by sobs.

The policy that emerged from this traumatic experience was, to say the least, disingenuous. While publicly proclaiming their fidelity to the constitution in order to reassure the French people, behind the scenes the king and queen mounted a concerted effort to persuade the European Powers to exert diplomatic pressure on France, backed by the threat of military force. The Powers should make two central demands – that the Assembly guarantee to respect previous French treaty obligations, and that the royal family should be set at liberty. Their instrument would be an 'armed congress' of the states most concerned, supported by troops, which would meet at a convenient location near the French border such as Aix-la-Chapelle. With his subjects' confidence bolstered by his oath to the constitution, Louis XVI would act as a mediator between the Assembly and the armed congress, enabling him both to regain his freedom and to recover his authority. As Marie Antoinette put it to Mercy-Argenteau on 28 September:

> If . . . the Powers find a swift and imposing way of speaking to us and demanding what they have a right to demand in the name of the security and equilibrium of Europe, we will regain confidence. The fear of an external force, which would however speak only the language of reason and that of the rights of all sovereigns, would soften the first shock, and could lead [the rebels] to ask the king to act as a mediator, which is the only role suitable for him, as much because of the love he bears for his people, as because in this way he will also be able to reimpose his authority on the *émigré* factions who, by the tone they are adopting and which will redouble if they play any part in the restoration of order, will plunge the king into another form of slavery . . . This is why I continue to think that a congress at Aix-la-Chapelle of all the Powers with an interest in the survival of the French monarchy, is the only real way to help us.[25]

The idea of a congress had been in circulation for some time before Louis XVI and Marie Antoinette adopted it. Bombelles claimed that it had first germinated in Turin in 1790, in discussions held in Artois's council.[26] Its first formal endorsement, however, came in a circular to all Austrian diplomatic representatives written by Kaunitz just after Varennes, on 17 July 1791.[27] Here, the old chancellor argued that the time was fast approching when the European Powers would have to unite against the common menace presented by revolutionary France. His preferred option was a congress, but already he foresaw that this might quickly give way to war.

The failure of the congress project, and the immense obstacles it faced from the beginning, have led most historians to dismiss it as an unworkable chimera from the start. According to Albert Sorel, the royal couple's plan was 'a prisoners' dream, troubled and incoherent, like the dreams of the sick; a fantastical conceit a hundred times abandoned because reason condemned it, and a hundred times resumed because it haunted the imagination'.[28] This is a colourful but unfair description. The odds may have been stacked against it from the beginning, but this does not mean the idea of a congress in itself was absurd and irrational. As a means of rescuing the French royal family, it was inadequate, but on a wider level it was a genuine attempt to resolve the issues raised by the Revolution and reconcile them with international law. Even Marie Antoinette, in the midst of her struggles in Paris, grasped this wider picture. On 19 October she wrote to Mercy-Argenteau:

> In the constitutional articles accepted by the king, there is one which certainly deals with the ratification of treaties; but, apart from the fact that I have no idea whether the Powers would wish to consent to this, what guarantee is currently given to previous treaties? This seems to me a point of such importance for the whole equilibrium of Europe, that the Powers must come together to discuss it.[29]

It was Kaunitz, in his circular of July 1791, who laid most stress on the congress as an an instrument of international law. In the face of the French threat, the chancellor was adamant that this must be defended, and the 'contagion' of revolutionary principles prevented from spreading. Yet Kaunitz was deeply reluctant to meddle in France's internal affairs. For him, the crucial point was that France should respect her international obligations, and this was why he advocated the congress. What was novel about his idea was that such a congress should be called not to make peace after a war, but beforehand to prevent one. It was to take twenty years of bloodshed before this proposal was revived, when the Congress of Vienna assembled in 1814 and the revolutionary wars finally came to an end. By this time Kaunitz was long dead, but an echo of his circular can be discerned in the agreement reached at Vienna that future European disputes should be resolved by regular congresses of the Powers.

Only the most intricate sophistry could have reconciled working for an armed congress with sincere acceptance of the constitution. How did the royal couple justify their double policy? The queen's attitude was straightforward. To her, the oath to the constitution was an outrage extracted under duress, and in no way binding. In a letter to Mercy of 26 August, just before Louis XVI took the oath, she made this view explicit:

> It is impossible, given the position here, for the king to refuse the oath. Believe me that this is the truth, since it is I who am telling you this. You have enough experience of me to know that I would prefer a nobler and more courageous path; but there is no point in courting certain destruction. Our only hope thus lies in the foreign Powers.[30]

The king's attitude was more complex. He set it out at length in a long memorandum to his brothers in September 1791, explaining his reasons for accepting the constitution. All historians acccept the document as genuine. It is a highly intelligent analysis, displaying an insight into the nature of the Revolution far superior to that shown by the queen and indeed by most contemporaries across the political spectrum. It is also a moving plea to the *émigrés* not to unleash the horrors of war: 'I know how much the nobility and clergy have suffered from the Revolution. . . . I too have suffered; but I sense that I have the courage to suffer yet more, in order to spare my people my own misfortunes.'[31]

To judge by this memorandum, Louis XVI genuinely intended to uphold the constitution. The king recognized that the mood of the country was firmly in favour of it, and that this state of affairs could only be changed over time and by experience: 'One cannot govern a nation against its will. This maxim is equally true at Constantinople as in a republic; opinion in our nation currently favours the rights of man, as absurd as these are.' There was no talk of forcing change by an armed congress; on the contrary, Louis argued that progress could only be achieved by convincing the people of the constitution's unworkability, and that this could only be done if he observed it scrupulously. On the sincerity of his oath, he was unambiguous:

> I have therefore decided to use the only course remaining to me, the joining of my will to the principles of the constitution. I am aware of all the difficulties, even the impossibility, of thus governing a great nation; but opposing it would have brought about a war that I wished to avoid, and would have prevented the people from fairly judging the constitution, because they

would only have seen that I was against it. In adopting its principles and executing them in good faith, [I will make the people] see the true cause of its misfortunes; public opinion will change; and since without this change new convulsions will be inevitable, I will have more chance of achieving a better state of things by my acceptance than by my refusal.[32]

The key difference between Louis XVI's policy as spelt out here, and that of Marie Antoinette, is the king's insistence that the French people's attachment to the constitution can only be changed by peaceful persuasion, not threats from abroad. The idea of the armed congress thus did not originate with Louis XVI. It is probable, however, that in the two months after his acceptance of the constitution he yielded to Marie Antoinette's forceful urging of the idea. As he had done when the plan for escaping from Paris was first put to him, he hesitated at first, then bowed to his wife's point of view.

Yet Louis also had to reconcile in his own mind his espousal of the armed congress with his oath to the constitution. Here, there were precedents for him to follow. In the past, the king had often inclined to the convenient fiction that the letter of his engagements was more important than their spirit. This was his way of squaring his conscience when he knew he had done something less than honourable; uneasy with the wider morality of his action, he took refuge in the small print. A notable example of this had been his pretence in May 1776 that his secret subsidy to the American rebels, which significantly accelerated the War of Independence, did not violate his treaty commitments to England. In exactly the same way, one can see him persuading himself that the concept of an armed congress, based not on actual force but merely the menace of it, could with a little stretching fit this definition of peaceful persuasion. For Louis XVI, one suspects, the distinction between threatening war and actually declaring it was all-important, even though it was essentially specious.

The most telling evidence that the king and queen had identical attitudes to the constitution and the armed congress comes from a well-known source, though up until now one ignored by historians. The standard text of Louis XVI's memorandum to his brothers is the copy in Mercy-Argenteau's papers in the State Archives in

Vienna. It has never been pointed out, however, that the only reason the document is there is because Marie Antoinette herself sent it to Mercy, enclosed with her letter to him of 28 September 1791.[33] If the queen had really been carrying on a secret policy at odds with the king's, how could she conceivably have sent to Mercy, for transmission to Vienna, the memorandum from her husband that would have made her own duplicity clear? Either she was monumentally stupid, in which case she can hardly have been the Machiavellian intriguer depicted by her critics, or she genuinely saw no contradiction between her husband's views and her own. The covering letter she sent with Louis's memorandum provides overwhelming evidence for believing the latter. Justifying the king's acceptance of the constitution, she paraphrases his words exactly:

> In any case, it was essential to appear to join in good faith with the people. If public opinion does not change, no human power can govern [France] in a contrary spirit. This reasoning is developed further in a memorandum that the king has just sent to the princes, and of which I am sending you a copy.[34]

The queen was also at one with her husband in her attitude to the prospect of war. At this stage, she viewed this with just as much horror as the king. This is clear from her letter to Leopold of 26 November:

> No, I am far from thinking of violent means. If we adopt violence, we shall perish by violence; that is the theme of all my letters, and this is why I insist so strongly on a congress; this is why I have always said that we must above all win over that class of people which is so numerous, which has up to now been so afraid, but which remains friendly to order and to monarchy, and whose horror of civil war and of the bloodthirsty republicans will finally give it the courage and unity it currently lacks.[35]

While his wife worked day and night for the armed congress, the king remained in the shadows. Once again, depression may have been a factor. The queen herself hinted at this to Mercy, in a letter of 16 August 1791 which echoes her comments back in 1788: 'You know the person I have to deal with; the moment one thinks one has persuaded him, a word, an argument, makes him change his mind without his even realizing it. It is for this reason that a thousand things simply cannot be attempted.'[36]

The queen's assertions are confirmed by other witnesses. On 28 September, Mirabeau's old friend la Marck, who continued to advise Marie Antoinette informally, sent Mercy a remarkable letter analysing Louis's state of mind. La Marck admitted that there was 'a host of areas in which he slipped away from the queen'.[37] However, he described this less in terms of Louis actively pursuing a separate policy than of a settled weakness and indecision that made his actions maddeningly inconsistent. The only solution la Marck saw was for the queen to become the undisputed centre of government, relying on the foreign minister Montmorin, who had the king's confidence, to control him on a day-to-day basis. La Marck's conclusion was damning:

As long as the queen is not the focus of policy, is not seconded by a capable minister, and is not aided where the king is concerned by somebody faithful with whom he has acquired the habit of feeling at ease, we can only expect great mistakes and a thousand dangers, because we have to admit that the king is incapable of ruling [underlined in the original] . . .[38]

This verdict may seem harsh, but it is echoed by other comments from those close to Louis XVI. In January 1791, Montmorin himself had given la Marck a vivid glimpse of the king's disassociated state, lamenting that when Louis 'spoke to him about his affairs and position, it seemed as if he were talking . . . about matters concerning the emperor of China'.[39]

This picture of a completely inert monarch does need some qualification. That September, just a few weeks after Marie Antoinette was lamenting his weaknesses to Mercy, the king was able to compose his long, closely reasoned and eloquent memorandum to his brothers. His absence from the records at this point may well be a result as much of his working methods as of his psychological state. He seems to have formulated his policy through writing detailed memoranda, sometimes addressed to others, sometimes for himself alone. He left the execution of his ideas to his wife. This routine comes across in a letter from the queen to Fersen of 25 November, enclosing instructions for Breteuil:

> Here is a note for the baron; it is an extract from a long memorandum that the king has written to account to himself for everything he has done recently. This paper is very well put together; but, as well as the fact that it contains some unnecessary arguments, it would have taken far too long to encode.[40]

The memorandum itself does not survive, but the enclosed extract does, and gives a revealing insight into the king's mind at this juncture. Significantly, Louis XVI talks indiscriminately of abiding by the constitution and promoting the armed congress; just like his wife, he clearly saw no contradiction between the two. 'A congress', he writes, 'would achieve the desired aim.' Yet a few paragraphs later he also writes:

> The king neither can nor should go back unilaterally on what has been done; the majority of the nation must desire this or be forced to it by circumstances, and in this case, [the king] must acquire confidence and popularity by acting according to the constitution; if he executes its provisions literally, all its vices will become obvious.[41]

By the end of November, the king's energies had revived. He was probably responding to the important political changes of the autumn. Its work completed with Louis's acceptance of the constitution, the Constituent Assembly disbanded, and elections were held for a new Legislative Assembly, which first met on 1 October. The new Assembly was very different from the old. This was a result of a 'self-denying ordinance' carried the previous May, which ruled that deputies to the Constituent Assembly should be ineligible to stand for the legislative. The prime mover of this proposal was Robespierre, who saw it as a means of depriving his moderate opponents in the Assembly of their seats and therefore their platform. The fact that it barred Robespierre himself from seeking re-election did not bother him unduly, since for the moment he was content to take up the post, which he had just been offered, of attorney-general to the new criminal tribunal of Paris.

At a stroke, the 'self-denying ordinance' robbed all those deputies who had helped shape the Revolution and now wished to control it, from Malouet to Barnave, of their authority. They stayed in Paris to help lead their party, but henceforth without formal political position. Initially, this did not seem vitally important; of the 745 new deputies, 345 joined the Feuillants. Yet no politicians of stature emerged from their ranks to succeed the triumvirs. In addition, the Feuillant Club itself, with its formal proceedings and discouragement of spectators, failed to capture public attention. By December, the moderates' influence had dramatically declined.

Their place was taken by the Jacobins. Although only 135 of the new deputies joined the Jacobin Club, they soon acquired a dominant political position. The club itself was one factor, its democratic ethos and packed meetings making it a focus for public debate in a way the Feuillants' never was. Another was the presence among the new Jacobin deputies of a handful of extraordinarily eloquent orators, soon dubbed the Girondins because three of them – Vergniaud, Gensonné and Guadet – came from the Gironde in south-west France. The name was not strictly accurate, since several members of the group came from elsewhere, while its leader, Jacques-Pierre Brissot, had been born in Chartres, imprisoned in Paris for sedition and for debt in London, and written hack journalism all over Europe. Finally, a smaller group soon emerged on the extreme wing of the Jacobins. It was known as the Mountain, because its deputies sat on the high seats on the left of the assembly, and it owed its allegiance to Robespierre.

From the start of the Legislative Assembly, the Girondins seized the initiative. As passionate supporters of the Revolution, they were determined to complete its work. This led them inevitably into a confrontation with the king. They were convinced that Louis's acceptance of the constitution was insincere, and although they never had proof of his secret policy, they could make a shrewd guess at its outlines. They therefore decided to smoke him out and force him to declare himself openly for or against the Revolution. In the first case, he would cease to be an obstacle for them, and in the second, he could be removed and replaced either by a more malleable monarch or by a republic. With unerring precision, they aimed at the three issues closest to his heart – religion, the *émigrés* and foreign policy.

The first battle was fought over the *émigrés*. On 14 October, in a shrewdly calculated move, the king issued a proclamation exhorting them to return and help him restore stability to France, and followed it up two days later with a similar letter to his brothers. This was the first fruit of his policy of regaining popularity by appearing faithful to the constitution, and it worked. The radicals were caught unprepared, and forced on to the defensive. But they soon struck back. A week later Brissot proposed to the assembly that the property of leading *émigrés* should be confiscated. The result, after heated debates, was the passage of a draconian decree on 9 November. The *émigrés* assembled on the frontier were declared suspect of conspiracy against France; those who had not returned by 1 January 1792 were liable to the death penalty and the sequestration of all their goods. Louis could not possibly support this, and on 11 November he defied the Assembly and vetoed the decree. The attempt to make the constitution work had lasted exactly two months.

The Girondins now moved to the religious question. The flashpoint here was the Civil Constitution of the Clergy, whose divisive provisions were leading to violence in many areas of France. This was worst in Avignon, which had been for centuries a papal enclave ruled from Rome. From the beginning of the Revolution, the territory had been completely split between those who demanded annexation to France and their opponents who remained loyal to the Pope. On 13 September, the Assembly unilaterally ended papal rule and united Avignon with France. The majority of Avignon's inhabitants wished to become French, it argued, and this overrode the rights and precedents on which papal sovereignty was based. The will of the people was the supreme law. If applied universally, this doctrine would undermine the foundations of every monarchy in Europe, and the Powers duly took note.

The sovereignty of Avignon, however, was inseparably linked to the religious issue. Its temporal ruler, the Pope, had openly rejected the Civil Constitution of the Clergy, and many priests throughout France had followed his example. In Avignon itself, this combustible mix of the sacred and the secular soon exploded in a bloody civil war. A few weeks after the annexation, the papal supporters lynched a pro-French municipal official. The annexationists' response was savage. Led by the aptly named Jourdan Coupe-Tête – Jourdan the Beheader – on 15 and 16 October they took over a tower in the papal palace where a group of their opponents had been imprisoned, and threw sixty-five to their deaths below.

To the Girondins in Paris, the culprits were not Jourdan and his band of murderers, but the Pope and his clerical allies. They demanded that all those priests who had refused to swear loyalty to the civil constitution should take a new civic oath. If they did not, they would be declared suspect and put under surveillance. On 29 November, these proposals regarding the 'refractory clergy', as they became known, were passed by the Assembly and sent to the king for approval. After agonizing for three weeks, Louis again used his veto.

The situation was now a stalemate. If Louis XVI chose to maintain his veto, the decrees on the *émigrés* and the refractory clergy were now blocked for two legislatures. On the other hand, having been forced to use the veto, the king was now isolated as never before. In this tense atmosphere, the Girondins moved in for the kill. The fateful method chosen was to embroil France with her neighbours. The issue, once again, was the *émigrés*. The frontal assault on them had failed, but a flank attack could be mounted, aimed not at the *émigrés* directly but at the Rhineland principalities that were sheltering them. This would force the king to take sides, either for France and the Revolution, or for foreign Powers and the counter-revolution. On 29 November, the same day that the Assembly passed the decree on refractory priests, a deputation was sent to the king. It demanded that he summon the electors of Mainz and Trier immediately to expel the armed *émigrés* gathered in their lands.

Louis's response to this offers further proof that by late autumn 1791 he had recovered his nerve. He saw that the Girondins had unwittingly played into his hands, and set out to call their bluff. He positively welcomed the removal of the *émigrés*, whose provocations posed a constant danger to his own safety, from the border. By taking the lead in demanding this, he could also regain some of the popularity he had lost through using the veto. On 14 December, he went to the Assembly himself and announced that he had issued an ultimatum to the Elector of Trier to disperse the *émigrés* he was harbouring by 15 January 1792. If the elector did not, he would be treated as an enemy of France. The Assembly's response was extraordinary. A storm of applause erupted from the deputies, mingled with cries of 'Long live the king of the French!', and went on for several minutes. Only the extreme Left refused to join in. The king had scored a personal triumph.[42]

The electors' response to the ultimatum was no less gratifying. Thoroughly alarmed at the prospect of a French invasion, they moved swiftly to comply. The *émigrés* were hustled out of their dominions, and within a few weeks the Assembly had received convincing assurances of this. For the moment at least, the *émigré* menace to the king's policy had receded.

This success, however, did not deflect the royal couple from their central aim, which remained the armed congress. Yet neither the king nor the queen could hope, from their semi-captivity in the capital, to conduct the intricate international diplomacy that their plan required. Once again they cast their eyes across the border, and towards Breteuil.

Chapter Eleven

WINTER 1791: BRETEUIL, THE POWERS AND THE PRINCES

FOR SOME WEEKS AFTER VARENNES, Breteuil's movements are unclear. On hearing the shattering news, he appears to have followed the plan he had previously announced to Mercy-Argenteau, and proceeded to Aix-la-Chapelle. On 16 July, Mercy, who was at Spa taking the waters, wrote to the Archduchess Marie Christine, governor of the Austrian Netherlands, with news of the baron: 'M. de Breteuil, who is at Aix-la-Chapelle, is menacing me with a visit; but I shall be careful in my dealings with him to give no purchase to his scheming activity.'[1] With friends like this, Breteuil needed no enemies. It is all the more surprising that within a month he had set up house next to Mercy's own residence in Brussels. This was to be his headquarters for the following year.

As usual, a remarkable ménage soon gathered around the baron. In addition to his daughter, granddaughter and the ever-present Bishop of Pamiers, he was joined in October by Mirabeau's old friend la Marck, who had sensibly decided that Paris was now too hot to hold him. The household was completed by a truly exotic couple. This consisted of an immensely wealthy Scottish nabob, Quintin Craufurd, who had made his money as British resident in Manila, and his mistress Eléonore Sullivan. Originally an Italian circus acrobat, Eléonore had used her ample charms to win the favours of the Duke of Württemberg, her husband Sullivan, and now Craufurd. As if her life was not complicated enough, at this point she was also having an affair with Fersen.

Another significant figure who gravitated towards Breteuil in Brussels was the celebrated royalist journalist Rivarol, who had just emigrated. The only problem with the newcomer was that he tended to monopolize conversation at dinner. This annoying habit was later recalled in merciless detail by Chateaubriand, in the *Mémoires d'outre-tombe*. At the time, the young Chateaubriand had just returned from America to join Condé's army, and his weatherbeaten appearance contrasted strongly with the glittering guests at the baron's table:

> I and my brother were invited to dinner by the baron de Breteuil; there I met the baronne de Montmorency, who was then young and beautiful ... martyred bishops in cassocks of watered silk wearing golden crosses [no doubt including the Bishop of Pamiers] ... and Rivarol, whom I saw then for the only time in my life. He had not been introduced to me, and I was struck by the language of this man, who was declaiming alone and was being listened to as if he were an oracle ... I was leaving [for the army] after dinner, and my haversack was behind the door ... My attitude and my silence unsettled Rivarol; the baron de Breteuil, noticing his unease, came to his aid. 'Where has your brother the chevalier come from?' he asked my brother. 'From Niagara,' I replied. 'From the cataract!' exclaimed Rivarol. I was silent. He ventured the beginning of a question: 'Monsieur is going? ...' 'Where there is fighting,' I interrupted. Dinner swiftly came to an end.[2]

Breteuil soon had more to occupy him than his social life. The failure of the flight to Varennes had left his own political position ambiguous and insecure. The most pressing issue was the status of his *plein pouvoir*. The validity of these powers, and with them the whole thread of Louis XVI's secret diplomacy, had by now become even more confused. The essential cause of this was the successful escape of Monsieur, the comte de Provence, which had major implications for the leadership of the royalist movement. Monsieur now supplanted Artois as the senior member of the royal family at liberty, and Bombelles for one immediately anticipated that he would brook no rivalry from Breteuil. In the face of this threat, Bombelles argued that the baron should stick to his guns. 'You are the sole, the only legal minister of the king,' he wrote to him on 2 July. 'Grasp your *plein pouvoir* firmly in your hands. Let it be the plume [a reference to the famous white plume — *le panache blanc* — of Henri IV] to which all true Frenchmen will rally.'[3]

As the marquis had foreseen, Provence's onslaught was not long in coming. On that very same day, 2 July, he addressed a short, cold note to Breteuil, ordering him to cease immediately all his activities on behalf of Louis XVI:

> Having been informed directly, Monsieur, that the intention of my brother the king is that during his captivity I undertake, in conjunction with the comte d'Artois, everything that may bring about his freedom and the good of the state by negotiating to this end with the Powers for whose help we hope, I can no longer believe that His Majesty wishes to extend any further the commissions and powers he may previously have issued. You should therefore regard as obsolete those which are in your hands, and only employ your zeal in conformity with what we ourselves prescribe to you. Indeed, we would be most happy to hear your views on the policy you consider most appropriate. In consequence, if you have anything to impart to us, we invite you to present yourself at Coblenz, where we are journeying without delay. After this advice, there is no need to mention that you yourself will be responsible for any action which does not accord with our own.
>
> Rest assured of my sentiments towards you,
> Louis-Stanislas-Xavier.[4]

Breteuil's reaction to this letter remains a subject of controversy. It is often stated that he fraudulently went on using his *plein pouvoir* even after he knew that it was no longer valid. (No contemporary, however, ever claimed publicly that the document itself was a forgery.) Breteuil's first accuser was the ex-minister Bertrand de Molleville in his influential *Secret Memoirs of the History of the Last Year of Louis XVI's Reign*. Bertrand writes that on receipt of Provence's letter, Breteuil hurried after the princes on their way to Coblenz, and caught up with them at Bonn. 'He unhesitatingly agreed', claims Bertrand,

> that *his powers were revoked*; but he begged Monsieur to leave in his hands this document, which he considered the most hon-ourable reward possible for his long services and his most precious family heirloom, giving his word of honour neither to make use of it nor to take part in the affairs either of France or of the princes, unless Their Royal Highnesses wished it and in conformity with the orders they saw fit to give him. Neverthe-less he continued to use these same powers without the princes' knowledge . . .[5]

There is certainly evidence that Breteuil momentarily lost heart in the face of Provence's hostility. In a letter of 12 August, Mercy-Argenteau, now back in Brussels from Spa, informed Kaunitz of the princes' campaign against the baron. Rather than taking one side or the other, however, he distributed his contempt equally between both:

> A few days before I left Spa, M. de Breteuil came to see me. He only stayed 24 hours, and neither said nor proposed anything substantial in terms of politics. Monsieur and M. le comte d'Artois want to push him aside; the intrigue which follows these two princes everywhere they go will never cease to act against anything that could lead to a sensible policy, not that I think M. de Breteuil is better qualified for this task; in this respect all these persons are alike.[6]

It is clear that Breteuil did see the princes at Bonn, and that the *plein pouvoir* was discussed. Provence himself confirmed this, in a curious note to his sister Mme Elisabeth in the Tuileries. Mme Elisabeth was an intransigent royalist, far more sympathetic to the princes than Louis XVI and Marie Antoinette, and Provence confided much more to her than he did to the king and queen. In case of interception, Provence disguised his letter in medical terminology, of which he was fond. The queen became 'the patient', 'the remedies prescribed by the Faculty' his own policy, and Breteuil alternatively 'the quack' and 'l'Olivisianello', an obscure Italianism:

> I should say that I am by no means content with our patient. All her consultations with the doctors have been favourable, yet she persists in giving her confidence to the charlatans who have already almost killed her, and if she does not turn to proper doctors, her illness will soon become incurable. Two of your friends, passing a few days ago through a town not far from here, encountered, in the inn where they had dined, the first and the worst of the quacks. They were curious to talk to him, and asked him for news of the patient. *L'Olivisianello*, who was still stupefied by her last attack, virtually admitted his ignorance and told them that he was giving up his medical practice. My two honest friends, who while having no great opinion of him, do not regard him as a complete ass, spoke to him of the remedies prescribed by the Faculty in such cases. He appeared convinced of their efficacy. But I now hear that the rascal has rushed to get hold of the patient again and persuade her that these remedies are too violent for her condition and that they will finish her off . . .[7]

Provence obviously enjoyed writing this letter, though one doubts that his code would have fooled anybody had it fallen into the wrong hands. It does not specifically state, as Bertrand de Molleville does, that Breteuil recognized that his powers had been revoked. Yet it implies something to that effect, and Monsieur clearly wanted his sister to believe that the baron had acted in bad faith.

The truth is rather purer and not so simple. Part of it is contained in a letter from Bombelles to his friend and confidant the chevalier de Las Casas, the Spanish ambassador to Venice, of 15 August 1791. This reveals that in setting himself up as the king's sole representative, Provence had in fact only been acting on the basis of a verbal message from Louis transmitted to him by a third party – hardly solid grounds for such a sweeping arrogation of authority. Ironically, Bombelles added, three weeks later Provence had indeed received a written *plein pouvoir* from his brother. This was not, however, as wide-ranging as he wished. It also contained instructions that he should cooperate with Breteuil — but naturally Provence 'had not breathed a word about this'.[8]

The available evidence bears Bombelles out on almost every point. On 7 July Louis XVI did write out a *plein pouvoir* for his brothers, which was smuggled out of the Tuileries and transmitted to them via Fersen. It was carefully framed:

> I entrust myself completely to my brothers' affection for me, to the love and attachment they bear their country, to the friendship of the sovereign princes my relatives and allies, and to the honour and generosity of the other sovereigns, to decide together on the manner and means of the negotiations whose aim must be the restoration of order and tranquillity to my kingdom; but I think that any use of force should be subordinated to negotiations. I give full powers to my brothers to treat to this end with whoever they wish, and to make a choice of the people they wish to employ in this diplomacy.[9]

This *plein pouvoir* was an answer to a letter written by Fersen on 27 June and smuggled into the Tuileries. Fersen had bluntly asked whether Provence or Artois should now be given full powers, and whether the choice of using either Breteuil or Calonne as chief adviser should be left to them or laid down by the king and queen. Louis XVI's reply shows his continuing caution with regard to his brothers, especially the hot-headed Artois, in its limiting of their powers to negotiations only, and specifically in ruling out the use of force. The identity of his policy and Marie Antoinette's is underlined by the fact that it was she who sent her husband's note to Fersen, and enclosed with it a letter of her own. This amplified the royal couple's reticence towards Provence and Artois, and their determination not to equip them with sweeping powers: 'The king thinks that he neither can nor should issue an unlimited *plein pouvoir*; but he sends this paper written in invisible ink, to be given to his brothers.'[10]

Bombelles's account is wrong on only one point. The instruction to the brothers to collaborate with Breteuil, which answered Fersen's question, is not in the king's note, but in the queen's covering letter. It reads: 'It is important that the b. de Bret. links up with the king's brothers and whoever they choose for this important negotiation.'[11] In the light of this, Marie Antoinette was particularly infuriated by

Provence's letter to Breteuil. She made this clear to Fersen on 31 October. At the same time, she revealed that Mme Elisabeth's indulgence for the king's brothers was tearing the royal family apart:

> Monsieur's letter to the baron has astonished and revolted us, but we must have patience and not show our anger too openly at this point; I shall however make a copy and show it to my sister [Elisabeth]. I am curious to see how she will justify it, given the situation we are in. Our domestic life is a hell; with the best will in the world, one can't discuss anything. My sister is so indiscreet, surrounded by intriguers, and above all dominated by her brothers abroad, that we cannot speak to each other, otherwise we would be quarrelling all day.[12]

Most significant of all is the queen's postscript to her letter, which discloses the identity of the third party who had allegedly given Provence his verbal authority to act as the king's sole representative. It turns out, in fact, to have been none other than Fersen. What had clearly happened was that Fersen, at his meeting with Monsieur just after Varennes, had spoken some words which Monsieur had subsequently twisted into a plenipotential power. The terms in which the queen alerted Fersen to this leaves little doubt of Provence's mendacity:

> My sister has shown me a letter from M[onsieur], dated from Brussels . . . in which he says that it was you who informed him that the king wished to entrust him with everything during his captivity: I warn you of this, in case it is being said in your vicinity, since as for us, we know very well where things stand. Adieu.[13]

Bombelles's testimony thus accords with virtually all the known facts, and exposes the exaggerations and half-truths of the version spread by Monsieur himself and then by Bertrand de Molleville. Breteuil, who was obviously deeply discouraged, may well have told the princes he intended to retire, and there is nothing at this point to suggest that his desire was not genuine. The situation had clearly changed with Provence's escape, and this only strengthened the baron's desire to quit the stage. If he was going to withdraw, however, he would do so on his own terms, reserving the right to return should events take a different course.

The ultimate blame for all this confusion lies with the king himself. He had responded to Provence's successful flight by issuing him and Artois with a limited authorization to negotiate in his name with the Powers. However, for whatever reason, he did not formally disavow Breteuil. This may have been because he wished to keep the baron up his sleeve as a counterweight to his brothers. It may also have been because of pressure from Marie Antoinette, who distrusted Provence and Artois even more than he did, and was determined to keep her candidate Breteuil in play to protect her own interests. In this respect it is significant that it was the queen, not the king, who added the instruction to Fersen that Breteuil should work with the princes.

The controversy surrounding Breteuil's position after Varennes is thus mostly ascribable to Louis XVI's own vacillation. It is quite possible that for some months after his recapture the king was indeed angry with Breteuil. Montlosier recalls him expressing displeasure when Breteuil's name was mentioned, and snorting: 'He was the one who got me into that Varennes escapade.'[14] Yet by the end of 1791 the baron had regained his confidence. Proof of this comes in a letter Louis wrote to Frederick William II of Prussia on 3 December, discussing the armed congress. In this, the king specifically stated: 'only the baron de Breteuil is apprised of my plans, and Your Majesty can pass on to him whatever he wishes'.[15]

This letter is extremely important, since it is the only document in Louis XVI's hand other than the *plein pouvoir* itself that explicitly accredits Breteuil. Because its authenticity too has been questioned by the Girault de Coursacs, it seemed advisable to submit it to the same handwriting experts who had examined the *plein pouvoir*. This time, however, they could find no indications that the document was not genuine.[16] There is thus no reason to doubt that Breteuil continued to enjoy the confidence of Louis XVI as well as Marie Antoinette after the flight to Varennes.

There remains the perplexing question of why Louis XVI turned back to Breteuil only three months after sidelining him in favour of Provence and Artois. The answer must lie in the rapid deterioration of his relations with his brothers during that time. The reconciliation between the king and the princes was short-lived. Louis composed his memorandum on his acceptance of the constitution to his brothers in the course of September 1791. Even before he had finished it he received a defiant letter from them which, to add insult to injury, they had openly published before sending to him. Disingenuously arguing that the king was now completely captive in Paris and had no means whatever of communicating his true feelings to them, they proclaimed that none of his public statements could therefore be believed, and that whatever he might say to the contrary, his real wish was that his brothers should rescue him by force, with the aid of the European Powers. This was tantamount to exploiting the Revolution to usurp the throne. Anything that might contradict the princes' assertion that their brother was simply a tool in the hands of the revolutionaries, like his September memorandum, they studiously ignored.

Louis XVI had to find some response to this flagrant betrayal, and the most obvious one was to reactivate Breteuil. The diplomatic initiative required to implement the armed congress was confided to him as the king's authorized representative. Just like the flight to Varennes, the aim was as much to frustrate the *émigrés'* designs as those of the National Assembly. Thus, four months after the worst setback of his career, the baron was once again Louis XVI's plenipotentiary, entrusted with his personal policy for ending the Revolution.

*

THE MISSION AHEAD OF Breteuil was complex and dangerous. Its success depended on the attitude of the Powers, above all Austria, to the worsening plight of the French royal family. Now on his way back from Italy to Vienna, Leopold II had followed every step of the flight to Varennes. At Padua he had received false news that Louis and Marie Antoinette had been arrested but had managed to escape to safety. He sat down and wrote his sister a euphoric letter:

> You know my affection, attachment and friendship for you, and you can easily imagine how I have felt these last few days, particularly when I heard you had been arrested. I thank God

for your happy deliverance. The king, the state, France, and all monarchies owe their deliverance and existence to your courage, your firmness and your prudence. If only I could be with you and the king, to embrace you and express the joy of a brother, friend and ally, and know that you are finally free of the dangers which have menaced you for so long! Everything I have is yours: money, troops, everything! Use them freely, I only wish to be of some use, and to prove my friendship on all occasions, but especially this one.[17]

When he finally learned the truth, Leopold's reaction was swift. On 6 July, he issued to the European Powers the 'Padua circular', calling for concerted action to liberate his sister and brother-in-law. This was also intended as a warning to revolutionary France to respect their persons and position. It was given added force by a major shift in European power politics. The Austro-Prussian *rapprochement*, about which Leopold had waxed lyrical to Bombelles at Cremona, was almost complete. This was greatly helped by the official ending of the Turkish war at the treaty of Sistova on 5 August, which eased Austria's eastern European difficulties that Prussia had been exploiting for so long. With France in chaos, Leopold needed a reliable new ally, and Prussia now seemed an acceptable partner. On 25 July, in Vienna, Austria and Prussia signed a joint convention, bringing them close to a formal alliance.

The situation in France was now firmly at the top of the European diplomatic agenda. It was Leopold and Frederick William of Prussia who took the next step. On 25 August 1791, they met at Pillnitz, the Elector of Saxony's summer residence outside Dresden, to seal their new-found friendship. The following day, however, their peaceful discussions were rudely interrupted by uninvited guests. These were Artois and his entire entourage, including Condé and Calonne. As at Mantua, the prince's aim was to browbeat his hosts into providing him with troops to intervene in France; again as at Mantua, he came armed with a shopping-list of 'points to be fixed'. This included the issuing of a manifesto threatening the Assembly with drastic punishment (and Paris with 'extermination'), if the royal family was harmed. Now that Provence was free, a further demand was added – that while the king and queen were captive, he be recognized as regent of

France. Leopold, who had had quite enough of Artois's unannounced visits, was furious. Calonne, garrulous and brimming with unworkable plans, he found particularly trying. 'Whenever I contradicted him,' the emperor later remarked, 'he would say: "Ah! I have just had a sublime idea!" – and it was another lunacy.'[18]

On all the *émigrés*' substantive demands, Leopold and Frederick William held firm. Provence's regency was vetoed, and the request for troops was met with the stock response the emperor had already used at Mantua – that this would have to await concerted action by all the major Powers. By this time, however, the two monarchs were desperate to be rid of their troublesome house-guests, and prepared to make one concession to speed them on their way. They agreed to Artois's request that they publish a manifesto. The result was the famous declaration of Pillnitz, which appeared on 27 August. It announced that the emperor and the king of Prussia regarded Louis XVI's situation as a matter of common interest to all the monarchs of Europe. Leopold and Frederick William invited their fellow rulers to join with them to ensure that Louis and Marie Antoinette were set at liberty and France stabilized on a monarchical basis. They expressed the hope that this concert could be brought about. 'In this case,' the declaration went on,

> Their Majesties the emperor and the king of Prussia are resolved to act promptly and in mutual accord, with all the force necessary to achieve the proposed common goal. In the meantime they will issue the orders required to set their troops in movement.[19]

On the surface the declaration of Pillnitz appeared very menacing, but in reality it was a paper tiger. The statement that Leopold and Frederick William would only march in the case of all the Powers agreeing to them doing so rendered their promise meaningless. Leopold, of course, was well aware of this, which is why he had inserted the condition in the first place. ' "In this case" (*Alors et dans ce cas*) is with me the law and the prophets,'[20] he wrote to Kaunitz. He had no intention of being dragged into another conflict so soon after the Turkish war.

Once Leopold was back in Vienna again, his policy became even more cautious. It was more difficult for *émigrés* to ambush him in his capital, and Kaunitz's influence was correspondingly strengthened. The chancellor was more than ever determined that Austria should not intervene in France, and his views had their effect on his master. The most convenient way out of the impasse would be if Louis XVI himself managed to achieve a compromise with the moderate revolutionaries and make the action foreseen in the declaration of Pillnitz unnecessary. This was why Leopold gave his backing to the king and queen's negotiations with the Feuillants that summer. For the same reason, he preferred to believe that Louis's oath to the constitution in September was freely given, despite Marie Antoinette's letters making clear that it was not. Rather than acknowledge this uncomfortable truth, he stopped writing to his sister and did not resume until January 1792. Kaunitz was particularly delighted by the king's acceptance of the constitution, and the excuse for inaction it provided. 'The cowardice and weakness of our good Louis XVI', he wrote, 'will get us off the hook.'[21]

If Austria, with all her diplomatic and blood ties to France, did nothing, then the prospect of the other Powers supporting an armed congress looked bleak. Prussia and Spain swiftly took their cue from Leopold, and backed away from the project. Breteuil's thankless task was to change this state of affairs, as the representative of a captive master without credit or resources. Yet he set about his work with determination and ingenuity.

The baron's first priority was to re-establish communications with the Tuileries. Since 8 July, when Marie Antoinette had sent the limited *plein pouvoir* for Louis XVI's brothers to Fersen, there had been no word from the king and queen. Then, in late September, the silence was broken. Breteuil and his colleagues breathed a sigh of relief. 'At last that correspondence so necessary to my unfortunate master has been resumed,'[22] wrote Bombelles to the Bishop of Pamiers. As before, the bulk of the royal couple's letters were written by Marie Antoinette. They were addressed to Fersen in Brussels, where he too had now taken up residence. Sometimes notes and memoranda from the king were enclosed. On other occasions, Louis seems to have written directly to Breteuil. Quite how contact came to be resumed remains mysterious; the queen merely told Fersen that she now had 'a safe method always at my disposal'.[23] This may well have been the courier network described by d'Allonville in his memoirs.

Now that he could be certain what the king and queen wanted, Breteuil launched his own diplomacy. He soon realized that Austria was backing away from the congress (this was confirmed by Fersen, who had been to Vienna in August and spoken at length to both Leopold and Kaunitz). His pre-Varennes strategy, which had revolved around Austria, now had to be modified, and a new diplomatic combination constructed. For this, Breteuil looked to the Northern Powers, Russia and Sweden. If they took the lead in championing the French royal cause, this could galvanize their fellow monarchs into action. The plan was bold. In carrying it out, Breteuil had one major asset, the friendship of Gustavus III. However, this was offset by the persistent enmity of Catherine the Great.

Gustavus was still at Aix-la-Chapelle, from where he had been hoping to join the liberated king and queen. The news of Varennes, far from crushing him, spurred him to frantic activity. On 5 July, he held a council at Aix with Provence, Artois and their advisers, and outlined a far-reaching yet wildly unrealistic project. Given Louis XVI's captivity, Provence should assume the title of regent, and recognize Gustavus as head of an armed international league to restore the French monarchy. The princes would invade France through Alsace with the *émigrés* and contingents raised from the German princes, in particular Hessians provided by the Landgrave of Hesse. Gustavus himself would deliver the *coup de grâce*, landing in Normandy at the head of 16,000 Swedish and 8,000 Russian troops, seizing control of the Seine and marching on Paris.

Not only was this scheme premature, the fact that it gave such a prominent role to the princes was most unwelcome. Breteuil moved as fast as he could to calm Gustavus's ardour and wean him away from Provence and Artois. He saw the king at Aix, and had a long conversation with him. At the end of July Gustavus left to return to Sweden, his old friendship with the baron reinforced. Yet this would not proceed without hiccups – Gustavus was temperamentally more inclined to the princes' bellicose fantasies than to Breteuil's sober diplomacy. The promises given at Aix had also made him a hero to the *émigrés*. As a Russian observer sarcastically remarked: 'They await him like the Messiah with a fleet from Gothenburg.'[24]

In fact, Gustavus did recognize Breteuil as Louis XVI's plenipotentiary, and on this basis the two men set up a secret correspondence. This is of particular significance, since Gustavus was the only European monarch whom Breteuil really trusted and to whom he could confidently impart his plans. The baron's letters to Gustavus are the most important surviving source as to his real thinking between the autumn of 1791 and the spring of 1792.

No sooner had the king arrived back in Sweden than the first squall blew up. Gustavus was shocked by the news that Louis XVI had accepted the constitution. To him, this was an abject betrayal of the monarchical cause. Unable to believe the oath was genuine, he wrote Breteuil an urgent letter to ask what was going on:

> I will need much explanation of the motives behind this action, which is so damaging to the dignity of the throne, and will fool nobody ... If the dangers of the situation forced the king into an insincere acceptance, I don't see why he had to adopt the forms he did, and demean his dignity and his person. All this must necessarily conceal a great design; which it is important for his friends to know ... I hope that you, M le baron, who are in a better position than myself to understand these mysteries, will not leave me in ignorance of what you know, and will give me the arms I need to defend the [French] court.[25]

Breteuil rushed to reassure Gustavus, and retain his friendship, in a long reply dated 11 November. In the course of this, he gave a detailed account of Louis XVI's reasons for accepting the constitution. It is the most explicit evidence we possess that the king took the oath in bad faith. Since so much of the baron's information came from Marie Antoinette via Fersen, it may be that he adopted her crude explanation of the action and ignored the king's more subtle approach. None the less, given all the evidence, this confidential letter from such a well-placed source as Breteuil is further evidence of Louis's and Marie Antoinette's shared sentiments towards the constitution:

> My only explanation, sire, for the king's oath is that His Majesty, hemmed in by the rebels, was in the most complete ignorance of what he could expect from the Powers; that he felt himself abandoned, having heard nothing from the emperor, or receiv-

ing from him only the faintest expressions of concern and even advice tending to the very course he eventually took: in this cruel position, without counsel or support, the king saw only the necessity and the importance of appearing to take the oath in good faith, so as to inspire confidence in the people and conciliate them enough to place more means of action at his disposal ... You will see, sire, that in order to gain time [for foreign help to arrive], the king could not refuse the assurances that the rebels were demanding as a guarantee of his faithful promise to abide by the constitution. The force of your noble spirit, of your principles and of your friendship for the king, sire, may recoil from this conduct, but Your Majesty can have no doubt that the king feels all the horror of his position and is actively seeking to change it; to think otherwise would be to forget his courage in leaving for Montmédy, and to ignore the fact that before implementing a new plan, the king must have a clear idea of the intentions of the Powers on whose friendship he relies, and of just how far they can or will express interest in his fate, so that he can conduct himself in consequence.[26]

Breteuil went on to outline to Gustavus the armed congress plan, and the diplomatic means he envisaged to achieve it. He proposed a modified version of the league projected at Aix-la-Chapelle, but aimed at securing the congress rather than an actual invasion of France. At its head would be not Gustavus, but the king of Spain as the senior reigning Bourbon after Louis XVI:

If it becomes certain that the emperor prefers to remain a tranquil spectator of our disorders, Your Majesty could turn this fatal resolution to advantage by linking up with Russia and the king of Prussia, to force the emperor into a more generous policy and convince Spain to place herself at the head of the league. It is true, sire, that we shall need to make sure of setting Spain in movement over these objects so as to overcome Spanish slowness. To fulfil this plan, overtures to the different Powers will be necessary to make known to them the true views of the king.[27]

By the time he next wrote to Gustavus, on 1 January 1792, Breteuil had had the benefit of two detailed sets of instructions from

Louis XVI. The first was the memorandum, the extract of which the queen sent to Fersen on 25 November. The king wholeheartedly endorsed the congress, but stuck to his view that the only way to regain the confidence of the nation was by scrupulously observing the constitution. He insisted forcefully that the *émigrés* should be contained. The second letter, dated 14 December, is the longest from Louis to Breteuil that we possess. The king began with a long explanation of why he had vetoed the decrees on the *émigrés* and the refractory clergy. He was adamant that if the former did not return to France, then at least they should disperse:

> In any established government, if expatriate citizens assemble in force with the aim of mounting an armed invasion of their country to destroy that government, with the support of foreign Powers, it becomes impossible for the head of state to tolerate such a thing, otherwise he would completely lose public confidence. This is precisely my position, and my feelings are shared by most articulate people ... This was my thinking when I accepted the constitution. I have written several times [to the *émigrés*] demanding that they disperse and move away; that they should not give cause for alarm that would force me to act against them, that they should spare me this cruel distress ...[28]

The king repeated that his authority could only be retrieved by reasoning and persuasion. Yet this letter makes quite clear that the catalyst to this had to be the foreign Powers and the congress. The other great advantage of giving the initiative to his fellow-rulers was that they would be able to contain the *émigrés* and prevent them from mounting some wild provocation. 'You know', Louis wrote to Breteuil, 'that my strategy has always been to hold back the *émigrés* and get the Powers to take the lead.'[29]

Echoing Kaunitz and Marie Antoinette, Louis was equally determined that the congress should carefully avoid pronouncing on France's internal affairs. Instead, it should be called as a response to the Assembly's violations of international law. In particular, the king thought that the summons issued to the Electors of Mainz and Trier to expel the armed *émigrés* could be presented as a threat to German liberties and thus a justification for the congress. Breteuil had already argued in his November letter to Gustavus that France's attacks on her neighbours offered the best excuse for intervention. The example he chose, however, was rather more solid than the king's – the annexation of Avignon.

Throughout this whole secretive correspondence, as proposal succeeded counter-proposal, the royal family was in acute danger. This forced them to formulate and communicate their instructions hurriedly and haphazardly, and to make public utterances that often contradicted their private views. Yet through all the clandestine messages and invisible ink, a consistent policy does emerge. Having accepted the constitution, the king would observe it to the letter, while looking to an armed congress of the Powers to enable him to regain the initiative. The king and queen were united in pursuing this goal. Where it would take them, however, was another matter.

*

THE FINAL MYSTERY surrounding the armed congress is its ultimate purpose. Like the flight to Varennes, it was a means, not an end. The end was a settlement to the Revolution on Louis XVI's terms. Yet precisely what these terms were, and whether they had changed at all since Varennes, has up until now remained unclear.

Louis and Marie Antoinette were vague in their letters about their aims for the congress – perhaps deliberately. Breteuil dropped one slight hint that the congress might foster a constitutional compromise. 'The king thinks', he wrote to Gustavus in January 1791, 'that this vigorous, yet conciliatory, measure will greatly help him in containing the domestic situation, and make it necessary for the strongest and most steadfast resolutions to be taken abroad.'[30] The key aspect of the plan was that Louis XVI should regain his liberty through acting as a mediator between the assembly and the Powers, but neither the king, the queen nor Breteuil gave any details about this.

Louis and Marie Antoinette may not have set out their political hopes for the congress in writing, but there is evidence that they did so verbally. In the winter of 1791–2, three trusted confidants managed to slip into the Tuileries from abroad to find out at first hand what their intentions were. In the first week of December, the Bishop of Pamiers made a secret visit of several days. At the end of the month, the wealthy Scot Craufurd journeyed to Paris, and stayed there until April 1792. Then, towards mid-February, Fersen himself arrived.

Quite how the bishop managed to get into Paris remains unclear. He must have disguised himself, since he was known in the capital. However arrogant and bumptious he may have been, one can only admire his courage; had he been discovered, immediate imprisonment was the kindest fate he could expect. At the Tuileries, Marie Antoinette rushed to greet him: 'You cannot imagine my joy at seeing the bishop,' she wrote to Fersen, 'I could not leave him for a moment.'[31] For the first time since Varennes, the queen was able to unburden herself to someone other than her husband. She described in detail her negotiations with her 'new acquaintances', the Feuillants; with his usual self-confidence, the bishop reprimanded her for not doing more in this direction. The terms in which Marie Antoinette described this discussion make her sound like a penitent schoolgirl: '[The bishop] was very severe with me; I thought I had done a lot and that he would admire my work: not a bit of it. He told me bluntly that I should have done a lot more.'[32]

Having given the queen her dressing-down, the bishop headed covertly back to Brussels. His visit underlined the usefulness of placing a more permanent confidential agent in Paris, who could see the royal couple regularly and transmit information and instructions more frequently than they were able to do. Quintin Craufurd, as brave as he was eccentric, volunteered for this dangerous task, and on Christmas Eve set off with Eléonore Sullivan. He stayed in Paris, in close touch with the queen, for almost four months, and his house in the rue de Clichy became a royalist 'safe house'. It was there that Fersen hid when he arrived in the capital on the evening of 13 February, disguised as a Swedish courier carrying despatches to Portugal.

Much has been written about Fersen's visit, because it provides the best evidence that he did indeed sleep with Marie Antoinette. He slipped into the Tuileries a few hours after his arrival, saw the queen alone in her apartments, and stayed concealed there until the morning. We know this because the last words in his journal entry for that day, partially obliterated by descendants anxious to preserve his reputation, read 'stayed there'.[33] Given that Fersen and Marie Antoinette were unquestionably in love, and now found themselves alone in the same rooms for a whole night, it does seem likely that they went to bed together. Whether this was the first time they had done so or was merely part of a long-standing physical relationship, will always remain a mystery.

The personal significance of Fersen's visit, however, has obscured its wider importance. During his stay in Paris Fersen had long policy discussions with the king and queen, of which he left a detailed account, both in his journal and in a long report to Gustavus III. These writings provide the best evidence we possess of Louis's and Marie Antoinette's real views in the last months of the monarchy. At times, Fersen records the king's words verbatim, beginning with a conversation on the evening of 14 February. Louis opened with a *cri de cœur* that revealed how much he had reflected on the Revolution and his part in it: 'Ah, we are in private and can talk freely. I know everybody blames me for weakness and indecision, but nobody has ever been before in a position like mine.' He went on to confess the great mistake he had made in 1789: 'I know that I missed my chance on 14 July; I should have left then . . .'[34]

Fersen's aim was to find out how the king and queen wished the armed congress to proceed, and what they expected from it. He had prepared a memorandum 'on the different methods of operation for the congress', which he read to them. He reported their reactions to Gustavus III in a despatch of 29 February, which has been published. The memorandum itself, however, has lain unnoticed in the Swedish State Archives until now.[35] It is a crucial document for two reasons. First, Fersen's account of Louis's and Marie Antoinette's response to his proposals only make sense when one reads the proposals themselves. Second, the text set out two possible goals for the congress, and asked the king and queen to choose between them. The choice the royal couple made indicates clearly their preferred basis for a settlement to the Revolution.

For Fersen, there were two ways for the congress to act, and each would have a different result. The first was to insist that no negotiation with the Assembly was possible while the king was in captivity. The Powers should therefore

demand as an essential precondition that the king and his family leave Paris within a fixed time for an agreed place close to the frontier, protected by troops and a guard chosen by himself, from where he will negotiate with the Powers over the different

objects of their demands, and from where the king will renew
fully or in part his acceptance of the constitution, or propose
those changes that experience has suggested to him are necessary.[36]

The second option was more complicated – and much riskier. In
this scenario the Powers would carefully avoid any mention of the
king's captivity, but act solely in the name of international law. They
would demand satisfaction on two issues – the annexation of Avignon
and the attacks on German liberties – and assurances on a third, the
sanctity of existing treaties. The aim of this ultimatum, whose terms
were calculated to be unacceptable to France, would be to push her
into war. 'In adopting this approach,' Fersen wrote,

> the Powers should be forewarned that the king's conduct cannot
> be anything other than that he has followed up until now . . .
> [He must] . . . appear to do willingly whatever is demanded of
> him; and even to declare war on them, taking all measures
> necessary on this score as to inspire enough confidence to put
> himself at the head of his army. . . . If he can achieve this goal,
> it will then be easy for him to find a secure position from where
> he can treat with the Powers, and with the assurance of their
> support dictate laws to his people.[37]

Here, in its final form, was the choice that had faced the king and
queen since October 1789 – whether to accept at least some aspects
of the Revolution or to fight it to the end. This fundamental conflict
had underlain both the rival plans of Mirabeau and Breteuil for escape
from Paris, and the later differences between Marie Antoinette and
Barnave. Fersen's first option mirrored Mirabeau's earlier scheme:
the king would leave Paris but use his freedom not to renounce the
constitution but to renegotiate it. Fersen's second option, however,
exactly echoed Breteuil's plan for the flight to Varennes. The king
would gain his freedom not through an agreed process, but through
subterfuge and military force. Once at liberty, he would not proceed
on the basis of the constitution, but cast it aside. Instead, backed by
loyal troops and the armies of the Powers, he would impose a
settlement on his own authority – 'dictate laws to his people'.

Through the expedient of the congress, Fersen was thus asking
Louis XVI to make a final decision between constitutional monarchy

and, if not absolute monarchy, then something very close to it. The essential issue was the source of sovereignty. Would the king consent to share this with the National Assembly, which even partial acceptance of the constitution would imply? Or would he instead disown the constitution and reassert his undivided authority? In this case, even if concessions had to be made to calm the situation, this would be by the king's grace, leaving his prerogative intact.

Louis XVI's response was unambiguous. 'I . . . presented to the king the two options contained in [my] memorandum,' Fersen informed Gustavus. 'He preferred the second, saying that it offered him the best chance of linking up with the congress.'[38] The king would thus use the congress not to renegotiate the constitution, but to re-establish the monarchy on his own terms. This was an uncompromising decision, but at least it was consistent. Having briefly yielded to the Feuillants' siren song, at the moment of truth Louis XVI ruled out any significant concession of authority.

In his despatch to Gustavus, Fersen went on to amplify this. He was determined to extract from the king and queen a clear indication of their ultimate political goals, and did this by relaying to them Gustavus's and Catherine the Great's strong opposition to any form of constitutional monarchy in France. His account of Louis's and Marie Antoinette's response is highly revealing. It depicts the king as initially hesitating, but then coming round to the queen's insistence on a virtual restoration of the absolute monarchy:

> I then declared to the king, on behalf of Your Majesty, his intention, and that of the empress of Russia, under no circumstances to suffer the establishment of a mixed government in France; to have no dealings with the rebels, but to restore the monarchy and the royal authority in all its plenitude. The queen seized on this solution with alacrity, and the king, although he desires it, appeared to think that this might be difficult to achieve; but I had no difficulty in proving to him that with foreign help, and certain as I was that it was impossible and that he was quite decided not to compromise with the rebels, nothing could be easier; in the end he was convinced, and assured me that he had no intention of negotiating with the rebels, half of whom, he said, have no power to do good, and the other half of whom have no desire to.[39]

This passage shows clearly that while there may have been differences of emphasis between Louis and Marie Antoinette, at heart they were in agreement. It is also significant that the argument by which Fersen finally won over the king concerned sovereignty. This was his assertion that any constitutional compromise would involve treating with rebels. If Louis did so, Fersen argued, he would fatally damage his authority. As was no doubt intended, this touched a nerve; gathering around him the shreds of his prerogative, the king replied that he would never bargain with insurgents.

The scene is so remarkable that one might doubt Fersen's veracity, except that his report to Gustavus tallies exactly with the account in his journal, which, since it was entirely private, he had no reason to embroider. The king, so jealous of his public authority, was in private deferring to a young Swedish nobleman who may well have just slept with his wife. Did Louis ever suspect that Fersen was Marie Antoinette's lover? His words to Fersen as recorded by the latter show both affection and complete trust – 'M de Fersen, whatever happens I will not forget what you have done for me', 'Ah, we are in private and can talk freely.' If Fersen and the queen were having an affair, either the king had no inkling of this, or on the contrary he was a complaisant husband, understanding and fully accepting the arrangement.

Whatever Louis XVI may have felt, such situations were familiar to Fersen. Whether or not he did sleep with Marie Antoinette on the first night of his visit, on the subsequent ones he went back to the rue de Clichy and slept with Eléonore Sullivan. This is clear from his diary. Indeed, at the rue de Clichy, a far more immediate menace than arrest by the revolutionary authorities was discovery by Quintin Craufurd, who had no idea that Fersen was his mistress's lover or even that he was currently in his house. For a week Fersen stayed hidden in an upstairs room, whiling away his leisure hours by reading novels. The Revolution had receded, replaced by *Les Liaisons dangereuses*.

Fersen's account contains one last puzzle. It is political rather than personal. If Louis had been so determined just a few months before to abide scrupulously by the constitution, how could he now contemplate overthrowing it by war? The most likely answer lies in the rapidly worsening situation in France, and the perceptible hardening this wrought in his stance. Between November 1791 and February 1792, the attacks of the Girondins, far from abating, had intensified. The king concluded that if it took a war to complete his discomfiture, then the Girondins were ready, indeed enthusiastic, for one. This recognition is clear from his letter to Breteuil of 14 December. After a long discussion of how the Powers should deal with the *émigré* issue, he added, 'There remains war, if it becomes inevitable,'[40] and outlined his policy should it break out. The impossibility of his position was driving this peaceable man to accept even a European conflict if it brought deliverance.

Here too, the king's sentiments were fully shared by the queen. By this time, the royal couple were coming to wish simply for an end, any end, to their ghastly predicament. Their state of mind is vividly portrayed by Fersen in his despatch to Gustavus III:

> In sum, I found the king and queen quite decided to endure anything rather than continue in their present situation, and following my conversation with Their Majesties I can assure you, sire, that they feel strongly that any compromise with the rebels is both useless and impossible, and that the only means of restoring their authority lies in force and foreign aid.[41]

On the evening of 21 February, Fersen took his leave of Louis and Marie Antoinette. They gave him tea, and he stayed on for supper. At midnight he left, and never saw them again.

*

AS THE WINTER wore on, one final drama was played out. Determined to end the divisions in the royalist camp, Breteuil made a last effort to impose the king's authority on the *émigrés*. The sabre-rattling and provocations from this quarter had not diminished since Varennes; if anything, they had increased now that the king's younger brother was at liberty.

Following Provence's successful escape from France on the night the king and queen left for Montmédy, he and Artois had jointly established themselves at Coblenz, at the invitation of their uncle Clement-Wenceslas, Elector of Trier. The elector put at their disposal the vast baroque palace of Schönbornlust just outside the town. There, they set up a court modelled exactly on Versailles, with all its etiquette, ranks and offices; all that was lacking was a country to sustain it. Both princes organized separate royal households surrounded by all the military trappings of the old monarchy, with troops of bodyguards and Swiss soldiers. Even some Guards units that had been abolished as an economy measure back in the 1770s were re-created, such as the Household Horse Grenadiers!

In private as well as in public, the manners of Versailles were maintained. Provence's marriage had long ceased to have any meaning as his wife slid increasingly into alcoholism. The comtesse de Provence lived at Schönbornlust, but her role as consort was taken over by her husband's mistress, Mme de Balbi, intelligent, witty and a formidable intriguer. The lifestyles of Monsieur's brother and his cousin were little different. Artois still lived openly with Mme de Polastron, the sister of Mme de Polignac, while Condé and his companion Mme de Monaco had been together so long she was treated as his *de facto* wife. Condé, however, did not live at Coblenz, but further down the Rhine at Worms, where he set about creating an army of refugee noblemen that eventually numbered 22,000. Even though it was chronically short of resources, this was still a substantial force, and one can see why its presence on France's borders so exercised the legislative assembly.

This kingdom of Cockaigne not only had an army, but also a diplomatic service, which was what worried Breteuil most. The duc de Polignac represented it at Vienna, the duc d'Havré at Madrid, the comte d'Esterhazy at St Petersburg and the baron de Roll at Berlin. Through these ambassadors, the princes claimed the sole right to speak for the French monarchy, and arrogated to themselves their elder brother's authority. The convenient fiction that Louis XVI was completely captive and could have no policy of his own was used to discredit any instructions from the Tuileries that did not accord with Provence's and Artois's views. It was urgent that the king bring his family under control.

Breteuil looked to Sweden and Russia to keep Artois and Provence in check. Above all, the baron relied on Gustavus III, who enjoyed the princes' trust as well as his own, to share the task of containing them. On 11 November 1791, he broached the subject to Gustavus as bluntly as he dared:

I cannot avoid repeating to Your Majesty that the king has good reason to fear the indiscretion of Coblenz, and as the misfortunes that stem from this are felt first of all by himself and his family, you cannot, sire, blame him for setting some limits to his confidence; if [the princes'] entourage are wounded by this reserve, this evil is preferable to that which would result from giving too much away. The only solution to this problem that I can see, sire, is Your Majesty's own influence over the princes. ... As for me, sire, this would please me all the more in that Your Majesty's covering of my own conduct would protect me from harsh judgements motivated by anxiety or bad faith. You can easily judge, sire, whether the emperor's lukewarm attitude is not in itself sufficient cause for his inactivity, and how cruel it is to be constantly attacked as the cause of [his] indifference when all the time I am trying to prod him into action.[42]

At the same time Breteuil was adamant that Provence should not declare himself regent, despite Gustavus's support for the idea back in July. 'I should not hide from Your Majesty,' he wrote,

that the king is on principle utterly opposed to the idea of Monsieur becoming regent. His Majesty thinks that the princes' actions in this regard will merely irritate rather than frighten [the rebels]. The king of Spain and the emperor are fully aware of the king's feelings and share them entirely. I do not think that either of these courts will ever accept this regency; only serious and well-coordinated measures on the part of the Powers themselves will make an impression on the rebels.[43]

Breteuil was so categorical about the regency that it seems likely he was acting on specific instructions from the king. Indeed, there is evidence that Louis XVI did write to him on the subject. In his memoirs, the comte d'Allonville reproduces a letter from Louis, undated but clearly from this period, formally ordering the baron to oppose Monsieur's regency. This also contains a postscript from Marie Antoinette endorsing her husband's words. Unfortunately, the original is lost and the only proof that it ever existed is this published version. However, d'Allonville's role in smuggling out the king and queen's secret correspondence does lend his story credibility. If it can be believed, it offers further confirmation that Louis XVI and Breteuil did write directly to each other, and not just via Marie Antoinette and Fersen.

The letter shows the king as determined not to cede his authority despite his predicament, and certainly not to his younger brother. 'I am informed, Monsieur le baron de Breteuil,' he wrote,

> that my very dear brother, Monsieur, comte de Provence, deceived as to my true situation and thinking me in chains, has thought it necessary to set up a central authority aimed at directing my empire, as if the throne was vacant or there was a royal minority: with God's help, this is not the case: apart from some crises, I enjoy the liberty necessary to a prince, and I, and I alone, should give orders in my kingdom.
>
> Therefore, Monsieur le baron, as soon as you receive this you should travel to Vienna, present yourself to our dear and puissant brother the emperor, and inform him of our intentions. You will also take action to entreat all the crowned heads, on my behalf and in my name, neither to accept nor recognize the above regency. The acts of this contradictory authority can only further irritate my people, and will infallibly provoke them to the worst excesses against myself. As long as I live I shall do all in my power to fulfil my duties and give peace and happiness to my peoples. If God should take me, the queen, my most worthy and honoured companion, will become regent in her own right. Her sound judgement, her good heart, her virtues assure me of the wisdom of her administration; her love for my son will redouble her personal resources and zeal. Adieu, my dear baron de Breteuil; in misfortune as well as prosperity I shall always be your good lord and your most sincere friend.

The queen then added her postscript:

> Monsieur le baron de Breteuil, the king being convinced that our brother's regency would present disadvantages, I add my own recommendation to his orders. Our intention is not to oppose Monsieur, but to prevent even greater misfortunes, and it seems that this measure would infuriate the whole of France. I beg you, Monsieur, never to doubt the lively gratitude I bear you; it will never lessen.[44]

The authenticity of this text is supported by one telling detail. In his letter to Gustavus, Breteuil paraphrases it very precisely. In particular, when emphasizing the bad impression Monsieur's regency would create in France, the baron even uses the same word as Louis: 'irritate'. This points to the fact that the document is genuine, and that d'Allonville did indeed publish a now vanished letter from Louis XVI to Breteuil.

If this is the case, then on one important point the baron clearly disobeyed the king. Contrary to his instructions, he did not undertake the journey to Vienna, but stayed put in Brussels. Presumably he did not wish to disturb the networks he had set up, and his proximity to Mercy-Argenteau and the Archduchess Marie Christine already gave him a privileged channel of communication to the emperor. Moreover, it was much easier to keep an eye on the princes from Belgium than from Austria.

By this time Coblenz needed watching more closely than ever. We shall never know whether Breteuil's plan to use Gustavus III to contain Provence and Artois would have worked, because in December 1791 it was torpedoed from an unexpected quarter – the king and queen themselves. Marooned in the Tuileries, Louis and Marie Antoinette had been pondering how best to reconcile the baron with the princes. This could not be done directly, as was made clear by the princes themselves. Writing to the king on 4 August, they had refused point-blank to work with Breteuil:

> His intrigues, his utterances, and his bad faith towards us are too notorious for anybody to believe that he was acting at our orders . . . This reason alone forbids us to promote a man whose incompetence is anyway too well known for him to be of any further use.[45]

A truce would have to be established indirectly, through a go-between. The king and queen cast about for a candidate, and eventually hit on the maréchal de Castries, the former minister of marine, who had emigrated in 1790 and was now living at Cologne.

Castries was a substantial figure, tough, able, respected by the princes and, in a more subtle way, every bit as stiff-necked as Breteuil. In late November 1791 he received a secret message in invisible ink from Louis XVI asking him to 'reach an understanding with the baron de Breteuil over the best way of dealing with Coblenz',[46] with both men acting as intermediaries. The marshal accepted the task with alacrity. Breteuil, however, was thoroughly annoyed. He knew Castries well; the two men had been ministerial colleagues in the 1780s and maintained a wary friendship. Since Castries now had the king's authority, if only for this particular mission, the baron would have to treat him, and by implication the princes, on an equal footing. This ran directly contrary to his own conception of how Provence and Artois should be dealt with: through orders, given by himself as Louis XVI's sole representative, and unquestioningly obeyed.

For the moment there was nothing for it but to put as good a face as possible on the setback. Breteuil swiftly wrote Castries a cordial note: 'Like yourself, I welcome anything that will prevent the ideas and measures of Coblenz taking the wrong political and military path. I add with the sincerity of friendship how much the division of this difficult task with you encourages and reassures me.'[47] For his part, by early January 1792 Castries had managed to extract the princes' consent to the arrangement, which he forwarded to Breteuil with a letter of his own asking how the new relationship should be managed.

The baron's reply, written on 20 January, was uncompromising. He firmly fixed the blame for the previous bad relations between the Tuileries and the princes on the latter. 'I agree with you', he wrote, 'that you must absolutely remove any false ideas that the Tuileries are in opposition [to the princes].'[48]

As to future relations, however, Breteuil's views were rigid.

> The king must be judge and master of what he ... should communicate to the princes for the common good, while on the other hand it is absolutely necessary that the princes do not permit themselves the slightest step without having previously submitted it to His Majesty and received from him authority to initiate and pursue it.[49]

In the meantime, Provence and Artois should pass on to him a detailed description of the state of their negotiations with the European courts and the means at their disposal.

None of this was particularly helpful, but it paled into insignificance beside an action Breteuil had taken just before writing this letter. Given the importance he now attached to the Northern courts, it had seemed sensible to send a representative there. His own close relations with Gustavus III made an emissary in Stockholm superfluous, but this was not the case with St Petersburg. Catherine the Great still bore Breteuil a grudge for not having aided her *coup d'état* thirty years before, and since her resources were infinitely greater than Gustavus's, it was urgent to placate her. Once again the choice fell on Bombelles, and on 31 December 1791 the long-suffering marquis set off for Russia.

The news of Bombelles's arrival in St Petersburg set off an explosion in Coblenz. Of all the major Powers, Russia had been the most generous to the princes, both in promises of support and, more concretely, with money. Their agent in St Petersburg, the comte d'Esterhazy, enjoyed great favour with Catherine. The choice of future representatives at the European courts was the most delicate issue outstanding between Breteuil and the princes. To them, his unilateral decision to supersede Esterhazy was bad enough. To supersede him with Bombelles, after the marquis's blazing row with Artois the previous May at Vicenza, seemed like a calculated insult.

Artois's fury was channelled to Breteuil through Castries. The marshal sent off an anguished letter, complaining bitterly of this breach of the spirit if not the letter of the new dispensation. He went on to outline a more positive path. It was obviously vital that no whisper of Breteuil's relations with the king and queen should reach France. Castries therefore proposed that Breteuil continue to direct their secret diplomacy from Brussels, but cover his activities by using the princes' representatives as his agents in the field. The phrasing of Castries's proposal is revealing, since it shows that the marshal himself had no doubts about the validity of Breteuil's powers:

> However one looks at it, Monsieur le baron, the more you show yourself, the more difficult it is for the king to proclaim fidelity to the constitution; you know the influence His Majesty has assigned you over the content of policy, this is the only worthwhile role to have. You draw up the plan, you set it in motion and give it direction, and it is for the princes to deal

openly with the [European] courts. It is in this way that I have always thought the king and the monarchy would be best served.[50]

Breteuil, however, was having none of it. He disingenuously expressed surprise and pain that Artois should have been so offended by Bombelles's mission to St Petersburg. The only reason he had not previously mentioned this, he added unconvincingly, was that discretion was the essence of the marquis's task, and that he had not wanted news of his arrival to precede him. Using the princes' emissaries in the future was also rejected, 'on the principle that to the king alone belongs the direction of his affairs'. Castries's observation that the baron's role had at all costs to be kept hidden, however, drew a more thoughtful response. It showed just how aware Breteuil was of the need for deep secrecy in all his activities, and of the tremendous peril the king and queen would face if these became generally known:

> You are quite right, Monsieur le maréchal ... I cannot too carefully conceal the role it has pleased His Majesty to entrust to me. I am strongly convinced of this necessity, and all my efforts for the last two years have been bent towards veiling my activities in the thickest obscurity. I am far from wishing to emerge from this now, and I have no need to make myself believed by pointing out all the dangers to which an alternative conduct would give rise.[51]

By this stage, Castries was not going to be fobbed off with a letter. He sent his son the duc de Castries, who alone had his confidence, to carry his protest about Bombelles to Breteuil. Armed with a list of questions his father had drawn up for him, the duke was to gain an interview with the baron and report back his conclusions on each point. It says something about the atmosphere of the times that Castries, like Bouillé just before Varennes, refused to entrust the most secret missions to any but the closest members of his family.

Castries's list of instructions and questions for his son survive, along with the latter's replies. Both documents form one more link in the chain of testimony, from Mercy-Argenteau to Kaunitz to Chamfort, attesting to the baron's faults. Castries's opening warning to his son bluntly confirmed these: 'The king's confidence in M. de Breteuil increases his natural tendency to pomposity and self-importance. The smallest success makes it difficult to reason with him, and . . . contradiction infuriates him to the point of brutality.' On a personal level, the duke's meeting with Breteuil went better than expected. The baron was charming to him and full of compliments for his father. Yet on the issues at stake, he was immovable. As the duke put it: 'He was more open with me than I had expected, but as regards the princes he is prime minister and stuffed with the royal supremacy.'[52]

Breteuil was so intransigent with Castries that one shares the latter's suspicion that he actually wanted the negotiations to fail. His motivation is obvious. He knew he had the confidence of the king and queen, and was unlikely to lose it if the arrangement with Castries proved unworkable. Despite the damage this would do the royal cause, he was probably confident that in any battle between the princes and himself for the ear of Europe's crowned heads, his claim to speak in the king's name would eventually prevail.

Throughout the Revolution, but especially after Varennes, Breteuil set his face against any compromise with the princes. His obstinacy in this respect was truly remarkable. For himself personally, it was a poor strategy because it eventually robbed him of his political role. But it is probable that he did not care. In agreeing to serve Louis XVI he had insisted that he alone should have the royal confidence, whether in treating with the Powers to restore the royal authority, or in forming a ministry after this had taken place. Sharing that confidence with the obstreperous and ultimately treacherous Provence and Artois formed no part of his plans. Indeed, in his letters to Castries there is a note of genuine anger in his references to the princes. Breteuil was an emotional man, and his reaction to their behaviour may well have been simple disgust.

Even as Breteuil was arguing with Castries, decisive proof of the princes' bad faith arrived in the Tuileries. Louis XVI's letter to his brothers of 16 October had urged them to return to France of their own free will, since otherwise they would place him in an impossible position. Receiving no answer, he wrote to them again in November, repeating his plea. Finally, in early December, he received a cold and deeply hypocritical reply from Provence, affecting to believe that Louis had been forced to write the letter. 'The order it contains to return to Your Majesty's presence,' Monsieur wrote, 'is not the expression of his own free will, and my honour, my duty, even my affection forbid me to obey it.'[53] The implication was that he would continue his provocations from beyond the Rhine, regardless of the fury this aroused in the Parisians, and the danger in which it placed his brother and sister-in-law. It was too much for Marie Antoinette. Reading the letter, she burst out: 'Cain! Cain! Monsieur is sacrificing us, murdering us! What a heart of stone! . . . There is nothing left for us to do but die.'[54]

Chapter Twelve

ENDGAME

IN THE NATIONAL ASSEMBLY, the Girondins were only briefly disconcerted by the king's triumph on 14 December 1791 over the dispersal of the *émigrés*. Undaunted, they stuck to their strategy of undermining him through attacking France's neighbours. Indeed, within two months they had provoked a crisis that led inexorably to war.

Ironically, it was the cautious Leopold II who provided the pretext. Even if he did not bother to reply to them, the desperate pleas of Marie Antoinette had had some effect, particularly in the context of the Assembly's sabre-rattling. In the course of December, his stance hardened perceptibly. The emperor sought a pretext for warning the French that he would not tolerate their provocations. He found it in the tangled question of the German princes in Alsace. When France had taken over the province in 1648, a number of German princes of the Holy Roman Empire had retained enclaves within it. Ever since 4 August 1789, it had been unclear whether the abolition of feudalism decreed by the Constituent Assembly applied also to these areas. The Assembly, naturally, maintained that it did; the German princes, unimpressed by the prospect of thus losing the income from their feudal dues, replied that it did not. Negotiations between the two sides had dragged on for two years, but were still incomplete. On 3 December, Leopold protested against the

Assembly's rejection of the princes' claims. He based himself on the sanctity of existing treaties, the very issue which Fersen was soon to recommend to the queen as an excuse for calling a congress.

Nor was this all. By this time even Kaunitz was coming to support a firm line. Although he had had no objection to the expulsion of the *émigrés* from Mainz and Trier, he wished to make it clear that further French aggression on the German side of the Rhine would not be tolerated. On 21 December, he handed the French ambassador a diplomatic note. This warned that orders had been given for Austrian troops to march to the aid of the Elector of Trier if French troops crossed his borders. If France did opt for war, the chancellor went on, she would find herself opposed not just by Austria, but by a concert of the European Powers.

This was just what the Girondins had been waiting for. The king may have trumped them over the *émigrés*, but Vienna had now presented them with an even more promising foe – the combined monarchies of Europe. On 24 and 31 December respectively, the Austrian notes were made public. They were read to the Assembly by Lessart, the new foreign minister, who had replaced the exhausted Montmorin the previous month. Delighted to seize a challenge they thought could only benefit them, the Girondin leader Brissot and his allies went on the offensive.

The Girondins' speeches in the Assembly during January 1792 were decisive in pushing France into war. They were an extraordinary blend of eloquence and self-delusion. From 14 to 24 January, in the crucial debate over Kaunitz's note of 21 December, all the group's leading orators – Brissot himself, Vergniaud, Guadet, Gensonné and their ally Isnard, deputy for the Var – rose to denounce Austria and her accomplices within France. From their deadly words materialized the fantasy of an 'Austrian committee' headed by the queen, working within the Tuileries to betray France to her native country. The leitmotiv of this onslaught was Austrophobia, ingrained for centuries in French public opinion, now used to present all royalists, but above all the queen, as in league with the ancestral foe. Yet the consequences were more fateful than even the Girondins could have imagined. By linking the enemy without to the enemy within, they were forging a weapon which, in more ruthless hands than their own, would soon unleash the bloodiest phase of the Revolution.[1]

It is difficult to gauge the Girondins' motivation at this point. Provoking a foreign war to compel the king to declare himself was a rational, if highly dangerous, strategy. Yet the Girondins did not do so in normal diplomatic, or even military, language, but in a flood of Messianic rhetoric that was bound to stir up uncontrollable passions. Either this was merely a tactic to whip up public opinion, or they had fallen under the spell of their own hypnotic words – more likely the latter. The Girondins' pseudo-religious devotion to the Revolution was such that they positively welcomed a war which would unmask its enemies outside and inside France, and enable it to crush them. This led them from the realms of sober politics into those of eschatology and its attendant spirit, paranoia. In a speech to the Jacobin Club of 30 December, Brissot pointed the way:

> Yes, we shall either prevail over all of them, nobles, priests and prince-electors, and establish our public credibility and prosperity, or we shall be defeated and betrayed . . . the traitors will be convicted in the end, they will be punished, and we shall finally be able to get rid of everything that prevents France from becoming a great nation. I admit, gentlemen, to only one fear – that we may not be betrayed. We need great acts of treason: therein lies our salvation.[2]

The 'Austrian committee' was indeed a fantasy, but it was symptomatic of the fog of suspicion that had now descended over all the actors in the Revolutionary drama. It had some basis in fact. The king and queen really did disapprove of the constitution, and the threats from Austria and the arming of the *émigrés* were genuine. Yet the Girondins fused all these elements together into one vast conspiracy to be exploited for their own domestic ends. They failed, or preferred not to see, that their foes were anything but united, that there were major disagreements between the Tuileries and Vienna, between the Tuileries and the *émigrés*, and between Vienna and the *émigrés*. To the Girondins, these opponents were simply different heads of the same counter-revolutionary hydra. For Brissot and his allies, charging the princes and Calonne with high treason, which they did on 1 January, was just one part of their wider attack on their foreign enemies.

The Girondins were remarkable orators, but without help they could not have brought the Assembly to the verge of mass hysteria. This help was provided by the Assembly's method of working, and even its physical layout. This bore little resemblance to other contemporary legislatures, such as the House of Commons. The Manège, the riding school next to the Tuileries where it met, was not just a forum for the deputies. The floor itself was overlooked by large public galleries, usually crammed with several hundred spectators. The speakers addressed their speeches as much to the gallery as to their fellow deputies, and the gallery responded in kind, cheering their heroes and howling down speakers with whom they disagreed. The atmosphere was more like a rowdy theatre than a parliamentary assembly.

In this setting, it was easy for the participants to be swept by waves of mass emotion. The echoes of this can still be seen in the minutes of the debates – 'repeated applause', 'the chamber resounds with applause', 'this surge of enthusiasm communicates itself to everyone present'. The focus was not on sober law-making, but rather on forging unity through demagoguery. It was in these conditions that the decision to go to war was taken.

Though often carried away, the Girondins never lost sight of their basic aim. This was to use the spectre of Austrian aggression to confound the king and queen. They did not know the exact nature of the royal schemes, but they could make a shrewd guess. Above all, they soon smelled out the armed congress plan. Whether this was the result of a leak is impossible now to know, but the public references to a concert of Powers against France in the Austrian notes and the declaration of Pillnitz were in themselves sufficient clues. Whatever the truth, from the start of the debate on Kaunitz's note, the congress was in the Girondins' sights. On the very first day, Gensonné rose and, in the name of the Assembly's diplomatic committee, presented a report on France's present relations with Austria. This was a blanket attack on the Franco-Austrian alliance since its inception, taking in the emperor, the queen and the shadow 'Austrian committee'. In this context, Gensonné denounced the intrigues for a congress, branding them a treasonable plot concocted by the court. This gave his ally Guadet, currently president of the Assembly, his chance. Rising from his official armchair, Guadet rushed to the podium and unleashed an inflammatory harangue:

15. *Above.* Marie Antoinette's personal seal, sent to Breteuil with the plein-pouvoir as a further token of royal confidence.

16. *Right.* Antoine Barnave: the only Revolutionary politician for whom Marie Antoinette felt 'a form of attraction'.

17. Georges-Jacques Danton, the chief organizer of the monarchy's overthrow on 10 August 1792.

18. The *plein-pouvoir* sent to Breteuil on 20 November 1790.

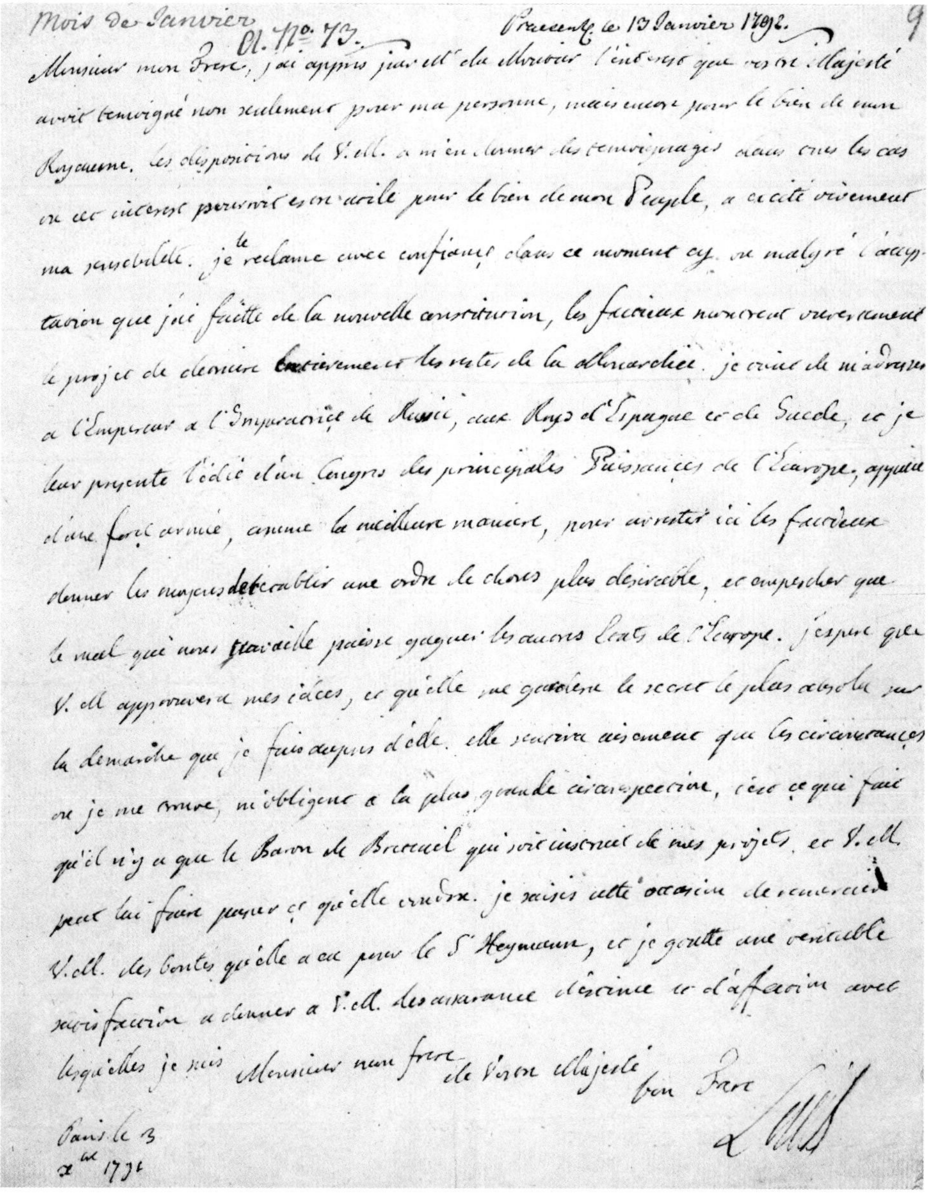
Mois de Janvier
A. No. 73.
Praesent. le 13 Janvier 1792.
9

Monsieur mon Frère, j'ai appris par M. du Moustier l'intérest que votre Majesté avoit temoigné non seulement pour ma personne, mais encore pour le bien de mon Royaume. les dispositions de V. M. a m'en donner des temoignages dans tous les cas où cet interest pourroit etre utile pour le bien de mon Peuple, a excité vivement ma sensibilité. je la reclame avec confiance dans ce moment cy, où malgré l'acceptation que j'ai faitte de la nouvelle constitution, les factieux montrent ouvertement le projet de detruire entierement les restes de la Monarchie. je viens de m'adresser a l'Empereur a l'Imperatrice de Russie, aux Roys d'Espagne et de Suede, et je leur presente l'idée d'un Congrés des principales Puissances de l'Europe, appuyé d'une force armée, comme la meilleure maniere, pour arreter ici les factieux donner les moyens de retablir un ordre de choses plus desirable, et empescher que le mal qui nous travaille puisse gagner les autres Etats de l'Europe. j'espere que V. M. approuvera mes idées, et qu'elle me gardera le secret le plus absolu sur la demarche que je fais auprès d'elle. elle sentira aisement que les circonstances où je me trouve, m'obligent a la plus grande circonspection, c'est ce qui fait qu'il n'y a que le Baron de Breteuil qui soit instruit de mes projets, et V. M. peut lui faire passer ce qu'elle voudra. je saisis cette occasion de remercier V. M. des bontés qu'elle a eu pour le Sr Heymann, et je goutte une veritable satisfaction a donner a V. M. des assurances d'estime et d'affection avec lesquelles je suis Monsieur mon Frere de Votre Majesté bon Frere

Louis

Paris le 3 xbre 1791

19. Louis XVI's letter of 3 December 1791, accrediting Breteuil to King Frederick William II of Prussia.

20. The assassination of Gustavus III.

21. *Taking of the Tuileries, Court of the Carrousel, 10th August 1792,* by Jean Duplessis-Bertaux.

22. Louis XVI in January 1793, the month of his execution. A charcoal drawing with chalk highlights by Joseph Ducreux.

23. *Above.* Valmy, the battle that saved the Revolution, by Jean-Baptiste Mauzaisse.

24. *Below.* The execution of Louis XVI.

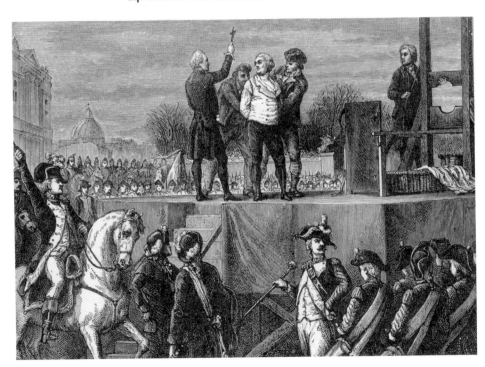

25. Marie Antoinette, dressed as a widow after her husband's execution, by Sophie Prieur, after a painting by Aleksander Kucharski.

26. Marie Antoinette on her way to execution, 16 October 1793, drawn from life by Jacques-Louis David.

27. *Above*. Bombelles
in old age, as Bishop
of Amiens.

28. *Left*. Mme de Matignon
in old age, drawn by her
daughter the duchesse
de Montmorency.

Let us mark out a place for traitors, and let it be the scaffold. Let us decree this instant that the French nation denounces as infamous, betrayers of the fatherland, and guilty of treason towards the nation, any agent of the executive power, any Frenchman who participates, directly or indirectly, either in a congress with the object of obtaining modifications to the constitution, in any form of mediation between the nation and rebels, or in any bargain with the German princes in Alsace.[3]

The effect was electric. To frantic applause and the waving of hats, the entire Assembly rose. Everybody – deputies, spectators, even the ushers – stretched their hands out towards the president's desk and shouted: 'Yes! We swear it! We shall live in freedom or die! The constitution or death!' Guadet's ferocious proposal was decreed by acclamation. It was a fateful moment. The deputies had just voted on to the statute book that most elastic term 'treason towards the nation' (*lèse-nation*). The most dangerous instrument of the Terror had been prepared.

The decree was brought to the Tuileries that same day. Realizing that to veto it would simply confirm all the suspicions that had dictated it, Louis XVI gave his sanction immediately. The Girondins' ruse had worked. The king could no longer pretend, even to himself, that working for an armed congress was remotely compatible with defending the constitution. If he persisted in his secret policy, there was now no possibility of reconciling it to the Revolution; instead he would be its enemy, and, at its starkest, guilty of 'treason to the nation' himself. The Girondins had finally succeeded in separating the king from France.

The debate on the Austrian note ended on 24 January. The result was another decree, voted that day, giving the emperor until 1 March to declare that he renounced any hostile intentions or acts against French independence or sovereignty. Silence, or an ambiguous response, would be taken as a declaration of war. Essentially, this was an ultimatum, to which Leopold could only accede at the price of abject humiliation.

By this time, the emperor had finally made up his mind to accept the French challenge. On 17 January, a meeting of the council of state was held in his presence and that of his son and heir, the

Archduke Francis. Having condemned the armed congress project the previous September, Leopold and his ministers now pushed for its revival. France should be summoned to disband her forces on the Rhine, respect the rights of the German princes in Alsace, return Avignon to the Pope, and guarantee to observe all existing treaties. At home, she should provide for the liberty and security of the royal family and uphold the monarchical form of government. The other Powers were invited to join with Austria in compelling France to accept these demands. The essential preliminary, however, was the support of Prussia. This fact lent further momentum to the *rapprochement* already under way. On 7 February 1792, the logical conclusion was reached, with the signing in Berlin of a treaty of alliance between Austria and Prussia.

This was Leopold's last major act as emperor. He died, suddenly and unexpectedly, on 1 March. In the fevered atmosphere of the time, it was immediately suspected that he had been poisoned by a French agent, but no evidence of this was found at the autopsy. The real cause of death was a sudden rheumatic fever, exacerbated by the demanding pace the emperor always set himself, both in the council chamber and the bedroom. Bombelles's prediction had come true: Leopold's activity had killed him.

The political impact of the emperor's death was simply to accelerate the drive to war. His son and successor, the twenty-three year-old Francis II, was infinitely less supple and intelligent than his father. Above all, he saw himself as a soldier, having recently served in the Turkish war. This further reduced any remaining chance of a negotiated solution to the crisis. The likelihood of conflict also threatened the primacy of Kaunitz. Now eighty-one, the chancellor found his measured, calculating policy towards France increasingly challenged by two younger colleagues, Philipp, Count Cobenzl and Anton, Baron Spielmann. As a result, his own tone with the Assembly became ever more strident. In a despatch of 17 February to Blumendorf, the Austrian chargé d'affaires in Paris, which was designed for communication to the French government, he condemned in menacing language 'the influence and violence of the republican party'.[4] He thought that this would cow the radicals and strengthen the moderates; in fact, it had precisely the opposite effect.

On 1 March, the foreign minister Lessart brought Kaunitz's

despatch to the Assembly to be read, along with his own reply to the previous Austrian notes. As an associate of the Feuillants, Lessart clung to the last tatters of their peace policy. His response to Vienna had therefore been timid and conciliatory. Hearing it, the Girondins were incensed, and their fury was roused to boiling-point by Kaunitz's subsequent despatch. Behind this Austrian aggression and the ministry's complaisant reply, they saw the hand of the king, and especially that of the queen. The royal couple's intrigues had to be checked, they decided, and this could only be done by making a Girondin foreign minister. An attack on the government would also have the beneficial effect of overawing the peace party. To drive the message home, Lessart was chosen as a sacrificial victim.

The plan was implemented on 10 March. As the Assembly was about to begin its session, the news of the emperor's death was received, which further inflamed the atmosphere. The likelihood that this would cause at least temporary confusion in Vienna emboldened the Girondins. Brissot rose and proposed that Lessart be impeached for neglect and betrayal of his duties and for compromising French honour and security. There was no substance to the charges, but the Girondins, undeterred, used their rhetoric to paint him as an agent of the familiar Austrian conspiracy. Beyond the hapless Lessart, of course, Brissot and his allies were taking aim at the royal family, and they did not bother to hide the fact. At the climax of the debate, Vergniaud mounted the rostrum and pointed dramatically at the Tuileries, clearly visible through the windows of the Manège. 'From this podium', he declaimed,

> one can see the place where treacherous counsels are leading the king astray ... terror and horror have often issued forth from this palace; they should enter it today in the name of the law! All inside it should know that only the king's person is inviolable, that the law will judge every criminal without distinction, and that not one guilty head will escape its blade![5]

These inflammatory words had their effect, the Assembly was moved to its usual transports, and the decree accusing Lessart was carried by a substantial majority. Vergniaud's speech, however, under-lined the dangers facing one particular inhabitant of the Tuileries –

the queen. It was widely reported that the Girondins wanted to put her on trial, on a charge of conspiring with the Austrian enemy. Another rumour, of which Breteuil in Brussels was quickly informed, was that she would be separated from the king and put into a convent. In this wider scheme, the fate of the foreign minister was of little importance. 'We'll let Lessart escape,' the deputies were over-heard muttering, 'but not the queen.'[6]

The most immediate legacy of the foreign minister's impeachment was a ministerial crisis. Two options faced the king. One was to defend his current ministers, moderates to a man and closely linked to the Feuillants, against a hostile Assembly now in full cry. The other was to surrender to the Girondins and give them the power they craved, in the expectation that under such crisis conditions this would prove a poisoned chalice. Louis chose the second path. Between 15 and 23 March, the Feuillant ministers departed and a Girondin government took their place. It contained three key figures: Roland, assiduously promoted by his dominating wife Manon Roland, at the interior, the Swiss speculator Clavière at finance, and the soldier, adventurer and former spy Dumouriez at the foreign ministry.

The net was drawing inexorably closer round the king and queen, and they were well aware of the fact. Both of them now faced the possibility that they would not survive. According to Bertrand de Molleville, Louis had for some time been convinced that he would shortly be assassinated. As for Marie Antoinette, even more directly menaced than her husband, she was so exhausted by the struggles of the past months that she viewed the approaching storm almost with relief. 'Everybody here is set on war,' she wrote to Fersen on 15 April, 'and so much the better if it resolves matters, because our position is no longer bearable.'[7] Under these desperate circumstances, the king and queen's policy shifted. The armed congress, they realized, was rapidly becoming irrelevant. Their priority now became self-preservation in the event of an armed conflict.

*

IF LOUIS'S AND Marie Antoinette's position inside France was worsening, their secret diplomacy abroad was becoming more coher-ent. Although the princes still had their representatives at the major

European courts, these were slowly becoming marginalized. This was because Breteuil's sole claim to speak in the king's name was now generally recognized. Most important, Louis XVI's letter to the king of Prussia of December 1791 had had the desired effect. Proof of this came in two cordial replies from Frederick William, one to Louis and one to the baron himself. In the second, Frederick William informed Breteuil that he was authorizing his ministers to negotiate with him alone over Prussian aid for the French monarchy. Even Breteuil's enemy Catherine the Great, despite her support for the princes, was forced to accept privately that he, not they, had Louis XVI's confidence. 'It is quite clear', she noted, 'that the baron de Breteuil is no less the king's man than the queen's, and that he has had plenipotential powers from Louis XVI for over nine months.'[8]

His position more secure than ever before, Breteuil could now extend his activities. To cement relations with Frederick William, in late January 1792 he sent an envoy of his own to Berlin, the thirty-year-old vicomte de Caraman. The youngest of Breteuil's protégés, Caraman had always been destined for a diplomatic career. At the age of eighteen, his parents had sent him on a grand tour of Europe, in the course of which he had met Frederick the Great, Catherine the Great, Joseph II, Gustavus III, Pitt the Younger and Charles James Fox. Caraman had first met Breteuil in Vienna in 1782, during the latter's embassy there. He had stayed for almost a year, and served his political apprenticeship by reading drafts of despatches back to Breteuil each morning while the baron dressed and powdered his hair, as was his habit, with his own hands. Later in life Caraman wrote his memoirs, and extracts dealing with his early life were published in the 1850s.[9] Tragically, the manuscript was then lost, and none of his recollections of the revolutionary era ever appeared. Caraman's actual despatches to Breteuil from Berlin do survive, however, and give much detail about his mission.

As a major if declining Power ruled by Louis XVI's own cousin Charles IV, Spain held an important place in the baron's diplomacy. He did not need to send an envoy to Madrid, since he already had one in place. This was none other than the duc de la Vauguyon, his former colleague in the Ministry of the Hundred Hours. After his resignation on 16 July 1789, la Vauguyon, who was still officially ambassador to Spain, had left Versailles to resume his embassy. Arrested at Le Havre by local revolutionaries, he had eventually been released and allowed to proceed. La Vauguyon had continued his embassy for a further eighteen months before finally resigning, but had prudently decided to stay on in Madrid. He had always got on well with the king, and went on enjoying his confidence even after he ceased to be ambassador. Breteuil, for his part, had never lost touch with la Vauguyon since the fall of his ministry. He knew he could not hope for a better-placed ally at the Spanish court, and the duke was delighted to be of service.

In St Petersburg, Bombelles was fighting an uphill battle against the polite hostility of Catherine the Great. After an exhausting winter journey, he arrived in the Russian capital on 26 January. He was carrying a letter from Marie Antoinette to the empress, begging for her support for the armed congress, backed up by two memoranda from Breteuil, one to Catherine and one to her chancellor, Count Ostermann. Yet he soon found that his hosts had reserved all their favour for the princes and their representative at St Petersburg, Count Valentin Esterhazy. The marquis was received by Ostermann on the very day of his arrival, but was kept kicking his heels for several weeks before Catherine herself agreed to see him.

Bombelles's most important audience with the empress took place on 17 March. At three in the afternoon he went to the Hermitage Palace, and was shown into the billiard-room. Catherine then arrived with Platon Zubov, the latest in her long line of younger lovers. Zubov soon left, and the empress drew up a chair next to the billiard table and motioned her guest to take an armchair opposite. Beneath her surface charm, however, Catherine was making no concessions. She spoke harshly of Louis XVI's vacillation and lack of energy, dismissed the armed congress plan as impracticable, and ended by pointedly praising Provence and Artois. Behind these words lay an eminently practical calculation. Russia could reap no solid gains from intervention in faraway France, whereas neighbouring Poland, currently even more unsettled than usual, seemed ripe for further partition. It was in the empress's interest that the Western Powers should be distracted by the problem of France, while she herself held back and waited for Poland to drop into her lap.

It was clear from this that Breteuil's projected Northern alliance to aid Louis XVI was unlikely to reach fruition. Increasingly depressed, Bombelles lingered in St Petersburg until late August and then departed. While Russia stood on the sidelines, the focus of events was shifting elsewhere.

The real breakthrough in the baron's diplomacy during these months was the sudden upsurge of Prussian goodwill. However, Breteuil had no illusions that this was disinterested. Frederick William II loudly proclaimed his sympathy for the plight of Louis XVI and Marie Antoinette, but his real aim was to enhance the power and prestige of his own kingdom. Frustrated of an expansionary war in the East by the end of the Turkish conflict, he now looked to the West. Breteuil soon received concrete proof of his real intentions. In late January 1792, a letter arrived from Frederick William's minister Schulenburg, pointing out that his master could not be expected to rescue Louis XVI without any regard for his own interests, and should be given some compensation for the trouble and expense involved. He was clearly hinting at the cession to Prussia of actual French lands, perhaps all or part of Alsace. Seriously alarmed, Breteuil rushed to deflect Prussian greed into less dangerous channels, proposing a financial rather than a territorial indemnity. Eventually his solution was accepted.[10]

More positively, the Prussians responded with enthusiasm to Breteuil's ideas for the armed congress. These were soon the object of detailed negotiations between the baron in Brussels and Schulenberg and Caraman in Berlin. The number of troops needed to support the congress was discussed, as were the precise demands it should make and at what point Louis XVI's mediation should be invoked. There was much debate about where exactly the congress should meet. Aix-la-Chapelle or Cologne were the most obvious locations. Citing his experience at the Congress of Teschen back in 1779, Breteuil pointed out that a small, quiet town would be preferable, as it would provide fewer diversions for the assembled diplomats and thus speed up their work. For this reason he strongly recommended Cologne,

> which really is extremely miserable: I insist on the importance of this because I remember that the frantic activity . . . that went into finishing the Congress of Teschen had much to do with the

dullness of the place; from which I concluded that congresses should always be held in a place offering the fewest possible distractions of society.[11]

The fact that Prussia and Austria had just signed a treaty of alliance further modified the situation. Although Berlin and Vienna still paid lip-service to the notion of a congress, it was clear that stronger measures were being actively prepared. Frederick William observed that the legislative assembly's ultimatum to Leopold of 24 January amounted to a declaration of war, and acted in consequence. The Duke of Brunswick, who had fought with Frederick the Great, was invited to Berlin to draw up plans for a military campaign against France, and the official French ambassador was sent packing. Austria proposed the joint mobilization of 80,000 men, and the Prussians agreed immediately.

This hardening of attitude towards revolutionary France chimed well with Breteuil's own feelings. He had worked for the armed congress because Louis XVI had ordered him to, but it is quite possible that he himself had little enthusiasm for it. Certainly the Bishop of Pamiers, on whom he was now heavily reliant, had opposed the congress from the start, feeling that it was too cumbersome and might not bring a decisive result. From January 1792, the baron came to see war as increasingly inevitable. His only fear was that France might start it before her opponents were prepared. For this reason, when the Assembly summoned the Electors of Mainz and Trier to expel the *émigrés*, he reluctantly counselled compliance, knowing that Austria and Prussia were not yet ready to act. He set out his thinking in his long letter of 1 January to Gustavus III, displaying as he did so some shrewd insights into the revolutionaries' motivation:

> The electors' prudent behaviour will not halt the rebels' aggression; the latter are telling each other that they will be attacked as soon as the campaigning season opens, and they think there is great advantage to be gained in anticipating this by ravaging twenty leagues of countryside before their attack can be contained by superior forces. They think that this first move will give their faction and their troops a great boldness, as well as a prestige which their pride will exaggerate; above all

they flatter themselves that this momentary apparent success will give their foreign proselytes powerful means of stirring up the population and rallying it to the slogans and standards of independence. You may know, sire, that to achieve this end they intend to emblazon in large letters on their standards: *Peace to the cottages, war to the castles*. They also think that they will raise the credit of the *assignats* for as long as they can maintain their troops on foreign soil. These, sire, are the reasons which impel the dominant party to launch their attack without delay, and which make me anticipate a recourse to arms. In this belief, and also in the conviction that the pace of events within France is outstripping our counter-measures outside, I have tried to impress upon Coblenz the necessity of combining firmness with prudence . . .[12]

The increasing likelihood of Austrian and Prussian intervention did not, in Breteuil's eyes, diminish the importance of Sweden and Russia. Austrian and Prussian resolve might falter at any moment, and if their help did finally materialize, it would certainly be at a price. In contrast to this, Sweden at least was relatively disinterested. Gustavus III did not fail to point this out, and warned Breteuil in March of the dangers of relying exclusively on the emperor and the king of Prussia:

The season is well advanced and Austria and Prussia will soon act and exclude the North. I leave it to you to judge what will happen to yourself, France and His Most Christian Majesty, should you be left to the mercy of those two Powers if they are not counterbalanced by those of the North.[13]

Gustavus still persisted in his plan of leading a Russo-Swedish expeditionary force against the Normandy coast, and Breteuil felt it prudent to encourage this. In general terms, it was important to keep the mercurial king's enthusiasm for the cause of Louis XVI burning brightly. More specifically, should Austria and Prussia call off their attack, Gustavus's plan would be the only hope.

The difficulty was money. Sweden was a poor country, and financially exhausted by the cost of her recent war with Russia. In addition, the Revolution had robbed Gustavus of the annual French subsidy he had enjoyed – indeed, one of his motivations in helping in attempts to restore Louis XVI's authority was to ensure its resumption. Financial aid had to be sought from somewhere, and Gustavus's roving eye settled on Spain. King Charles IV was clearly not about to send troops across the Pyrenees to help his cousin, but his kingdom had substantial economic resources, derived not least from the gold and silver mines of South America. To unlock this door, Gustavus needed a key that only Breteuil could provide – the duc de la Vauguyon, with his extensive connections at the Spanish court. These were vital to counteract the notoriously stately pace at which the Spanish government did business: 'It is your task, Monsieur le baron,' wrote Gustavus, 'to find the best means of speeding up Spanish slowness.'[14]

La Vauguyon set to work, and by late February his efforts had begun to pay off. Charles IV intimated that he would furnish sixteen million *reales* to Gustavus immediately, and as much as could be raised thereafter.[15] Then came a serious blow. The Spanish leading minister, Count Floridablanca, who was favourable to the French royal cause, fell from power. He was replaced by his long-standing rival, Count Aranda, who was correspondingly lukewarm about aiding Louis XVI. La Vauguyon's negotiations began to languish. This put Breteuil in an unenviable position, since the pressure from Gustavus was growing rapidly. Bouillé, who had now entered the Swedish service, had drawn up for the king a detailed plan of operations for a landing on the French coast, and he was impatient to put it into effect. It was now clear, however, that funds from Spain would not be forthcoming. All Breteuil could do was express his frustration in increasingly colourful terms:

> I am charmed that Your Majesty is pleased with the plan of campaign that M. de Bouillé has sent him; it would be dreadful if mere lack of money were to prevent its implementation. I could drink my own blood, sire, seeing this obstacle in the way of your first steps, when it is so clear that abundant means will swiftly follow them.[16]

Despite his fervour for the French royal cause, Gustavus also had to attend to his own kingdom. The Swedish nobility, always turbulent, had attempted to exploit his difficulties during the war with Russia to regain their former power. In the spring of 1789, however, he had managed to turn the tables on them by summoning a Diet in Stockholm, arresting the principal noble leaders, including Fersen's own father, and promulgating a new constitution that turned Sweden into a virtually absolute monarchy. Gustavus was only able to do this by gaining the support of the non-noble estates in the Diet. Louis XVI would have done well to remember this when he opened his own Estates General just one month later.

In January 1792, Gustavus held another successful Diet, where measures were passed to stave off the state bankruptcy that loomed following the Russo-Swedish war. By this time, however, a number of nobles had grown tired of opposing the king by constitutional methods, and resolved to assassinate him. Just how widely the conspiracy extended remains mysterious, but some sources claim that it encompassed almost half the Swedish aristocracy. They chose as their instrument a fanatical and disgruntled former army officer, Jakob Johan Anckarström. Soon, rumours of the plot were beginning to leak out, so it became imperative to act at once. When it was announced that Gustavus would be attending the last masked ball of the season at the Stockholm opera house on 16 March, the conspirators decided to kill him there.

At 11 p.m. on the 14th, the king arrived at the opera house accompanied by his chief equerry, Baron Essen, and a small group of courtiers, and sat down to supper in the private apartment he kept there. During the meal, an anonymous letter was brought to Gustavus, warning him that an attempt on his life would be made that night at the ball. Yet the king, whose personal courage had always been remarkable, brushed aside the advice, and put on a tricorne hat, a Venetian silk cloak, and a half-mask which in no way concealed his identity. He then stepped out into the royal box with Essen to observe the ball in progress below. He immediately noticed a group of guests in black cloaks and half-masks whispering together, who hurriedly dispersed as soon as they saw him. Gustavus continued to stand, quite immobile, in full view of the partygoers below, for fifteen minutes. Then, turning to Essen, he quipped: 'They have lost a good opportunity of shooting me. Come, let us go down.'[17]

On entering the grand saloon where the ball was taking place, the king was immediately recognized, and toured the throng before disappearing briefly into the Green Room. Anckarström and his companions, who were observing his every movement, quickly made their dispositions. The moment Gustavus and Essen stepped back into the saloon, the black cloaks swept forward, trapping them on both sides. One of the conspirators then tapped the king on the shoulder to indicate him to Anckarström, and uttered the prearranged words: 'Adieu, beau masque [Farewell, fine mask]!' Anckarström immediately fired a pistol containing two bullets, fourteen scraps of lead and iron and a few nails for good measure into the king's back.

Held upright by the assailants pressing against him, Gustavus did not fall, but would certainly have been finished off if another equerry and a guardsman, alerted by the muffled shot, had not rushed to his aid. Quite conscious, the king was helped back up to his apartment, while the news of what had happened quickly spread.

Anckarström, who had dropped his weapons in the scuffle, was swiftly arrested when these were traced back to him, and soon afterwards the principal conspirators were under lock and key. Anckarström suffered the prescribed penalty for regicide: flogging, amputation of the hand that had done the deed, and beheading. There were, however, no other executions. The king himself lingered for two more weeks before dying on 29 March. Since his son was still a minor, a regency was established under his brother Charles, who had no intention of embarking on foreign adventures. All Swedish plans to rescue the French royal family died with Gustavus III.

Breteuil received the news of the attempt on the king's life on 1 April. His reaction, according to Fersen who observed it, was one of consternation. The next despatches announced Gustavus's death. Writing to Bombelles, Breteuil made no secret of his grief:

> Like myself, you will today be mourning this great man; you know how attached I had been to him since his childhood, and all his generosity to me. I cannot sufficiently express to you the extreme pain of my heart, and the darkness which this terrible event throws over my spirit and my soul.[18]

The baron had good reason to mourn the passing of Gustavus III. Anckarström's pistol shot had robbed him of a friend of thirty years' standing and Louis XVI and Marie Antoinette of their only disinterested ally. From now on, Breteuil's task would be harder and bleaker.

*

As Austrian and Prussian intervention drew closer, so too did the prospect of an end to the Revolution. For Breteuil this had a special significance. In the spring of 1792, he was once again in the position he had been in just before the flight to Varennes. If the king and queen were indeed rescued and their authority restored, it was obvious that the baron would be their prime minister. As before, his first task would be to find a settlement to the upheavals of the past three years. How much, if at all, had his views on the subject changed since Varennes, and what light do they shed on the policy of Louis and Marie Antoinette themselves?

On this vital issue, posterity is once more indebted to Bombelles. During his mission to St Petersburg, the marquis kept up a substantial correspondence with Breteuil, which has largely survived. In it, the baron was candid about his political views and strategy. There was a particular reason for this. Ever since Varennes, the princes and their emissaries had been mounting a campaign aimed at discrediting him. Above all, they sought to portray him as a *deux-chambres*, in league with the moderate revolutionaries to bring about a French constitutional monarchy based on a two-chamber parliament. Their aim in this was to present him as a traitor to France's 'antique constitution', prepared to compromise with a revolution that the rest of Europe held in horror.

Nothing could have been further from the truth. Breteuil remained what he always had been, a partisan of the traditional three orders rather than the two-chamber legislature championed by the *monarchiens*. He himself rejected the charge of being a *deux-chambres* in a despatch to Bombelles of 16 March 1792. Here, he suggested ways in which the marquis could dispel Catherine the Great's suspicion that he was prepared to compromise Louis XVI's authority. Was it likely, Breteuil pointed out, that a man who had defended the king's rights so stoutly against the princes would adopt a different policy towards revolutionaries and rebels? 'It will surely not escape Her Majesty', he wrote, that it would have been easier for me to be much more complaisant towards the princes, and you will not find it difficult to drive home the message that a mealy-mouthed *monarchien* or *monarchiste*, happy to bargain with the rights of the king, would not have taken the approach I have towards his brothers. I flatter myself that the long-standing esteem which the empress has for me will give force to your words, and destroy all the slanders she has been told about me. You could recall how the unfortunate Archbishop of Sens [Loménie de Brienne], whose aim was the destruction of the royal authority and the monarchy and always found me strongly opposed to the treacherous ideas he insinuated to the king by abusing his virtues, nicknamed me the *louisquatorʒian*, to paint me as an extremist in my support of the rights of the crown.[19]

In fact, Bombelles needed no encouragement to defend his master. On his own initiative he drew up a written defence of Breteuil, and read the entire document to Catherine the Great at his audience on 17 March 1792. The deadliest charge he cited, and the one he took most care to refute, was that 'M. de Breteuil had a plan ready to put into action the moment the king was free [at the time of Varennes], which included the formation of two chambers and a new constitution abolishing all the rights of the clergy, nobility and magistrature'.[20]

Interestingly, for Bombelles support for the *deux-chambres* was indistinguishable from Anglomania, the desire to impose an English-style constitution on France through a two-chamber parliament. To clear Breteuil's name on the first count, his method was to rebut the second:

It is . . . a fact that M. de Breteuil, while respecting the English form of government, has never thought for one instant that [it] was suitable for France, and that he has always worked for, and has never suggested to the king any other constitution than, the restoration of the one under which France has flourished for many centuries.[21]

It is clear from this evidence that Breteuil's general constitutional views did not change after Varennes, and that they remained as conservative as before. How, in this new climate of confrontation and war, did he propose to put them into effect? The most detailed

account of his aims and strategy at this juncture is provided by the
Bishop of Pamiers. On 7 March, while the baron was laid up with a
severe attack of gout, the bishop wrote a long letter on his behalf to
Bombelles in St Petersburg. Its central section discussed Austrian
policy towards the Revolution. Like Breteuil, the bishop was convinced that Austria's real aim for France was a constitutional
monarchy that would keep her weak in the future. Yet he predicted
that this goal would be quickly frustrated if the royal family did
regain their liberty. 'The emperor is strangely deceived', he wrote,

> if he thinks that once the rebels are defeated and the king free,
> His Majesty will still be obliged to make an unsound compro-
> mise with the agitators, by which he would have to cede a large
> part of his legitimate authority . . . The king once at liberty will
> find, in his nobility and his faithful subjects, and in the Swiss
> and Hessian troops he will be able to take into his pay, sufficient
> means to regain and maintain his legitimate and tutelary
> authority.[22]

These lines make one fact clear. In the wake of a successful
invasion of France, the political settlement Breteuil and his colleagues
wished to impose was quite uncompromising. Instead of a negotiated
solution, the royal authority would be reimposed, by force if
necessary. Just as they had planned in the spring of 1791, when
preparing the king's flight from Paris, their main instrument would
be Swiss troops, reinforced this time by Hessians. The continuity
with policy before Varennes was underlined by the fact that with this
letter the bishop enclosed the highly conservative plan Breteuil had
sent to Luxembourg the previous May in readiness for Louis XVI's
successful escape. Bombelles should use it, he wrote, to dispel any
last doubt in Catherine the Great's mind that Breteuil was a closet
constitutionalist. Again, the bishop's words make his purpose plain:
'I do not think you could have a more decisive proof with which to
destroy those charges, which nothing can justify, of *monarchiste* or
monarchien, and apostle of the two chambers.'[23]

The plan was ready; it only remained to put it into effect. The
acceleration of the crisis made the calling of a congress much less
likely, and this delighted the bishop. He had always suspected that if
it did meet, the emperor would exploit it to open negotiations with

the Assembly. A straight fight, in his view, offered the best chance of restoring the royal power. The Austro-Prussian alliance, and Berlin's sudden conversion to counter-revolution, brought this much closer. The bishop did not hide his satisfaction from Bombelles, writing:

> You can see, my dear marquis, that no one any longer is thinking of a congress, and I am certainly much relieved, for it was a pure product of necessity, and the resolve of the court of Berlin, by forcing the emperor's hand, will enable us to dispense with this measure.[24]

War was looming, and to some at least it was welcome. Breteuil may have been in bed with gout, but his closest collaborator was in his element. With unwavering faith in the royal authority, and thinking more of battle plans than the cure of souls, the Bishop of Pamiers looked forward eagerly to the conflict.

*

IN PARIS, the ministerial crisis had brought to power the man who would finally touch off the explosion. This was General Charles François Dumouriez, the new foreign minister. Fifty-three years old, 'tough and wiry, with an ordinary, almost ugly face, agreeable expression, and bold, darting eyes',[25] Dumouriez was to play a central role in this crisis of the Revolution. He had an adventurous past; having fought in the Seven Years War, he had then become a spy for Louis XV. Falling foul of ministerial intrigues, he had been imprisoned in the Bastille before being released at Louis XVI's accession. In 1778, he had become the military commander at Cherbourg, a post he held until 1790. In foreign policy, his guiding principle was a deep hatred of Austria.

Dumouriez's path to the Girondins had lain through this Austrophobia. Yet he was by no means as radical in domestic politics as they. He lacked their passionate commitment to the Revolution; he distrusted the popular movement and his ideal was a constitutional monarchy that would guarantee order. This principle also dovetailed with his immense personal ambition. Stability and order would only return if France's present political chaos was ended, and he intended to achieve this himself with the help of the military. As the first revolutionary politician to trace out this path, bringing the army to the centre of the political stage, Dumouriez anticipated Napoleon.

Externally, Dumouriez was convinced that Austria was bent on exploiting the Revolution to invade and dismember France. The best form of defence, he decided, was attack. A French invasion of Belgium would throw the Austrians into confusion, while the Belgians' recent uprising against Vienna would make them willing prey for revolutionary propaganda. At the same time, Dumouriez planned a diplomatic offensive to isolate his enemy. He was a great admirer of Frederick the Great, and dreamed of an alliance with Prussia. He also wished to win over some of the smaller German states. By this time, of course, any *rapprochement* with Prussia was a pipe-dream, but the new foreign minister was undeterred. He pressed forward down the final slope into war.

Provocation was Dumouriez's method. On 27 March he addressed a further ultimatum to Austria. In deliberately insulting language, he warned that if by 15 April she had not formally renounced the armed congress project and ceased her build-up of troops on the Rhine, France would consider herself at war. When Kaunitz received this note, he exploded with fury. Echoes of his wrath reached the vicomte de Caraman in Berlin. 'The interests of all Europe having previously failed to move [the chancellor],' wrote Caraman to Breteuil, 'he was driven wild by the insolences of M. Dumouriez, to whom he wishes to prove that his ancient hands can still inflict blows.'[26] The Austrian reply was a curt rejection of the French demands. It arrived in Paris on the night of 14–15 April, and was discussed at a council of ministers three days later. It was at this meeting that the decision to fight was finally taken.

A formal declaration of war, however, could only come from the king. As the prospects for the congress had receded, Louis XVI had come to accept that armed conflict was inevitable, and had already begun to adapt his policy in consequence. He was determined, however, that if the war went badly, as he was convinced it would, the Girondins should not be able to dodge responsibility by throwing the blame on him. He demanded that each minister should set out his signed opinion on the matter in his own hand, and that these should be published, which was done. Satisfied, Louis agreed to support their decision. On the morning of 20 April 1792, he appeared in the

Assembly, which was already surrounded by a huge crowd. Inside, the floor and galleries were packed. First, Dumouriez read a report prepared by the ministers, accusing Austria of systematically betraying her alliance with France ever since its inception in 1756. Then, in a flat, faltering voice, the king proposed that war be declared on Austria.

Louis then left the hall, and the deputies began to debate the proposal. Patriotic frenzy soon took hold. One by one, the Girondin orators rose to stoke it. 'The people want war,' declaimed Mailhe, 'you must swiftly surrender to its generous impatience. You will give liberty perhaps to the entire world.' 'I believe,' cried his colleague Merlin, 'that we must bring war to the kings and peace to the people!'[27] Amid transports of enthusiasm, and with only seven dissenting votes, war was declared. With a few brief pauses, it would last for twenty-three years.

*

IF THE ASSEMBLY thought that hostilities could be limited to Austria, it was sorely mistaken. Frederick William II viewed the assault on his ally as an attack on himself, and accelerated his military preparations. By the middle of July, France was at war with Prussia and, for good measure, the kingdom of Sardinia.

In the spring of 1792, the state of the French army belied the deputies' confident rhetoric. Ever since 1789, insubordination among the troops had been growing. The reaction of many officers, who as nobles had particular reasons for disliking the Revolution anyway, was to emigrate. Between 15 September and 1 December 1791 alone, 2,160 officers left France. The regiments which spearheaded Dumouriez's grand offensive into Belgium were thus ill equipped to sustain a campaign. The army of the North began its attack on 28 April 1792. It was disposed in three columns, commanded respectively by Generals Dillon, de Biron and La Fayette. Just outside Tournai, Dillon's column ran into Austrian artillery fire. The result was ignominious panic, retreat turned into rout, and the general himself was swept along in the flood. The troops then turned on Dillon, accusing him of betraying them, and sent him under arrest back to Lille. Hardly had he arrived there than he was dragged from his carriage, stabbed and bayoneted to death, and his body publicly burned in the city's main square.

The other columns met a similar fate. Biron's soldiers, like Dillon's, fled at the first contact with the enemy in their advance on Mons, blaming the fiasco on their general. Biron too was arrested, but fortunately escaped lynching. With the rest of the army in full flight, La Fayette was compelled to beat a hasty retreat. If the Austrians had followed up their advantage then and there, they could have gained a decisive victory. However, they too were unprepared, their commanders were cautious, and they were waiting for their Prussian allies. It was a fateful precedent. Over the coming year, the French would owe their survival to the hesitations of their enemies.

These disasters led to further upheavals in Paris. In the panicking city, popular paranoia, fuelled by rumours of counter-revolutionary plots, was mounting steadily. The authorities hurried to match the mood of the people. On 18 May all foreigners in Paris were placed under surveillance. In this atmosphere, it was easy for the Girondins once again to blame Louis XVI. The bad news from the front, Brissot claimed, was caused not by the troops' cowardice but by the machinations of the 'Austrian committee' in the Tuileries. As before, the aim was to force Louis either to declare himself openly opposed to the Revolution, or to surrender to it completely. Between 27 May and 8 June, the Girondins passed through the Assembly three more decrees designed to flush him out of cover. The first was directed at that favourite target, the refractory clergy, who were now to face deportation if they did not take the oath to the constitution. The second was intended literally to disarm the king, by abolishing the guard the constitution allowed him. To overawe him further, a camp of 20,000 National Guards from the provinces, whose revolutionary sentiments could be relied upon, was to be set up just outside Paris. Since their arrival was timed to coincide with the annual feast of the Federation on 14 July, they would be known as *fédérés*.

The king drank some, but not all, of this poisoned chalice. He agreed to disband his constitutional guard, which was now replaced by units of the Paris National Guard. In this weakened state, however, it would have been sheer suicide to countenance a hostile force of 20,000 at the gates of the capital. Louis therefore decided to veto this decree, as well as the one concerning refractory priests, which he saw as yet another violation of his conscience.

When he told his ministers his intentions, the result was a political crisis. The minister of the interior, Roland, wrote a public letter which he then read to Louis, demanding that he sanction the decrees immediately. 'Much more delay,' he warned, 'and a grieving people will see in its king the friend and accomplice of conspirators.'[28] This was tantamount to an accusation of high treason, and could not be tolerated. On 13 June, invoking one of his few remaining powers, the king dismissed Roland, along with Clavière and the minister of war, Servan. Dumouriez remained, but was shifted from foreign affairs to the war ministry. He thought he could now dominate policymaking, but realized after only a few days that the king did not intend to follow his advice. Concluding that there was nothing further to be done in Paris, he resigned in turn and went off to a command at the front. The political situation was collapsing, and his real faith had always been in the army.

The Girondins hastened to pick up the gauntlet Louis had thrown down. Within days, they had an added reason for doing so. From his command on the border, La Fayette had viewed the developments in the capital with alarm. He still retained some prestige, and it was time to throw it into the balance. He wrote an open letter to the Assembly, which was read out on 18 June. In harsh tones, he demanded the suppression of the popular clubs and a reinforcement of royal authority. Briefly asserting themselves, the deputies of the Right and Centre rose in applause and voted that the letter be published and distributed. Behind La Fayette's menacing phrases, backed as they were by an army, loomed the shadow of a *coup d'état*.

The Girondins riposted with their own weapon – the people of Paris. They organized a mass demonstration for 20 June. Ostensibly this was to present a petition calling for the reinstatement of the Girondin ministers and the withdrawal of the king's vetos, but its real aim was to overawe the Assembly and break the remaining royal power for good. That morning, a crowd 8,000 strong, armed with muskets, pikes and bludgeons, converged on the city centre. The Assembly was invaded, and the entire procession filed through it, singing and shouting revolutionary slogans. A pike was brandished on which a calf's heart was impaled, above the inscription: 'The heart of an aristocrat'. Fortified by this show of strength, the crowd moved on to the Tuileries.

The royal family awaited the mob's arrival with stoicism. The king was just emerging from a severe bout of depression. That May, according to Mme Campan, he had fallen into a form of stupor, and had not uttered a single word for ten days on end, except those necessary when playing backgammon with Mme Elisabeth. On one occasion, he even failed to recognize his son, and asked who the child was. As with the Girondins' provocations the previous December, the Assembly's attacks forced Louis out of this black despair. He well knew what price he might pay for his resistance. When he heard what was planned for 20 June, he wrote a brief note to his confessor: 'I have finished with men; I look to Heaven. Great misfortunes are expected tomorrow; I shall have courage.'[29]

At four in the afternoon the crowd broke into the Tuileries, the National Guard doing nothing to stop them. They stormed up the main staircase, dragging a cannon behind them. They advanced through the upper rooms, smashing down the doors with axes and pikes, until they found the king standing in an anteroom. Mme Elisabeth, who was beside him, threw herself forward to protect him, but was quickly hustled off to safety. In the meantime, some courtiers had rushed the queen and her children into the *salle du conseil*, and pushed them behind a makeshift barrier of upturned tables and furniture. The room was soon invaded by the mob, which pressed up against the barricade hurling abuse, but did no more.

The focus of the people's fury was the king. Backed into the embrasure of a window, with only a few loyal grenadiers and attendants around him, he faced the angry demonstrators, separated from them only by a table. One of the grenadiers told him not to be afraid. In answer, Louis took the man's hand and placed it on his chest. 'Feel my heart,' he said, 'it is quite calm.' The petition demanding the recall of the Girondin ministers and the withdrawal of the vetos was read to him, punctuated by loud shouts of 'No aristocrats! No veto! No priests!' Pistols and sabres were thrust in his face. Throughout this terrifying ordeal Louis remained composed and good-humoured. A red cap of liberty was pushed towards him on the end of a pike, and he put it on. A bottle of wine was presented to him, with the demand that he drink his visitors' health, and he toasted the people of Paris. On the issues of principle, however, he stayed absolutely firm: he would neither reappoint the ministers nor sanction the decrees.

An impasse had now been reached. It was only broken by the arrival of Pétion, who had accompanied the royal family back from Varennes and was now mayor of Paris and an ally of the Girondins. Although he knew exactly what was going on, he had studiously refrained from intervening, hoping that the king would either be killed or forced to agree to the petition. Yet by six in the evening even Pétion was compelled to act, and he made his way to the Tuileries. He greeted the king with the most threadbare of excuses: 'Sire, I have just this minute learned of your situation.' 'That is very surprising,' replied Louis, 'since this has been going on for at least two hours.'[30] At 8 p.m., the crowd finally left the palace. The royal family were still alive, but they had stared death in the face.

In the short term, the brutal invasion of the palace and the king's remarkable courage created a reaction in favour of the monarchy. Loyal addresses flooded in from the provinces, condemning what had taken place. This was even echoed in the capital itself, where a petition protesting at the events of 20 June collected 20,000 signatures. The department of Paris suspended Pétion from his functions as mayor. Yet if the king had won this round, the final confrontation had only been postponed. Royalist volunteers enlisted to guard the Tuileries, while loyal units of the National Guard braced themselves for a fight. On the other side, the popular forces regrouped to plan their next offensive. The endgame was rapidly approaching.

*

THE CONDUCT OF the king and queen during the last weeks of the monarchy has often seemed confused and hesitant. They made no bold move to break the hostile forces closing in on them, and remained consistently on the defensive. Historians have concluded from this that they had no coherent policy, and were by now simply hapless victims of events beyond their control. This is not the case. The passivity of Louis XVI and Marie Antoinette formed part of a deliberate strategy, and reflected, *in extremis*, an ultimate choice.

The most significant development during these days, on the

royalist side, was that the moderate revolutionaries made one last attempt to save the crown. This eleventh-hour effort was the Feuillants' swansong, and its central figure was La Fayette. Shocked by the news of 20 June, the general left his post at the frontier and rushed to Paris. On 28 June, he made a speech in the Assembly, demanding once more the closure of the clubs and the restoration of order. He had his own plans for achieving the latter. The following day, a review of the 2nd Legion of the National Guard was to be held in the Champs-Elysées. La Fayette proposed to go there with the king, rally the soldiers and march on the Jacobin Club. Marie Antoinette, however, had lost none of her dislike and distrust of La Fayette, and was determined not to place the monarchy in his debt. She arranged for Pétion to be warned of what was afoot, and the review was cancelled.[31]

A few weeks later, the Feuillants made a further overture to the king and queen. La Fayette again played a crucial role, but the scheme was broader based and better worked out. It revolved around the army of the Rhine, commanded by La Fayette, and the army of Flanders, led by another moderate, General Luckner. Under the pretence of swapping positions, the armies would unite near the border at La Capelle. La Fayette would then go personally to Paris and excort the royal family to Compiègne, where the troops would now have marched. Louis XVI would then convoke the majority of the Assembly to Compiègne. He would forbid the Austrian and Prussian armies to advance any further, negotiate a truce, mediate between his subjects and the foreign invaders, and propose a revised constitution that reinforced the royal authority.[32]

The plan reads like a compendium of every attempt to end the Revolution by compromise since Mirabeau defected to the court. All the familiar elements were present – an open royal departure from Paris, residence at Compiègne, at a safe distance but not too far from the capital, and modification but not overthrow of the constitution. The moderates' pet project, the two chambers, was also revived, for the last time. This is clear from a report by Mercy-Argenteau to Kaunitz. True to their old policy, the Feuillants wanted Austrian backing. They therefore sent a secret emissary, named Masson de Saint-Amand, to Brussels to ask for support. 'M. de Saint-Amand', wrote Mercy, outlined the whole system at great length. It consists of dividing the legislature into two chambers, one of which as the upper chamber would be made up of notable persons, elected for a whole parliament and eligible not by right as nobles, but as the wealthiest property-holders; nobility will be restored in France, but without exclusive privileges, and only enjoying titles, coats of arms, decorations, etc. on a courtesy basis. A permanent legislature would remain the basis of the constitution, and the king would be given powers approaching those which the English have assigned to their monarch.[33]

Confirmation of this conversation is provided by Masson de Saint-Amand himself. When Duport, who as a leading Feuillant had strongly supported the plan, was arrested soon after the fall of the monarchy, several incriminating letters were found on his person. Though anonymous, they were clearly from Masson de Saint-Amand, reporting on his mission to Mercy. Naturally, they used a code to guard against interception, but this was of the most rudimentary kind: Mercy became 'the mother's' (i.e. Austria's) business agent, Louis XVI 'the husband', and the second legislative chamber 'a spare room for his friends'. Masson wrote to Duport:

> I have just had my second conversation with the mother's business agent, and I was more satisfied than I had hoped. . . . The aim is to end the husband's illness, see him housed more comfortably and able to get some fresh air, and with enough space to keep a spare room for his friends.[34]

The means of effecting this salutary cure were also discussed. Echoing what the Bishop of Pamiers had earlier written to Bombelles, Mercy thought that this would be best achieved by Swiss troops. In Masson's letter, these were charmingly disguised as 'Swiss herbs'. Fortified by this 'foreign remedy', the convalescent 'husband' would then complete his recovery at a town with a bracing north wind, no doubt Compiègne:

> The mention of a foreign remedy surprised me, but [added the business agent] do not be alarmed, there is a very simple one, and that is Swiss herbs. I am sure these will restore the ease of digestion necessary to [the husband's] health. He won't have to

travel to the Alps to find them, but can simply have them brought to him, and then he can choose a healthy place for himself on his estates – he has plenty of choice – but the airiest and most exposed to the north wind would be best.[35]

If Masson thought he had won over Mercy, however, he was deceived. In his despatch to Kaunitz, the ambassador dismissed the overture with his usual cool contempt. It was, he said, simply proof of the desperation and 'state of nullity to which the Feuillant leaders are now reduced'.[36] He particularly objected to the fact that Masson had no formal accreditation, and used this as an excuse not to commit himself to his proposals. Whatever the Austrians may have thought in the past, now was not the time for negotiation.

Most decisively of all, after agonized deliberation the king and queen themselves rejected the Feuillants' plan. For a time they were divided, with Louis favouring it and Marie Antoinette opposed. This is clear from the latter's note to Fersen, dated 11 July:

> The const[itutionalists], together with La Fayette and Luckner, want to escort the king to Compiègne the day after the [festival of the] Federation. The king is disposed to lend himself to this project; the queen is combating it. The outcome of this great matter, which I am far from approving, is still in doubt.[37]

Much has been made of this last-minute disagreement between Louis XVI and Marie Antoinette. This is because once again it seems to mirror a deeper political divergence between husband and wife. In favouring the Feuillants' plan, the king was putting himself in the hands of moderate revolutionaries who would never have permitted a return to absolute monarchy. It was precisely for this reason that the queen threw her weight against the scheme. Yet once again Louis finally yielded to Marie Antoinette. He refused the increasingly desperate offers of Duport and La Fayette, and told the latter to go back to his army. At the last, he conformed to the behaviour pattern evident throughout the Revolution and noted by Fersen on his last visit: initial hesitation and willingness to compromise, swiftly overcome by the urgings of his wife.

In reaching this conclusion, Louis and Marie Antoinette reaffirmed the decision they had already made together twice before, in the spring and then the autumn of 1791. For the third and final time, they turned down the offer of a compromise settlement to the Revolution based on a constitutional monarchy. Instead, they staked their lives on the most dangerous course of all. They would hold out in Paris, and hope to survive long enough to be rescued by the invading foreign armies. This was because a full-blooded restoration of the royal authority could now be achieved only by Austrian and Prussian arms. To the king and queen, this prize was worth the gamble, although the odds were shortening every day.

In one area, Marie Antoinette did take action of which her husband may have been unaware. On 26 March in a letter to Mercy-Argenteau, and in notes to Fersen of 5 and 23 June and 11 July, she passed on information about French war plans from what she had gleaned from discussions in the *conseil*. From the revolutionaries' point of view, this was treason, although it is unlikely that the queen herself would have recognized it as such. Had this evidence been produced at Marie Antoinette's trial, it would massively have strengthened the case for the prosecution. Fortunately for her, however, it remained safely in the hands of her confidants abroad.[38]

It is a measure of the efficiency of royalist spies that Provence and Artois almost immediately got wind of the Feuillants' intrigue. On 10 July, they addressed a memorandum to Breteuil, with copies to all the European courts, asking for his assurance that the rumours were without foundation. In particular, they were alarmed by reports that the king was about to declare a truce that would bolster the Feuillants' position. Some of the princes' fear was genuine. Yet, as usual, they were also trying to discredit Breteuil by insinuating that if secret negotiations were indeed afoot, then he himself must be involved in them. As Fersen put it in his diary:

> The princes have written a foolish memorandum that is insolent towards the king, claiming that through weakness he is working with the constitutionalists to ask for a truce and negotiations, and that we must not listen to him; they have sent this to the baron for him to reply ... Calonne says that the baron will surely not respond, thus implying that he supports this policy.[39]

It is clear from Fersen's diary that Breteuil replied to the princes' memorandum. This reply has never been published. A copy does exist, however, preserved by Fersen himself and now in his papers in the Swedish State Archives. It starkly outlines the baron's own attitude to negotiations with the revolutionaries at this point. In line with his previous policy, Breteuil resolutely opposed them. The document also provides confirmation of the king and queen's basic unwillingness to compromise. The baron was well informed about the deliberations of the Tuileries. Had he seriously suspected that his sovereigns would adopt the compromise put forward by the Feuillants, he would never have dared to reject the possibility as categorically as he did. What was more, he did it in the king's name:

> It would be too unjust to support that His Majesty had any other [views] than those dictated by his interests, his glory and his courage; in the king's present cruel position he is obliged to listen to his enemies and often to pretend to share their opinions, but the king has the right to hope, and even to demand, that his wishes not be confused with those of his captors.
>
> The king is well aware that the constitutionalists are quite as untrustworthy as the Jacobins; His Majesty has had all too much proof that the differing views of these factions have always been united in their wish to destroy the crown; we can therefore be certain that he will never delude himself that either has any intention of restoring his rights. To regain these, the king counts solely on the courage and fidelity of the princes and the French nobility, and on the Powers whose friendship and high principles have brought them to his aid.[40]

On the issue of the truce itself, Breteuil was no less forthright. He admitted that the first he had heard of the rumour was through the princes' own memorandum, but he vigorously denied that it could have emanated from the king: '[The baron] can easily believe that these fraudulent overtures are coming from the Jacobins or constitutionalists, but he has no hesitation in affirming that they are in no way authorized by the king.'[41]

The passivity of Louis XVI's and Marie Antoinette's policy in the final days of their reign should not be mistaken for incoherence. The only active strategy possible was to accept La Fayette's and the

Feuillants' plan, and make a break for Compiègne. Since this meant
endorsing a fully constitutional monarchy, the king and queen
rejected it. The one remaining course was to remain in Paris and
wait for the invading armies. This was the option the royal couple
chose, though they were quite aware that by the time the Austrians
and Prussians arrived, they themselves might no longer be alive to
welcome them. Those who seek proof of the king and queen's
moderation at this juncture will be disappointed. Admirers of bravery,
on the other hand, will not. As the Bishop of Pamiers put it to
Bombelles: 'Our sovereigns' outlook remains the same; the courage
and firmness I myself have witnessed have not faltered, and I hope
that these virtues, so necessary in their position, will sustain them to
the end.'[42]

*

By July 1792, an invasion of France was imminent. An army of
80,000 men, commanded by the Duke of Brunswick, was massing in
the Rhineland. Its centre was formed by 42,000 Prussians, supported
by 5,500 Hessians. Its flanks were made up of Austrian troops, 15,000
on the right under Clerfayt, and 14,000 on the left under Hohenlohe.
It was not anticipated that the disorganized French forces facing them
would put up serious resistance. Brunswick's plan was to advance
into Champagne, brush them aside, and march straight for Paris.

It was obvious that the Austro-Prussian entry into France would
bring to a head the dangers facing the royal family. How best to
confront them was a delicate and agonizing question. In the Tuileries,
the king and queen were concerned above all that the princes should
not do what they had threatened just before the flight to Varennes,
and issue a provocative manifesto. This, they were convinced, would
infuriate the people of Paris and place their own lives in serious
jeopardy. Immediately after war was declared, in May 1792, Louis
XVI sent the moderate royalist journalist Jacques Mallet du Pan to
the maréchal de Castries in Cologne with a draft manifesto. At first
sight, it seems odd that the document was given to Castries and not
to Breteuil. In fact, it is not surprising, given the baron's parlous
relations with the princes, which had recently deteriorated even
further after his despatch of Bombelles to St Petersburg. Louis XVI's
overriding aim was to rein in his brothers; he had a much better

chance of doing this with Castries, whom he had brought into play precisely for this purpose, than with Breteuil.

The document that Mallet du Pan presented to Castries was carefully judged. It deliberately avoided detail, but insisted simply on the safety and freedom of the royal family, and the restoration of order and the Catholic religion within France. The king stressed particularly that any manifesto 'should menace only the rebels and not France as a whole; it should not reflect any feelings of animosity or vengeance'.[43] Castries was sceptical at first, but Mallet du Pan eventually won him round, and the marshal agreed to send him on to meet the princes.

By this time, however, it was too late. Delayed by various misadventures, Mallet du Pan arrived in Cologne only after the events of 20 June in Paris. In the interim, the situation had deteriorated dramatically. The invasion of the Tuileries appalled the *émigrés*, and made even the most moderate of them think of vengeance. Under these circumstances, it was hardly to be expected that the princes would show restraint. Most important of all, after the royal family's ordeal at the hands of the Paris crowd, the tone of their letters altered markedly. In particular, Marie Antoinette, who had previously echoed her husband's sentiments about the manifesto, now changed tack. The invasion of the palace brought home the immediacy of the peril facing herself and her family; in her desperation, she concluded that only fear of reprisal would prevent a repetition. 'Everything is lost', she wrote to Mercy-Argenteau on 4 July,

> if the rebels are not halted by fear of imminent punishment. They want the republic at any price; to achieve it, they have resolved to murder the king. A manifesto must be issued making the National Assembly and Paris responsible for his safety and for that of his family.[44]

By the time Mallet du Pan reached the princes, his mission had been overtaken by events. Not even the Austrians now placed any faith in moderate language, and the Prussians were as bellicose as Provence and Artois. Fersen, intent on saving the woman he loved and driven to distraction by her latest despairing letters, was also working behind the scenes. In collaboration with the marquis de

Limon, an *émigré* of dubious reputation who had the confidence of the princes, he drew up an alternative manifesto, notably more menacing than Mallet du Pan's version. This gained general approval, and on 25 July it was published over the signature of the invading army's commander, the Duke of Brunswick.

The 'Brunswick manifesto' is one of the most notorious documents in modern history. Its beginning, however, was almost conciliatory, stressing that Austria and Prussia had no desire to meddle in France's internal politics, and demanding only that Louis XVI be set free to take up residence near the frontier – the primordial goal that both the flight to Varennes and the armed congress had failed to achieve. It went on, however, to employ the direst threats to forestall a repeat of 20 June. If 'the least violence or outrage' was offered to the royal family, the invaders would 'exact an exemplary and forever memorable vengeance by giving Paris over to martial law and complete destruction'. As Marie Antoinette had recommended, the deputies of the National Assembly and the capital's officials were made personally responsible for the safety of the king and queen, on pain of 'military punishment without hope of pardon'.[45]

Published on 25 July, the Brunswick manifesto was available in France three days later. As so often in the revolutionary conflict, it had precisely the opposite effect from the one intended. It tried to distinguish loyal from rebellious Frenchmen, but in doing so virtually outlawed the most vital group in the whole country, which held the fate of the royal family in its hands – the people of Paris. Reading Brunswick's blood-curdling threats, the Parisians concluded that their city would be sacked if the invaders reached it, and that therefore they had nothing to lose. Another factor further inflamed the situation. Although Louis XVI had vetoed the establishment of an armed camp outside Paris for the *fédérés* arriving for the 14 July celebrations, hundreds of the latter, all committed revolutionaries, gathered in the capital anyway.

The Girondins still dominated the Assembly, but events were swiftly slipping from their grasp. As on 20 June, they planned to use the people of Paris to force Louis XVI to capitulate to them, restoring them to the ministry and allowing them to govern in his name. They baulked, however, at actually deposing the king and proclaiming a republic. This gave the radicals their chance. The

Parisian districts, known as sections, most of which were by now openly republican, began calling for an end to the monarchy. On 3 August and again on the 6th, they presented mass petitions to the Assembly demanding the king's dethronement. The deputies promised to debate the issue three days later, on the 9th. When the day dawned, however, it was clear there was no majority for deposition. The sections, which some weeks ago had set up a permanent central committee, decided on an armed uprising that night.

The leaders of the rebellion were diverse but formidable. Through his own 'self-denying ordinance' of 1791, Robespierre had disqualified himself from standing for the legislative assembly. Since mid-July he had been vice-president of the Jacobin Club, using it as a platform for urging the overthrow of Louis XVI. The central figures in the rising, however, were Danton and Santerre. Thirty-three years old in 1792, Georges-Jacques Danton was a prosperous lawyer who now held a legal post in the Paris municipal government. Since the outbreak of the Revolution he had been one of the chiefs of the popular movement, basing his power on the Cordeliers Club, which was even more radical than the Jacobins. A massive, stocky man with a scarred face, allegedly the result of being gored by a bull as a child, Danton was an energetic organizer and the greatest popular orator of the era. Antoine Santerre, forty, was a wealthy Parisian brewer who had played an important part in the storming of the Bastille, and in July 1791 had orchestrated the ill-fated demonstration on the Champ-de-Mars. As colonel of a battalion of National Guards, he took charge of the military aspects of the planned coup.

At midnight on 9 August, the church bells in central and eastern Paris began to ring the tocsin, as a signal to begin the insurrection. The final decision to set the people marching was taken at 3.30 a.m. by the delegates of the nineteen most radical Parisian sections meeting at the Hôtel de Ville. Since there were forty-eight sections in all, the revolutionaries were six short of a majority, but this was no time for procedural niceties. It was agreed that two armed columns would converge on the Tuileries. The *fédérés* and the National Guards from south of the river would march along the Left Bank, while Santerre would lead the National Guards of the eastern sections along the Right Bank. The aim was to occupy the palace and dethrone the king, by force if necessary.

In the Tuileries, the royal family passed a sleepless night, interrupted by the tolling of the tocsin. The interior of the building was a hive of martial activity. The core of the defence was 800 Swiss Guards, backed up by roughly 1,250 loyal National Guards. Throughout the last hours, royalist volunteers had also been making their way to the palace. There were around 200 of them, mostly former members of the king's bodyguard and constitutional guard. A few, however, were old friends and servants of Louis XVI himself, like the ex-foreign minister Montmorin. By the early morning, some of the National Guard were beginning to waver, but the Swiss remained firm. Silent and disciplined, they awaited the day in battle formation.

It has usually been assumed that the defenders of the Tuileries were overwhelmingly outnumbered by their attackers, and that from the outset resistance was useless. In fact, recent researches have shown that this is far from the truth.[46] Certainly Paris was astir – Louis was at one point told that 20,000 people were on the march – but the insurgents' effective force was much smaller. The Left Bank column probably numbered no more than 1,100, and Santerre's Right Bank column around 1,500. At dawn on 10 August, both sides were fairly evenly matched.

As in July 1789, what ruined the royal cause was not the troops themselves, but weak and indecisive leadership. No attempt was made to master the situation or turn it to the advantage of the monarchy. Instead, in the face of a flagrant *coup d'état*, the king and his advisers maintained a bizarre deference to constitutional authority. The Assembly, with no armed force at its disposal, was reduced to irrelevance, but the bodies that administered the capital, the Department of Paris and the municipal government, or Commune, were still theoretically functioning. Instead of taking decisions of their own, Louis XVI, his ministers and his military commanders allowed themselves to be manipulated by both the Department and the Commune, and this was their undoing. At 4.30 a.m., the general in overall charge of the defence, the marquis de Mandat, was persuaded to obey a summons to report to the Commune at the Hôtel de Ville. He did not realize that the revolutionary sections were in the process of overthrowing the existing municipality, and proclaiming themselves an 'insurrectionary Commune'. By 7 a.m., Mandat was under arrest; by 10.30 a.m., he had been murdered.

At about the time Mandat left the Tuileries to meet his death, the king emerged from his bedchamber, where he had snatched a few hours' sleep. On this, the last occasion where his leadership could have made a difference, he once again provided none. Not even his appearance inspired confidence. He was wearing a violet coat and breeches, and looked anxious and dishevelled. His hair had not been dressed since the previous evening, and was flattened down on one side where he had been lying. At 5 a.m. he withdrew to meet with his confessor, and was gone for over half an hour. In his absence, the central figure in the palace became the senior official of the Department of Paris, Pierre-Louis Roederer. Since it was hoped that the politically moderate Department might prove a useful counterweight to the Commune, Roederer had been summoned in the course of the night to the Tuileries. He was a shrewd, experienced politician, but had no stomach for a confrontation with the people of Paris. He was determined to avoid bloodshed, even at the price of a royal surrender.

It was Marie Antoinette who gave Roederer his first opening. With the king still closeted with his confessor, she turned to him and asked him what should be done. Roederer promptly replied that the royal family should not try to resist, but instead take refuge in the Assembly. The queen, however, rebuffed him. 'It is time to find out who will overcome,' she replied, 'the king and the constitution, or the rebels.' At this point, the tide was running in favour of putting up a fight. Louis XVI reappeared, buckled a sword to his side, and decided to review his troops. First he went out on the balcony at the front of the palace, and was greeted by shouts of 'Vive le roi!' Then he descended into the courtyard and inspected the Swiss and National Guards drawn up there.

Then the king made a fatal mistake. Instead of returning inside, he proceeded towards the side of the palace abutting on to the Seine. The National Guards stationed there, a company of gunners, were of far more dubious loyalty. Instead of 'Vive le roi!' they shouted 'Vive la nation!' and this visibly disconcerted Louis. He compounded his error by walking over to the garden side of the Tuileries, to the Terrasse du Bord de l'Eau, where the National Guards battalions were frankly hostile. By this time, Louis had been spotted by a crowd of armed Parisians who had infiltrated the opposite side of the garden and now made towards him howling abuse. He was only rescued by a group of ministers and loyal officers who rushed out of the palace and linked arms to protect him. The beleaguered party retreated slowly to safety, surrounded by demonstrators bellowing, 'Down with the fat pig!'[47]

Back in the Tuileries, the king went into the *salle du conseil*, where he was joined by his family, ministers and military commanders. His shaken state gave Roederer his chance to renew the attack. Roederer was aided by the fact that the National Guards who had insulted the king had promptly left their posts and deserted. 'Your Majesty has not five minutes to lose,' he warned. 'There is no safety except in the Assembly.' As Louis remained silent, Marie Antoinette tried desperately to bolster his resolve. Rather than seek the protection of the deputies, she told Roederer, she would be nailed to the walls of the palace. Roederer faced her down. 'If you oppose this measure, Madame,' he replied, 'you will be responsible for the lives of your husband and your children.' The queen flushed with fury but said nothing; in any case it was too late. What remained of the king's will had been broken by the brutal spelling-out of the threat to his family. He raised his right hand and said simply, 'Let's get started. Since we are going to the Assembly, there's nothing further to do here.'

This was Louis XVI's final failure. Presumably his aim was to keep alive, by whatever means, even fleeing to the Assembly, until the imminent Austro-Prussian invasion could rescue him. Yet he must have known that divesting himself of his last loyal defenders would place him entirely at the mercy of his enemies. In this ultimate crisis, his worst shortcoming was starkly revealed: he would neither lead himself, nor permit anybody else to do so. As a result, the defence of the Tuileries fell apart. Although less intelligent than Louis, Marie Antoinette instinctively rose to the situation. She knew that this was the decisive moment, and that only a showdown could save the crown. Once her husband had agreed to leave the Tuileries, despite her frantic efforts to persuade him otherwise, she could not publicly contradict him. Yet had the queen and not the king led the defence of the palace, supported by a resolute commander, the history of France might well have been different.

The king's abandonment of the Tuileries was in effect an abdication. What followed was a ghastly tragedy. When the decision to leave for the Assembly became known in the palace, there was a general stampede. Courtiers and ministers jostled round the royal family while an escort of 150 Swiss and 300 National Guards formed up. At 8.30 a.m. the cortège moved off. Yet for a reason that has never been established, the troops who remained behind – roughly 600 Swiss and a few loyal National Guards, supported by the royalist volunteers – were left no orders. Ultimately the king was responsible, but at this point he had more to occupy him than military matters. More to blame were the two senior Swiss commanders, Colonel Maillardoz and Major Bachmann, who accompanied the escort to the Assembly, but issued no instructions to their subordinates before departing. The only explanation of this dereliction of duty is that they assumed that once the royal family had left the Tuileries, any cause of conflict would be removed. This was, however, an unwarranted assumption. The agony of the monarchy once again revealed the incompetence of its senior officers.

The crown's remaining forces were left in the hands of a very old man. This was the maréchal de Mailly, aged eighty-four. Yet the overall chain of command had been broken, leaving the initiative to individual company captains. Under these circumstances, all that was left was the basic military pride of each unit. In the absence of clear orders, this meant above all not laying down their arms. Yet this was precisely what their attackers insisted they do. When, just after 9 a.m., the *fédérés* moved across the courtyard and entered the great hall of the palace, the tension reached breaking-point. Summoned to surrender, the commander stationed there, Captain Durler, refused. A sergeant standing next to him added: 'We are Swiss, and the Swiss only abandon their arms with their lives.' Scuffles broke out, and shots were fired. A full-scale battle immediately exploded.

Left to themselves, the defenders quickly took the offensive. The maréchal de Mailly directed a murderous fire from the palace windows into the ranks of the *fédérés*, while Captains Durler and de Salis-Zizers led a charge that cleared the courtyard and penetrated into the Place du Carrousel. The insurgents fled, leaving over 300 dead on the ground. By this time, however, the Swiss were running dangerously short of ammunition, and pulled back to the Tuileries to make a final stand. At this moment, the comte d'Hervilly, the former deputy commander of the constitutional guard, came running over to the palace from the Assembly through a storm of shot, bringing a belated order from the king himself to cease fire and withdraw.

The Tuileries was then evacuated in two stages. Durler and Salis-Zizers led a detachment of 150 Swiss over to the Assembly. Crossing the Tuileries Gardens, they were subjected to heavy fire and suffered many casualties, but were able to reach their destination. The second group, composed of the remaining Swiss and royalist volunteers, was less fortunate. It set off towards the Place Louis XV (now Place de la Concorde) at the far end of the gardens, in order to disperse there, but was cut to pieces on the way. Back at the palace, there was a general massacre as the Parisians and National Guards moved in to finish off the domestic servants and the wounded Swiss. As usual, the defenceless suffered most. They were killed, stripped, their heads paraded on pikes and their bodies mutilated. Just how many died will never be known.

Over at the Assembly, the royal family had been crammed into the reporters' box behind the president's chair, separated from the debating chamber by a grille. Crowds of armed Parisians were massing around the building, and the sounds of fighting from the Tuileries were clearly audible. Inside, under the eyes of the packed galleries, the deputies were soon confronted with a deputation from the insurrectionary Commune demanding new elections. The Girondins had unleashed the crisis by pushing France into war. Fittingly, it was they who now made the final capitulation. Guadet, whose speeches had done so much to inflame the Assembly against Austria, gave up the president's chair to his colleague Gensonné. Then Vergniaud rose and proposed that the king be suspended from his functions and the Assembly replaced by a new national convention elected by universal manhood suffrage. The deputies assented by a show of hands. At a stroke, both the monarchy and the constitution had been swept aside.

The king watched the destruction of his authority from behind the reporters' grille. His will may have deserted him, but his lucidity had not. From the moment he had decided to leave the Tuileries, he had known what the likely consequences would be. The point was reinforced by a symbolic incident on the way to the Assembly. A Jacobin newspaper had written that the monarchy would be swept away by the autumn. As they crossed the gardens, the royal family saw that many trees were already bare, and that the leaves had been piled into heaps by the gardeners. The dauphin amused himself by kicking them up on to the legs of the courtiers walking in front of him. 'Ah,' Louis remarked, 'the leaves are falling early this year.'[48]

Chapter Thirteen

ROYAL BLOOD

NINE DAYS AFTER the storming of the Tuileries, on 19 August 1792, the Duke of Brunswick's army invaded France. Their advance was rapid. The border town of Longwy was swiftly besieged. The defending commander, Colonel Lavergne, was prepared to make a fight, but was opposed by the civilian authorities, who feared the destruction to property a full-scale assault would bring. On 23 August, Longwy capitulated. Brunswick moved on to the vital city and fortress of Verdun. The same thing happened here; after an initial bombardment, the city fathers panicked and forced the senior officer, Colonel Beaurepaire, to seek terms. On 3 September, Verdun surrendered, but Beaurepaire committed suicide rather than sign. The road to Paris now lay open.

Breteuil arrived in Verdun on the evening of 6 September. Two compelling factors demanded his presence at the front. A swift march on Paris was essential if the royal family were to be rescued, yet Brunswick was a cautious commander, and it was possible that even at this stage the Austrians might attempt to negotiate with the enemy. The baron's influence might well tip the scales in favour of boldness. Furthermore, on 29 August, his bugbears the princes had crossed the frontier with a small force of 4,500 *émigrés*. Fearful that their entry into France might alienate the local population, Brunswick kept them well back from the fore, but once on French soil their pretensions soared. With the king, queen and dauphin now prisoners of the Assembly, Provence was more determined than ever to be recognized as regent of the kingdom. The vicomte de Caraman, currently at Prussian headquarters, warned Breteuil that the only way to combat these claims was in person. When the baron agreed to make the journey, Caraman was delighted. 'I shall go to Luxembourg on 28 [August], Monsieur le baron, and await you there . . .' he wrote. 'We have not a moment to lose.'[1]

The showdown took place the day after Breteuil arrived in Verdun. A conference was called in his lodgings, with the regency the sole item on the agenda. The baron, however, held the trump card. This was the confidence of the king of Prussia who, thirsting for military glory, had accompanied his army. Louis XVI's letter of 3 December 1791 had convinced Frederick William II that Breteuil really did speak for the king of France, and this gave the baron an authority that his rivals lacked. Frederick William's central role in the unfolding campaign in turn ensured that his allies followed his example. During that crucial autumn of 1792, the Powers accorded Breteuil the status of his master speaking *ex cathedra*.

The conference began on the evening of 7 September. Provence and his allies argued that it was essential to organize a government on French soil as quickly as possible to challenge the revolutionaries in Paris, and that this could only be done through a regency. A council of regency would have to be set up, and Breteuil's reward would be to head it. The baron's position, in contrast, was that in six weeks' time Brunswick's army would be in Paris anyway to liberate the king, so a regency now was simply not worth the trouble. His opponents' reply carried some force: it was highly unlikely that the royal family would still be in the capital by the time Brunswick arrived, since by then they would probably have been carried off into the southern provinces as hostages. Breteuil grudgingly accepted the point, and agreed that if the king were to be taken off to the Midi, Provence should become regent.[2]

The manoeuvres of the next few days are difficult to follow. Clearly, if Breteuil were to head the council of regency, there would be no room for Calonne. By this point the baron's great rival was also being loudly blamed for the *émigré* army's disastrous lack of organization and resources. On 15 September he was dismissed by the princes, having spent most of his fortune over the past two years in their service. Despite this, the compromise solution to the regency issue put forward soon encountered obstacles. As a delaying tactic, Breteuil had earlier persuaded the Austrian representative at the conference, the Prince of Reuss, to demand that the question be referred back to Vienna. The Austrian government, however, simply refused to give an answer. So Provence did not become regent after all; eventually he had to take the title unilaterally in January 1793, after the king's execution. It was hardly an auspicious beginning to his new relationship with Breteuil.

With Calonne at least out of the way, the baron could devote himself to administering the captured French territory, which Brunswick made over to him. For the first – and last – time during the Revolution he held real power within France, and his actions gave a foretaste of what his ultimate triumph would have entailed. Wherever possible, the baron restored the old regime. He made this plain to Fersen on 17 September. 'Yesterday . . . I reinstated the bishop, the canons and the monks [of Verdun],' he boasted. 'Not a single constitutional priest remains.'[3] This intransigence could have been foreseen. In late August, Fersen noted a conversation between Breteuil and Mirabeau's old friend la Marck in Brussels. La Marck remarked that in the event of victory some aspects of France's 'ancient constitution' should be retained, 'whereupon . . . the baron de Breteuil replied that he had never had and never would have any other aim than to return everything to its former state'.[4]

The least pleasant aspect of Breteuil's brief exercise of power was his desire for vengeance. The only way to restore order, he was convinced, was to hand down exemplary punishments to cow the populace. 'I have spared nothing to impress upon the Duke of Brunswick the necessity for great severity,' he wrote to Fersen from Verdun, 'but his character is mild, and his present principles make him recoil from that harshness which is so clearly needed.'[5] In particular, the baron wished Brunswick to make an example of Varennes, which was only a few miles away, by having it completely destroyed. In this, however, he was to be disappointed – it was to take another German invasion, that of the First World War, to inflict significant damage on the town.

Breteuil's sentiments must be seen in the context of the recent events in the capital. Just a few days before, on 2 and 3 September, the Paris crowd had risen, broken into the prisons and butchered 1,400 people as suspected counter-revolutionaries. Breteuil himself knew several of the victims. He was also far from alone in his thirst for revenge. 'Clemency', wrote Fersen at this time, 'would be extremely pernicious';[6] indeed, it was he, not the baron, who first urged the destruction of Varennes. Even moderates caught the infection. Mallet du Pan warned against any 'harmful pity'.[7] Not to be outdone, Mercy declared on 24 September that 'if the Jacobins were not exterminated and an example made of France, every country . . . would sooner or later be ruined'.[8] The following day he went further, adding that 'severity was the only way, and that the four corners of Paris should be set on fire'.[9] Like the September massacres, such reactions showed that the Revolution had spilled over into civil war.

A final problem that concerned Breteuil at this point was the fate of La Fayette. On hearing of the overthrow of the monarchy, the general had done all he could to reverse it. He summoned his troops to renew their oath to the king and the constitution, preparatory to unleashing them on the Jacobins. The soldiers, however, refused. Only one road remained for La Fayette, and it led to the frontier. On 21 August, he crossed the border with twenty officers and gave himself up to the Austrians. The illustrious prisoner was soon the subject of an undignified tug-of-war. The Austrians were inclined to give him privileged status as a potential instrument of some future negotiation; their allies opposed this. A diplomatic conference was held which Breteuil attended as Louis XVI's representative. It issued a communiqué claiming that their prisoner's existence was 'incompatible with the security of all European governments'.[10] La Fayette was sent into close confinement in a series of Prussian and Austrian fortresses. He was not released until 1797.

The fate of France, however, would be decided not by Breteuil in Verdun but by Brunswick on the battlefield. Eerily, the theatre of conflict was the forest of the Argonne, through which the royal family's *berline* had trundled just eighteen months before on the road to Varennes. Dumouriez, who had taken command of the French army after La Fayette's defection, occupied a strong defensive position amid its hills and woods. Unable to mount a frontal assault, on 12 September Brunswick moved to turn the enemy flank. Covering himself by a feint at Dumouriez's right and centre, he launched his main attack on his left around Croix-aux-Bois. The French were thrown back in disorder, and the Argonne line was broken. Brunswick now had a good chance of catching and smashing Dumouriez's main force. Yet he failed to seize it. He stayed in camp until 18 September, allowing his opponent to escape due south. By the time Brunswick resumed his advance, Dumouriez had found a secure new position. Again, it held striking echoes of the flight to Varennes; its centre was Sainte-Ménehould, and it extended back to the windmill at Valmy, which the royal family had passed on their route east from Châlons.[11]

The reason for Brunswick's action remain mysterious. The two most likely ones are his own innate caution, allied to growing problems of supply. The Prussian commissariat was rapidly breaking down under the strain of maintaining an army on enemy soil. It had attempted to feed the troops from its own reserves, but this soon proved impossible, since the field bakeries and grain stores were way behind the lines. As a result, the hungry soldiers soon took to looting, and this further alienated the already hostile French peasantry. Rumours soon spread of stragglers being murdered and isolated detachments ambushed by partisans. With food and morale dwindling, Brunswick was in no mood to take risks.

Given this difficult situation, the duke was disposed to lend an ear to the old refrain that the swiftest route to Paris might lie through negotiations. His chief encouragement in this came from Breteuil. It was not, however, a question of a compromise with the constitutional party that would involve political sacrifices, but of a simple 'turning' of Dumouriez that would speed the destruction of the Revolution by military force. The idea the baron put forward came from the French royalist journalist Rivarol, who had recently emigrated to Brussels. Rivarol's sister, the baronne d'Angelle, was Dumouriez's mistress, and as such an ideal conduit for Austrian and Prussian propositions to the general. The plan first germinated before Breteuil left for the front; one of the first things he did on reaching Verdun was to send Fersen detailed instructions on how to conduct the intrigue in his absence. 'What Rivarol and I agreed,' he wrote, was that his sister, who is currently still in Paris, should immediately leave to join Dumouriez ... and that Rivarol should meet her secretly on the frontier to give her our instructions. Rivarol assures me that she is a woman of spirit; if Rivarol does not report back to the bishop [of Pamiers], then the bishop must ask him what is happening about the matter I broached with him regarding his sister, and then you and he can follow it up. Dumouriez ... must be asked – if his army is attacked by the Duke of Brunswick and retires under the walls of the capital – to persuade his army to declare for the king ... bring it over to the Prussian army, and make peace in Paris itself. I could set no limit to the reward Dumouriez and his friends would be entitled to ask in such circumstances.[12]

The French commander, however, was not about to listen to such propositions, even in the form of pillow-talk. The Prussians had already sent emissaries to him, but he had torn up the letters they brought in front of them with the words: 'I shall reply with cannon-fire.' On 14 September, Brunswick sent a further envoy to the French camp, his confidant Major von Massenbach, but the general refused to see him. Dumouriez was not for turning – yet.[13]

Faced with this rebuff, Brunswick hesitated once more. By now he had added reason, since his slow pursuit of the French had allowed them to bring up reinforcements under Beurnonville and Kellermann. Until his own right wing under Clerfayt caught up, he would be heavily outnumbered. Brunswick's instinct was to consolidate his forces and then continue with a war of manoeuvre. At this point, however, political considerations came to the fore. Blood-curdling reports were still coming in from Paris, and it was feared that if the army did not drive straight on the capital, there might soon be no royal family left to rescue. Frederick William II in particular was insistent on a rapid advance. He was egged on by Breteuil, who was constantly at his side. The baron had already seen the opportunity presented by the French retreat to get between them and the capital. 'The rebels have avoided battle', he wrote to Mercy-Argenteau on 17 September, 'but have sustained serious losses. They have been forced to leave the road to Paris open to our armies. It is said they wish to await us in the plains of Champagne; this is much to be desired.'[14]

On 18 September, Brunswick moved out of camp; the following day, on a direct order from Frederick William, he swooped
down behind Dumouriez's army, menacing the Châlons road and his
route back to Paris. The positions were now reversed. Brunswick
stood between Dumouriez and the rest of France; Dumouriez stood
between Brunswick and Germany. It was clear that the following day
would bring a battle. That evening, in its bivouacs, the Prussian
army prepared for combat. The scene was described by Goethe, who
was there in the entourage of his master, the Duke of Saxe-Weimar.
It was the prelude to a strange meeting:

> Among the faces and figures illuminated in the circle of firelight,
> I saw a middle-aged man whom I thought I recognized. When
> I became certain, I went up to him, and he was not a little
> surprised to see me there. It was the marquis de Bombelles,
> whom I had met in Venice two years before.[15]

Bombelles had travelled a long way to arrive at Goethe's campfire.
At the end of August, he had abandoned his fruitless mission in
St Petersburg and attached himself to the Prussian army. The next
day would decide his entire future – glorious return to Versailles as
foreign minister, or a life of exile. That night, however, he was prey
to gloomy presentiments. As Goethe recalled Bombelles's charm and
hospitality in Venice, the marquis suddenly burst out:

> Don't speak of those things! They are too far away; and even
> then, when I was entertaining my noble guests with apparent
> sincerity, anxiety was gnawing at my heart; I foresaw what
> would happen in my country; I envied you your carefree
> ignorance of the danger that menaced you in turn; I prepared
> myself in silence for my fate. Soon after, I had to quit my
> honourable position and begin the wanderings that have finally
> brought me here.[16]

Just after six the following morning, the Prussian advance guard
under Prince Hohenlohe-Ingelfingen moved on to the Châlons road.
It was raining, and a thick fog covered the ground. Almost immediately, the French guns opened up, and the battle of Valmy began.
The attacking Prussians were faced by a solid French position in the
form of a semi-circle, with its right on the small hill of Mount Yron,

its centre under Kellermann pushed forward around the windmill of Valmy, and its left anchored on the road. The arrival of reinforcements had also given Dumouriez a local superiority of roughly 60,000 to 30,000. At noon, when the Prussians had completed their leisurely deployment, the morning fog lifted to disclose not the disorderly rabble they were expecting, but a firm and well-disciplined enemy.

The shock was as much mental as military. Since Dillon's ignominious rout in April, followed by La Fayette's defection and the collapse of Longwy and Verdun, the Prussians had become half convinced that the French would never stand and fight. Now they were clearly prepared to do so. This was because Dumouriez's army contained just enough veterans to stiffen the raw recruits. Just under half of the infantry were new volunteers, but the rest were professionals from the line army, as were all the cavalry and, crucially, the artillery. The Prussians had more guns than the French – fifty-eight to forty – but the French ones were better handled and kept up a fire that badly dented their opponents' *élan*. Reluctantly, at 1 p.m., Brunswick ordered a frontal attack. The Prussians formed into two lines with parade-ground precision and set off across the valley separating them from the French position. The enemy artillery began to inflict heavy casualties. At this moment Kellermann decided to rally his troops. Placing his hat on the point of his sword, he rose in his stirrups and shouted, 'Vive la nation!' With one voice, his soldiers echoed the slogan. A few seconds afterwards, the attackers stopped in their tracks.

This was more than a psychological turning-point. By this time, France had made an impression not just on the Prussians' minds, but on their bowels. A few days before the battle, a serious dysentery epidemic had struck in Brunswick's camp and laid low a significant number of his troops. The soldiers now advancing across the valley were cold, wet and ill-fed. The French gunfire was becoming murderous, and it was clear that their infantry was not about to turn and run. Having advanced against his better judgement, Brunswick swiftly concluded that Kellermann's position could not be carried. After just 200 yards, he ordered a retreat.

Ever since, argument has raged over this decision – whether it was justified, a disastrous error, or even black treachery. In fact,

Brunswick had actually been approached before the war to command the French armies, and the *émigrés* later seized on this to allege that he was in French pay and had been bribed to pull back his forces. No convincing proof of this has ever emerged. The duke's vindication or otherwise lies in an imponderable – whether or not the French would have stood if the Prussians had got to close quarters. One of Napoleon's best marshals, Gouvion Saint-Cyr, who fought in the Valmy campaign, claimed afterwards that they would not. There is some evidence to back him up: just four days before, during the retreat from the Argonne, 10,000 of Dumouriez's men had taken to their heels at the sight of 1,500 Prussian cavalry. Attacking a superior French force at Valmy was certainly risky. Yet having accepted a bold course of action in the first place, it was illogical of Brunswick not to press it home. As Albert Sorel put it: 'He executed a bold plan half-heartedly, and exposed himself to all the perils of rashness while securing none of its benefits.'[17]

The artillery exchange rumbled on until nightfall, but the moment of decision had passed. Under cover of darkness and heavy rain, the French left the battlefield, but they had won a tremendous moral victory. They had stood up to the fearsome regiments of Frederick the Great, and with their army still in the field Brunswick was not about to push on to Paris. Contrary to expectations, there would be no quick end to the campaign.

The Prussians may have been discouraged, but Dumouriez for his part was far from confident. Brunswick had not beaten him, but neither had he beaten Brunswick. A resolute Prussian counter-attack that put his infantry properly to the test could still have disastrous consequences. The general decided the time had come to re-open negotiations. His motivation for doing so remains mysterious. He claimed to his superiors in Paris that this was simply a ruse; aware of the logistical problems facing the king of Prussia, he boasted that if he could keep him talking for eight days, 'his army will be completely defeated, of its own accord, without a battle'.[18]

It is more likely that Dumouriez was keeping his options open. He certainly convinced Frederick William's emissary, Colonel von Manstein, of his sincerity, and did not blink when the latter presented him with a peace proposal based on the liberty of Louis XVI and the return of order to France. A truce was agreed. Manstein returned in delight to the Prussian camp, where the conviction grew that a French surrender was imminent. This was shared by Frederick William and Brunswick himself. A letter from Breteuil, who had been told the news in Verdun, to his daughter Mme de Matignon back in Brussels, makes this absolutely clear:

> I am certain that Dumouriez, harassed by hunger and unable to extricate his forces, has requested to capitulate. The king of Prussia had the goodness to let me know this yesterday. The Duke of Brunswick has accorded a truce of twenty-four hours that should have ended at midday yesterday, so I have no doubt that the rebel army has already surrendered at the moment of writing. I hope to receive the news in the course of the day and will send it on to you immediately by a dispatch-rider. It is 1 o'clock in the afternoon.[19]

Breteuil's hopes were soon dashed. Whatever Dumouriez's intentions may have been on 23 September, when Manstein visited him, by the time the baron wrote to his daughter on the 26th he had turned his back on the talks. The decisive factor was the news, which the general received on the evening of the 23rd, that two days previously the republic had been declared in Paris. It was clear that the government's political resolve had not cracked, and that if he continued his equivocal conduct towards the enemy he might find himself arraigned for treason. Dumouriez immediately wrote to Manstein, informing him of what had happened and adding that he would have to await orders from his superiors to resume negotiations. The truce was at an end.

Isolated on enemy soil, faced by superior French forces and menaced by hunger and disease, the Prussians had no option but to retreat. On 12 October they evacuated Verdun and fell back towards the Rhine. This sudden reversal of fortune when victory had seemed so near shattered Breteuil. 'You know and share', he wrote to Fersen,

> all the misfortunes that our army's withdrawal brings us, just when we thought we had everything to hope for. I cannot hide from you that this turn of events has crushed my soul and my spirit; I am overwhelmed, and will need several days to recover. If I were less alone, perhaps I would pull myself together more

quickly, especially if I could discuss things with you; none the
less, I am glad that you are not here in the midst of our distress
– you would only be upset by everything you saw and heard.[20]

Just when the baron thought things could not get any worse, they
did. A week later, he received news that his sugar plantation in
St Domingue, his only substantial asset outside France, was now
menaced by the slave revolt that had been raging on the island for a
year. 'We will be reduced to penury if I lose my plantation,' he
wrote to Mme de Matignon. 'For myself, I think I could bear it,
but I could not survive seeing you, dear child, and Caroline [his
granddaughter Mme de Montmorency] reduced to that condition.
I embrace you. I embrace the bishop.'[21]

Breteuil's personal disasters shrank to nothing beside the wider
significance of Valmy. The battle saved the Revolution and ushered
in a new age. The British historian T. C. W. Blanning puts it
succinctly:

> One must agree with Marshal Foch – 'The wars of kings were
> at an end; the wars of peoples were beginning.' This turned
> out to be terrible news for all mankind, but in the short term,
> the French revolutionaries had every reason to feel proud of
> themselves.[22]

*

VALMY, NOT THE EVENTS of 10 August, sealed the fate of the royal
family. They had survived the storming of the Tuileries, but
Brunswick's defeat put paid to their hopes of liberation. It does not
follow automatically that if the duke had won a victory they would
have been rescued. If the Prussians had advanced on Paris the government might well have evacuated the capital and taken the royal
family with it as hostages. Fersen and Breteuil feared that the king
would be taken to the Cévennes and surrounded by an army of
Protestants, though this may reflect their vivid imaginations rather
than reality. Yet the loss of Paris would have been a tremendous
blow to the revolutionaries, and probably hastened Louis XVI's
release.

As it was, the king and queen got the worst of both worlds.
Valmy postponed their salvation indefinitely, while the *coup d'état* of

10 August had given their most hard-line opponents in Paris a substantial slice of power. Roland, Clavière and Servan, the three Girondin ministers Louis had dismissed in June, were immediately restored to office. The dominating figure in the new government, however, was Danton, who was appointed minister of justice. Behind him loomed the true victor of 10 August, the insurrectionary Commune of Paris. With the National Guards and armed Parisians at its disposal, it entirely overshadowed the Legislative Assembly, which was in any case about to be superseded by the National Convention.

For two days after the storming of the Tuileries, the royal family had been kept cooped up in the stenographers' box in the Assembly by day and moved to a nearby convent by night. On the evening of 13 August, they were transferred under heavy guard to the keep of the medieval fortress of the Temple in the east of the capital. Ironically, before the Revolution this had been Artois's Paris residence. They were joined in captivity by the marquise de Tourzel, and by the queen's old friend the princesse de Lamballe. The prisoners soon settled into a routine that was constricted but comfortable. They occupied two floors in the tower, where they led an entirely domestic life. There was only one valet, but a substantial kitchen staff – two chefs and eleven under-cooks. After breakfast at nine, Louis took charge of the dauphin's lessons. Following his own preferences, these were mostly in Latin and geography. He even devised an exercise in which maps were put before his son with certain countries cut out, which the boy then had to fit back in to demonstrate his knowledge.

After a walk outside, the family dined at two. The king's appetite was undiminished by misfortune; he normally took three courses, with red and white wine for the first two, and half a bottle of champagne and a glass of liqueur with dessert. Understandably, he then took a nap. From six to nine, he continued the dauphin's lessons or played with him, while Marie Antoinette and Mme Elisabeth did embroidery. Then came a light supper, after which Louis retired and read until midnight. Between August 1792 and January 1793, he read 250 volumes, from Tacitus to Tasso to Buffon to Hume. Remarkably, he also set about translating Horace Walpole's *Historic Doubts on the Life and Reign of King Richard III*, which had first appeared in 1768, from English into French. His translation was published posthumously in 1800.[23]

Outside, however, the situation was deteriorating rapidly. Under pressure from the Commune, a special tribunal was set up on 17 August to try political criminals, and especially those who had fired on the people in the battle for the Tuileries. The first to be condemned was Louis Collenot d'Angremont, the administrative secretary of the National Guard, who was accused of betraying the popular cause. The instrument of his punishment was a new machine designed to aid painless decapitation, named after its inventor the former deputy Dr Guillotin, which had been in sporadic use since the previous April. This 'guillotine' was now moved to the Place du Carrousel in front of the Tuileries, and Collenot d'Angremont went under its blade on 21 August. He was followed three days later by the king's close confidant and intendant of the civil list, Arnaud de la Porte.

As the Austro-Prussian invasion began, the capital was seized by panic. A makeshift police state came into being, as on Danton's orders armed patrols took to the streets on 'domiciliary visits', searching houses for weapons and dragging off suspected traitors into custody. Their arm reached even into the Temple; on the night of 19–20 August, Mesdames de Tourzel and Lamballe were arrested and taken away. Roughly 3,000 people suffered the same fate in the last weeks of August, filling the prisons to bursting-point. This created a new problem. In the fevered popular imagination, the hapless detainees became magnified into a monstrous fifth column, counter-revolutionary 'brigands' poised for the signal to break out of captivity and massacre all good citizens in their beds. These fantasies were assiduously encouraged by the more inflammatory radical newspapers, Marat's *L'Ami du peuple* and Hébert's *Le Père Duchesne*. Parisian men became unwilling to volunteer for the front, fearing that they might be leaving their families behind to be butchered.

Rumours of the fall of Verdun reached Paris on 2 September. The realization that nothing now lay between Brunswick and the capital touched off the powder-keg of popular paranoia. Gangs of armed assassins formed, backed by the crowd. That afternoon twenty-four refractory priests being transported to the prison of the Abbaye (formerly the abbey of Saint-Germain-des-Prés) were set upon in the rue de Buci and several were killed; the survivors were finished off at the end of their journey. Kangaroo courts were then set up in most of the other prisons, and 'popular justice' dispensed with swords, knives and hatchets. In all, around 1,400 people, none remotely dangerous, were killed over the next five days. Fewer than a third of them were priests, nobles, or political suspects; the rest were ordinary criminals. Thirty-seven were women. Two of the victims were former ministers. Montmorin was butchered at the Abbaye. Lessart was murdered on 9 September, when a convoy carrying forty-five state prisoners from Orléans to Paris was intercepted at Versailles and massacred.

In the Temple, Louis and Marie Antoinette could sense that something was amiss; they heard the tocsin ringing, and the distant clamour of the crowd. Two municipal officials then appeared, and in menacing tones outlined the situation to the king:

> Sir, you do not know what is happening in Paris . . . the people are infuriated and demand vengeance . . . it is you who have unleashed against us a ferocious enemy determined to massacre us and cut the throats of our wives and children. We know that our death has been decreed, but before we are immolated, you and your family will perish by the hands of those who guard you.[24]

The following afternoon, as the royal family were sitting down to dinner, a violent commotion broke out below the windows. They must have thought the previous day's threat was about to be carried out. Then Louis XVI's valet, Cléry, who had looked outside, rushed into the room looking horror-struck. He was immediately joined by another municipal officer, who announced that the people were insisting the family show themselves to counter a rumour that they had escaped. He added that he opposed this demand. Then four members of the crowd appeared, accompanied by a further protesting official, repeating that the prisoners should go to the window. The dignitaries continued to resist this, whereupon one of the visitors turned brutally on the king: 'They are trying to hide from you that the crowd want to show you the head of Mme de Lamballe, to show you how the people revenges itself on tyrants. I advise you to appear to them unless you want them to come to you.'[25] Marie Antoinette fainted dead away.

Since 20 August, the princesse de Lamballe had been held at the prison of La Force. She was brought before a makeshift 'court', condemned, and immediately hacked to death. Her body was stripped and mutilated, her head cut off, placed on a pike and taken to the Temple to be displayed to the queen, her lesbian lover of popular legend.

After this horror, Louis and Marie Antoinette had few illusions as to their fate if Brunswick did not arrive soon. Over the next weeks, the net around them tightened yet further. The National Convention first met on 20 September, and the following day voted unanimously to abolish the monarchy. At four that afternoon, a cavalcade was heard approaching the Temple. Trumpets sounded and a stentorian voice announced the proclamation of the republic. The king, who was reading, did not look up from his book. Then came the news of Valmy. The royal family prepared itself for the worst.

On 3 December, the Convention decreed that Louis XVI should be put on trial, on the central charge of 'conspiring against liberty and an attempt against the safety of the state'. It had been encouraged in this decision by the discovery in the abandoned Tuileries the previous November of a secret cupboard, the famous *armoire de fer*, containing some of the king's secret papers. The most incriminating documents had naturally been burned before 10 August, but in the current climate what remained was still damaging, especially the king's correspondence with Mirabeau and La Fayette. The legal grounds for arraigning Louis were dubious in the extreme, and certainly unsupported by the constitution of 1791, but this was a quintessentially political trial. On 11 December, Louis XVI was brought to the bar of the Convention. Thirty-five separate indictments were read to him, which he had to answer without benefit of counsel. In general, he acquitted himself well.

The urgent priority was now to find a legal team. The first person the king approached was the famous barrister Tronchet, who agreed to take the brief, but only with great reluctance. His lack of enthusiasm, however, was made up by the commitment of the junior counsel appointed, an eloquent advocate from Bordeaux named de Sèze. Finally, and touchingly, the seventy-two-year-old former minister Malesherbes, magistrate, botanist and one of the ornaments of the French Enlightenment, offered his services, which were accepted. 'I have been summoned twice', wrote Malesherbes, 'to the council of the man who was my master at a time when this function was coveted by everyone; I owe him the same service when it is a function which many people find dangerous.'[26]

*

OVER THE BORDER, Breteuil watched with growing anxiety the clouds gathering round the royal family. Even before Valmy, with the Prussians advancing, he had been casting around for the best way to save their lives. Now, with the march on Paris ignominiously thrown back, this became his most urgent concern.

In his efforts to preserve the king and queen, the baron left the realm of mainstream diplomacy and entered the murky world of treason and espionage. By their very nature, his clandestine activities are difficult to reconstruct – anybody the revolutionary authorities caught helping him faced a short route to the guillotine. Yet it is clear from Fersen's papers and diary that Breteuil did have several well-placed agents and sympathizers inside France. Over the months that followed, he drew them together into an informal network. Their first – but not their only – task was to keep the king and queen from the scaffold.

The linchpin of this conspiracy was the most legendary royalist secret agent of the Revolution, Jean, baron de Batz. Much has been written about the still mysterious role Batz played in Paris in 1794, at the height of the Terror, but the extent of his connection with Breteuil has been generally overlooked. Born in Gascony in 1754, Batz was, appropriately enough, a descendant of d'Artagnan. After some years in the army he had established himself in Paris at the height of the speculative boom of the late 1780s. He soon joined a group of financiers who aimed to make profits from a downturn on the stock exchange. His principal colleague in this 'bear' syndicate was Breteuil himself, along with the future Girondin finance minister Clavière. The partnership may have been sealed by a more intimate bargain – an English spy later claimed that for a time Batz shared the favours of the baron's mistress Mme de Brancas.[27]

At the outbreak of the Revolution Batz, who had been elected to the Estates General as deputy for the nobility of Tartas, immediately put his financial resources at the disposal of the royal cause. His role in the financial planning of Breteuil's Ministry of the Hundred Hours has already been discussed. It says much for Batz's nerve that while the baron and his colleagues were fleeing abroad, he continued to sit unmolested in the Assembly. Indeed, by the summer of 1790 he was president of its important committee for the liquidation of the debt. In this capacity he conceived an audacious plan for creating an emergency secret fund for Louis XVI to draw on. The holders of venal offices in the royal household which the Assembly had suppressed were approached and asked to cede a percentage of the sum reimbursed to them to the crown. Since most were convinced royalists, they usually agreed. By July 1792 Batz had raised 512,000 livres in this way, as the king himself noted in his diary.[28]

Batz's political intrigues were inseparable from his financial activities. Certainly the wealth and reputation he derived from the latter smoothed his path in and around the Assembly. Above all, it allowed him to cultivate a wide range of friends and allies on all sides of the ideological spectrum, from royalists to the most extreme revolutionaries. This made him extremely useful to Breteuil. It is unclear whether the two men remained in contact during the early part of the Revolution, but they had definitely resumed relations by the spring of 1792. The following July, Batz emigrated. At the beginning of September, he was in Brussels, where he saw Fersen and discussed with him ways of ensuring the royal family's safety as Brunswick's army advanced on Paris. He then left for Verdun to find Breteuil, carrying with him a letter to the baron from Fersen. He did not know that it contained a distinctly uncomplimentary passage about himself. '[This letter]', wrote Fersen,

> will be brought to you, M. le baron, by the baron de Batz; permit me to add to my respect and attachment for you one plea – not to appear to have too much confidence in the baron de Batz, and only to speak of him as a man whose merit you appreciate in its proper place, but whom you are only using at the moment because of his banking connections, and to find out useful details. You know as well as I, M. le baron, that the baron de Batz does not have the best reputation, and that many

people regard him as an adventurer; your enemies will not fail
to say that you only confide in and surround yourself with this
type of person. Please excuse these observations, M. le baron,
but I hope that you will only see in them further proof of
my sincere devotion and desire to assure you the success you
deserve. Could you not use the baron de Batz to enter into
negotiations with the rebels?[29]

Fersen's snobbish distaste for Batz is evident from this passage,
but the only politically significant line is the last. Fersen was well
aware that Batz was close to his – and Breteuil's – pre-revolutionary
partner in speculation, Clavière, who had just been reinstated as
finance minister after 10 August. If the royal family's situation in
Paris were to deteriorate dramatically in the near future, Clavière's
influence would be a powerful card to play. Yet Breteuil felt that
these considerations were premature. A time would no doubt come
for secret dealings, but the most propitious moment would be after a
decisive victory in the field. 'My own opinion', he wrote to Fersen,

> ... is that when the army gets close to Paris ... we should try
> to begin a negotiation, and sacrifice everything to rescue the
> king, the queen and the royal family; I would bait my traps
> most carefully if I could tempt those rogues in Paris. Any other
> type of approach would only sting their pride, and might even
> increase their rage and madness. I would not hesitate to ask the
> king of Prussia to offer them a full and generous pardon, if he
> won a battle tomorrow; I would even beg His Majesty to add
> secretly to this a promise of rewards to the most important, and
> therefore the most guilty, rebels. I would hope that these pacific
> and well-meaning overtures, allied to a victory and the conse-
> quent panic in the capital, would bring success.

On the subject of Batz, Breteuil was careful to reassure Fersen. 'I
feel the same way as you about the baron de Batz,' he wrote, 'and
thank you for your comments on the subject; you know that I am
only cultivating him at present in the hope of securing through him
important financial resources for the first moments of the king's
administration.' Yet the baron added a note that showed he was also
thinking of Batz as a go-between in an eventual negotiation with the
revolutionary government:

If the Duke of Brunswick gives battle, we shall see what opportunities a victory might open up for ... a conciliation. Perhaps the baron de Batz will make the sacrifice of going to Paris; yesterday at least he seemed willing to do so, and I shall try to keep him to that decision. I can think of no one with better contacts on the spot.[30]

Batz, however, was not the only instrument the baron had to hand. Two more of his associates from pre-revolutionary days were still in Paris and in positions of influence: Antoine-Omer Talon and Maximilien Radix de Sainte-Foy. Talon was a former magistrate who had been closely linked to Mirabeau in his efforts to save the monarchy in 1790 and 1791. Sainte-Foy, Talon's uncle and associate in his dealings with Mirabeau, was a remarkable and exotic figure, a former diplomat and financier with a reputation for sharp practice.[31] He had gained powerful connections in revolutionary politics, both as an informal adviser to the Assembly's diplomatic committee, and as the friend and financial agent of Dumouriez.

Sainte-Foy, who had known Breteuil from his days as a diplomat, kept in contact with him at intervals throughout the Revolution. In July 1789, he collaborated with Batz in the financial planning for the Ministry of the Hundred Hours. He was also involved at this time in an attempted reconciliation between the duc d'Orléans, another of his patrons, and the crown. He was certainly back in contact with Breteuil by 1792. That July, Sainte-Foy wrote to the baron urging a negotiated settlement to the Revolution. According to Fersen, he argued that the moment was ripe for Brunswick to 'organize a truce, a national convention and a congress, that this was the only way to break up the Assembly and make the necessary changes in the constitution, and that this could never be achieved by force'.[32]

On 11 August, Sainte-Foy wrote again to Breteuil, giving him details of the events of the previous day in Paris. A great collector himself, he seemed more concerned by the architectural damage inflicted on the Tuileries than by the fact the monarchy had been overthrown. 'The château was not burned,' he informed the baron, 'only the temporary barracks and accessory buildings that bad taste had caused to be put up unnecessarily between the palace courtyards and the Carrousel ... The statues in the public squares are being torn down, which is a real barbarism.'³³

Sainte-Foy's aesthetic pose, however, concealed genuine courage. At some risk to himself, he had walked over to the Tuileries to see what was going on. By that time, the crowd had broken into the palace cellars. 'More than ten thousand bottles of wine,' he told Breteuil, 'whose remains littered the courtyard, had made everybody so drunk that I quickly ended my rather imprudent inspection, amid two thousand intoxicated people brandishing loaded firearms which they were handling most carelessly.' Sainte-Foy concluded with a serious political point: 'We are going to have that national convention that I thought of earlier, but which I wanted convoked by the king and on different principles, that is to say that I wished it to comprise only property-owners.'³⁴ Breteuil showed Sainte-Foy's letters to Fersen, who immediately decided that he, rather than Batz, would be the best agent to use in Paris. On 28 September, when it still seemed that Dumouriez might surrender, Fersen broached this idea to the baron, and proposed an elaborate means of communicating secretly with Sainte-Foy:

> On the basis of what several people have said to me ... about Sainte-Foy being closely connected with the duc d'Orléans, and given my knowledge of his character and links with yourself, I thought that he is the man who could be of most use to us in Paris. I have therefore had the idea ... of sending Sainte-Foy a note warning him to heat with a candle any letters from you, Mme de Matignon or the bishop. I will ... then write to him with the proposals for Dumouriez that you drew up with Rivarol, and if he sends a reply, I will pass it on to you. It would be helpful, M. le baron, if you could give me a letter for Sainte-Foy outlining this ... It should appear to deal only with unimportant subjects and Mme de Matignon could then insert between the lines the propositions you wish to make.³⁵

The defeat at Valmy, and Brunswick's retreat, temporarily put a stop to Breteuil's intrigues with Batz and Sainte-Foy. There was now no question, at least in the short term, of a victorious Prussian army opening negotiations from a position of strength as it advanced on Paris. The plan had to be modified: it was now simply a matter of saving the king's life. At this point, Talon entered the scene. In late October, he wrote to Breteuil from London, where he had been forced to flee following the discovery of his secret correspondence with Louis XVI in the *armoire de fer*. Now he offered his services to the baron, claiming that he could be 'useful, but really extremely useful, to the king'. His proposal was that Breteuil should send an agent to London to see him and concert joint action, but he does not seem to have received a response. Talon's role in the story, however, was by no means over.

Frustrated at these setbacks, Batz now decided to take matters into his own hands. As the king's trial reached its climax, he decided to attempt a rescue himself. At the beginning of January 1793, he went back to Paris to set this in motion. He carried with him, as he later recalled, an official authorization. Although he did not say who signed it, it was most likely from Breteuil:

> Convinced of the importance of the services that can be expected of the baron de Batz's loyalty and his attachment to the king and the royal family, we invite him to return to France and use all possible means to liberate the king, the queen and their family. 2 January 1793.[36]

*

ON 26 DECEMBER Louis XVI made his second, and final, appearance before the convention. De Sèze rose for the defence and spoke, with great passion, for three hours. The king then made a short concluding speech. It was clear that he expected to die, and that his words were addressed more to posterity than to his audience:

> Speaking to you perhaps for the last time I declare to you that my conscience reproaches me with nothing ... I have never feared a public examination of my conduct; but my heart is rent at finding in the indictment the imputation that I wished to shed the blood of the people and above all that the misfortunes of 10 August should be attributed to me.
>
> I confess that the manifold proofs I have given at all times of my love for the people and the manner in which I have always conducted myself seemed to me sufficient proof that I

took little heed of exposing myself to spare its blood, and to remove such an imputation from me for ever.[37]

The verdict was now in the hands of the Convention. It was decided in a series of votes, which began on the morning of 25 January and continued for thirty-seven hours. The first motion put before the deputies, on whether Louis was guilty of conspiring against liberty and the safety of the state, was carried with no dissenting voices, but twenty-seven abstentions. The second, on whether the king's punishment should be decided by the people in a referendum, was rejected by a wide margin. The crucial vote was on the penalty to be inflicted. The result could not have been more dramatic. Of the 721 deputies present, 361 voted for death without conditions, 286 for imprisonment or banishment, 46 for death but with a postponement of the sentence, 26 for death but demanding a debate on the question of postponement, and two for imprisonment in irons. The majority for unconditional death was thus only one vote.

On the morning of 17 January, Malesherbes went to the Temple to tell Louis the verdict. Halfway though he broke down and fell weeping at the king's feet. The two men then parted and never met again. Meanwhile, in the convention, a final effort was being mounted to secure a reprieve. A motion was introduced calling for the sentence to be delayed, but went down to defeat by seventy votes. On the evening of 20 January, Louis was informed that he would be executed within twenty-four hours. The king made three requests: a three-day stay of execution to prepare himself for death, a confessor of his own choice, and a last meeting with his family, from whom he had been separated since the beginning of his trial. The first was denied; the second two were granted.

A few hours later Louis XVI saw his family for the last time. It was a profound and tragic moment. Against all the odds – an ancestral feud, markedly different personalities, little physical attraction and initial sexual dysfunction – Louis and Marie Antoinette had found a kind of love. What had brought them together were the children now gathered around them. There were no witnesses to what was said, but the king's valet Cléry observed some of the scene through the glass in an adjoining door. Marie Antoinette, the children and Mme Elisabeth did not yet know the verdict, and Cléry saw them sway and weep as Louis broke the news to them. The dauphin clung to his father's knees. The family remained stricken in this tableau for an hour and three-quarters. The only one of the group to survive, Louis's daughter Marie-Thérèse, recalled that the king told Marie Antoinette about his trial, then gave religious instruction to his son and exhorted him to pardon those who had condemned him to death. As they parted for the last time, Marie-Thérèse threw herself at her father's feet and collapsed in a dead faint.

The one thing that resisted all these traumas was the king's appetite. At 11 p.m. he sat down to supper, consuming two wings of chicken, some vegetables, some wine mixed with water, and for dessert some finger-biscuit and a little Malaga wine. At 12.30 p.m. Louis retired to bed, and to judge from his loud snores was soon asleep.

The king woke at about 5 a.m. on 21 January. The priest he had chosen was already in attendance. This was Henry Essex Edgeworth, a forty-seven-year-old Irishman from County Longford who had previously been Mme Elisabeth's confessor. Louis took communion at a makeshift altar improvised by Cléry. Just before nine, Santerre and a group of municipal officials arrived to take him to his death. One of them was the former priest turned extreme revolutionary, Jacques Roux, to whom Louis tried to give a packet of his personal effects and his will to pass to Marie Antoinette. 'I am not here to do your errands, but to take you to the scaffold,' replied Roux brutally. The parcel was handed to someone else. The king then stamped once on the floor, and said in a loud voice: 'Partons! [Let's go!]' The group went out into the courtyard, where a closed carriage was waiting. Louis got into it, accompanied by Edgeworth and two gendarmes.

In the meantime, the baron de Batz had been making his preparations. He had sent out a summons to 500 royalist sympathizers to gather on the route to the scaffold for an attempt to rescue the king. The king's journey would take him from the Temple west-wards along the northern boulevards to the Place de la Révolution (formerly Place Louis XV, and today the Place de la Concorde), where the guillotine had been set up. Batz calculated that the best spot to intercept the procession was the intersection between the boulevard Bonne-Nouvelle and the rue de Cléry. At this point the road mounted a slope and was dominated on one side by a steep embankment. Batz's plan was to mass his supporters on the embankment, rush the closed carriage as it slowed down on the incline, and hurry the king away in the confusion into an adjoining house where a hiding-place had been prepared. It is not clear what Batz intended to do next, but he probably planned to smuggle Louis out of France to safety in England.

Batz was at his post early on the morning of 21 January with a few chosen companions, waiting anxiously for the bulk of the conspirators to arrive. As the minutes ticked by and nobody appeared, he grew more and more worried. By this time 130,000 soldiers and National Guardsman were on the streets, turned out in force expressly to prevent the type of action Batz was contemplating. Most likely it was this that put off the baron's accomplices. It did not, however, discourage Batz. As the carriage came into view with its escort, he drew his sword and, at the head of his little party, rushed into the road in front of the horses, shouting, 'To me, all those who wish to save the king!' There was no movement from the crowd. As the National Guards rushed towards him, Batz slipped away down a nearby street. The carriage itself barely paused; it is probable that Louis XVI was not even aware that an attempt had been made to rescue him.[38]

Fittingly for such a devout Catholic, the king's last moments were impregnated with religious imagery. At about 10 a.m. the carriage reached the foot of the guillotine and Louis got out. The executioner and his assistants, who were waiting, made a move to tie his hands. Shocked, Louis began to resist. He was only restrained by an interjection from Edgeworth: 'Sire, in this further outrage I see only a final resemblance between Your Majesty and the God who will be his recompense.' The king slowly mounted the steep steps of the scaffold. Edgeworth, who was supporting him, exclaimed: 'Son of St Louis, ascend to Heaven!' Walking across the platform, the king then attempted to address the vast crowd: 'Frenchmen! I die innocent of the crimes of which I have been accused. I forgive those who are guilty of my death, and I pray God that the blood you are about to shed may never be required of France.' Characteristically, his last thought was to uphold the traditional Church: 'I only sanctioned upon compulsion the Civil Constitution of the Clergy . . .'

At this point Santerre, determined to cut the scene short, signalled for the drums to beat, and Louis's final words were drowned out. The executioners rushed towards the king, bound him to the plank, tipped it horizontally and released the blade. Unfortunately, Louis's neck was so fat that it was not severed at the first stroke, and a scream was heard. It was all over in a matter of seconds. At 10.22 a.m., the executioner reached into the basket to display the king's head to the people. The hair had not even been disarranged.[39]

*

THE EXECUTION OF Louis XVI horrified Europe. In the House of Commons, the prime minister Pitt the Younger termed it 'the foulest and most atrocious deed which the history of the world has yet had occasion to attest'. Spain immediately expelled the French ambassador, and within two months had joined the war on the side of Austria and Prussia. In St Petersburg, Catherine the Great was so shocked by the news that she took to her bed. The Russian court was ordered into full mourning for six weeks.

For Breteuil, the king's death was merely the greatest in a catalogue of disasters. After Valmy, he had returned to Brussels, but not for long. Flushed with success, Dumouriez swiftly put into execution his pet project, the invasion of Belgium. On 6 November 1792, he routed the Austrians opposing him at Jemappes. Amid scenes of panic, the government of the Austrian Netherlands, accompanied by crowds of *émigrés*, fled from the capital. Breteuil, Fersen, Mercy-Argenteau, Craufurd and Eléonore Sullivan were carried along with the flood. After the initial chaos, however, the baron does not seem to have been unduly inconvenienced. On 11 November, Fersen found him at Maastricht, sitting down to dinner with twenty of his closest friends. By December he had established himself, alongside the refugee government of Belgium, at Düsseldorf.

Throughout these months the war continued to expand. Alarmed by France's occupation of Belgium and increasing control of the Channel and North Sea coast, England had been growing steadily more hostile. On 1 February 1793, the two countries went to war.

A fortnight later, Dumouriez launched an invasion of Holland. This time, however, the revolutionary juggernaut was halted. On 18 March, in a furious battle at Neerwinden, the French were decisively defeated by the Austrians under the Prince of Coburg.

Dumouriez's setback had important political consequences, with which Breteuil was soon deeply involved. By this time the general was both deeply discontented with his political position and fearful for his personal safety. Although he had opportunistically declared himself a republican after Valmy, he was basically a constitutional monarchist, and profoundly out of sympathy with the radical turn the Revolution was taking. He knew he was suspect to the new government, and was currently under sureveillance by the political commissars it had sent, in an ominous foretaste of the Russian Revolution, to the army. He had also criticized the sweeping reforms the Convention had decreed in Belgium. Now, in the wake of Neerwinden, Dumouriez began to think seriously about taking sides. It would be wrong, however, to see this as a complete volte-face. Rather, it was simply a resumption of the overtures he had first made to the Prussians the previous September.

Much has been written about the 'treason of Dumouriez'. Yet the central role played in it by Breteuil has been curiously neglected. In fact, it was probably to the baron that Dumouriez made his first approach. The scene was London, where Breteuil had travelled in early February 1793 to attempt to persuade the English government to issue a declaration to France demanding that the lives of Marie Antoinette and her children be spared. According to Fersen, Breteuil was contacted there by a secret emissary of Dumouriez, one of his former aides-de-camp named Toustaing.[40] This go-between brought a series of proposals from the general, which unfortunately Fersen did not note in his diary. Probably they were similar to those that the baron had previously tried to smuggle to Dumouriez via Rivarol's sister before Valmy.

The aims of the negotiation became clearer as it developed. Dumouriez would declare against the republic, march his army on Paris, rescue the surviving members of the royal family and restore the monarchy. In exchange, he would be guaranteed a leading role in the new dispensation. Yet at the same time Breteuil was involved in other clandestine intrigues to save the queen and her children, which may or may not have been linked to this one. Just before Toustaing's arrival, Talon, who was still in London, brought a French banker named Ribbes to see the baron. Ribbes had connections with Danton, but at heart he was a devoted royalist who in February 1792 had offered his services to Louis XVI. Ribbes now offered to try to secure a decree from the Convention (presumably through Danton's influence) releasing Marie Antoinette and her family in exchange for 6 million livres payable once the prisoners were on foreign soil.[41]

Breteuil immediately went to see Pitt the Younger with both Dumouriez's and Talon's proposals, hoping for political support for the former and a loan of 6 million livres for the latter. Yet Pitt refused both requests. The baron, his suspicion of England never far from the surface, concluded that this was because the prime minister had little desire to see either France restored to her former position or her royal family saved. Accordingly, he came away with a low opinion of Pitt. According to Fersen, he remarked that Pitt 'had little grasp of foreign policy, which he does not understand at all, hiding his mediocrity by silence; yet he has a perfect mastery of domestic affairs, and especially of the intrigue necessary to keep his place and popularity'.[42]

Pitt's hostility doomed Talon's project for the time being. Dumouriez's plan, however, was not so dependent on English participation, and it was on this that Breteuil now pinned his hopes. On 10 March he arrived back in Düsseldorf. His first action was to send the vicomte de Caraman to Mercy-Argenteau, who was currently at Wesel, to inform him of Dumouriez's approach and gain Austrian support. Mercy's reply, though cautious, was essentially positive:

> The arrangement with M. Dumouriez is in fact nothing more than a simple conjecture on the part of the person who has formed it. We are still some way from this point to its actual confirmation by the object of our plans. However, I still think this goal should be pursued, because even if it does not produce real advantages, it will at least have no ill-effects, as long as we proceed in a manner that does not compromise us.
>
> We must suppose that our intermediary will have enough credit with M. Dumouriez to need no accreditation apart from his own word.[43]

Mercy went on to outline two conditions that, to him, were crucial. The first was that Dumouriez would bring over to the Austrians as prisoners the two sons of the duc d'Orléans who were currently serving on his staff. This was because, like most of his colleagues, he had an exaggerated idea of Orléans's influence on the revolutionary government. He was convinced that if the duke's sons were captured, they could be held as hostages against the safety of Marie Antoinette and her family. The second stipulation was military: that Dumouriez deliver up at least one frontier fortress to his new masters, to speed up their advance on Paris. These were certainly substantial demands, but then a great deal was at stake.

The identity of the mysterious go-between Mercy mentions is intriguing. There are strong grounds for believing that it was Breteuil's other correspondent, Radix de Sainte-Foy. At this point the ubiquitous Sainte-Foy was constantly shuttling between Paris and Dumouriez's army. Conveniently, he possessed a property on the frontier, at Mont Saint-Martin,[44] and this would have been ideally situated for conducting the necessary secret negotiations. The fact that such a well-connected figure was in all probability now working for the royalist cause shows the calibre of the network Breteuil had set up, and just how far it reached into the Revolutionary government. By March 1793, it must have seemed to the baron that his careful cultivation of these contacts was about to pay off.

On 1 April, Dumouriez arrested the political commissars attached to his army and declared against the Convention. At eleven that night, he issued a proclamation to his troops announcing his intention of restoring order and the constitution of 1791. By this fact alone, Marie Antoinette's son would become Louis XVII. 'It is time', the general declaimed,

> that the army makes known its will, purges France of assassins and agitators and returns to our unfortunate country the repose it has lost through the crimes of its representatives. It is time to reinstate a constitution which we swore to uphold for three successive years, which gave us liberty and which alone can preserve us from licence and anarchy.[45]

On the other side, hopes were high that this time a decisive blow had been struck against the Revolution. Fersen's main preoccupation, naturally, was with Marie Antoinette's safety. He was also determined that a sound political adviser should be despatched to her as soon as possible, to fortify against the perfidious counsels that would no doubt soon reach her from Mercy. As he put it in his diary:

> I proposed to [Breteuil] that someone should be sent to see the queen at the moment of her deliverance, to enlighten her as to her situation and to outline her course of action to her in contrast to the ideas M. de Mercy will not fail to send her in writing.[46]

Presumably Fersen feared that the Austrian desire for a constitutional monarchy in France, and perhaps territorial gain at her expense, would be revived.

Oddly, Fersen did not volunteer to go to Paris himself. Instead, the intrepid Bishop of Pamiers agreed to perform the task. The means by which he proposed to do so underlined the hidden but important role Sainte-Foy was now playing in these events. On 7 April, Fersen noted: 'The Bishop of Pamiers is due to leave tomorrow; he is to head towards the French army and try to see Dumouriez through Sainte-Foy.'[47] Once again, the bishop was where he liked to be, in the thick of the action, although the prospect of approaching a substantial army whose dispositions were still in doubt cannot have been very tempting.

The following morning Fersen was sitting writing a note to the queen when the bishop came into his room and told him 'that Dumouriez's army had risen against him, and that he had fled across the frontier to Mons with all his staff'.[48] The news was accurate. The bulk of Dumouriez's troops in the field had initially declared for him. However, he had failed to win over the garrisons of the vital fortresses of Lille, Valenciennes and Condé. This, coupled with resolute proclamations from the Convention denouncing him as a traitor and recalling the soldiers to their loyalty, had led to a growing tide of defections. By the evening of 5 April, the situation was hopeless. In despair, Dumouriez fled to the Austrians, bringing with him only 458 infantrymen and 424 cavalry.

Coming only six months after Valmy, Dumouriez's failure was a further crushing blow for Breteuil. Not only was a quick ending to the Revolution once again out of sight, but it was possible that the French government's narrow escape might dispose it to even more extreme measures. The baron confided these fears to Mercy on 10 April. Above all, his thoughts were with Marie Antoinette, whom he now termed 'the queen mother', and her son:

> I am sure, my dear count, that you find like me that in these terrible circumstances, the events which unceasingly batter our morale and spirits are crowding in too fast for our frail constitutions. As for myself, I admit that I no longer have the strength to withstand such shocks. Just as I was rejoicing at Dumouriez's decision, my hopes for the benefits it would secure had to be drastically revised. The state to which the rebel army is now reduced should give us great advantages, but to make best use of these developments and calculate their consequences, I will need reassurance that this is more likely to paralyse the villains with fear than to incite them to that ghastly fury which usually guides their conduct. One can only shudder at this thought, although opinion in Paris, allied to the concerted actions of several provinces, gives some cause for comfort regarding the position of the king and the queen mother. I don't know when we will next get news from Paris; if you receive any, please do me the kindness of sending it on to me, because at the moment I have no positive information on a subject . . . that absorbs all the feelings of my soul.[49]

*

AS BRETEUIL HAD predicted, Dumouriez's defection did indeed contribute to a lurch to the Left in Paris. The day after the general crossed the frontier, the convention decreed the establishment of a nine-man emergency executive, known as the Committee of Public Safety. A special court to deal with political crimes, the Revolutionary Tribunal, had already been set up on 10 March. The Girondins, whose enthusiasm in beginning the war was only equalled by their incompetence in prosecuting it, incurred particular blame for Dumouriez's treason. On 2 June, National Guards from the radical sections, accompanied by a large crowd, surrounded the Convention, and Brissot, Vergniaud, Guadet, Gensonné, Clavière, Pétion and twenty-six of their colleagues were arrested. Power passed into the hands of the hardline Jacobins, dominated by Danton.

It was now a race against time to save the queen. Even before the fall of the monarchy, there had been talk of putting her on trial; the establishment of the Revolutionary Tribunal now put her in immediate peril. Yet over the next few months there were at least two serious attempts to rescue Marie Antoinette, the second of which came very close to success. The organizer of both was the baron de Batz. Whether he was acting on his own initiative or as Breteuil's agent is unclear. At the end of January 1793, Batz and Breteuil met in London, where the former had fled after his failed attempt to save Louis XVI from the scaffold, and the fate of the queen and her family was almost certainly discussed. Yet there is no further record of Breteuil's involvement in the dangerous work Batz now undertook.[50]

After the king's execution, Marie Antoinette, her two children and Mme Elisabeth remained in the Temple. One day in early February 1793, the queen was amazed to see the comte de Jarjayes, her erstwhile go-between in her correspondence with Barnave, come into her room. Jarjayes hurriedly outlined to her a plan he had concocted with Batz. In the course of an inspection of the prisoners' quarters by a patrol of National Guards secretly sympathetic to their plight, Marie Antoinette and Mme Elisabeth would disguise themselves as one of their number, while the two children would be carried out enveloped in the guardsmen's greatcoats. The royal family would then be smuggled to safety in England.

Obviously, none of this could have been attempted if Batz and Jarjayes had not possessed a well-placed network of co-conspirators in the revolutionary administration itself. This was in fact the case. It remains mysterious how this came about, and whether Batz's collaborators were motivated by promises of material reward, were secret royalists, or simply felt pity for the captive queen and her family. Perhaps it was a mixture of all three factors. Batz's two most crucial allies in his efforts to liberate the royal family were Michonis, a lemonade-seller who was also a municipal officer and inspector of prisons, and Cortey, a National Guard officer with shared responsibility for the security of the Temple. Yet Batz's network extended all over Paris. Only this can explain how, after his return to France on 9 February 1793, he was able to remain at liberty throughout the Terror.

The rescue attempt had to be postponed several times through various mishaps, but at last all was set for 21 June. The date was chosen because both Cortey and Michonis would be on duty that day. At six that evening, a patrol of thirty National Guards, commanded by Cortey, set out for the Temple. In their ranks marched Batz himself, under the assumed name of Forget. The party entered the Temple, took command, and were about to put their plan into action when suddenly the cobbler Antoine Simon, another municipal officer who had become the royal family's principal gaoler, appeared. Probably he had been alerted by a suspicious attendant in Marie Antoinette's retinue. He brought an order from the Commune for Michonis' arrest. It was clearly now impossible to proceed. Michonis, however, was able to satisfy the Commune that there had been nothing suspicious about his conduct, and he was soon back at his post. It may well be that he got off so lightly because his interrogators were themselves in the pay of Batz.

Soon afterwards, the conditions of Marie Antoinette's imprisonment worsened. On the night of 3 July, she was separated from her son, who was taken to the floor below and put under the charge of Simon and his wife. The parting was a ghastly affair; the queen stood over the boy's bed, refusing to give him up, and was only subdued by the threat of violence. For two whole days afterwards, she could hear her son sobbing in the rooms below, begging to be returned to his mother. Knowing that every day the young Louis was taken for a walk by his gaolers and passed by the adjoining tower, Marie Antoinette climbed up there every day and often waited for hours for a glimpse of her son.

It is possible that this brutal separation was directly linked to Batz's previous rescue attempt. It is likely that the events of 21 June had raised the government's suspicions, even if nothing had been conclusively proved. The most important prisoner by far in the Temple was Louis XVII; if he managed to escape, the royalist cause would have a king in waiting. It therefore made sense to remove him from his mother and aunt, both incorrigible counter-revolutionaries who were presumably alert to any possibility of rescue. And who better to guard the boy than Simon, whose presence of mind had foiled the plot in the first place? The human feelings of the victims took distinctly second place; for the revolutionary as for the old regime, the grim logic of *raison d'état* had taken over.

Worse was to follow. In the early morning of 2 August, Marie Antoinette herself was taken from the Temple and moved to the Conciergerie prison next to the Palais de Justice on the Île de la Cité. The lack of warning, the hurried departure, the transfer in darkness; all bear the trademarks of the modern police state. The implication of the action was obvious. The Conciergerie was for prisoners about to be condemned, the 'antechamber of death'. The queen's quarters there were a far cry from the relative comfort of the Temple. She was put in a cell eleven and a half feet square, which she had to share with one female servant and two gendarmes.

It was it these grim circumstances that the last, and most famous, effort to save the queen was made. This was the 'Carnation Conspiracy'. Although the principal roles were played by Michonis and another royalist agent, the chevalier de Rougeville, it is probable that much of the plot was again organized by Batz from his various hiding-places in Paris. The first move was made on 28 August. By this time Michonis was again functioning as an inspector of prisons, with authority extending to the Conciergerie. In this capacity, he brought the chevalier de Rougeville to see Marie Antoinette. The queen recognized him immediately; it was he who, on 20 June 1792, had helped save her life by pushing her behind a table when the crowd invaded the Tuileries. Probably Rougeville was in love with her: Fersen refers to him as 'spending all his time in her antechambers and following her everywhere'[51] before the Revolution.

Up until now, Marie Antoinette had steadfastly refused to escape without her children. Yet the family's current separation meant that her presence was no longer of any use to them. In these circumstances, she was prepared to acquiesce in Rougeville's scheme. The surveillance was such that nothing could be arranged verbally. Rougeville entered Marie Antoinette's cell with a bunch of carnations, in which was concealed a note. The amazed queen was trembling too much to take the flowers, so Rougeville placed them behind the stove, whispering that they contained a message. After the visitor had left, Marie Antoinette quickly read the scribbled lines, which told her to be ready the following Friday. She was allowed no writing implements, so she pricked out a reply indicating agreement with a pin on a scrap of paper. She then entrusted this to a young guard named Gilbert, who she thought was sympathetic to her plight.

It is unclear what happened next. According to the official sources, instead of smuggling Marie Antoinette's message to Rougeville, Gilbert informed his superior officer. He may indeed have felt pity for the queen, but he valued his own skin more. However, other accounts claim that at 11 p.m. on the Friday in question, 2 September, Marie Antoinette was indeed escorted out of her cell by Michonis and her two guards, on the pretext of being transferred back to the Temple. In fact, so the story goes, this was simply a cover story; Rougeville was waiting outside the prison with a carriage to take her to safety. Yet just before the group reached the prison gates Gilbert, who was one of the party, for whatever reason refused to let them proceed further, and the queen had to return to captivity.

Whichever version is the truth, the consequences are not in doubt. Michonis was again arrested, and this time he was not released. Rougeville, however, was hidden by Batz and managed to flee France. It was Marie Antoinette, once again, who suffered most. A fortnight after the discovery of the Carnation Conspiracy, she was put into solitary confinement. By this time, her health had begun to decline dramatically. She had lost a great deal of weight, and her hair was now quite white. Her eyesight had deteriorated, and she was experiencing severe period pains that gave rise to haemorrhages. With her simple black or white dress and a plain bonnet on her head, she had become an old woman in mourning for her husband. The contrast with the young woman Burke had seen twenty years before at Versailles, 'full of life, and splendour, and joy', could not have been more cruel.

Finally, at 6 p.m. on 12 October, Marie Antoinette was summoned before the Revolutionary Tribunal for a preliminary examination. Everything was designed to break her spirit; it was known that her period pains had begun and were particularly severe, and again the hours of darkness had been chosen for the ordeal. The revolutionary tribunal sat in what had been the *grand'chambre* of the *parlement* of Paris in the Palais de Justice. The Stygian atmosphere of the proceedings was deepened by the fact that the only light came from two flickering candles. This played on the sombre costumes of the judges and the nodding black plumes on the front of their hats.

Beyond, in the gloom, the queen could hear but not see an unknown number of spectators, which clearly unsettled her.

Thirty-five accusations were put to Marie Antoinette. The principal ones were that she had sent millions to her brother the emperor to be used against France, organized the flight to Varennes, and persuaded her husband to veto the decrees against the *émigrés* and refractory priests in November 1791. The queen denied all the accusations, showing considerable presence of mind in her answers. When asked, for example, whether she regretted that her son would never be king, she simply replied: 'I shall never regret anything for my son when his country is happy.' The examination ended, and the trial was scheduled for the following Monday, 14 October.

In the absurdly short time given her to prepare her defence, Marie Antoinette worked with Chauveau-Lagarde, the twenty-eight year-old lawyer assigned to her case. At eight o'clock on the Monday morning, she again appeared before the Revolutionary Tribunal. Facing her were five judges, and to her right sat the jury. Behind her the public benches were crowded with spectators. There was little written evidence for the prosecution, which was provided instead by forty-one witnesses. The calibre of this is indicated by the testimony of the second witness, Roussillon, who described having seen many empty wine bottles under the queen's bed after the storming of the Tuileries, which led him to conclude that she had plied the Swiss Guards with drink to incite them to attack the people.

The fourth witness, however, was of a different mettle. This was Hébert, the radical journalist and now deputy prosecutor of the Commune. Hébert testified that during a visit to Louis XVII in the Temple, the boy had confessed to him that his mother and aunt had taught him to masturbate, and that Marie Antoinette had committed incest with him. These charges were the culmination of every pornographic libel published against the queen since she had arrived in France. Once again, they were designed to portray her as an unnatural mother and wife, whose private debauchery matched her public treasons.

It is certainly true that, after repeated interrogations, the young Louis had been forced to sign a confession detailing Hébert's claims. Our own age, more familiar with the brainwashing of children than the eighteenth century, can judge these assertions at their proper value. Even at the time, Hébert's accusations completely backfired. Marie Antoinette at once realized that her persecutors had gone too far. Summoned to respond to the question, she rose from her chair and replied: 'If I have not answered, it is because nature refuses to answer such a charge against a mother.' There was a murmur of sympathy from the crowd, even some shouts of support, and the court had to be called to order.

Returning to her seat, Marie Antoinette leaned over to Chauveau-Lagarde. 'Was there too much dignity in my answer?' she asked. Mystified, Chauveau-Lagarde replied: 'Madame, be yourself and you will always do right, but why do you ask?' 'Because', the queen responded, 'I heard a woman of the people say to her neighbour: "See how proud she is!" '[52] This was a remarkable exchange. Before the Revolution, Marie Antoinette had taken acting lessons at Versailles and proved herself an accomplished amateur actress. Now, even as her life hung in the balance, she saw her trial as a stage. Not only was she seeking to justify herself, she was also trying to win the audience over to her side.

The result of the trial, however, was never in doubt. The following day, after the speech for the defence and the prosecution's summing-up, the jury retired. After an hour, it returned with a unanimous verdict of guilty. The presiding judge, Hermann, then rose and condemned Marie Antoinette to death. According to the usual practice, the sentence was to be carried out within twenty-four hours.

The queen spent her last hours writing a farewell letter to her sister-in-law. Mme Elisabeth never received it. Marie Antoinette's guard handed it to the public prosecutor Fouquier-Tinville, who kept it. When Fouquier-Tinville was himself executed after the Terror, it was seized by the revolutionary tribunal, and only came to light in 1816.

It is to you, my sister, that I write for the last time. I have just been condemned, not to a shameful death for that is reserved only for criminals, but shall now go to rejoin your brother. Innocent, like him, I hope to show the same firmness in my last moments. I am calm, as one is when one's conscience is clear. I am profoundly sad at leaving my dear children; you know that I only lived for them and for you, my good and tender sister. . . . My son must never forget his father's last words, which I never cease to repeat to him: he must never seek to avenge our death!

I must speak to you about a matter that is very painful to my heart. I know how much distress this child has caused you. [This was a reference to the young Louis's 'confession' that Mme Elisabeth had helped to abuse him.] Forgive him, my dear sister; think of his young age, and how easy it is to make a child say almost anything, without even understanding it. The day will come, I hope, when he will only value the more greatly your kindness and tenderness for us both . . .

I ask pardon of everybody I know, and of you in particular, my dear sister, for any pain I might unwittingly have caused them. I forgive my enemies the harm they have done me. I bid goodbye here to my aunts and to all my brothers and sisters. I had friends; the thought of being separated from them for ever and of their grief is one of my greatest regrets in dying; they should at least know that right up until my last moment I was thinking of them . . .[53]

At eleven o'clock on the morning of 16 October, Marie Antoinette was led out into the courtyard of the Conciergerie. Awaiting her there was the final barbarity; not a closed carriage that would permit her to die with decency like her husband, but the open tumbril reserved for common criminals. The queen's composure momentarily deserted her at the sight, and she hastily had to relieve herself by the wall. The lapse was quickly over. The queen climbed into the cart, her hands tied behind her back, and set off on her last journey. As she passed through the crowds, the painter David, a committed Jacobin, made the famous sketch of her sitting bolt upright, her face drawn, an expression of grim disdain on her features. Although drawn with hate, the picture none the less captures the great dignity of the condemned woman.

Throughout her life Marie Antoinette had striven to emulate her redoubtable mother, who in 1740 had saved her empire by mounting a horse and rallying her people. In the last years of her life, she often invoked the memory of the dead empress. In August 1791 she had written to Mercy-Argenteau: 'My blood flows in my son's veins, and

I hope that one day he will prove himself a true grandson of Maria Theresa.' In February 1792 she had reminded Kaunitz of his past services to the empress, and assured him that 'come what may, her daughter will show the same mettle as her mother'. Marie Antoinette kept her promise. In her last moments, as the tumbril turned into the Place de la Révolution and she mounted the scaffold, she showed herself worthy of Maria Theresa.

Chapter Fourteen

AFTER THE DELUGE

THE FRENCH MONARCHY had been wrecked, and Louis XVI and Marie Antoinette had perished with it. Yet there were many more victims than the king and queen. Even the survivors were not to escape unscathed; the rest of their lives was shaped by the struggle against the Revolution and its legacy.

Between 1793 and 1815 France experienced political instability, military glory and blood-letting on a grand scale. In July 1794 the dictatorship of Robespierre and the Jacobins was overthrown and replaced by the more moderate but considerably more corrupt and inefficient Directory. This regime in turn was swept aside in 1799 by the ambitious and brilliant general Napoleon Bonaparte, who ruled autocratically as first consul and then emperor of the French until 1814. Perhaps a quarter of a million French people died during the Terror and the civil war that accompanied it. A further 1.4 million Frenchmen died in the twenty-three-year war that had begun in April 1792 and ended only with the fall of Napoleon.

The continuing vicissitudes of the royal family mirrored this sombre background. After the queen's execution, her children and sister-in-law remained imprisoned in the Temple. A few months later Mme Elisabeth in turn left to face the Revolutionary Tribunal, accused of sending money to the *émigrés* and conspiring to attack the people on 10th August. Borne up to the end by her profound religious faith, she was executed on 10 May 1794. The fate of the young Louis XVII was even more ghastly. For six months after his mother's death he was put into solitary confinement in a filthy cell, amidst his own excrement. In these conditions he swiftly developed the disease that had earlier killed his older brother, tuberculosis of the bones. According to official sources, he died in the Temple on 8 June 1795, aged ten. There have been endless rumours since that he was in fact smuggled to safety and a substitute put in his place. However, a recent DNA test carried out on the preserved heart of the boy who died in the Temple has proved beyond reasonable doubt that he was indeed Louis XVII.

The only prisoner of the Temple to survive was Louis and Marie Antoinette's daughter Marie-Thérèse. In December 1795, aged seventeen, she was exchanged by the revolutionary government for the political commissars Dumouriez had arrested in April 1793, and whom he had delivered to the Austrians when he crossed the frontier. After spending some years with her mother's family in Vienna, in 1799 she married the comte d'Artois's eldest son, the duc d'Angoulême. Marie-Thérèse returned to France in 1814 at the restoration of the monarchy, only to be forced to flee once more by the revolution of 1830. She died in exile in Austria on 19 October 1851, leaving no children.

Despite becoming an avowed Jacobin and even voting for his cousin Louis XVI's death in the convention, the duc d'Orléans did not escape the scaffold. He was executed less than a month after Marie Antoinette, on 6 November 1793. In contrast, Louis XVI's aunts Adélaïde and Victoire met natural deaths, though not without some last hair-raising adventures. As the French armies advanced into Italy in 1797, Mesdames Tantes fled Rome and took refuge with their Bourbon cousins in Naples. Within a year, however, Naples too was menaced with invasion, and the two old ladies had to pack up again. They took ship at Bari on 5 February, just as the French troops were entering the town, heading for Trieste. It was the start of a truly horrific two-month voyage, in a tiny, overcrowded boat, buffeted by terrible winter storms. After a much-needed stopover in Corfu, Mesdames Tantes finally arrived at Trieste. Mme Victoire, exhausted by her tribulations, died there a month later, on 8 June 1799, and Mme Adélaïde followed her the next year.

After the death of Louis XVII, the comte de Provence succeeded him as Louis XVIII, even though for nineteen years he was merely a king in exile. After a life of obscurity in Russia's Baltic provinces and then in England, his moment finally came in 1814. In April that year, after a series of military defeats, Napoleon abdicated as emperor of the French, and the monarchy was restored. The price of this restoration, however, was a constitutional charter that the new king agreed to observe. On 3 May, aged fifty-nine, ill, obese, but still dignified and shrewdly intelligent, Louis XVIII returned to the capital he had fled on the night of 20 June 1791. Apart from Napoleon's brief return in 1815 during the Hundred Days, Louis reigned until his death in 1824. Determined like Charles II of England not to 'go on his travels again', he proved a pragmatic and peaceable ruler, trying to steer a middle way between the political extremes created by the Revolution.

Since Louis XVIII had no children, he was succeeded by his younger brother, the comte d'Artois. As Charles X, the new king soon showed that he had learned nothing over the last forty years. By his determination to reinstate the clergy and nobility in as many of their former privileges as possible, Charles decisively alienated the moderates on whose support the restored monarchy depended. In July 1830 his policy led to a confrontation with the Chamber of Deputies, which swiftly led to a revolution. After three days of street-fighting – the 'trois glorieuses' – the army was forced to abandon Paris, and the king and his family had to flee. They went first to England before settling at Gorizia on what is now the Italian-Slovenian border. It was there that Charles died on 6 November 1836. In 1830 as in 1789, he had proved the nemesis of his family. To bring down the French monarchy once is a misfortune; to do so twice seems like carelessness.

The Terror took a heavy toll among both royalists and revolutionaries. In September 1793 Malesherbes, who had defended Louis XVI at his trial, offered the same service to Marie Antoinette, although this was declined. On 20 December, he and his family were arrested at their château and imprisoned in Paris. Accused on the flimsiest of evidence of counter-revolutionary activities, Malesherbes was guillotined on 24 April 1794 in the Place du Trône-Renversée (now Place de la Nation), along with his daughter, his son-in-law and one of his granddaughters. He was seventy-three.

Barnave wrote his last letter of advice to the queen on 5 January 1792. Shortly afterwards, realizing that his influence on events was over, he retired from politics to his native Grenoble. According to Mme Campan, the last favour he asked from Marie Antoinette was to kiss her hand. On the fall of the monarchy he was arrested. Transferred from Grenoble a year later to face the Revolutionary Tribunal, he was executed on 29 November 1793. Fersen, who regarded him as a rival for the queen's affections, noted the event with satisfaction. 'Barnave', he remarked cruelly, 'died like a coward.'[1] There is no evidence to support this assertion.

Breteuil's former friend the astronomer Bailly, first president of the National Assembly and mayor of Paris, also died on the scaffold. Charged with shedding the blood of the people in the 'massacre' of the Champ-de-Mars, he was executed on 12 November 1793. It was decreed that he should die symbolically at the site of his crime. However, the crowd who gathered on the Champ-de-Mars for the spectacle decided at the last minute that this would be to dishonour the memory of the victims. The guillotine was dismantled and re-erected on a dunghill on the banks of the Seine, and it was there that Bailly met his death.

Few of the Girondins escaped the Revolutionary Tribunal. Brissot, Vergniaud, Gensonné and nineteen of their colleagues were executed on 31 October 1793. As their sentence was read out one of their number, Valazé, stabbed himself to death. None the less, so that the law could be carried out to the letter, his corpse was placed in the tumbril and guillotined anyway.

A few months later, the revolutionary government disintegrated. It was torn in two between Hébert and his followers, who wished to accelerate the Terror, and Danton and his faction, the so-called 'indulgents', who were growing sick of the bloodshed and wished for political normalization. It was left to Robespierre and his allies to hold things together. This they did by eliminating first the 'Hébertists' and then the 'indulgents'. With bizarrely twisted logic, both sides were accused of involvement in an international conspiracy that linked corrupt Parisian speculation with counter-revolution. Significantly, the baron de Batz was denounced as its chief instigator.[2]

Just how much of this 'foreign plot' was genuine remains mysterious to this day. Still, it served its purpose. On 24 March 1794, Hébert, whose incendiary prose had done so much to stoke revolutionary violence, was sent to the guillotine trembling with fright. Danton, who followed Hébert on 5 April, did not share his weakness. With the sunset behind him, the great orator and man of action stepped on to the scaffold, as though, one observer wrote, 'he was emerging from the tomb rather than about to enter it'.[3]

The death of Danton tore the soul out of the Jacobin dictatorship. Robespierre and his colleagues grew increasingly isolated, from both the popular movement in the streets and the deputies in the convention. To the latter, Danton's fall was proof that in the prevailing paranoid atmosphere, even the most eminent revolutionaries were no longer safe. Finally, on 27 July 1794 (9th Thermidor in the new republican calendar), they rose in revolt. Robespierre and his friends were denounced on the floor of the Convention, arrested, and after making an inept attempt to raise the people of Paris in their favour, swiftly guillotined. It was the last great political bloodbath of the Revolution.

Breteuil had spent the two years after 1792 in Germany and Belgium. Ever since Brunswick's retreat from France, his position had been delicate. He was now head of the princes' council, but still had grave reservations about Provence becoming regent. However, as the prospect of rescuing Louis XVI receded over the horizon, the baron began to face the inevitable. On 2 October 1792, he outlined his predicament to Fersen:

> I am no longer able to combat [the regency] with the hope of the king's speedy liberation, and though I am absolutely sure that neither our policy nor [the princes] will derive any benefit from this chimerical regency, since it is and will remain without force or territory, I can no longer oppose it without being accused of pig-headedness; I think therefore that I shall keep my own council and let the Powers decide; if they decide in favour, I neither can nor will take the credit; if they veto it,

I will be innocent of blame, though I hardly expect this to be recognized. In any case, if this regency is established and the Powers want me at the head of the council, do you think that I should follow my inclination, which would be to refuse, or that my respect and attachment for the king demand from me this further sacrifice? It would cost me a lot, but I would not refuse if it were necessary. Rest assured that I will certainly have neither the confidence of the regent nor his brother, and will be unceasingly tormented by the others.[4]

As things turned out, the Powers made no decision at all, and so the question of Provence's regency was postponed indefinitely. As he had predicted, Breteuil got most of the blame. As the princes and their tattered band of follows retreated before the French armies, he continued to act as their chief adviser, but the task grew increasingly uncongenial. Eventually, at the end of December, the *émigré* court was given permission to settle at Hamm in Westphalia. A few months later, Breteuil and the princes parted company. The baron returned to Brussels, now reoccupied by the Austrians, while on 19 November 1793 Provence left for Verona.

However, Breteuil's counter-revolutionary activities did not end there. There is suggestive, if not conclusive, evidence that during the reign of Terror he was involved with important royalist networks inside France whose aim was to undermine the Jacobin dictatorship from within. The principal figure in these intrigues, once again, was the baron de Batz. By his own account, in late 1793 Batz conceived a plan of wrecking the Revolution by setting the various factions in the government at loggerheads through the use of wholesale bribery and corruption. As he himself put it at the time:

How can such a formidable power [the revolutionary government], before which all heads are bowed in silence, be brought down? I would reply that such a regime is by its very nature a form of delirium, a convulsive state; and that any such violent action is by definition, according to the immutable laws of nature, of short duration, and that the jealousies, suspicions, hatreds and divisions it produces will set the participants against each other and drag them towards the abyss they themselves have opened; that preparing these divisions and accelerating them by sowing mistrust and exacerbating rivalries is, in the absence of armed force, the only effective way of conspiring against such a government and hastening its prompt collapse.[5]

Batz's project may seem visionary, but there is evidence that he implemented at least part of it. In the course of 1792, he had speculated on the new paper currency, the *assignats*, and devoted part of the considerable profits he made to setting up a financial reserve for Louis XVI to draw on if he ever regained his freedom. Now, at the end of 1793, despite leading a semi-clandestine existence in Paris, he used his financial acumen to gain the friendship of a number of influential and more or less corrupt Jacobin politicians, several of whom were close to Danton. At this time, substantial fortunes were being made in speculation, especially in the shares of the French East India Company. There was soon a public outcry against this profiteering, whereupon the Convention decreed the suppression of joint-stock companies and societies, including the East India Company, on 24 August 1793. It is probable that Batz himself, through the deputies he knew, helped frame the decree, and did so in such a way that one group of Jacobins who had been speculating benefited at the expense of their rivals, thus setting the two factions at each other's throats. It is certainly the case that the tangled affairs of the East India Company lay at the root of the mutual denunciations which the followers of Danton and Hébert were soon throwing at each other, and which were instrumental in destroying both groups in turn.[6]

Not the least mysterious aspect of this extraordinary story is the part Breteuil may have played in it. It is unclear whether Batz conceived his plan on his own initiative, or whether he was in fact working as the baron's agent. It is certain that as early as 1792 Batz, in conjunction with other royalist bankers in Paris, maintained a highly placed informer in the Jacobin Club, and passed the information gleaned from this source to Breteuil in Brussels. That April, for example, Batz sent Breteuil a report on the parlous state of the French army. As Fersen noted in his diary:

The baron de Batz writes from Paris that nothing is ready nor will be before 20 May, that resignations are flooding in from all directions, that M. de Grave, the minister of war, has told M.

Dumouriez that he wants to resign and wants nothing further to do with the distortions of the truth that the Assembly is demanding from him, that the revolutionaries are in great difficulties and will be lost if Prussia joins with Austria and if their troops arrive by 20 May, that there is only 17 million left in the royal treasury. This baron de Batz is an intriguer, but he, Laborde de Méréville, Boyd and Company and Walckiers (all prominent bankers) have a member of the Jacobins' secret council on their payroll who tells them everything.[7]

This is only one source, but it is an extremely important one. It indicates that individual Jacobins were not averse to taking bribes from counter-revolutionaries, and that more than one may have been playing a double game. It also shows that in April 1792 Batz was already perfecting his tactic of corrupting, dividing and spying on the revolutionary leaders. Bizarrely, although a full edition of Fersen's diaries was published in Sweden between 1924 and 1936, this particular passage was omitted, and has never been published.[8] The diaries' editor, the eminent revolutionary scholar, Alma Söderhjelm, did not even insert the customary dots to indicate that it had been left out. One wonders why she would not admit that perhaps all was not as it seemed at the Jacobin Club.

There is one further intriguing connection between Breteuil and Batz during this period. Among the various weapons to hand in the struggle against the Revolution, the baron certainly contemplated economic warfare. In mid-December 1792, he sent the Austrian government an elaborate plan to destroy the credit of the *assignats* by flooding France with forged notes. According to Breteuil, a secret fund had been set up to aid Louis XVI, which was still in the coffers of various Parisian bankers. It consisted of the equivalent of 150 million *assignats* in gold, silver and letters of exchange. However, because the *assignat* had gone up in value since the fund had been created, selling it off now would involve a loss for the bankers concerned. The latter, claimed the baron, were prepared to deliver their holdings to the Austrians and Prussians in exchange for 150 million forged *assignats*. At a stroke, Vienna and Berlin would gain a massive sum in real effects, and France's new paper currency would be wrecked by a wave of counterfeit notes.[9]

Behind Breteuil's proposal, one detects two hands – those of Batz and the Bishop of Pamiers. The bishop was fascinated by public finance, and had constantly harped on the necessity of ruining the *assignats*. When Batz visited Breteuil in Verdun in September 1792, he almost certainly talked to the bishop as well. After reassuring Fersen on the 12th of that month that he was only cultivating Batz 'in the hope of securing from him great financial resources to aid the king at the outset of his administration', the baron added: 'The bishop has told you of his plan, and the use to which we intend to put it.'[10] Although it is unclear whether this is a reference to Batz or the bishop, it may well be that the plan evoked is the one concerning the forged *assignats*.

One obvious link between Breteuil and Batz is the baron's mention, in his memorandum outlining the plan, of the fighting fund that had been set up for the king. Between the autumn of 1791 and the summer of 1792, Batz had made several trips abroad on behalf of the French government to negotiate the sale of *assignats* on the international money market against solid cash. Some of these solid effects had gone to make up the reserve earmarked for the king. It was surely to these that Breteuil was referring in his memorandum when he spoke of the 'fund of 150 millions in gold, silver and bills of exchange . . . constituted by the efforts and through the credit of the greatest banking houses of Paris to be paid for in *assignats* by Louis XVI'.[11]

Most remarkable of all, Breteuil also claimed that he would be able to get hold of the actual plates and type-moulds currently being used to manufacture the *assignats*. 'Certain devoted servants of the king of France inside the country', he wrote, 'are in a position to procure the type-moulds produced by the very plates from which the *assignats* are printed.'[12] Of all the royalist agents working within France only Batz, with his extensive financial connections and deep involvement in the *assignat* trade, would have been capable of performing this service. In his memorandum, Breteuil also mentions several times the presence of an intermediary in Paris between the bankers and the Powers. It is probable that this mysterious person was Batz himself.

Breteuil's plan was submitted to the Emperor Francis II for his approval, but that moralistic monarch was horrified by the proposal, and killed it off with one sentence: 'Such an infamous project is not to be considered.'[13] Without the backing of the Powers, the scheme for flooding France with forged *assignats* had to be abandoned. Yet as Batz's subsequent career showed, the idea of undermining the Revolution by financial means was far from dead.

There is no firm evidence linking Breteuil to the 'foreign plot' of 1794 allegedly masterminded by Batz and which led to the downfall of first Hébert and then Danton. It is clear, however, that, in their efforts on behalf of the royalist cause, Breteuil and Batz did have dealings with a number of prominent revolutionaries and their associates. At the very least, these intrigues helped to create that heavy atmosphere of paranoia and distrust which impelled France's ruling faction to tear itself apart.

Throughout the grimmest period of the Terror, Batz led a charmed life. His co-conspirators were not so lucky. On 17 June 1794 fifty-four of them, charged with abetting the counter-revolution, were guillotined *en masse*. Since they had plotted against the nation, they were taken to their deaths in red shirts, signifying that they were parricides. Among them were Cortey and Michonis, who had helped Batz try to rescue Marie Antoinette. Yet Batz himself did not see the inside of a prison until October 1795, when he was arrested for his part in the royalist uprising of 13th Vendémiaire. He was soon released, however, and retired to his château of Chadieu in the Auvergne. At the restoration of the monarchy he was made military commandant of the department of the Cantal. He died of apoplexy at Chadieu on 10 January 1822.[14]

From 1793 to 1798, Breteuil's movements are difficult to follow. For at least some of this time he lived in London. In February 1796, he filed a lawsuit in the Court of Chancery, giving his address as Hanover Square. Picturesquely, the documents describe the baron as:

> an emigrant from the kingdom of France ... driven from thence or obliged to flee therefrom to avoid death as for his attachment to the royal family of that kingdom. He is obnoxious to the persons who exercise the powers of government in that kingdom and ... has not been in France since the beginning of the year 1791 [this was a mistake, since Breteuil's emigration dated from July 1789].[15]

The object of litigation was a large sum of money, 200,000 livres, left in England by Breteuil's cousin, the duc du Châtelet, who had been executed under the Terror in December 1793. Claiming that the duke had died intestate, the baron had obtained letters of administration over his estate as next-of-kin. However, the holder of the funds in England, one George Yelverton Kendall, maintained that du Châtelet had in fact made a will, and that as he himself was holding the money in trust he would only give it up to the rightful heirs. Conveniently, they were in France, and contacting them was not only difficult but dangerous. The outcome of the case is not clear. If Breteuil had indeed managed to obtain the 200,000 livres, this would have made a major difference to his financial situation.

By 1798 at the latest, the baron had decided to move back to the continent. In July 1798 he informed Bombelles, who was now with the remnants of Condé's army, that he had found a pleasant house standing in grounds just outside Hamburg. Soon afterwards, he moved in with his usual household: his daughter Mme de Matignon, his granddaughter Caroline, her husband the baron de Montmorency, and, of course, the Bishop of Pamiers. Despite all the upheavals of war and revolution, this unorthodox family group had remained inseparable.

During this period, one notable change in Breteuil's character became apparent. As with so many of the *émigrés*, the vicissitudes of the Revolution made him turn to religion. Remembering the baron's famous arrogance, the historian and politician Sénac de Meilhan remarked cynically to Bombelles: 'He has finally bowed his head.'[16] Bombelles, however, who was extremely devout himself, indignantly rebutted the insinuation. He was thus particularly pleased when, in the course of a letter of April 1798, Breteuil wrote that he wished his new home to be close to a town and added: 'I would prefer this to be a Catholic town, but if not, that the Catholic religion should be sufficiently tolerated there for nothing to hamper my religious observances, and for me to be able to fulfil them regularly.'[17]

Changes in the wider world, however, soon affected the little household. In November 1799, in the *coup d'état* of 18th Brumaire, Napoleon Bonaparte overthrew the weak and chaotic Directory and became, as first consul, the effective ruler of France. It was soon apparent that he was restoring to the country an order and stability that it had lacked since the outbreak of the Revolution. To all but the most diehard *émigrés*, it became clear that a return of the Bourbons was now farther away than ever. After a decade of hardship and exile, many began to think of taking the road home. Napoleon himself facilitated this. Anxious to 'heal the wounds of the Revolution', in 1800 he declared an amnesty for returning *émigrés*.

The first member of Breteuil's family to respond to this olive-branch was Mme de Matignon. In the spring of 1801, she returned to France and what remained of her former life. The Bishop of Pamiers did not accompany her at first, but rather touchingly stayed in Hamburg to keep her old father company. Breteuil moved into lodgings while the family house was put up for sale, but the bishop visited him every weekend to share his cutlets.[18]

This state of affairs was clearly temporary. Mme de Matignon had departed to see how the land lay for the rest of the family at home. The news she sent back must have been reassuring, for by the end of 1802, Breteuil was back in Paris after an enforced absence of thirteen years. The return to France of such a luminary of the old monarchy was a considerable propaganda coup for the new regime. Indeed, Napoleon judged it politic to receive the baron himself. Echoes of the meeting reached Bombelles in the depths of central Europe. On 18 December, he noted in his diary 'the extraordinary reappearance in France of the baron de Breteuil, and his short audience with the first consul'. He added that Fouché, the minister of police and a former Jacobin, had been shocked by his master's cordiality to Breteuil, remarking that if things went on like this he would soon be allowing Louis XVIII himself to come back. 'Certainly,' Napoleon apparently replied, 'as long as he does not bear arms against the republic.'[19]

Breteuil was grateful for this benevolent reception; so grateful, indeed, that he underwent a change of allegiance. The last freely chosen minister of Louis XVI became, in his last years, a convinced Bonapartist. Partly it was realism; by now the baron had concluded that a restoration of the monarchy was impossible, and that in its absence the government of Bonaparte was at least reasonably moderate and orderly. To this was no doubt added his personal distaste for Louis XVIII and his brother. He knew better than anybody how much they had contributed to Louis XVI's misfortunes, and he was also well aware that he could hope for nothing from them. Finally, reconciliation with the new French government offered the baron a chance to recoup his battered fortune. In particular he sought to recover two of his properties which had been expropriated, his town house in Paris and the Pavillon du Mail at Saint-Cloud.

In fact, Breteuil was already deriving some income from his Paris house. It was currently inhabited by two of Napoleon's aides-de-camp, Savary and Lauriston. The actual owner, however, was none other than the former Director Barthélemy, who before the Revolution had been Breteuil's embassy secretary in Vienna and had more recently helped pave the way for his return. Barthélemy made over the profit from the house to Breteuil; this generous action was just one example of the small ways in which the *émigrés* and their friends helped each other to survive the Revolutionary years.[20] Yet the baron was still determined to regain the title to his possessions. In January 1804, he sought an interview for this purpose with Napoleon's chief architect, Fontaine. As the latter recalled in his diary:

> He took his solicitations to the point of coming to see me. As much from duty as from obligation, I profited from a favourable opportunity to present this request from a former minister of Louis XVI to the first consul in a positive light. [The baron] was only asking for the honour of being admitted to pay homage to the first consul, in spite of the poor condition of his fortune, his town house and his pavilion at Saint-Cloud, and of the few resources still remaining to him.[21]

These manoeuvres seem to have had the desired effect. Napoleon did not return Breteuil's properties, but he did give him a pension. In exchange, the baron discreetly went the rounds of the faubourg Saint-Germain in Paris, rallying support for the new dispensation among the returning *émigrés*. This was enough for Napoleon to recall him favourably during his own exile on St Helena. In the diary of General Bertrand, one of his companions there, he is recorded as saying:

> M. de Breteuil was always well disposed to me. He did not want any position, but probably a bit of money instead. I gave him an annuity of 10,000 francs as compensation for his pavilion in the gardens of Saint-Cloud. He often went round the inhabitants

of the faubourg Saint-Germain urging them to be reconciled with me, and since he had been a member of the queen's party [a reference to Marie Antoinette] many people listened to him. He told them ... that their cause was lost; that they had been beaten, and that they were lucky that the government was in the hands of someone who had arrived there honourably, through his victories, and was willing to include them in his system. Woe to those who left it too late![22]

The baron was now seventy-four. Although he still frequented the remaining aristocratic salons of the capital, he was a figure from a vanished age. The main preoccupation of his last years was securing his family's future. His hopes rested in particular on his granddaughter Caroline de Montmorency, and his nephew Charles de Breteuil. No doubt on his advice, both integrated swiftly into the new regime, Caroline as one of Josephine Bonaparte's ladies-in-waiting, and Charles as one of the new administrative elite. Indeed, in the tradition of Bombelles, Fersen and the Bishop of Pamiers, Charles became the last of Breteuil's substitute sons. On his regular visits to the salon of Talleyrand, now foreign minister, the baron lost no opportunity to advance his nephew's career. This comes across clearly in his last extant letter. It was written on 14 December 1804 to Charles, who was now in Germany working for Jollivet, the prefect of the newly-annexed department of the Bas-Rhin. The old man's concern for his nephew, down to the most minute aspects of his health and domestic arrangements, is present in every line:

> I ... must ask you not to throw yourself into an excess of work or study that could damage your health, which needs constant attention, in just the same way that your mind and spirit require occupation. Your reason, my friend, must dictate the way you go about your work. I am delighted that you are enjoying your employment in diplomacy, my son (how much I wish that you were), and I am equally glad that this idea was suggested by the foreign Powers themselves in memory of my ancient services.
>
> You did well to write to M. d'Hauterive [director of the archives of the foreign ministry] ... whom I often meet at M. de Talleyrand's ...
>
> It is good news that you have managed to find lodgings

opposite M. Jollivet's residence, and doubly agreeable for you that this minister has invited you to dine with him every day; your slender financial resources will benefit from this amiable arrangement.

My child, we all send you a thousand greetings, and as for me I embrace you, and repeat how much I love you.[23]

There is one distressing aspect of Breteuil's declining years. In the late 1790s, he fell out with Bombelles, and the breach was never healed. The cause was money. In November 1791, knowing his patron to be financially distressed, the marquis had generously loaned him most of his savings, amounting to 30,000 livres. On the 25th of that month, Breteuil made out an IOU agreeing to pay Bombelles 5 per cent interest on the sum per year, and to reimburse the entire capital in six years' time. The baron, however, did not repay the loan in 1797, and even the interest payments soon dried up. By this time, Bombelles was in virtual penury, with six children to support. The matter was made more galling when the baron airily informed his protégé that he had had no difficulty in raising the 80,000 livres necessary to buy his house outside Hamburg.[24]

From this point on, relations between the two men deteriorated rapidly. Breteuil took to avoiding Bombelles. In August 1801, just before his return to France, he made a visit to Vienna to spend a month with a former mistress, Countess Hoyos. He did not, however, find the time to see his former protégé, who was living nearby at Brünn. Instead, he wrote him a stilted letter, mixing expressions of regret at the impossibility of a meeting with laments about his own poverty. Understandably, Bombelles was deeply offended, particularly since reports had reached him that Breteuil had in fact travelled in style through Germany. 'A man claiming to be in the depths of penury', he wrote on 7 September,

journeys from Hamburg to Vienna spending money hand over fist on the way . . . to pay a nostalgic visit to a lady whom he flaunted on his arm during his embassy in Vienna. He tells me in his letter: 'I am coming to spend a month with my friend Countess Hoyos; the long trip and the bad roads have not fatigued me too greatly.' He travels over 400 leagues for this lady, yet a further twelve seem too many to see an old friend who has weathered every vicissitude to stay faithful to him. He gives a month to this lady and has not even an hour to spare for his friend . . .[25]

Bombelles's anger at his old patron was probably justified. It is difficult to establish the precise state of Breteuil's fortune at this point, but he was certainly not poor. He had his pension from Napoleon, to which was added a substantial inheritance, perhaps as much as 15,000 livres a year, when his cousin the marquise de Créquy died aged eighty-nine in 1803. The baron had also benefited from the generosity of Fersen, who some years previously had bailed him out by making a notional purchase of his now worthless plantation on St Domingue. At any rate, in September 1801 Breteuil's credit was still good enough for his Hamburg bankers, the house of Chapeaurouge, to advance him 12,000 livres for the use of Mme de Matignon when she arrived in Paris.[26]

The most charitable interpretation of the baron's conduct was that old age, coupled with the upheavals of the past fifteen years, had affected his personality. Since 1789 he had lived a life of constant insecurity, and he may well have reacted to this by becoming a miser. In addition, his health was now extremely poor – he was afflicted by gallstones as well as his usual gout – and this cannot have improved his temper. None of this excuses his treatment of Bombelles, but perhaps it makes it a little easier to understand. Finally, after several titanic rows with Bombelles's sister, the marquise de Travanet, who had also returned to Paris and was pressing her brother's case, an accommodation was reached. Breteuil resumed his interest payments to Bombelles, though it is unclear whether the capital sum was ever restituted.

Breteuil died at his daughter's Paris house, 163 rue Sainte-Dominique, early in the morning of 2 November 1807. A politician to the last, he was determined that his final illness should not harm his family's interests. Napoleon and Josephine were currently at Fontainebleau, and the baron's granddaughter Caroline, now duchesse de Montmorency, was in attendance. Hearing that her grandfather was very ill, she immediately returned to Paris. This did not please the baron at all. As Caroline's husband, the duc de Montmorency, put it in his diary:

My wife came back from Fontainebleau. My grandfather-in-law
rallied over the next four or five days, giving the doctors a little
hope. He even wanted my wife to return to Fontainebleau;
she agreed, fearing that a refusal would upset my grandfather-
in-law, who needed some favours done at court.[27]

The next few days are described by the duke in minute detail.
'My wife left [for Fontainebleau]', he wrote,

on 29 October. But she did not stay there long, for my
grandfather-in-law's condition soon became alarming and on the
31st I sent her a message to return. She arrived at midnight, and
my grandfather-in-law died on 2 November at one o'clock in
the morning in the seventy-seventh year of his life, remaining
calm and collected to the last. He had received all the sacraments
a fortnight before. Towards the end he went off food because
he could keep nothing down; he had frequent attacks of
diarrhoea. Three hours before his death he demanded some
medicine. He was so insistent that we could not oppose him.
We gave it to him, and as he was getting out of bed to bring it
up he fainted. We thought that he was dead; his eyes had
already rolled upwards. We brought him round with smelling-
salts, but he finally died three hours afterwards, while making
the sign of the cross. A few moments before his death my wife
gave him something to drink, and he said to her: 'It's all over,
I can see nothing more.'[28]

The duchesse de Brancas and the Bishop of Pamiers had stayed with
Breteuil to the last, and were left keepsakes in his will. The bishop
received a watch and chain set in diamonds; the duchesse de Brancas
a blue porcelain vase supported, appropriately, by two bronze satyrs.[29]

Breteuil was a remarkable and contradictory man, an extraordinary mixture of kindness and brutality, calculation and emotion,
generosity and avarice. His political career was even more paradoxi-
cal. A staunch conservative, he was none the less deeply influenced
by the Enlightenment and became, in the mid-1780s, a reforming
minister. During the Revolution, he was even accused of wishing to
bargain away the rights of the crown. In reality, while committed to
removing its abuses, he wished to restore as much of the old regime
as possible, and viewed constitutional monarchy with great suspicion.

Breteuil has also been taxed with insatiable ambition. Certainly he was fond of power and position, and at various points in his career aimed at becoming a prime minister. Yet he also often spoke of the tribulations of politics and expressed a wish to retire into private life. The Revolution put this desire to the test. A great realist, Breteuil can have had few illusions about the likelihood of rescuing the royal family once they had been taken to Paris after the October days. None the less, he soldiered on in Solothurn and Brussels, with no resources and a tiny staff, at the thankless task of gaining disinterested support for the French crown from the cynical monarchs and statesmen of Europe. If ambition inevitably played some part in this, so too did loyalty and devotion.

Bombelles outlived Breteuil by fifteen years. In September 1800 his wife Angélique died, leaving him devastated. Soon afterwards, he renounced his worldly career and went into holy orders. In 1806 he became curate of Oppersdorf in Prussian Silesia, and two years later dean of Oberglogau. On 21 November 1807, he received news of Breteuil's death from his eldest son. 'A letter from Louis,' he wrote in his diary,

> informs me today that the baron de Breteuil whom I loved so much, and who through an unfortunate love of money did me such an injustice, has departed this life. May God have extended His mercy to him in the last moments of his existence.[30]

Happily, Bombelles's fortunes improved at the restoration of the Bourbons. In 1816, he was appointed almoner to the duchesse de Berry, the daughter-in-law of his old enemy Artois. Then, in August 1817, he was elevated to the see of Amiens. The fact that the new bishop had six children from his previous life gave rise to some comic incidents. Once, accompanied by two of his sons, he went to an embassy reception. At the entrance, an usher asked the guests for their names. 'Announce the Bishop of Amiens and his sons,' replied Bombelles. The usher looked at him aghast. Taking pity on the poor man, Bombelles gently corrected himself: 'Announce the Bishop of Amiens and his nephews.'[31]

Bombelles died on 5 March 1822. After remarkable adventures and many hardships, he had finally reached a safe harbour. A highly culti-vated and sensitive man, he was politically even more conservative

than Breteuil, yet throughout his career showed extraordinary qualities of honesty and fidelity. His devotion to his children, who entered
Austrian service, was certainly repaid. His eldest son Louis ended as
Austrian minister to Denmark; the third, Henri-François, became
governor to the future Emperor Franz Joseph. His second son
Charles, however, had the most striking destiny of all. Having
served in both the Austrian and French armies, in 1830 he was
appointed grand master of the court of Parma. The ruling duchess
was none other than the former Empress Marie Louise, Napoleon's
second wife, who had retired there after her husband's abdication.
She and Charles fell in love and were married secretly on 17 February
1834. When Marie Louise died in 1847, Charles de Bombelles
returned to France, where he lived at Versailles until his own death
in 1855.

Fersen was shattered by Marie Antoinette's execution and never
fully recovered. The brutal manner of her death had horrified him.
'That she should have been alone in her last moments without
consolation,' he wrote on 21 October 1793, 'with nobody to speak to
or to whom to impart her last wishes, makes one shudder. The
monsters of hell! No, without vengeance, my heart will never be at
peace.'[32]

Fersen never did get his vengeance, and his heart never found
peace. Instead, he returned to Sweden, from where he was forced to
watch the ever-increasing expansion of the French revolutionary
empire. In 1797, he gained an opportunity to meet its new rulers face
to face. In November of that year, he was nominated as Swedish
representative to the congress called at Rastadt to draw up a peace
between France and the Holy Roman Empire. At nine in the evening
of 28 November, he had an interview of half an hour with Napoleon.
The latter, however, refused to deal with Fersen because of his links
with the old monarchy; and specifically because he 'had been the late
queen's lover'. Humiliated, Fersen was compelled to withdraw from
the congress.

His fortunes improved a few years later. In 1799 the young King
Gustavus IV, the son of Gustavus III, made him chancellor of the
University of Uppsala, in 1800 a knight of the Order of the Seraphim,
Sweden's highest decoration, and the year after that the grand marshal
of the kingdom. Yet despite these honours Fersen remained reserved,

aloof and alone. He never married. He continued his relationship with Eléonore Sullivan for a few years after Marie Antoinette's death, but in 1799 Quintin Craufurd finally found out about it, there was a tremendous row, and the affair petered out.[33] Fersen did, however, stay in touch with Breteuil. Indeed, in August 1801 he acted as a go-between for Breteuil in his belated interest payments to Bombelles. Fersen's sister and Mme de Matignon continued corresponding even after his death.

In 1810, European politics finally caught up with Fersen. After an uneasy peace, in April 1805 war again broke out between France and her neighbours. That October, Gustavus IV declared war on the French. The decision proved disastrous; Russia, decisively defeated by Napoleon at Austerlitz and then Friedland, changed sides, and in 1808 attacked and occupied Sweden's Finnish provinces. In March 1809, Gustavus himself was forced to abdicate by a military coup, and his descendants were excluded from the succession. Gustavus's uncle assumed the throne as Charles XIII, but since he was childless a new heir had to be found. Eventually the choice fell on Prince Christian August, a member of the neighbouring Danish royal family.

This decision was strongly political. The French Revolution had deeply divided Sweden's political class, between liberals who favoured an accommodation with France, now the dominant Power on the continent, and conservatives who felt the Revolution and its heirs should be fought to the bitter end. Fersen, needless to say, was a pillar of the conservative party. Charles XIII and the new crown prince, however, were liberals. When Christian August dropped dead of a sudden stroke at a military review on 28 May 1810, many suspected he had been poisoned as part of a conservative plot to restore the rights of the exiled Gustavus IV's young son to the throne. Fersen was accused of organizing this conspiracy. There was almost certainly no truth in these allegations.

Fersen was warned that it would be unwise for him to take part in the prince's funeral in Stockholm, but as one of the highest-ranking officials in the kingdom he insisted on attending. It is unclear whether a plot had been actually formed against his life; it is more likely that certain of the liberals, assuming there would be some sort of popular demonstration against Fersen, saw this as a means of bringing the conversatives to heel and were thus disinclined to prevent it. Certainly, inadequate measures were taken to deal with the possibility of trouble. On the day itself, in accordance with protocol, Fersen set out at the head of the cortège in the grand marshal's carriage.

As soon as the carriage reached the city centre, it was assailed by a barrage of paving-stones, which broke its windows and injured the grand marshal in the face. He managed to escape into a nearby house, with an escort of sixteen men. The house was then besieged, and the only resolution to the situation the escort's commander could see was to accompany Fersen to a safe place, appeasing the crowd by a promise that he would be put on trial.

The moment the party left the house, it was again assailed by the crowd and Fersen was separated from his protectors. He was dragged into an adjoining square, savagely beaten with sticks and umbrellas, and handfuls of his hair were torn out. All of this took place in full view of a battalion of the royal guard. Not only did they do nothing, but after a moment, inexplicably, the two generals commanding them turned their horses around and cantered away. Fersen was then dragged into the town hall, but the door of the guardhouse where he was being held was soon forced by the mob. Hauled out into the courtyard, he was attacked once more, and finally finished off by one of his assailants jumping on his rib-cage. Chillingly, it was 20 June, the anniversary of the flight to Varennes.[34]

The two other main protagonists in the royal family's escape from Paris are buried not only in the same city, but in the same cemetery. In 1794, Mercy-Argenteau was made Austrian ambassador to London. Soon after his arrival, however, he fell ill. He died on 25 August and was buried in old St Pancras churchyard. In the following years the area around St Pancras became home to many French *émigrés*. Among them was General de Bouillé, who spent the last years of his life there writing his memoirs. He died on 14 November 1800 and was also laid to rest in the churchyard. The cemetery was later obliterated by the Midland Railway, but in 1877 the philanthropist Baroness Burdett-Coutts converted what remained into a public garden, which still exists. The graves of Bouillé and Mercy-Argenteau, however, have been lost forever.

Dumouriez too ended his days in England. In 1803 he was appointed as military adviser to the British government, becoming one of the first theoreticians of partisan warfare. His views proved of great importance in the Peninsular War, helping Wellington's army to exploit the military potential of the Spanish guerillas against the French. A few years later, on 20 June 1815, the duc d'Orléans's son Louis-Philippe, also an exile in London, drove up to town from Twickenham to learn the latest news from the continent. On a street-corner in Hammersmith he spotted Dumouriez gesticulating wildly, stopped to see what was the matter, and learned from the old man the news of the victory of Waterloo.[35] Dumouriez survived for a further eight years, dying on 14 March 1823 at Turville Park in Buckinghamshire. He is buried in the parish church of Henley-on-Thames.

Of all Louis XVI's and Marie Antoinette's secret advisers during the Revolution, the Bishop of Pamiers lived longest. Like Breteuil and Fersen, his hopes too were blighted by the executions of the king and queen. As the Prussian army invaded France in 1792, Breteuil had drawn up a list of candidates for the ministry he expected to form shortly; the bishop was to have charge of the finances. In contrast, after 1793 the future held only a life of exile. In 1793, the bishop travelled to England to beg Pitt the Younger to intercede with the French government for Marie Antoinette's life, but without success. Yet his visit bore fruit in other ways. He met Edmund Burke and had a long conversation with him, which he later published as a pamphlet. Now extremely rare, the work forms an intriguing link between the last defenders of Louis XVI and Marie Antoinette, and the founder of modern conservatism.[36]

The bishop was profoundly affected by his stay in England. To the end of his life, he remained fascinated by the English constitution and fiscal system, publishing in 1817 a lengthy comparison of taxation in France and England. His visit even influenced his taste in architecture. The Château of Courtalain, where he often stayed under the Empire and the Restoration, is today approached via a Strawberry Hill Gothic gatehouse and is surrounded by an English landscape garden, both of which he designed.

Having moved to Hamburg with Mme de Matignon and her father in 1798, the bishop returned with them to France in 1802. He resigned his see as part of Napoleon's religious settlement, and lived in discreet retirement in Paris. The restoration of 1814, however, and the triumph of the monarchy in which he had never ceased to believe, paved the way for his return to political life. In this new world, the bishop had one particularly strong card to play: the continuing affection of Louis XVI's and Marie Antoinette's daughter, the duchesse d'Angoulême, who never forgot his efforts on behalf of her parents during their last years. This link was reinforced by the closeness to the duchess of other members of the bishop's family; his brother the vicomte d'Agoult, was her master of the horse, and his sister-in-law the vicomtesse was her first lady-in-waiting and greatest friend.

For a brief moment, this new dawn was menaced by Napoleon's return from Elba and the start of the Hundred Days. The upheaval, however, was soon brought to an end at Waterloo, and the bishop's prospects brightened still further. At the second restoration of the Bourbons, a campaign was mounted, presumably backed by the Angoulêmes, to make him finance minister. It is probably no coincidence that the bishop chose this moment to publish a project for a new national bank, which he claimed he had first submitted to Louis XVI in 1791. It is also significant that this pamphlet appeared under the imprint of Adrien Egron, printer to the duc d'Angoulême. In the light of this suggestive evidence that the bishop retained both political ambitions and powerful backers, one should take with a pinch of salt the modest disclaimer in his preface:

> The restoration of Louis XVIII to the throne of his fathers, in fulfilling the dearest and most ardent of my wishes, has certainly not affected my resolution never to come out of retirement and return to public life; my age has in any case reinforced this vow that I took after the loss of Louis XVI.[37]

Despite this burst of literary activity, the intrigue failed and the former finance minister, Baron Louis, stayed in place. Yet from his anchorage in the royal household the bishop was able to wield considerable influence behind the scenes. His political ideal remained France's pre-revolutionary 'antique constitution'. He particularly regretted that, under the constitutional charter drawn up by Louis XVIII, the 'two chambers' had finally triumphed over the traditional three orders. He did not, however, endorse absolute monarchy, and insisted that the true principles of the 'antique constitution' had always included consent to taxation by a representative body. More generally, he realized that the Revolution had changed France irrevocably, and that it was impossible to put the clock back to 1789. He made the point almost poetically in a pamphlet of 1815. Having warned against the dangers of too rapid constitutional change, he added:

> A no less dangerous folly, after a revolution of twenty-five years, would be to attempt to retrace our steps along a path made impassable by obstacles, to arrive back at the place where we began and whose ruins would offer no shelter from storms.[38]

The Bishop of Pamiers makes his last appearance in the memoirs of Count Molé, minister for the navy in 1817–18, and eventually one of King Louis-Philippe's prime ministers under the July monarchy. Molé recalls attending a secret political meeting in December 1818 with the bishop and the ultra-royalist parliamentary leader Villèle. He draws a splendidly vituperative portrait of the bishop, although this was partly a literary device to underline the contrast between pre- and post-revolutionary royalism:

> This interview ... had little result, but my passion for observation found much to satisfy it. The elegant bishop, old relic of the corruption of an age which could never return, and the plebeian royalist, himself the child of a revolution whose principles he attacked, formed a most instructive and piquant contrast. The first, handsome, polished, powdered, solemn, obsequious, but hollow, ignorant, narrow, blinded by prejudices and hardened by personality. The other, of an ignoble ugliness, increased by his clumsiness and untidiness, yet composed in manner, free in spirit and language, at bottom shrewd and contained beneath an artless appearance, contemptuous of the bishop and all his kind, who were grovelling at his feet and expecting him to fulfil their most cherished hopes.[39]

The Bishop of Pamiers died in Paris on 21 July 1824, aged seventy-seven. Mme de Matignon survived him by seven years, until 1833. Her daughter the duchesse de Montmorency lived out an agreeable, if loose, life in Paris; a contemporary police report speaks euphemistically of her 'more than gallant conduct'. She died in 1851.

*

THE LIVES OF Breteuil, Bombelles, Fersen and the Bishop of Pamiers, fascinating in themselves, become more than the sum of their parts when put together. Throughout the French Revolution, they were the only people Louis XVI and Marie Antoinette really trusted. It was to them that the king and queen turned to implement their true policy in these years, at considerable risk to all involved. Since the royal couple understandably destroyed their most secret and compromising papers before the fall of the monarchy, this policy can only be fully reconstructed by examining the careers and ideas of Breteuil and his collaborators.

A study of the baron and his network dispels many enduring myths about the attitude of Louis XVI and Marie Antoinette towards the French Revolution. The king and queen were neither as reactionary as French historians have traditionally thought, nor as liberal as some more recent writers have claimed. Despite Breteuil's best efforts, had they regained their freedom after October 1789 they would probably have been unwilling or unable to restore the old regime completely. Yet the concessions they were prepared to make, to which the declaration of 23 June forms the most credible guide, would not have satisfied even the most moderate of their opponents. Under these circumstances, the royal authority could only have been restored by civil war or foreign invasion.

Another crucial question that must be answered is whether, as has been recently claimed, Marie Antoinette pursued a separate policy to her husband's during the Revolution, and even stooped to forgery to pass it off as his own. The handwriting expertise employed here supports the conclusion that on one occasion, the queen did indeed do just that. But this discovery, however sensational it may at first seem, should be put in perspective. At certain moments Marie Antoinette may have 'embroidered' her husband's real views in order to further her own. Yet she always knew that to have any real credibility, her own plans would at some point have to be endorsed by Louis. If she did misrepresent the king, her aim was never more than to buy time in which to bring her perennially indecisive husband round to her own opinion. In this, she was always successful, so that throughout the Revolution, despite undoubted tensions, a joint royal policy was preserved.

Breteuil's papers, contained in the indispensable archives of Bombelles and Fersen, clear up one further enigma. Many contemporaries, and subsequent historians, have claimed that at various points after 1789 Louis XVI and Marie Antoinette were prepared to compromise with their more moderate opponents, and settle the Revolution on the basis of an English-style monarchy resting on a bicameral legislature. Breteuil's unpublished letters and memoranda make it absolutely clear that this was never contemplated. For the king and queen, this involved an unacceptable dilution of royal authority. In July 1792, they even preferred the dangers of Paris to rescue by La Fayette's army, precisely because they thought this would mean endorsing a fully constitutional monarchy. Louis XVI and Marie Antoinette have often been portrayed as weak and vacillating. Far from it; their policy between 1789 and 1792 was entirely consistent, and highly conservative. They were prepared to die for their beliefs, and ultimately did so.

The king and queen's trust in their closest confidants was well founded. Deeply conscious of the perils to which discovery of their real plans would expose the royal couple, Breteuil and his collaborators kept carefully, and successfully, in the background. Their discretion was such that the crown's enemies never got wind of what it really intended. Indeed, the baron and his colleagues carried their secrets with them to the grave. Fersen and Bombelles kept diaries, but, unlike almost all their contemporaries, neither they, Breteuil nor the Bishop of Pamiers ever published memoirs. Of the baron's little network, only Fersen became well known because of his love affair with the queen. Thanks to their silence, the mystery of Louis XVI's and Marie Antoinette's true policy towards the French Revolution has endured to this day. Yet such discretion, though vital at the time, is no longer a matter of life and death. It is time for Breteuil and his friends to emerge from the shadows.

Appendix by Bruno Galland and Susan Wharton

LOUIS XVI'S LETTER TO THE BARON DE BRETEUIL

The letter attributed to Louis XVI, addressed to the baron de Breteuil, is written on a single sheet of paper measuring 153 × 101 mm (the sheet was originally larger, but the margins have been cut down). It is written on the recto only, on the upper three-quarters of the page. The verso is blank except for the date '20 novembre'. The paper is watermarked, but of the watermark only the characters '& FILS' can be distinguished.

For many years the document was kept in a frame for public display at the Château de Breteuil, which may explain the yellowish tone of the paper and its brittleness, as well as the trimming of the margins. It is still kept at the Château de Breteuil, but is now housed in an archival quality folder, and a facsimile is displayed in the frame in its place.

This document, hereafter referred to as *Br*, has been compared with a number of original documents in the Archives Nationales (AN) in Paris, and most closely with the following:

— a letter by Louis XVI to M. de Boisgelin, requesting his resignation as master of the wardrobe, Versailles, 15 July 1788: AN K684, nos 168–9 (*Bo*)
— a letter by Louis XVI to the duc d'Orléans, about relations with England, 30 June 1790: AN C184, dossier 116, no. 33 (*Or*)
— a letter by Louis XVI to the Bishop of Clermont, sending Easter greetings, 1791: AN C187, dossier 134, no. 5 (*Cl*)

Layout

The position of the text on the page is similar to comparable documents in the king's own hand.

The first line is 10 mm from the top edge of the paper, as it is in the three documents used for comparison. The left-hand margin is very narrow (11 mm, the same as *Cl*). The right-hand margin is non-existent, since certain words, such as the last word in the sixth line, touch the very edge of the paper (as in *Bo* and *Cl*). The lower portion of the sheet is blank.

The absence of a date is frequent in the king's letters; neither *Cl* nor *Or* is dated in the text.

General characteristics of the handwriting

The hand of *Br* is small and slopes to the right, with harsh, thick and angular penstrokes. As a result, several words are difficult to read, such as *couronne* in line 4: the *o*, *r* and *e* appear to be formed of a single oblique stroke and are difficult to distinguish from the connecting strokes of the *u* and *n*. This hand is noticeably different from that found in letters written by Louis XVI at a similar period. The king's hand is small and slopes to the right, but although it is harsher at the end of his reign than at the beginning, it is more rounded, the *o* being formed of two strokes, similar to a *v*, but curved and separated so that the two strokes are quite distinct. The line is less firm than in *Br*.

It is also noticeable that in *Br* the interlinear spaces are sometimes irregular (for example, between lines 10 and 11). The king's own hand is more regular, and the interlinear spaces do not vary between the beginning and the end of the line.

Some notable features

Most of the letters or groups of letters found in *Br* can be seen in other letters by the king, including certain distinctive features such as the capital *M* in *Monsieur* which is surmounted by a dot (cf. *Or*, line 1). However, other letter forms are peculiar to *Br* and are not found in the other letters used for comparison:

— As already noted, the *o* and *e* are so squashed that the loop is difficult to make out. While this trait can be found elsewhere in the king's correspondence, it is not a regular feature and there are always examples of the same letter being written in a more rounded fashion (see in particular *Cl*).

— The bar of the final *t* is systematically long and flowing to the right (cf. *connoissant*, line 1, *permettant*, line 4, *but*, line 14); this is not found in other letters, and the bar of the *t* does not slope upwards in such a consistent manner (the rounded *t* of *but* can be found in *Or*, but only in the intermediate position, as in *intention*, line 8; in *Cl* the bar of a final *t* is sometimes short and parallel with the baseline).

— In the final group -*eʒ* (*connoisseʒ*, *fereʒ*) the *ʒ* has a tail flowing clearly below the line; this feature can be found in other documents, but is much less marked, and the tail generally finishes with a flick to the right, which is hardly seen at all in *Br* (cf. line 13, *fereʒ*).

The signature

It is not possible to draw any firm conclusions on the basis of the signature alone. It is slightly smaller than others, but Louis XVI's signatures vary enormously in size. In *Bo* the *i* is 15 mm high, in *Cl* only 5 mm, and in *Br* 3 mm. The formation of the signature matches those in the other three letters.

Overall conclusion

In our opinion, the characteristic features of the hand of *Br*, which is harsher than the hand of the other three pieces used for comparison, and the resulting individual traits of this hand, would argue against its being in Louis XVI's own hand.

LOUIS XVI'S LETTER TO THE KING OF PRUSSIA OF 3 DECEMBER 1791

We have not been able to examine the original of this letter, which is in Berlin. On the basis of a photograph it is evidently not possible to form any definitive conclusions about the hand. However, solely on the basis of the photograph, we have not observed any features of the hand to imply that it was not an autograph letter signed by Louis XVI.

Dr Bruno Galland,
Conservateur en chef, Chargé de la Section Ancienne,
Archives Nationales,
Paris

Dr Susan Wharton,
Director in the Department of Printed Books and Manuscripts,
Sotheby's.

July 2001

NOTES

INTRODUCTION

1. M. Lenz, 'Die Vorbereitung der Flucht Ludwigs XVI (Oktober 1790 bis Juni 1791): ein Beitrag zur kritik der französischen Memoirenliteratur', *Historische Zeitschrift*, 72 (1894), 236–7.

One THE KING AND HIS FAMILY

1. G. Lefebvre and A. Terroine, *Recueil de documents relatifs aux séances des États-généraux*, vol. 1, *Mai–juin 1789: les préliminaires, la séance du 5 mai* (Paris, 1953), p. 206.
2. Ibid., p. 247.
3. See J. Hardman, *Louis XVI* (New Haven and London, 1993), pp. 39–40, and E. Lever, *Louis XVI* (Paris, 1986), pp. 275–8.
4. *Louis XVI and the comte de Vergennes: correspondence, 1774–1787*, ed. J. Hardman and M. Price (Voltaire Foundation, Oxford, 1998), p. 5.
5. Cited in Lever, *Louis XVI*, p. 146.
6. See P. Girault de Coursac, *L'Éducation d'un roi* (Paris, 1972), pp. 195–211, and P. and P. Girault de Coursac, *Le Voyage de Louis XVI autour du monde* (Paris, 1985).
7. Girault de Coursac, *L'Éducation d'un roi*, pp. 193–5.
8. Hardman and Price, *Louis XVI*, pp. 89–90.
9. Cited in Girault de Coursac, *L'Éducation d'un roi*, p. 149.
10. V. Cronin, *Louis and Antoinette* (London, 1974), p. 41.
11. Horace Walpole to John Chute, 3 October 1765, in *Letters of Horace Walpole*, ed. P. Cunningham (9 vols, London, 1891), vol. 4, p. 414.
12. *Souvenirs-portraits du duc de Lévis (1764–1830)*, ed. J. Dupâquier (Paris, 1993), p. 355. The standard biography of Louis-Stanislas-Xavier is P. Mansel, *Louis XVIII* (London, 1981).

13. A Britsch, *La Maison d'Orléans à la fin de l'ancien régime: la jeunesse de Philippe-Egalité, 1747–1785* (Paris, 1926), pp. 290–308.

14. E. Burke, *Reflections on the Revolution in France* (London, 1986, Penguin Classics edn, p. 169.

15. Hardman, *Louis XVI*, p. 24.

16. E. Welwert, 'L'éminence grise de Marie Antoinette', *Revue de l'histoire de Versailles et de Seine-et-Oise*, 23 and 24 (1921–2).

17. *Correspondance secrète du comte de Mercy-Argenteau avec l'empereur Joseph II et le prince de Kaunitz*, ed. A. von Arneth and J. Flammermont (2 vols, Paris, 1889–91), vol. 1, p. 84.

18. For Mercy's biography see comte de Pimodan, *Le comte F.-C. de Mercy-Argenteau* (Paris, 1911).

19. Marquis de Bombelles, *Journal*, ed. J. Grassion, F. Durif and J. Charon-Bordas (4 vols, Geneva, 1978–98), vol. 2, p. 208.

20. Ibid., p. 236.

21. Girault de Coursac, *L'Éducation d'un roi*, pp. 286–9.

22. Kaunitz to Mercy, 5 January 1781, *Correspondance secrète*, vol. 1, p. 12.

23. Marie Antoinette to Joseph II, 22 September 1784, *Marie Antoinette, Joseph II und Leopold II, ihr Briefwechsel*, ed. A. von Arneth (Leipzig, Paris and Vienna, 1866), p. 39.

24. S. Zweig, *Marie Antoinette: the portrait of an average woman* (London, 1933), p. 21. There are also two excellent recent biographies of the queen: A. Fraser, *Marie Antoinette: the journey* (London, 2001), and E. Lever, *Marie Antoinette: the last queen of France* (London, 2001).

25. Cited in D. E. D. Beales, *Joseph II*, vol. 1, *In the Shadow of Maria Theresa* (Cambridge, 1987), pp. 374–5.

26. See J. Hardman, *French Politics 1774–1789: from the accession of Louis XVI to the fall of the Bastille* (London, 1995), p. 200.

27. M. Price, *Preserving the Monarchy: the comte de Vergennes, 1774–1787* (Cambridge, 1995), pp. 22–9.

28. Mercy to Kaunitz, 1 March 1787, *Correspondance secrète*, vol. 2, p. 80.

29. Cronin, *Louis and Antoinette*, p. 132.

30. Ibid., p. 135.

31. See D. L. Wick, 'The court nobility and the French Revolution: the example of the Society of Thirty', *Eighteenth-century Studies* (1980), pp. 279–81.

32. L. Hunt, *The Family Romance of the French Revolution* (London, 1992), pp. 104–6.

33. The best biography of Fersen is H. A. Barton, *Hans Axel von Fersen: aristocrat in an age of revolution* (Boston, Mass., 1975); the best treatment of his relationship with Marie Antoinette is A. Söderhjelm, *Fersen et Marie Antoinette* (Paris, 1930).

34. Söderhjelm, *Fersen et Marie Antoinette*, pp. 382–90.

35. Cronin, *Louis and Antoinette*, p. 343.

36. Barton, *Fersen*, p. 72.

Two THE MONARCHY IN 1789

1. For the theory of the absolute monarchy, see M. Antoine, *Le Conseil du roi sous le règne de Louis XVI* (Geneva, 1970), pp. 2–43. For its practice from the reign of Louis XIV onwards, see W. Beik, *Absolutism and Society in Seventeenth-century France: state power and provincial aristocracy in Languedoc* (Cambridge, 1985); R. Mettam, *Power and Faction in Louis XIV's France* (London, 1988), and W. Doyle (ed.), *Old Regime France* (Oxford, 2001).

2. W. Doyle, *The Oxford History of the French Revolution* (Oxford, 1989), p. 16.

3. For the eighteenth-century *parlements* and their relations with the crown, see J. H. Shennan, *The Parlement of Paris* (Ithaca, NY, 1968); J. Egret, *Louis XV et l'opposition parlementaire* (Paris, 1970); J. Swann, *Louis XV and the Parlement of Paris* (Cambridge, 1995), and B. Stone, *The Parlement of Paris, 1774–1789* (Chapel Hill, North Carolina, 1981) and *The French Parlements and the Crisis of the Old Regime* (Chapel Hill, North Carolina, 1986).

4. See J. Brewer, *The Sinews of Power: war, money and the English state, 1688–1783* (London, 1989; 1994 edn), pp. 89, 130.

5. The best analysis of this phenomenon is J. F. Bosher, *French Finances 1770–1795: from business to bureaucracy* (Cambridge, 1970).

6. See J. Hardman, *French Politics 1774–1789: from the accession of Louis XVI to the fall of the Bastille* (London, 1995), p. 134.

7. For an example of this view see E. Lavaqueray, *Necker, fourrier de la Révolution* (Paris, 1933). More recently, however, Necker's reputation has revived significantly; see R. D. Harris, *Necker, Reform Statesman of the Ancien Regime* (Berkeley, Calif., 1979).

8. Brewer, *The Sinews of Power*, p. 116.

9. For Calonne, the standard biography is still R. Lacour-Gayet, *Calonne: financier, ministre, contre-révolutionnaire* (Paris, 1963).

10. E. N. White, 'Was there a solution to the ancien régime's financial dilemma?', *Journal of Economic History*, vol. 49, no. 3 (September 1989), 545–68.

11. C. A. de Calonne, Lettre adressée au roi le 9 février 1789 (London, 1789), p. 74.

12. S. R. N. Chamfort, *Maximes et pensées, caractères et anecdotes*, ed. P. Grosclaude (2 vols, Paris, 1953–4), vol. 2, p. 121.

13. This was coined by Jean Egret for the title of his classic work, *La Pré-révolution française, 1787–1788* (Paris, 1962).

14. Mercy to Joseph II, 14 August 1787, *Correspondance secrète du comte de Mercy-Argenteau avec l'empereur Joseph II et le prince de Kaunitz*, ed. A. von Arneth and J. Flammermont (2 vols, Paris, 1889–91), vol. 2, p. 112.

15. This is the conclusion of Louis XVI's most scholarly biographer, see J. Hardman, *Louis XVI* (New Haven and London, 1993), p. 126.

16. J. F. Marmontel, *Mémoires*, ed. J. Renwick (2 vols, Clermont-Ferrand, 1972), vol. 2, p. 339.

17. J. L. H. Campan, *Mémoires sur la vie privée de Marie-Antoinette, reine de France et de Navarre* (2 vols, London, 1823), vol. 2, pp. 29–30.

18. The most influential view of the *parlements* as reactionary was propounded by Marcel Marion in several early twentieth-century works, especially *Dictionnaire des institutions de la France au 17ème et 18ème siècles* (Paris, 1923) and *Le Garde des sceaux Lamoignon et la réforme judiciaire de 1788* (Paris, 1905). This view only began to be substantially revised fifty years later, with the publication of Jean Egret's *Louis XV et l'opposition parlementaire 1715–1774* (Paris, 1970).

19. Egret, *La Pré-révolution française*, p. 306.

20. Marquis de Bombelles, *Journal*, ed. J. Grassion, F. Durif and J. Charon-Bordas (4 vols, Geneva, 1978–98), vol. 2, pp. 216–17.

21. *Lettres de Marie Antoinette*, ed. M. de la Rocheterie and the marquis de Beaucourt (2 vols, Paris, 1895–6), vol. 2, p. 128.

22. Ibid., p. 123.

23. Egret, *La Pré-révolution française*, p. 324. For a more sympathetic view of Necker's policy at this time, see R. D. Harris, *Necker and the Revolution of 1789* (Lanham, 1986).

24. Egret, *La Pré-révolution française*, p. 323.

25. *Mémoire autographe de M. de Barentin, chancelier et garde des sceaux,*

sur les derniers conseils de Louis XVI, ed. M. Champion (Paris, 1844), p. 73.

26. Mirabeau to Brémond-Julien, 27 March 1789, cited in G. Chaussinand-Nogaret, *Mirabeau* (Paris, 1982), p. 119.

27. N. Hampson, *Prelude to Terror: the constituent assembly and the failure of consensus, 1789–1791* (Oxford, 1988), p. 40.

Three BRETEUIL IN 1789

1. Archives Breteuil, Château de Breteuil, Yvelines, LAB, 1ère série, papiers divers.

2. Marquis de Bombelles, *Journal*, ed. J. Grassion, F. Durif and J. Charon-Bordas (4 vols, Geneva 1978–98), vol. 1, p. 73.

3. A. Chevalier, *Claude-Carloman de Rulhière, premier historien de la Pologne, sa vie et son œuvre historique* (Paris, 1939), pp. 22–3.

4. *Recueil des instructions données aux ambassadeurs et ministres de France depuis les traités de Westphalie jusqu'à la Révolution française: Russie*, ed. A. Rambaud (Paris, 1890), pp. 118, 195–218.

5. The only study in English of Gustavus is R. Nisbet Bain, *Gustavus III and his contemporaries* (2 vols, London, 1894).

6. O. G. von Heidenstam, *La Fin d'une dynastie* (Paris, 1911), pp. 73–4.

7. Archives Breteuil, 1767 dossier, correspondance, divers.

8. A. Söderhjelm, *Fersen et Marie Antoinette* (Paris, 1930), p. 163.

9. Bombelles, *Journal*, vol. 1, p. 284.

10. *Correspondance secrète du comte de Mercy-Argenteau avec l'empereur Joseph II et le prince de Kaunitz*, ed. A. von Arneth and J. Flammermont (2 vols, Paris, 1889–91); Kaunitz to Mercy, 1 April 1777, vol. 2, p. 492; Kaunitz to Mercy, 19 February 1778, vol. 2, p. 523; Kaunitz to Mercy, 2 August 1784, vol. 1, p. 278.

11. Ibid., Mercy to Kaunitz, 23 June 1781, vol. 1, p. 47; Mercy to Kaunitz, 30 September 1783, vol. 2, p. 218; Mercy to Kaunitz, 17 June 1783, vol. 1, p. 193.

12. Ibid., Joseph II to Mercy, 1 January 1779, vol. 2, p. 535.

13. S. R. N. Chamfort, *Maximes et pensées, caractères et anecdotes*, ed. P. Grosclaude (2 vols, Paris, 1953–4), vol. 1, pp. 132–3.

14. Bombelles, *Journal*, vol. 1, p. 83.

15. Prince de Ligne, *Amabile*, ed. J. Vercruysse (Paris, 1996), p. 97. For Ligne's biography, see P. Mansel, *Le Charmeur de l'Europe: Charles-Joseph de Ligne, 1735–1814* (Paris, 1992).

16. Goltz to Frederick, 21 August 1774, cited in *Correspondance secrète*, vol. I, pp. 13–14.

17. *Mémoires de Bailly* (3 vols, Paris, 1821), vol. I, p. 308.

18. Chevalier, *Rulhière*, pp. 46–7.

19. Letter from the lawyer Royer to Breteuil, 16 June 1781, enclosing extract from the will of Mme H. C. Vriesen, dated 9 April 1770. Archives Gontaut-Biron, Château de Courtalain, Eure-et-Loir, folder 2.

20. Bombelles, *Journal*, vol. I, p. 124.

21. Ibid.

22. *Mémoires de Barras*, ed. P. Vergnet (Paris, 1946), p. 92.

23. Breteuil to the princesse de Guéméné, 7 May 1777, Archives Départementales des Yvelines, E450; Bombelles to Breteuil, 24 August 1782, ibid., E449.

24. Abbé Georgel, *Mémoires pour servir à l'histoire des evénéments à la fin du 18ème siècle depuis 1760 jusqu'en 1806–10* (6 vols, Paris, 1817), vol. I, p. 555.

25. Bombelles, *Journal*, vol. 2, p. 170.

26. Mercy to Kaunitz, 20 August 1781, in *Correspondance secrète*, vol. I, p. 55.

27. Price, *Preserving the Monarchy: the comte de Vergennes, 1774–1787* (Cambridge, 1995), pp. 25–8.

28. See L. S. Greenbaum, 'Jean-Sylvain Bailly, the baron de Breteuil and the "four new hospitals" of Paris', *Clio Medica*, vol. 8, no. 4 (1973), 261–84.

29. See R. M. Rampelberg, *Le Ministre de la maison du roi 1783–1788: baron de Breteuil* (Paris, 1975), pp. 185–6.

30. The best account of the diamond necklace affair is still F. Mossiker, *The Queen's Necklace* (New York, 1961). For its cultural implications see S. Maza, *Private Lives and Public Affairs: the causes célèbres of pre-revolutionary France* (Berkeley, Calif., 1993), pp. 167–212. For its political context see Price, *Preserving the Monarchy*, pp. 174–84.

31. Bombelles, *Journal*, vol. 2, pp. 206–7.

32. Ibid., pp. 211–13.

33. *Mémoires de Bailly*, vol. I, p. 308.

34. Breteuil to Bombelles, 16 March 1792, Bombelles papers, Burg Clam, Upper Austria.
35. Bombelles, *Journal*, vol. 2, pp. 215–16.
36. Ibid., p. 260.

Four THE SUMMER OF 1789

1. J. Hardman, *Louis XVI* (New Haven and London, 1993), p. 149.
2. Comtesse d'Adhémar, *Souvenirs sur Marie Antoinette, archduchesse d'Autriche, reine de France, et sur la cour de Versailles* (4 vols, Paris, 1836), vol. 3, pp. 156–7.
3. Ibid.
4. Cited in Egret, *La Pré-révolution française, 1787–1788* (Paris, 1962), p. 362.
5. M. Price, 'The "Ministry of the Hundred Hours": a reappraisal', *French History*, vol. 4, No. 3 (1990), 319–21.
6. *Mémoires du marquis de Ferrières* (3 vols, Paris, 1822), vol. 1, p. 35.
7. Mercy to Joseph II, 4 July 1789, in *Correspondance secrète du comte de Mercy-Argenteau avec l'empereur Joseph II et le prince de Kaunitz*, ed. A. von Arneth and J. Flammermont (2 vols, Paris, 1889–91), vol. 2, p. 255.
8. Marquis de Bombelles, *Journal*, ed. J. Grassion, F. Durif and J. Charon-Bordas (4 vols, Geneva 1978–98), vol. 2, p. 299.
9. *Mémoire autographe de M. de Barentin, chancelier et garde des sceaux, sur les derniers conseils de Louis XVI*, ed. M. Champion (Paris, 1844), pp. 195–6.
10. Comte de Saint-Priest, *Mémoires*, ed. baron de Barante (2 vols, Paris, 1929), vol. 1, p. 223.
11. Saint-Priest to Louis XVI, undated but 22 June 1789, in G. Lefebvre and A. Terroine, *Recueil de documents relatifs aux séances des États-généraux*, vol. 1, *Mai-juin 1789* (Paris, 1953), (ii), p. 197.
12. J. Necker, *De la Révolution française* (4 vols, Paris, 1797), vol. 1, p. 253.
13. Chevalier de Coigny to the Bishop of Soissons, 20 June 1789, in d'Adhémar, *Souvenirs*, pp. 170–5.
14. Barentin to Louis XVI, 22 June 1789, in *Lettres et bulletins de Barentin à Louis XVI, avril–juillet 1789*, ed. A. Aulard (Paris, 1915), no. 53.

15. Hardman, *Louis XVI*, p. 153.

16. Saint-Priest to Louis XVI, undated but 22 June 1789, in Lefebvre and Terroine, *Recueil*, vol. 1(ii), p. 197.

17. For the full text of the declaration of 23 June, see ibid., pp. 273–86.

18. Ibid., p. 284.

19. P. Mansel, *The Court of France, 1789–1830* (Cambridge, 1988), p. 190.

20. Hardman, *Louis XVI*, p. 154.

21. Lefebvre and Terroine, *Recueil*, vol. 1(ii), p. 27.

22. *Mémoires de C. C. Flahaut, comte de la Billarderie d'Angiviller*, ed. Louis Bobé (Copenhagen and Paris, 1933), p. 158. D'Angiviller was director of the king's buildings, and had been a close friend of Louis XVI since childhood.

23. Mercy to Joseph II, 4 July 1789, *Correspondance secrète*, vol. 2, p. 254.

24. *Mémoires de d'Angiviller*, p. 158.

25. Lefebvre and Terroine, *Recueil*, vol. 1(ii), p. 35.

26. Cited in ibid., p. 27.

27. Cited in ibid., p. 28.

28. Bombelles, *Journal*, vol. 2, p. 261.

29. Ibid., p. 297.

30. Ibid., p. 339.

31. Lefebvre and Terroine, *Recueil*, vol. 1(ii), pp. 278–9.

32. Bombelles, *Journal*, vol. 2, pp. 343–4.

33. Ibid., p. 344.

34. P. Caron, 'La tentative de contre-révolution de juin–juillet 1789', *Revue d'histoire moderne et contemporaine*, vol. 8 (1906–7), 5–34 and 649–78. My own article cited above, 'The "Ministry of the Hundred Hours": a reappraisal', challenged Caron's conclusions. However, I have revised my own argument in this current chapter in the light of the new evidence I have discovered in the Bombelles papers.

35. Caron, 'La tentative', 30.

36. *The Times* (London), 17 July 1789.

37. Cited in Caron, 'La tentative', 25.

38. Ibid., 27–8.

39. Ibid., 25.

40. *Mémoires du duc des Cars* (2 vols, Paris, 1890), vol. 2, p. 64.

41. Archives Gontaut-Biron, Château de Courtalain, Eure-et-Loir, folder 2.

42. Saint-Priest, *Mémoires*, vol. 2, pp. 83–4.

43. J. Egret, *La Révolution des notables: Mounier et les monarchiens, 1789* (Paris, 1950), pp. 87–8.

44. *Mémoires de Bailly* (3 vols, Paris, 1821), vol. 1, p. 326.

45. Ibid., p. 391.

46. Bombelles, *Journal*, vol. 2, p. 298.

47. *Mémoires de Bailly*, vol. 1, p. 325.

48. Bombelles, *Journal*, vol. 2, p. 303.

49. *Mémoires de d'Angiviller*, pp. 168–9.

50. *Lettre de M. de la Vauguyon au Prétendant* (Paris, 1797), pp. 7–8.

51. Ibid., p. 8.

52. Bombelles to Ostermann, 31 January 1792, Bombelles papers, Burg Clam, Upper Austria, Missions 1790–1792 volume, fo. 255.

53. Bombelles, *Journal*, vol. 2, p. 299.

54. Bombelles, mémoire, Bombelles papers, Missions 1790–1792 volume, fo. 256.

55. Caron, 'La tentative', 26.

56. Cited in J. J. Guiffrey, 'Documents inédits sur la journée du 14 juillet 1789', *Revue historique*, vol. 1 (January–June 1876), 500.

57. Broglie to Louis XVI, 31 July 1789, Archives Nationales, Paris, série C, 221, no. 86.

58. Necker, *De la Révolution*, vol. 2, p. 2.

59. Jacob-Nicolas Moreau, *Mes souvenirs* (2 vols, Paris, 1898), vol. 2, p. 438.

60. Ibid.

61. *Mémoires du duc des Cars*, vol. 2, p. 80.

62. Baron R. M. von Klinckowström, *Le comte de Fersen et la cour de France* (2 vols, Paris 1877–8), vol. 2, pp. 6–7.

63. Duc de Sérent, 'Note sur les motifs qui ont déterminé le départ de Monseigneur le comte d'Artois et de ses enfants dans la nuit du 15 au 16 juillet 1789', Bombelles papers.

64. Ibid.

65. S. F. Scott, *The Response of the Royal Army to the French Revolution* (Oxford, 1978), p. 57.

66. Ibid., p. 62.

67. Ibid., p. 60.

68. *Mémoires du duc des Cars*, vol. 2, p. 82.

69. Scott, *The Response*, p. 80.

70. Egret, *La Révolution des notables*, p. 96.

71. *Mémoires de Bailly*, vol. 2, pp. 43–4.
72. Archives Nationales, Paris, série F17, 372, fo. 110.
73. *Journal d'émigration du comte d'Espinchal*, ed. E. d'Hauterive (Paris, 1912), p. 26; Bombelles, *Journal*, vol. 2, p. 345.

Five THE TURN OF THE SCREW

1. W. Doyle, *The Oxford History of the French Revolution* (Oxford, 1990 edn), p. 16.
2. Published in J.-L. Soulavie, *Mémoires historiques et politiques du règne de Louis XVI* (6 vols, Paris, 1801).
3. Cited in G. Chaussinand-Nogaret, *1789* (Paris, 1988), pp. 140–1.
4. B. Shapiro, *Revolutionary Justice in Paris, 1789–1790* (Cambridge, 1993), pp. 90–2.
5. *Mémoires de Malouet*, ed. baron Malouet (2 vols, Paris, 1868), vol. 1, p. 342, and n.1.
6. J. Hardman, *Louis XVI* (New Haven and London, 1993), p. 171.
7. *Mémoires de Malouet* (2 vols, Paris, 1868), vol. 1, p. 342; E. Lever, *Louis XVI* (Paris, 1985), p. 533.
8. 'Récit de ce qui s'est passé à Versailles et à Paris depuis la 5 jusqu'à vendredi 9 octobre 1789', Haus-Hof-und-Staatsarchiv, Vienna, Frankreich Varia 48, Nachtrag 1786–1793.
9. A. Mathiez, *Étude critique sur les journées des 5 et 6 octobre 1789* (Paris, 1899), pp. 58–9; Shapiro, *Revolutionary Justice*, pp. 95–8, 114–20.
10. Published in A. Mousset, *Un témoin inconnu de la Révolution: le comte de Fernan Nuñez* (Paris, 1924), p. 228.
11. Breteuil to Lous XVI, 8 November 1789, Archives Nationales, Paris, C221, no. 114.
12. Ibid.
13. Ibid.
14. 'Don patriotique, dettes et retranchements 1790–1791', 'État des revenus de M. le baron de Breteuil pour servir à déterminer sa contribution patriotique', Archives Gontaut-Biron, Château de Courtalain, Eure-et-Loir, folder 2.
15. *Souvenirs et fragments pour servir aux mémoires de ma vie et de mon temps par le marquis de Bouillé (Louis-Joseph-Amour), 1769–1812*, ed. P.-L. de Kermangant (3 vols, Paris, 1908–11), vol. 1, pp. 176–8.

16. G. Chaussinand-Nogaret, *Mirabeau* (Paris, 1982), p. 223.

17. 'Mémoire fait par le comte de Mirabeau, après les evénéments des 5 et 6 octobre 1789, et remis à Monsieur, comte de Provence, frère du roi, le 15 octobre par le comte de la Marck', in *Correspondance entre le comte de Mirabeau et le comte de la Marck*, ed. A. de Bacourt (3 vols, Paris, 1851), vol. 1, pp. 364–82. This particular quotation is on p. 369.

18. A. Sorel, *L'Europe et la Révolution français* (8 vols, Paris, 1885–1905), vol. 2, pp. 128–9.

19. Hardman, *Louis XVI*, p. 182.

20. On 31 August 1790, General de Bouillé stormed the town of Nancy, which was being held by mutinous regiments of his army, and reimposed order on his rebellious troops. One mutineer was broken on the wheel, twenty-two were hanged, and thirty condemned to the galleys for thirty years each. See *Souvenirs et fragments*, vol. 1, pp. 148–75.

21. Louis XVI to Bouillé, 4 November 1790, in F. Feuillet de Conches, *Louis XVI, Marie Antoinette, Mme Elisabeth: lettres et documents inédits* (6 vols, Paris, 1864–73), vol. 4, p. 463.

22. *Lisez et frémissez; par l'auteur d'Ouvrez les yeux, de Bon Dieu, que les Français sont bêtes, etc.* (Paris, 1790), p. 15.

23. Château de Breteuil. There is a good translation in Hardman, *Louis XVI*, p. 187.

24. Breteuil to Bombelles, 12 March 1791, Bombelles papers, Burg Clam, Upper Austria, Missions 1790–1792 volume.

25. P. and P. Girault de Coursac, *Enquête sur le procès du roi Louis XVI* (Paris, 1982), *Sur la route de Varennes* (Paris, 1984), *Le secret de la reine: la politique personnelle de Marie Antoinette pendant la Révolution* (Paris, 1996). Their views on the planned escape from Paris are summarized in *Enquête*, pp. 240–56.

26. Girault de Coursac, *Enquête*, pp. 224–5.

27. Ibid. p. 227.

28. See below, p. 369–72.

29. See below, p. 371–2.

Six Mirabeau versus Breteuil

1. Marquis de Bouillé, *Mémoires*, ed. S. A. Berville and J. F. Barrière (Paris, 1821).

2. Ibid., p. 183.

3. Ibid., pp. 197–8.

4. Ibid., pp. 199–200.

5. Ibid., pp. 200–201.

6. Mercy to Marie Antoinette, 27 April 1791, in *Marie Antoinette, Joseph II und Leopold II, ihr Briefwechsel*, ed. A. von Arneth (Leipzig, Paris and Vienna, 1866), p. 161.

7. This quotation is from Mirabeau's fourth note to the court, 26 June 1790, in *Correspondance entre le comte de Mirabeau et le comte de la Marck*, ed. A. de Bacourt (3 vols, Paris, 1851), vol. 2, p. 57.

8. Bombelles to Breteuil, 10 April 1791, Bombelles papers, Burg Clam, Upper Austria, Missions 1790–1792 volume, fo. 209.

9. 'Copie d'une lettre de M. le baron de Breteuil à Mgr comte d'Artois, 6 décembre 1790', Bombelles papers. These are bound into the Missions 1790–1792 volume, but the pages are not numbered.

10. 'Copie de la réponse de Mgr comte d'Artois à une lettre de M. le baron de Breteuil du 6 décembre 1790', Turin, 15 December 1790, Bombelles papers.

11. Marie Antoinette to Leopold II, 19 December 1790, in *Lettres de Marie Antoinette*, ed. M. de la Rocheterie and the marquis de Beaucourt (2 vols, Paris, 1895–6), vol. 2, p. 203.

12. Cited in G. de Diesbach, *Histoire de l'émigration, 1789–1814* (Paris, 1984 edn), p. 109.

13. Marie Antoinette to Leopold II, 1 June 1791, in *Lettres*, vol. 2, p. 246.

14. 'Copie de la lettre écrite à Mgr le comte d'Artois par M. le baron de Breteuil le 8 février 1791', Bombelles papers.

15. Ibid.

16. 'Copie de la réponse de Mgr comte d'Artois à une lettre de M. le baron de Breteuil du 8 février 1791', Venice, 21 February 1791, ibid.

17. Bombelles, *Journal*, ed. J. Grassion, F. Durif and J. Charon-Bordas (4 vols, Geneva, 1978–98), vol. 3, pp. 194–5.

18. Marquise de Fouquet to Calonne, n.d. but March 1791, Public Record Office, London, PC1/125/383.

19. Ibid.
20. Bombelles, *Journal*, vol. 3, p. 195.
21. Ibid., p. 196.
22. Ibid., p. 197.
23. Ibid., p. 113.
24. Ibid., p. 199.
25. Ibid., p. 196.
26. Ibid., p. 209.
27. *Mémoires de Malouet*, ed. baron Malouet (2 vols, Paris, 1868), vol. 2, pp. 12–13.
28. 'Copie de la lettre de Worms', 29 March 1791, Papiers du vicomte de Mirabeau, Archives Nationales, Paris, Archives Privées 119, 1, dossier 1.
29. Bouillé, *Mémoires*, p. 216.
30. Bombelles, *Journal*, vol. 3, p. 210.
31. Breteuil to Bombelles, 12 March 1791, Bombelles papers, Missions 1790–1792 volume. The folios of this letter are not numbered.
32. Bombelles to Breteuil, 10 April 1791, ibid., fo. 209.

Seven PREPARATIONS

1. Marquis de Bombelles, *Journal*, ed. J. Grassion, F. Durif and J. Charon-Bordas (4 vols, Geneva, 1978–98), vol. 3, p. 176 n. 28.
2. Cited in J. Sperber, *Revolutionary Europe, 1780–1850* (London, 2000), p. 54.
3. Leopold II still lacks an English biographer. The standard German biography is A. Wandruska, *Leopold II* (2 vols, Vienna, 1963–5).
4. HHStA, Sammelbände 71, fo. 23.
5. Ibid.
6. Ibid.
7. Mercy to Kaunitz, 22 January 1791, in *Louis XVI, Marie Antoinette, Mme Elisabeth: lettres et documents inédits*, ed. F. Feuillet de Conches (6 vols, Paris, 1864–73), vol. 1, p. 445.
8. Breteuil to Mercy, 3 April 1791, HHStA, Frankreich Varia 48. The folios of Breteuil's letters to Mercy in Frankreich Varia 48 are not numbered.
9. Ibid.
10. Ibid.

11. Breteuil to Mercy, 20 April 1791, ibid.

12. Ibid.

13. Breteuil to Mercy, 17 May 1791, ibid.

14. Bombelles papers, Burg Clam, Upper Austria, Missions 1790–1792 volume. The folios of this letter are not numbered.

15. Bombelles to Breteuil, 3 April 1791, ibid., fo. 201.

16. R. Lacour-Gayet, *Calonne: financier, reformateur, contre-révolutionnaire* (Paris, 1933), p. 324.

17. Bombelles to Breteuil, 3 April 1791, Bombelles papers, Missions 1790–1792 volume, fos 205–6.

18. Bombelles, *Journal*, vol. 3, pp. 215–16.

19. HHStA, Frankreich Varia 44, fo. 16.

20. Bombelles to Breteuil, 3 April 1791, Bombelles papers, Missions 1790–1792 volume, fo. 201.

21. *Louis XVI, Marie Antoinette, Mme Elisabeth*, vol. 2, pp. 33–4.

22. Baron R. M. von Klinckowström, *Le Comte de Fersen et la cour de France* (2 vols, Paris, 1877–8), vol. 1, p. 96 n. 1.

23. Ibid.

24. Ibid., p. 94.

25. Comte d'Allonville, *Mémoires secrets, de 1770 à 1830* (5 vols, Paris, 1838–41), vol. 2, pp. 212–13.

26. V. Cronin, *Louis and Antoinette* (London, 1974), p. 318.

27. Fersen to baron Taube, 18 April 1791, in Klinckowström, *Le Comte de Fersen et la cour de France*, vol. 1, p. 105.

28. Marie Antoinette to Mercy, 20 April 1791, in *Lettres de Marie Antoinette*, ed. M. de la Rocheterie and the marquis de Beaucourt (2 vols, Paris, 1895–6), vol. 2, p. 234.

29. Bombelles, *Journal*, vol. 3, p. 217.

30. Breteuil to Bombelles, 13 April 1791, Bombelles papers, Missions 1790–1792 volume. The folios of this letter are not numbered.

31. Bombelles to Breteuil, 23 April 1791, ibid., fo. 214.

32. Bombelles, *Journal*, vol. 3, p. 217.

33. Ibid., p. 219.

34. Reproduced in ibid., pp. 220–1.

35. Ibid., p. 221.

36. Ibid., p. 222.

37. Breteuil to Fersen, 30 April 1791, in Klinckowström, *Le Comte de Fersen et la cour de France*, vol. 1, p. 110.

38. Bombelles, *Journal*, vol. 3, p. 222.

39. Bombelles to Breteuil, 6 May 1791, Bombelles papers, Missions 1790–1792 volume, fo. 217.

40. 'Mémoire de M. de Bombelles à sa majesté sur ce que M. de Breteuil demande au nom du roi', HHStA, Frankreich Varia 42, fo. 424.

41. Klinckowström, *Le Comte de Fersen et la cour de France*, vol. 1, pp. 106–7.

42. Leopold II to Marie Antoinette, 2 May 1791, in *Marie Antoinette, Joseph II und Leopold II, ihr Briefwechsel*, ed. A. von Arneth (Leipzig, Paris and Vienna, 1866), p. 162.

43. Bombelles, *Journal*, vol. 3, p. 226 n. 28.

44. Ibid., p. 228.

45. Marie Antoinette to Mercy, 1 and 5 June, and to Leopold II, 1 June 1791, in *Marie Antoinette, Joseph II und Leopold II*, pp. 167–72.

46. Ibid., pp. 177–9.

47. Marie Antoinette to Leopold II, 22 May 1791, ibid., p. 166.

48. HHStA, Frankreich Varia 44, fos 11–20.

49. Ibid., fos 12–13.

50. Breteuil to Leopold II, 27 May 1791, HHStA, Frankreich Varia 44, fo. 17.

51. HHStA, Frankreich Varia 44, fo. 25.

52. Breteuil to Artois, 14 May 1791, Bombelles papers, Missions 1790–1792 volume. The folios of this letter are not numbered.

53. Breteuil to Artois, 22 May 1791, ibid.

54. Artois to Breteuil, 10 June 1791, ibid.

55. Cited in P. and P. Girault de Coursac, *Enquête sur le procès du roi Louis XVI* (Paris, 1982), p. 233.

56. Bombelles, *Journal*, vol. 3, p. 232.

57. Ibid., pp. 236–7.

58. Breteuil to Leopold II, 27 May 1791, HHStA, Frankreich Varia 44, fo. 16.

59. Klinckowström, *Le Comte de Fersen et la cour de France*, vol. 1, p. 121.

60. See Bombelles to Breteuil, 3 April 1791, Bombelles papers, Missions 1790–1792 volume, fo. 202. For a thorough recent study of Anglo-French relations at this juncture, see J. Black, *British Foreign Policy in an Age of Revolutions, 1783–1793* (Cambridge, 1994), pp. 346–76.

61. Breteuil to Bombelles, 13 April 1791, Bombelles papers, Missions 1790–1792 volume. The folios of this letter are not numbered.

62. *Lettres de Marie Antoinette*, vol. 2, pp. 220–1.

63. 'Mémoire de M. de Bombelles à sa majesté sur ce que M. de Breteuil demande au nom du roi', HHStA, Frankreich Varia 42, fo. 424.

64. Bombelles to Breteuil, 28 May 1791, Bombelles papers, Missions 1790–1792 volume, fo. 225.

65. Bombelles to Leopold II, 23 May 1791, HHStA, Frankreich Varia 42, fo. 430.

66. Mercy to Marie Antoinette, 7 March 1791, in *Marie Antoinette, Joseph II und Leopold II*, pp. 149–50.

67. Fersen to Taube, 18 April 1791, in Klinckowström, *Le Comte de Fersen et la cour de France*, vol. 1, p. 101.

Eight THE FLIGHT TO VARENNES

1. For these details of the flight to Varennes see marquis de Bouillé, *Mémoires*, ed. S. A. Berville and S. F. Barrière (Paris, 1821), p. 410, Bouillé, *Souvenirs et fragments pour servir aux mémoires de ma vie et de mon temps, 1769–1812*, ed. P.-L. de Kermangant (3 vols, Paris, 1908–11), vol. 1, pp. 203–9, 227–42, and duc de Choiseul, *Relation du départ de Louis XVI le 20 juin 1791* (Paris, 1822), pp. 38–9. For a careful recent treatment of the flight, see M. de Lombarès, 'Varennes ou la fin d'un régime', *Revue historique de l'armée* (1961) no. 3, pp. 33–56; no. 4, pp. 45–62; no. 5, pp. 23–36.

2. Choiseul, *Relation*, p. 43.

3. Cited in G. Lenôtre, *Le Drame de Varennes* (Paris, 1905), p. 40.

4. Ibid., p. 24.

5. Marie Antoinette's note is in HHStA, Familienkorrespondenz 26, fo. 5; Louis XVI's words to Fersen are in baron R. M. Klinckowström, *Le Comte de Fersen et la cour de France* (2 vols, Paris, 1877–8), vol. 1, p. 2.

6. These descriptions of the *berline* are cited in J. Hardman, *Louis XVI* (New Haven and London, 1993), p. 193, and Lenôtre, *Le Drame de Varennes*, pp. 59–60.

7. *Mémoires de Mme la duchesse de Tourzel*, ed. J. Chalon (Paris, 1969), p. 194.

8. Ibid., 195.

9. Lenôtre, *Le Drame de Varennes*, p. 61.

10. Cited in *Mémoires de Mme de Tourzel*, p. 455 (note for p. 195).

11. Marquis de Bombelles, *Journal*, ed. J. Grassion, F. Durif and J. Charon-Bordas (4 vols, Geneva, 1978–98), vol. 3, p. 243.
12. HHStA, Frankreich Varia 48.
13. Ibid.
14. Bombelles, *Journal*, vol. 3, p. 245.
15. Ibid., p. 246.
16. Bombelles papers, Burg Clam, Upper Austria, Missions 1790–1792 volume, fo. 236.
17. Ibid., 'Note communiquée à M. Steiger, avoyer de Berne, contenant les demandes à faire aux cantons helvétiques après la liberté du roi'.
18. Cited in Lenôtre, *Le Drame de Varennes*, p. 69. See also Lombarès, 'Varennes', *Revue historique de l'armée* (1961) no. 3, pp. 46–52.
19. Choiseul, *Relation*, p. 84.
20. Lenôtre, *Le Drame de Varennes*, p. 76.
21. Ibid., p. 108.
22. Choiseul, *Relation*, pp. 93–4.
23. Ibid., p. 94.
24. 'Details du voyage du roi et de la reine à Montmédy, et de leur arrestation à Varennes dans le Clermontois, le 22 juin 1791', HHStA, Frankreich Varia 45, fo. 18.
25. Klinckowström, *Le Comte de Fersen et la cour de France*, vol. 1, p. 3.
26. Lenôtre, *Le Drame de Varennes*, p. 172.
27. Ibid., pp. 177–8.
28. Klinckowström, *Le Comte de Fersen et la cour de France*, vol. 1, p. 130.
29. Choiseul, *Relation*, pp. 50, 53.
30. Ibid., pp. 55–6.
31. Bombelles papers, Fontanges manuscript, 'Infandum . . . jubes renovare dolorem', fo. 1.
32. Ibid., fo. 46.
33. Ibid., fos. 46–7.
34. Ibid., fo. 48.
35. Ibid.
36. Lenôtre, *Le Drame de Varennes*, p. 268.
37. Bouillé, *Souvenirs et fragments*, vol. 1, p. 285.
38. Ibid., pp. 287–8.
39. Klinckowström, *Le Comte de Fersen et la cour de France*, vol. 1, p. 140.
40. Bombelles, *Journal*, vol. 3, p. 250.

Nine THE KING'S SECRET

1. Bombelles papers, Burg Clam, Upper Austria, Missions 1790–1792 volume, fo. 236.
2. Cited in J. Hardman, *The French Revolution: the fall of the ancien régime to the Thermidorian reaction, 1785–1795* (London, 1981), pp. 130–1.
3. Ibid., p. 126.
4. *Lettres de Marie Antoinette*, ed. M. de la Rocheterie and the marquis de Beaucourt (2 vols, Paris, 1895–6), vol. 2, p. 218.
5. Baron R. M. Klinckowström, *Le Comte de Fersen et la cour de France* (2 vols, Paris, 1877–8), vol. 1, p. 110.
6. Ibid., p. 123.
7. Ibid., p. 129.
8. Ibid., p. 128.
9. Ibid., p. 131.
10. Memorandum, 'Envoyé à Luxembourg. Partie de Soleure le vendredi 27 mai 1791', Bombelles papers.
11. Bishop of Pamiers to Bombelles, Brussels, 9 March 1792, ibid.
12. Memorandum, 'Envoyé à Luxembourg', ibid.
13. Ibid.
14. Ibid.
15. Ibid.
16. Ibid.
17. Ibid.
18. Marquis de Bouillé, *Mémoires*, ed. S. A. Berville and J. F. Barrière (Paris, 1821), pp. 192–5.
19. Duc de Choiseul, *Relation du départ de Louis XVI le 20 juin 1791* (Paris, 1822), p. 34.
20. Bouillé, *Mémoires*, pp. 192–3.
21. Choiseul, *Relation*, p. 35.
22. Bouillé, *Mémoires*, p. 280.
23. Ibid.
24. Klinckowström, *Le Comte de Fersen et la cour de France*, vol. 1, p. 128.
25. J. Chaumié, 'La correspondance du chevalier de Las Casas et du marquis de Bombelles, ambassadeurs de France et d'Espagne sous la Révolution', *Revue d'histoire diplomatique*, January–June and July–

December 1950, pp. 99–142, and January–June and July–December 1951, pp. 76–129.

26. Bishop of Pamiers to Bombelles, Brussels 9 March 1792, Bombelles papers.

27. Bombelles diary unpublished ms., vol. 71, fos 99–100, Bombelles papers.

Ten THE KING AND THE CONSTITUTION

1. *Mémoires de Weber concernant Marie Antoinette, archiduchesse d'Autriche et reine de France et de Navarre*, ed. S. A. Berville and J. F. Barrière (2 vols, Paris, 1822), vol. 2, pp. 143–4.

2. *Marie Antoinette et Barnave: correspondance secrète, juillet 1791–janvier 1792*, ed. A. Söderhjelm (Paris, 1934), p. 21.

3. J. L. H. Campan, *Mémoires sur la vie privée de Marie-Antoinette, reine de France et de Navarre* (2 vols, London, 1823), vol. 2, pp. 175–6.

4. *Marie Antoinette et Barnave*, pp. 27–34.

5. *Lettres de Marie Antoinette*, ed. M. de la Rocheterie and the marquis de Beaucourt (2 vols, Paris, 1895–6), vol. 2, p. 319.

6. Marie Antoinette to Mercy, 26 August 1791, ibid., p. 279.

7. Ibid., pp. 265–6.

8. G. Michon, *Essai sur l'histoire du parti feuillant: Adrien Duport* (Paris, 1924), p. 291.

9. *Lettres de Marie Antoinette*, vol. 2, p. 266.

10. Ibid., pp. 257–8.

11. HHStA, Familienkorrespondenz 26, Cahier A und B, fo. 24.

12. Mercy to Laborde, 20 July 1791, ibid., fos 25–6.

13. Mercy to Blumendorff, 13 July 1791, ibid., fo. 25.

14. Marie Antoinette to Mercy, 21 August 1791, in *Lettres de Marie Antoinette*, vol. 2, p. 276.

15. *Marie Antoinette, Joseph II und Leopold II, ihr Briefwechsel*, ed. A. von Arneth (Leipzig, Paris and Vienna, 1866), pp. 198–203.

16. *Mémoires de Malouet*, ed. baron Malouet (2 vols, Paris, 1868), vol. 2, pp. 72–7.

17. Michon, *Adrien Duport*, pp. 325–31.

18. Comte de Montlosier, *Souvenirs d'un émigré (1791–1798)*, ed. comte de Larouzière-Montlosier and E. d'Hauterive (Paris, 1951), pp. 54–5.

19. *Lettres de Marie Antoinette*, vol. 2, p. 267.

20. Campan, *Mémoires*, vol. 2, pp. 175–6; Montlosier, *Souvenirs*, pp. 54–5.

21. Marie Antoinette to Fersen, 7 December 1791, in *Lettres de Marie Antoinette*, vol. 2, p. 346.

22. Ibid., p. 345.

23. Louis XVI to Breteuil, 14 December 1791, in *Louis XVI, Marie Antoinette, Mme Elisabeth: lettres et documents inédits*, ed. F. Feuillet de Conches (6 vols, Paris, 1864–73), vol. 4, pp. 297–8.

24. Campan, *Mémoires*, vol. 2, p. 158 n.1.

25. *Lettres de Marie Antoinette*, vol. 2, pp. 313–15.

26. 'Précis des motifs pour le rassemblement d'un congrès', Bombelles papers, Missions 1790–1792 volume, fo. 266.

27. A. Sorel, *L'Europe et la Révolution française* (8 vols, Paris, 1885–1905), vol. 2, pp. 232–4.

28. Ibid., p. 274.

29. *Lettres de Marie Antoinette*, vol. 2, p. 318.

30. Ibid., p. 279.

31. *Louis XVI, Marie Antoinette, Mme Elisabeth*, vol. 2, p. 330.

32. Ibid., pp. 332–3.

33. *Lettres de Marie Antoinette*, vol. 2, pp. 312–13.

34. Ibid.

35. HHStA, Familienkorrespondenz 26, Dossier D.

36. *Lettres de Marie Antoinette*, vol. 2, p. 275.

37. HHStA, Frankreich Varia 44, fo. 52.

38. Ibid., fos 53–4.

39. La Marck to Mercy, 26 January 1791, in *Correspondance entre le comte de Mirabeau et le comte de la Marck*, ed. A. de Bacourt (3 vols, Paris, 1851), vol. 3, p. 30.

40. *Lettres de Marie Antoinette*, vol. 2, p. 337.

41. Baron R. M. von Klinckowström, *Le Comte de Fersen et la cour de France* (2 vols, Paris, 1877–8), vol. 1, pp. 231–2.

42. For this episode, see T. C. W. Blanning, *The Origins of the French Revolutionary Wars* (London, 1986), pp. 99–102.

Eleven WINTER 1791: BRETEUIL, THE POWERS
AND THE PRINCES

1. HHStA, Frankreich Varia 42, fo. 234.
2. François-René, vicomte de Chateaubriand, *Mémoires d'outre tombe*, ed. P. Clarac (3 vols, Paris, 1973), vol. 1, p. 366.
3. Bombelles diary, unpublished ms., vol. 45, fo. 7, Bombelles papers, Burg Clam, Upper Austria.
4. 'Copie d'une lettre de Monsieur frère du Roi à M. le baron de Breteuil', ibid.
5. A. F. Bertrand de Molleville, *Mémoires particulières pour servir à l'histoire de la fin du règne de Louis XVI* (2 vols, Paris, 1816), vol. 1, p. 377.
6. HHStA, Frankreich Varia 44, fo. 16.
7. Provence to Mme Elisabeth, 6 August 1791, in *Louis XVI, Marie Antoinette, Mme Elisabeth: lettres et documents inédits*, ed. F. Feuillet de Conches (6 vols, Paris, 1864–73), vol. 1, pp. 204–5.
8. Cited in J. Chaumié, 'La correspondance du chevalier de Las Casas et du marquis de Bombelles, ambassadeurs de France et d'Espagne sous la Révolution', *Revue d'histoire diplomatique* (January–June and July–December 1951), 136–7.
9. *Louis XVI, Marie Antoinette, Mme Elisabeth*, vol. 2, p. 156.
10. Marie Antoinette to Fersen, 8 July 1791, in *Lettres de Marie Antoinette*, ed. M. de la Rocheterie and the marquis de Beaucourt (2 vols, Paris, 1895–6), vol. 2, p. 257.
11. Ibid., pp. 256–7.
12. Ibid., pp. 322–3.
13. Ibid., p. 332.
14. Comte de Montlosier, *Souvenirs d'un émigré (1791–1798)*, ed. comte de Larouzière-Montlosier and E. d'Hauterive (Paris, 1951), p. 44.
15. Geheimes Staatsarchiv, Berlin, PK, I. HA Geheimer Rat, Rep. 11 Auswärtige Beziehungen, Frankreich, Nr 89 Fasz. 298, Bl. 9, 10.
16. See Appendix p. 371–2.
17. *Marie Antoinette, Joseph II und Leopold II, ihr Briefwechsel*, ed. A. von Arneth (Leipzig, Paris and Vienna, 1866), p. 181.
18. A. Sorel, *L'Europe et la Révolution française* (8 vols, Paris, 1885–1905), vol. 2, p. 257.
19. Ibid., p. 256.

20. Ibid., p. 257.

21. Ibid., p. 277.

22. Bombelles to Bishop of Pamiers, 15 November 1791, in marquis de Bombelles, *Journal*, ed. J. Grassion, F. Durif and J. Charon-Bordas (4 vols, Geneva, 1978–98), vol. 3, p. 261.

23. Marie Antoinette to Fersen, 26 September 1791, in *Lettres de Marie Antoinette*, vol. 2, p. 311.

24. Ivan Simolin to Count Ostermann, 8/19 August 1791, in *Louis XVI, Marie Antoinette, Mme Elisabeth*, vol. 2, p. 241.

25. Cited in N. Åkeson, *Gustaf III:s forhallande till franska revolutionen* (2 vols, Lund, 1885), vol. 2, pp. 225–6.

26. Riksarkivet, Stockholm, Gallica 524, de Breteuil folder.

27. Ibid.

28. *Louis XVI, Marie Antoinette, Mme Elisabeth*, vol. 4, p. 298.

29. Ibid., p. 300.

30. Riksarkivet, Gallica 524, de Breteuil folder.

31. Marie Antoinette to Fersen, 7 December 1791, in *Lettres de Marie Antoinette*, vol. 2, p. 342.

32. Ibid.

33. A. Söderhjelm, *Fersen et Marie Antoinette* (Paris, 1930), p. 247.

34. Baron R. M. von Klinckowström, *Le Comte de Fersen et la cour de France* (2 vols, Paris, 1877–8), vol. 2, p. 6.

35. 'Mémoire sur les différentes manières d'opérations pour le congrès', Riksarkivet, Stockholm, Gallica 499, 'Bilaga til Gr. Fersens underdaniga depecher af Brusse den 29 Februarii'.

36. Ibid.

37. Ibid.

38. Fersen to Gustavus III, 29 February 1791, in Klinckowström, *Le Comte de Fersen et la cour de France*, vol. 2, p. 180.

39. Ibid., p. 181.

40. *Louis XVI, Marie Antoinette, Mme Elisabeth*, vol. 4, p. 302.

41. Fersen to Gustavus III, 29 February 1791, in Klinckowström, *Le Comte de Fersen et la cour de France*, vol. 2, p. 182.

42. Riksarkivet, Gallica 524, de Breteuil folder.

43. Ibid.

44. Comte d'Allonville, *Mémoires secrets de 1770 à 1830* (5 vols, Paris, 1838–41), vol. 2, pp. 283–5.

45. 'Copie d'une lettre adressée au roi par les princes ses frères le 4 du mois d'août 1791', HHStA, Frankreich Varia 44 fos 25–6.

46. Duc de Castries, *Le Maréchal de Castries: serviteur de trois rois* (Paris, 1979 edn), p. 165.

47. Ibid., pp. 165–6.

48. 'Copie de la réponse de M. le baron de Breteuil à la lettre de M. le maréchal de Castries', Bombelles papers.

49. Ibid.

50. 'Copie d'une lettre de M. le maréchal de Castries à M. le baron de Breteuil', 6 February 1792, Bombelles papers.

51. 'Copie de la réponse de M. le baron de Breteuil à la lettre de M. le maréchal de Castries du 6 février', Bombelles papers.

52. Castries papers, Archives Nationales 306 AP 26, 'Instructions de mon père pour moi lorsque je fus envoyé à Bruxelles au baron de Breteuil, et mes réponses. Le 6 février 1792'.

53. Provence to Louis XVI, 3 December 1791, *Louis XVI, Marie Antoinette, Mme Elisabeth*, vol. 4, p. 261.

54. Cited in E. Daudet, *Histoire de l'émigration: Coblentz* (Paris, n.d), p. 123.

Twelve ENDGAME

1. For this account of the Girondins and the drive for war, I have relied on A. Sorel, *L'Europe et la Révolution française* (8 vols, Paris, 1885–1905), vol. 2, pp. 299–321, and T. C. W. Blanning, *The Origins of the Revolutionary Wars* (London, 1986), pp. 96–113.

2. Cited in F. Furet, *Penser la Révolution française* (Paris, 1978), p. 110.

3. Cited in Sorel, *L'Europe et la Révolution*, vol. 2, p. 360.

4. Ibid., p. 397.

5. Ibid., pp. 400–1

6. Baron R. M. von Klinckowström, *Le Comte de Fersen et la cour de France* (2 vols, Paris, 1877–8), vol. 2, p. 14.

7. Ibid., p. 230.

8. *Louis XVI, Marie Antoinette, Mme Elisabeth: lettres et documents inédits*, ed. F. Feuillet de Conches (6 vols, Paris, 1864–73), vol. 2, p. 348.

9. 'Mémoires du duc de Caraman', *Revue contemporaine*, vol. 1 (April – May 1852), 30–41, 187–202, and vol. 2 (June – July 1852), 54–73.

10. J. Flammermont, *Négociations secrètes de Louis XVI et du baron de Breteuil avec la cour de Berlin, décembre 1791 à juillet 1792* (Paris, 1885), pp. 15–16, 17–18, 18 n. 1.

11. Ibid., pp. 15–16.

12. Riksarkivet, Stockholm, Gallica 524, de Breteuil folder.

13. Gustavus II to Breteuil, 13 March 1792, in N. Åkeson, *Gustaf III:s forhallende till franska revolutionen* (2 vols, Lund, 1885), vol. 2, p. 251.

14. Gustavus III to Breteuil, February 1792, ibid., p. 246.

15. J. Chaumié, *Les relations diplomatiques entre la France et l'Espagne de Varennes à la mort de Louis XVI* (Bordeaux, 1957), pp. 77–8.

16. Breteuil to Gustavus III, 25 March 1792, Riksarkivet, Gallica 524, de Breteuil folder.

17. This account of Gustavus III's assassination is based on R. Nisbet Bain, *Gustavus III and his contemporaries* (2 vols, London, 1894), vol. 2, pp. 184–202.

18. Breteuil to Bombelles, 19 April 1792, Bombelles papers, Burg Clam, Upper Austria, Missions 1790–1792 volume.

19. Breteuil to Bombelles, 16 March 1792, ibid.

20. 'Observations lues à l'impératrice de Russie à l'audience du 17 mars 1792', response 5, ibid.

21. Ibid.

22. Bishop of Pamiers to Bombelles, 7 March 1792, ibid.

23. Ibid.

24. Ibid.

25. Sorel, *L'Europe et la Révolution française*, vol. 2, p. 407.

26. Caraman to Breteuil, 8 May 1792, in Klinckowström, *Le Comte de Fersen et la cour de France*, vol. 2, p. 270.

27. Sorel, *L'Europe et la Révolution française*, vol. 2, p. 433.

28. Cited in M. Clemenceau-Jacquemaire, *Vie de Mme Roland* (2 vols, Paris, 1929), vo. 2, p. 54.

29. Cited in J. Hardman, *Louis XVI* (New Haven and London, 1993), p. 217.

30. Ibid., p. 218.

31. G. Michon, *Essai sur l'histoire du parti feuillant: Adrien Duport* (Paris, 1924), pp. 405–7.

32. Ibid., pp. 415–16.

33. Mercy to Kaunitz, 30 May 1792, in H. Glagau, *Die franzósische*

Legislative und die Ursprung der Revolutionskriege, 1791–1792 (Berlin, 1896), pp. 361–2.

34. Michon, *Adrien Duport*, p. 420.
35. Ibid., p. 421.
36. Glagau, *Die französische Legislative* p. 361.
37. *Lettres de Marie Antoinette*, ed. M. de la Rocheterie and the marquis de Beaucourt (2 vols, Paris, 1895–6), vol. 2, p. 415.
38. These are published in ibid., pp. 391–2, 399, 402, 415.
39. Klinckowström, *Le Comte de Fersen et la cour de France*, vol. 2, p. 22.
40. 'Réponses du baron de Breteuil à la note des princes', Riksarkivet, Stafsundsarkivet, Hans Axel von Fersens samling, vol. 17.
41. Ibid.
42. Bishop of Pamiers to Bombelles, 9 March 1792, Bombelles papers.
43. Duc de Castries, *Le Maréchal de Castries: serviteur de trois rois* (Paris, 1879 edn), p. 173.
44. *Lettres de Marie Antoinette*, vol. 2, p. 407.
45. Sorel, *L'Europe et la Révolution française*, vol. 2, p. 510.
46. R. Allen, *Threshold of Terror: the last hours of the monarchy in the French Revolution* (Stroud, 1999), pp. 80–1.
47. Ibid., pp. 69–71. I have based my account of the events of 10 August on Allen's work, the most up-to-date we currently possess.
48. Cited in Hardman, *Louis XVI*, p. 221.

Thirteen ROYAL BLOOD

1. Caraman to Breteuil, 23 August 1792, in Baron R. M. von Klinckowström, *Le Comte de Fersen et la cour de France* (2 vols, Paris, 1877–8), vol. 2, p. 352.
2. 'Résumé d'un débat chez le baron de Breteuil', 8 September 1792, Public Record Office, PC1/128/178.
3. Klinckowström, *Le Comte de Fersen et la cour de France*, vol. 2, p. 373.
4. Ibid., p. 31.
5. Breteuil to Fersen, 12 September 1792, ibid., p. 367.
6. Fersen to Breteuil, 11 September 1792, ibid., p. 366.
7. A. Sorel, *L'Europe et la Révolution française* (8 vols, Paris, 1885–1905), vol. 3, p. 3.

8. Ibid., p. 37.

9. Ibid.

10. Marquis de La Fayette, *Mémoires* (6 vols, Paris, 1816), vol. 4, p. 250.

11. This account of the Valmy campaign is based on T. C. W. Blanning, *The French Revolutionary Wars* (London, 1996), pp. 71–82.

12. Breteuil to Fersen, 12 September 1792, in Klinckowström, *Le Comte de Fersen et la cour de France*, vol. 2, p. 370.

13. A. Chuquet, *Les Guerres de la Révolution*, vol. 2, *Valmy* (Paris, 1929), pp. 128–33.

14. HHStA, Frankreich Varia 48.

15. Cited in comte Fleury, *Les Dernières années du marquis et de la marquise de Bombelles* (Paris, 1906), p. 312.

16. Ibid., p. 313.

17. Sorel, *L'Europe et la Révolution française*, vol. 3, p. 42.

18. Ibid., p. 56.

19. 'Extrait d'une lettre du baron de Breteuil à Mme de Matignon', 26 September 1792, Riksarkivet, Stockholm, Stafsundsarkivet, Hans Axel von Fersens samling, vol. 12.

20. Breteuil to Fersen, 2 October 1792, in Klinckowström, *Le Comte de Fersen et la cour de France*, vol. 2, p. 378.

21. Breteuil to Mme de Matignon, 22 October 1792, ibid., p. 387.

22. Blanning, *The French Revolutionary Wars*, p. 82.

23. J. Hardman, *Louis XVI* (New Haven and London, 1993), p. 223; H. Walpole trans. Louis XVI, *Règne de Richard III, ou doutes historiques sur les crimes qui lui sont imputés*, ed. Roussel l'Epinal (Paris, 1800). See also C. Duckworth, 'Louis XVI and English history: a French reaction to Walpole, Hume and Gibbon on Richard III', *Studies on Voltaire and the Eighteenth Century*, 176 (1979), 385–401.

24. F. Hue, *Dernières années du règne et de la vie de Louis XVI* (Paris, 1816), pp. 359–60.

25. Hardman, *Louis XVI*, p. 224.

26. Cited in ibid., p. 228.

27. Cited in G. Bord, *La Fin de deux légendes: Léonard et le baron de Batz* (Paris, 1909), pp. 111–13.

28. Baron de Batz, *La Vie et les conspirations de Jean, baron de Batz* (Paris, 1908), p. 393.

29. Fersen to Breteuil, 6 September 1792, in Klinckowström, *Le Comte de Fersen et la cour de France*, vol. 2, pp. 360–1.

30. Breteuil to Fersen, 12 September 1792, ibid., pp. 369–71.

31. On Talon, see A. Doyon, 'Maximilien Radix de Ste-Foy', *Revue d'histoire diplomatique*, July–September 1966, pp. 232–70, October–December 1966, pp. 314–54.

32. Klinckowström, *Le Comte de Fersen et la cour de France*, vol. 2, p. 24.

33. Ibid., p. 348.

34. Ibid., p. 349.

35. Ibid., p. 377.

36. Baron de Batz, *Les Conspirations et la fin de Jean, baron de Batz* (Paris, 1911), p. 546.

37. Cited in E. Lever, *Louis XVI* (Paris, 1985), pp. 654–5.

38. Batz, *La Vie et les conspirations*, pp. 433–44.

39. Lever, *Louis XVI*, p. 665.

40. Klinckowström, *Le Comte de Fersen et la cour de France*, vol. 2, p. 65.

41. Ibid., p. 86.

42. Ibid., pp. 64–5.

43. Mercy to Breteuil, 17 March 1793, HHStA, Frankreich Varia 48.

44. 'Interrogatoire du citoyen Sainte-Foy, du 25 septembre 1792', in *Recueil des pièces imprimées d'après le décret de la convention nationale* (2 vols, Paris, 1793).

45. A. Chuquet, *Les Guerres de la Révolution*, vol. 5, *La Trahison de Dumouriez* (Paris, n.d.), pp. 178–9.

46. Klinckowström, *Le Comte de Fersen et la cour de France*, vol. 2, p. 67.

47. Ibid.

48. Ibid., pp. 67–8.

49. HHStA, Frankreich Varia 48.

50. Batz, *Les Conspirations et la fin*, pp. 123–90.

51. Klinckowström, *Le Comte de Fersen et la cour de France*, vol. 2, pp. 100–101.

52. V. Cronin, *Louis and Antoinette* (London, 1974), pp. 387–8.

53. *Lettres de Marie Antoinette*, ed. M. de la Rocheterie and the marquis de Beaucourt (2 vols, Paris, 1895–6), vol. 2, pp. 441–4.

Fourteen AFTER THE DELUGE

1. Fersen, bulletin to the Swedish government, 8 December 1793, Riksarkivet, Stockholm, Gallica 500.

2. Baron de Batz, *Les Conspirations et la fin de Jean, baron de Batz* (Paris, 1911), p. 256.

3. Quoted in C. Hibbert, *The French Revolution* (London, 1982 edition), p. 244.

4. Baron R. M. Klinckowström, *Le Comte de Fersen et la cour de France*, (2 vols, Paris, 1877–8), vol. 2, pp. 378–9.

5. Batz, *Les Conspirations et la fin*, pp. 30–1.

6. The best account in English of this episode is N. Hampson, 'François Chabot and his plot', *Transactions of the Royal Historical Society*, 5th series, vol. 26 (1976), pp. 1–15. In addition to the works cited above, see also A. Mathiez, *Un procès de corruption sous la Terreur: l'affaire de la Compagnie des Indes* (Paris, 1920) and A. de Lestapis, *La 'Conspiration de Batz'* (Paris, 1969).

7. Entry for 25 April 1792, Riksarkivet, Stafsundsarkivet, vol. 5.

8. A. Söderhjelm, *Axel von Fersens dagbok* (4 vols, Stockholm, 1924–36), vol. 1, pp. 192–3.

9. Breteuil's memorandum is published in A. Ritter von Vivenot, *Quellen zur Geschichte der deutschen Kasierpolitik Österreichs während der französischen Revolutionskriege, 1790–1801* (5 vols, Vienna, 1873–90), vol. 2, pp. 440–4.

10. Klinckowström, *Le Comte de Fersen et la cour de France*, vol. 2, p. 371.

11. Vivenot, *Quellen*, vol. 2, p. 442.

12. Ibid.

13. Ibid., p. 437.

14. For Batz's activities in 1794 and his later life, see Batz, *Les Conspirations et la fin*, pp. 256–543.

15. Public Record Office, C12/952/13/.

16. Entry for 3 March 1798, Bombelles diary, unpublished ms., vol. 66, fo. 99, Bombelles papers, Burg Clam, Upper Austria.

17. Entry for 19 April 1798, ibid., fo. 193.

18. Entry for 26 April 1802, ibid., vol. 74, fo. 215.

19. Entry for 18 December 1802, ibid., vol. 25, fo. 340.

20. École des Beaux-Arts, Paris, 'Journal et notes de Pierre Fontaine, premier architecte de l'empereur', fo. 58, entry for 31 January 1804. I am grateful to Philip Mansel for drawing this source to my attention.

21. Ibid.

22. Général Bertrand, *Cahiers de Sainte-Hélène: journal 1818–1819*, ed. P. Fleuriot de Langle (Paris, 1959), p. 454.

23. Archives Breteuil, 1ère série LAB 1783–1786, à 1791, 1792, 1793, 1807.
24. Entry for 27 July 1798, Bombelles diary, unpublished ms., vol. 67, fo. 49.
25. Ibid., vol. 73, fo. 132.
26. For the Créquy inheritance see ibid., entry for 28 July 1803, vol. 67, fo. 55, and Archives Gontaut-Biron, folder 2, 'Inventaire après-décès de dame Caroline de Froullay, veuve de Louis Marie de Créquy, 25 pluviôse an onze'. For Fersen's generosity see A. Söderhjelm, *Fersen et Marie Antoinette* (Paris, 1930), p. 376, and for Breteuil's credit in 1801 Archives Gontaut-Biron, folder 3, 2ème liasse, 'Lettres et correspondance avec MM. de Chapeaurouge, banquiers à Hambourg, 1800–1805', Chapeaurouge to Breteuil, 2 September 1801.
27. Journal of Anne-Charles, duc de Montmorency, Archives Gontaut-Biron, Château de Courtalain, Eure-et-Loir.
28. Ibid.
29. 'Compte d'exécution testamentaire de feu M. de Breteuil', statement by Bishop of Pamiers, 11 March 1808, and of duchesse de Brancas, 15 March 1808, ibid.
30. Bombelles diary, unpublished ms., vol. 84, fo. 135.
31. Comte Fleury, *Les Dernières années du marquis et de la marquise de Bombelles* (Paris, 1906), p. 369 n. 1.
32. Klinckowström, *Le Comte de Fersen et la cour de France*, vol. 2, p. 96.
33. H. A. Barton, *Count Hans Axel von Fersen: aristocrat in an age of revolution* (Boston, Mass., 1975), pp. 266–7.
34. Ibid., p. 375.
35. Cited in Lord Acton, *Lectures on the French Revolution* (London, 1920 edn), p. 223.
36. C.-C. d'Agoult, *De l'intérêt des puissances de l'Europe, et celui de la France, au rétablissement de son antique forme de gouvernement* (Paris, 1814). The only extant copy of this pamphlet that I know of is in the Collection Grégoire in the Bibliothèque des Amis de Port-Royal, Paris.
37. C.-C. d'Agoult, *Projet d'une banque nationale* (Paris, 1815), p. ii.
38. C.-C. d'Agoult, *Lettres à un jacobin; ou réflexions politiques sur la constitution d'Angleterre et la Charte Royale, considérée dans ses rapports avec l'ancienne constitution de la monarchie française* (Paris, 1815), p. 117.
39. Marquis de Noailles (ed.), *Le Comte Molé, 1781–1855, sa vie – ses mémoires* (8 vols, Paris, 1925), vol. 4, p. 191.

BIBLIOGRAPHY

PRIMARY SOURCES

PUBLIC HOLDINGS

ARCHIVES NATIONALES, PARIS (AN)

Série C 221.

Série F17372.

AP 119, 1, dossier 1 (papiers du vicomte de Mirabeau).

306 AP 26 (Chartrier de Castries).

ÉCOLE DES BEAUX-ARTS, PARIS

Journal et notes de Pierre Fontaine, premier architecte de l'empereur.

ARCHIVES DÉPARTMENTALES DES YVELINES, VERSAILLES

E449, 450 (Bombelles papers).

HAUS-HOF-UND-STAATSARCHIV, VIENNA (HHStA)

Frankreich Varia 42, 44, 45, 48.

Familienkorrespondenz, 26.

Sammelbände 17.

RIKSARKIVET, STOCKHOLM

Gallica 499, 500, 524 (de Breteuil folder).

Stafsundsarkivet, Hans Axel von Fersens samling, vols 5, 12, 17.

GEHEIMES STAATSARCHIV PREUSSISCHER KULTURBESITZ,
BERLIN

I. HA Geheimer Rat, Rep. 11 Auswärtige Beziehungen, Frankreich, Nr 89
Fasz. 298, Bl. 9, 10.

PUBLIC RECORD OFFICE, LONDON (PRO)

PC1/125/383, PC1/128/178, C12/952/13.

PRIVATE HOLDINGS

FRANCE: ARCHIVES BRETEUIL, CHÂTEAU DE BRETEUIL,
YVELINES

LAB, 1ère série, 1783–1786 à 1791, 1792, 1793, 1807.

LAB, 1ère série, papiers divers.

1767 dossier, correspondance, divers.

ARCHIVES GONTAUT-BIRON, CHÂTEAU DE COURTALAIN,
EURE-ET-LOIR

Folder 2:
— Letter from the lawyer Royer to Breteuil, 16 June 1781, enclosing
  extract from the will of Mme H. C. Vriesen, dated 9 April 1770.
— Don patriotique, dettes et retranchements, 1790–1791, État des revenus
  de M. le baron de Breteuil pour servir à déterminer sa contribution
  patriotique.
— Inventaire après-décès de dame Caroline de Froullay, veuve de Louis
  Marie de Créquy, 25 pluviôse an onze.

Folder 3, 2ème liasse:
— Lettres et correspondance avec MM. de Chapeaurouge, banquiers à
  Hambourg, 1800–1805.
— Compte d'exécution testamentaire de feu M. de Breteuil (statement by
  Bishop of Pamiers, 11 March 1808, and of duchesse de Brancas, 15
  March 1808).
— Journal of Anne-Charles, duc de Montmorency.

Austria: Burg Clam, Upper Austria

Bombelles papers
— Missions 1790–1792 volume.
— Correspondance de Mgr comte d'Artois avec M. le baron de Breteuil.
— Correspondance de M. le baron de Breteuil avec M. le maréchal de Castries.
— 'Copie d'une lettre de Monsieur frère du Roi à M. le baron de Breteuil'.
— Memorandum, 'Envoyée à Luxembourg. Partie de Soleure le vendredi 27 mai 1791'.
— Bishop of Pamiers–marquis de Bombelles, Brussels 9 March 1792.
— Duc de Sérent, 'Note sur les motifs qui ont déterminés le départ de Mgr le comte d'Artois et de ses enfants dans le nuit du 15 au 16 juillet 1789'.
— F.-G. de Fontanges, Archbishop of Toulouse, ms.: 'Infandum . . . jubes renovare dolorem'.

Journal du marquis de Bombelles (unpublished volumes)
— Vols 25, 45, 66, 67, 71, 73, 74, 84.

PRINTED PRIMARY SOURCES

Comtesse d'Adhémar, *Souvenirs sur Marie Antoinette, archiduchesse d'Autriche, reine de France, et sur la cour de Versailles* (4 vols, Paris, 1836).

C.-C. d'Agoult, *De l'intérêt des puissances de l'Europe, et celui de la France, au rétablissement de son antique forme de gouvernement* (Paris, 1814).

———— *Projet d'une banque national* (Paris, 1815).

———— *Lettres à un jacobin; ou réflexions politiques sur la constitution d'Angleterre et la Charte Royale, considérée dans ses rapports avec l'ancienne constitution de la monarchie française* (Paris, 1815).

Comte d'Allonville, *Mémoires secrets, de 1770 à 1830* (5 vols, Paris, 1838–41).

Mémoires de C. C. Flahaut, comte de la Billarderie d'Angiviller, ed. Louis Bobé (Copenhagen and Paris, 1933).

Mémoires de Bailly, ed. S. A. Berville and J. F. Barrière (3 vols, Paris 1821).

Mémoire autographe de M de Barentin, chancelier et garde des sceaux, sur les derniers conseils de Louis XVI, ed. M. Champion (Paris, 1844).

Lettres et bulletins de Barentins à Louis XVI, avril–juillet 1789, ed. A. Aulard (Paris, 1915).

Mémoires de Barras, ed. P. Vergnet (Paris, 1946).

Général Bertrand, *Cahiers de Sainte-Hélène: journal 1818–1819*, ed. P. Fleuriot de Langle (Paris, 1959).

A. F. Bertrand de Molleville, *Mémoires particulières pour servir à l'histoire de la fin du règne de Louis XVI* (2 vols, Paris, 1816).

Marquis de Bombelles, *Journal*, ed. J. Grassion, F. Durif and J. Charon-Bordas (4 vols, Geneva, 1978–98).

Marquis de Bouillé, *Mémoires*, ed. S. A. Berville and J. F. Barrière (Paris, 1821).

Souvenirs et fragments pour servir aux mémoires de ma vie et de mon temps par le marquis de Bouillé (Louis-Joseph-Amour), 1769–1812, ed. P.-L. de Kermangant (3 vols, Paris, 1908–11).

E. Burke, *Reflections on the Revolution in France* (London, 1986, Penguin Classics edn).

C. A. de Calonne, *Lettre adressée au roi le 9 février 1789* (London, 1789).

J. L. H. Campan, *Mémoires sur la vie privée de Marie-Antoinette, reine de France et de Navarre* (2 vols, London, 1823).

'Mémoires du duc de Caraman', *Revue contemporaine*, vol. 1 (April–May 1852), 30–41, 187–202, and vol. 2 (June–July 1852), 54–73.

Mémoires du duc des Cars (2 vols, Paris, 1890).

S. R. N. Chamfort, *Maximes et pensées, caractères et anecdotes*, ed. P. Grosclaude (2 vols, Paris, 1953–4).

François-René, vicomte de Chateaubriand, *Mémoires d'outre-tombe*, ed. P. Clarac (3 vols, Paris, 1973).

Duc de Choiseul, *Relation du départ de Louis XVI le 20 juin 1791* (Paris, 1822).

Journal d'émigration du comte d'Espinchal, ed. E. d'Hauterive (Paris, 1912).

Mémoires du marquis de Ferrières (3 vols, Paris, 1822).

Axel von Fersens dagbok, ed. A. Söderhjelm (4 vols, Stockholm, 1924–36).

Abbé Georgel, *Mémoires pour servir à l'histoire des événements à la fin du 18ème siècle depuis 1760 jusqu'en 1806–10* (6 vols, Paris, 1817).

F. Hue, *Dernières années du règne et de la vie de Louis XVI* (Paris, 1816).

Baron R. M. von Klinckowström, *Le comte de Fersen et la cour de France* (2 vols, Paris, 1877–8).

Marquis de La Fayette, *Mémoires* (6 vols, Paris, 1816).

Souvenirs-portraits du duc de Lévis (1764–1830), ed. J. Dupâquier (Paris, 1993).

Prince de Ligne, *Amabile*, ed. J. Vercruysse (Paris, 1996).

Lisez et frémissez; par l'auteur d'Ouvrez les yeux, de Bon Dieu, que les Français sont bêtes, etc. (Paris, 1790).

Louis XVI, Marie Antoinette, Mme Elisabeth: lettres et documents inédits, ed. F. Feuillet de Conches (6 vols, Paris, 1864–73).

Louis XVI and the comte de Vergennes: correspondence, 1774–1787, ed. J. Hardman and M. Price (Voltaire Foundation, Oxford, 1998).

Mémoires de Malouet, ed. baron Malouet (2 vols, Paris, 1868).

Lettres de Marie Antoinette, ed. M. de la Rocheterie and the marquis de Beaucourt (2 vols, Paris, 1895–6).

Marie Antoinette, Joseph II und Leopold II, ihr Briefwechsel, ed. A. von Arneth (Leipzig, Paris and Vienna, 1866).

Marie Antoinette et Barnave: correspondance secrète, juillet 1791–janvier 1792, ed. A. Söderhjelm (Paris, 1934).

J. F. Marmontel, *Mémoires*, ed. J. Renwick (2 vols, Clermont-Ferrand, 1972).

Correspondance secrète du comte de Mercy-Argenteau avec l'empereur Joseph II et le prince de Kaunitz, ed. A. von Arneth and J. Flammermont (2 vols, Paris, 1889–91).

Correspondance entre le comte de Mirabeau et le comte de la Marck, ed. A. de Bacourt (3 vols, Paris, 1851).

Comte de Montlosier, *Souvenirs d'un émigré (1791–1798)*, ed. comte de Larouzière-Montlosier and E. d'Hauterive (Paris, 1951).

Jacob-Nicolas Moreau, *Mes souvenirs* (2 vols, Paris, 1898).

J. Necker, *De la Révolution française* (4 vols, Paris, 1797).

Marquis de Noailles (ed.), *Le Comte Molé, 1781–1855, sa vie – ses mémoires* (8 vols, Paris, 1925).

Recueil des pièces imprimées d'après le décret de la convention nationale (2 vols, Paris, 1793).

Recueil des instructions données aux ambassadeurs et ministres de France depuis les traités de Westphalie jusqu'à la Révolution française: Russie, ed. A. Rambaud (Paris, 1890).

Comte de Saint-Priest, *Mémoires*, ed. baron de Barante (2 vols, Paris, 1929).

J.-L. Soulavie, *Mémoires historiques et politiques du règne de Louis XVI* (6 vols, Paris, 1801).

Mémoires de Mme la duchesse de Tourꝫel, ed. J. Chalon (Paris, 1969).

Lettre de M. de la Vauguyon au Prétendant (Paris, 1797).

A. Ritter von Vivenot, *Quellen ꝫur Geschichte der deutschen Kasierpolitik Österreichs während der franꝫösischen Revolutionskriege, 1790–1801* (5 vols, Vienna, 1873–90).

Letters of Horace Walpole, ed. P. Cunningham (9 vols, London, 1891).

H. Walpole (trans.), Louis XVI, *Règne de Richard III, on doutes historiques sur les crimes qui lui sont imputés*, ed. Roussel l'Epinal (Paris, 1800).

Mémoires de Weber concernant Marie Antoinette, archiduchesse d'Autriche et reine de France et de Navarre, ed. S. A. Berville and J. F. Barrière (2 vols, Paris, 1822).

SECONDARY SOURCES

Lord Acton, *Lectures on the French Revolution* (London, 1920 edn).

N. Åkeson, *Gustaf III:s forhallande till franska revolutionen* (2 vols, Lund, 1885).

R. Allen, *Threshold of Terror: the last hours of the monarchy in the French Revolution* (Stroud, 1999).

M. Antoine, *Le Conseil du roi sous le règne de Louis XVI* (Geneva, 1970).

H. A. Barton, *Hans Axel von Fersen: aristocrat in an age of revolution* (Boston, Mass., 1975).

Baron de Batz, *La Vie et les conspirations de Jean, baron de Batꝫ* (Paris, 1908).

——— *Les Conspirations et la fin de Jean, baron de Batꝫ* (Paris, 1911).

D. E. D. Beales, *Joseph II*, vol. 1, *In the Shadow of Maria Theresa* (Cambridge, 1987).

W. Beik, *Absolutism and Society in Seventeenth-century France: state power and provincial aristocracy in Languedoc* (Cambridge, 1895).

J. Black, *British Foreign Policy in an Age of Revolutions, 1783–1793* (Cambridge, 1994).

T. C. W. Blanning, *The Origins of the French Revolutionary Wars* (London, 1986).

—— *The French Revolutionary Wars* (London, 1996).

G. Bord, *La Fin de deux légendes: Léonard et le baron de Batz* (Paris, 1909).

J. F. Bosher, *French Finances 1770–1795: from business to bureaucracy* (Cambridge, 1970).

J. Brewer, *The Sinews of Power: war, money and the English state, 1688–1783* (London, 1994 edn).

A. Britsch, *La maison d'Orléans à la fin de l'ancien régime: la jeunesse de Philippe-Egalité, 1747–1785* (Paris, 1926).

P. Caron, 'La tentative de contre-révolution de juin–juillet 1789', *Revue d'histoire moderne et contemporaine*, vol. 8 (1906–7), pp. 5–34 and pp. 649–78.

Duc de Castries, *Le maréchal de Castries: serviteur de trois rois* (Paris, 1979 edn).

J. Chaumié, 'La correspondance du chevalier de Las Casas et du marquis de Bombelles, ambassadeurs de France et d'Espagne sous la Révolution', *Revue d'histoire diplomatique*, January–June and July–December 1950, 99–142, and January–June and July–December 1951, 76–129.

—— *Les relations diplomatiques entre la France et l'Espagne, de Varennes à la mort de Louis XVI* (Bordeaux, 1957).

G. Chaussinand-Nogaret, *Mirabeau* (Paris, 1982).

—— *1789* (Paris, 1988).

A. Chevalier, *Claude-Carloman de Rulhière, premier historien de la Pologne, sa vie et son oeuvre historique* (Paris, 1939).

A. Chuquet, *Les Guerres de la Révolution*, vol. 2, *Valmy* (Paris, 1929).

—— *Les Guerres de la Révolution*, vol. 5, *La trahison de Dumouriez* (Paris, n.d.).

M. Clemenceau-Jacquemaire, *Vie de Mme Roland* (2 vols, Paris, 1929).

V. Cronin, *Louis and Antoinette* (London, 1974).

E. Daudet, *Histoire de l'émigration: Coblentz* (Paris, n.d.).

G. de Diesbach, *Histoire de l'émigration, 1789–1814* (Paris, 1984 edn).

W. Doyle, *The Oxford History of the French Revolution* (Oxford, 1989).

—— (ed.), *Old Regime France* (Oxford, 2001).

A. Doyon, 'Maximilien Radix de Sainte-Foy', *Revue d'histoire diplomatique*, July–September 1966, 232–70; October–December 1966, 314–54.

C. Duckworth, 'Louis XVI and English history: a French reaction to Walpole, Hume and Gibbon on Richard III', *Studies on Voltaire and the Eighteenth Century*, 176 (1979), 385–401.

J. Egret, *La Révolution des notables: Mounier et les monarchiens, 1789* (Paris, 1950).

———— *La Pré-révolution française, 1787–1788* (Paris, 1962).

———— *Louis XV et l'opposition parlementaire* (Paris, 1970).

J. Flammermont, *Négociations secrètes de Louis XVI et du baron de Breteuil avec la cour de Berlin, décembre 1791 à juillet 1792* (Paris, 1885).

Comte Fleury, *Les Dernières années du marquis et de la marquise de Bombelles* (Paris, 1906).

A. Fraser, *Marie Antoinette: the journey* (London, 2001).

P. Girault de Coursac, *L'Éducation d'un roi* (Paris, 1972).

P. and P. Girault de Coursac, *Enquête sur le procès du roi Louis XVI* (Paris, 1982).

———— *Sur la route de Varennes* (Paris, 1984).

———— *Le Voyage de Louis XVI autour du monde* (Paris, 1985).

———— *Le Secret de la reine: la politique personnelle de Marie Antoinette pendant la Révolution* (Paris, 1996).

H. Glagau, *Die französische Legislative und die Ursprung der Revolutions-kriege, 1791–1792* (Berlin, 1896).

L. S. Greenbaum, 'Jean-Sylvain Bailly, the baron de Breteuil and the "four new hospitals" of Paris', *Clio Medica*, vol. 8, no. 4 (1973), 261–84.

J. J. Guiffrey, 'Documents inédits sur la journée du 14 juillet 1789', *Revue historique*, vol. 1 (January–June 1876).

N. Hampson, 'François Chabot and his plot', *Transactions of the Royal Historical Society*, 5th series, vol. 26 (1976), 1–15.

———— *Prelude to Terror: the constituent assembly and the failure of consensus, 1789–1791* (Oxford, 1988).

J. Hardman, *The French Revolution: the fall of the ancien régime to the Thermidorian reaction, 1785–1795* (London, 1981).

———— *Louis XVI* (New Haven and London, 1993).

———— *French Politics 1774–1789: from the accession of Louis XVI to the fall of the Bastille* (London, 1995).

R. D. Harris, *Nector Reform Statesman of the Ancien Régime* (Berkeley, Calif., 1979).

———— *Necker and the Revolution of 1789* (Lanham, 1986).

O. G. von Heidenstam, *La Fin d'une dynastie* (Paris, 1911).

C. Hibbert, *The French Revolution* (London, 1982 edn).

M. Hochedlinger, *Die Krise der Österreichischen Außlandspolitik 1787–1792:*

Österreich, die 'Französische Frage' und das Ende der Ära Kaunitz (2 vols, Vienna, 1997).

L. Hunt, *The Family Romance of the French Revolution* (London, 1992).

R. Lacour-Gayet, *Calonne: financier, réformateur, contre-révolutionnaire* (Paris, 1963).

E. Lavaquéray, *Necker, fourrier de la Révolution* (Paris, 1933).

G. Lefebvre and A. Terroine, *Recueil de documents relatifs aux séances des États-généraux*, vol. i, *Mai–juin 1789: les préliminaires, la séance du 5 Mai* (Paris, 1953).

G. Lefebvre, *Recueil de documents relatifs aux séances des États-généraux*, vol. i (2), *la séance du 23 juin* (Paris, 1962).

G. Lenôtre, *Le Drame de Varennes* (Paris, 1905).

A. de Lestapis, *La 'Conspiration de Batz'* (Paris, 1969).

E. Lever, *Louix XVI* (Paris, 1985).

——— *Marie Antoinette: the last queen of France* (London, 2001).

M. de Lombarès, 'Varennes ou la fin d'un régime', *Revue historique de l'armée* (1961), no. 3, pp. 33–56; no. 4, pp. 45–62; no. 5, pp. 23–36.

P. Mansel, *Louis XVIII* (London, 1981).

——— *The Court of France, 1789–1830* (Cambridge, 1988).

——— *Le Charmeur de l'Europe: Charles-Joseph de Ligne 1735–1814* (Paris, 1992).

M. Marion, *Le Garde des sceaux Lamoignon et la réforme judiciaire de 1788* (Paris, 1905).

——— *Dictionnaire des institutions de la France au 17ème et 18ème siècles* (Paris, 1923).

A. Mathiez, *Étude critique sur les journées des 5 et 6 octobre 1789* (Paris, 1899).

——— *Un procès de corruption sous la Terreur: l'affaire de la Compagnie des Indes* (Paris, 1920).

S. Maza, *Private Lives and Public Affairs: the causes célèbres of pre-revolutionary France* (Berkeley, Calif. and Los Angeles, 1993).

R. Mettam, *Power and Faction in Louis XIV's France* (London, 1988).

G. Michon, *Essai sur l'histoire du parti feuillant: Adrien Duport* (Paris, 1924).

F. Mossiker, *The Queen's Necklace* (New York, 1961).

A. Mousset, *Un témoin inconnu de la Révolution: le comte de Fernan Nuñez* (Paris, 1924).

R. Nisbet Bain, *Gustavus III and his contemporaries* (2 vols, London, 1894).

Comte de Pimodan, *Le Comte F.-C. de Mercy-Argenteau* (Paris, 1911).

M. Price, 'The "Ministry of the Hundred Hours": a reappraisal', *French History*, vol. 4, no. 3 (1990), 319–21.

———— *Preserving the Monarchy: the comte de Vergennes, 1774–1787* (Cambridge, 1995).

R. M. Rampelberg, *Le Ministre de la maison du roi 1783–1788: baron de Breteuil* (Paris, 1975).

S. F. Scott, *The Response of the Royal Army to the French Revolution* (Oxford, 1978).

B. Shapiro, *Revolutionary Justice in Paris, 1789–1790* (Cambridge, 1993).

J. H. Shennan, *The Parlement of Paris* (Ithaca, NY, 1968).

A. Söderhjelm, *Fersen et Marie Antoinette* (Paris, 1930).

A. Sorel, *L'Europe et la Révolution française* (8 vols, Paris, 1885–1905).

J. Sperber, *Revolutionary Europe, 1780–1850* (London, 2000).

B. Stone, *The Parlement of Paris, 1774–1789* (Chapel Hill, North Carolina, 1981).

———— *The French parlements and the crisis of the old regime* (Chapel Hill, North Carolina, 1986).

J. Swann, *Louis XV and the Parlement of Paris* (Cambridge, 1995).

A. Wandruska, *Leopold II* (2 vols, Vienna, 1963–5).

E. Welwert, 'L'éminence grise de Marie Antoinette', *Revue de l'histoire de Versailles et de Seine-et-Oise*, 23 and 24 (1921–2).

E. N. White, 'Was there a solution to the ancien régime's financial dilemma?', *Journal of Economic History*, vol. 49, no. 3 (September 1989), 545–68.

D. L. Wick, 'The court nobility and the French Revolution: the example of the Society of Thirty', *Eighteenth-century Studies* (1980).

S. Zweig, *Marie Antoinette: the portrait of an average woman* (London, 1933).

INDEX